This journal belongs to

....

'The past is another land, and we cannot go to visit. So if I say there were dragons, and men rode upon their backs, who alive has been there, and can tell me that I'm wrong?'

SPRING
WETTINGS

'I was not a natural at the Heroism business. I had to work at it. This is the story of becoming a Hero the Hard Way.'

Hiccup Horrendous Haddock the Third

TOOTHLESS
Hiccup's disobedient little
dragon

·↑

This is Toothless, in a hibernation sleep.

STOICK the VAST

I Declare a BLOOD FEUD!!

Fishlegs

'Fishlegs was a tall, spindly runner-bean of a boy, who had eczema as well as asthma, and was allergic to wheat and dairy. Not to mention dragons.'

SOME FIERY DRAGON JOKES:

Q: What's as big as a Seadragonus Giganticus Maximus but weighs nothing?
A: Its shadow!

Q: What do you call a deaf Driller Dragon?
A: Anything you like — he can't hear you!

Q: What do you find inside Wartihog's clean nose?
A: Finger prints!

Q: What do Stoick the Vast, Mogadon the Meathead and Baggybum the Beerbelly all have in common (besides bad breath and excessive sweating)?
A: They all have the same middle name!

Q: What's the best way to catch a Basic Brown dragon?
A: Have someone throw it at you.

Q: How do Vikings send secret messages?
A: By norse code!

Q: How do you know when a Seadragonus Giganticus Maximus is under your bed?
A: When your nose hits the ceiling.

Q: What do you get when a Sniffer Dragon sneezes?
A: Out of the way!

One day the great god Thor decided to come down to Earth and challenge Thwettibot the Hero to a rock-lifting contest. After a day of lifting rocks, Thwettibot conceded defeat. 'You did well!' said the god graciously, 'for I am Thor.' 'You're Thor?' said Thwettibot. 'Listhen Mithter, I'm tho thore, I can barely thtand up!'

Don't forget to BREATHE Toothless

HA! HA! HA! HA! HA! HA! HA! HA! HA!

Camicazi

'The indomitable Heir to the Bog-Burglar Tribe, whose hair looks like it has been vigorously back-combed by squirrels.'

Camicazi riding her Rocket Ripper, Typhoon, very low over the Murderous Mountains.

'He was a seven-foot giant with a mad glint in his one working eye and a beard like exploding fireworks.'

'We're all
snatching precious
moments from
the peaceful
jaws of time.'

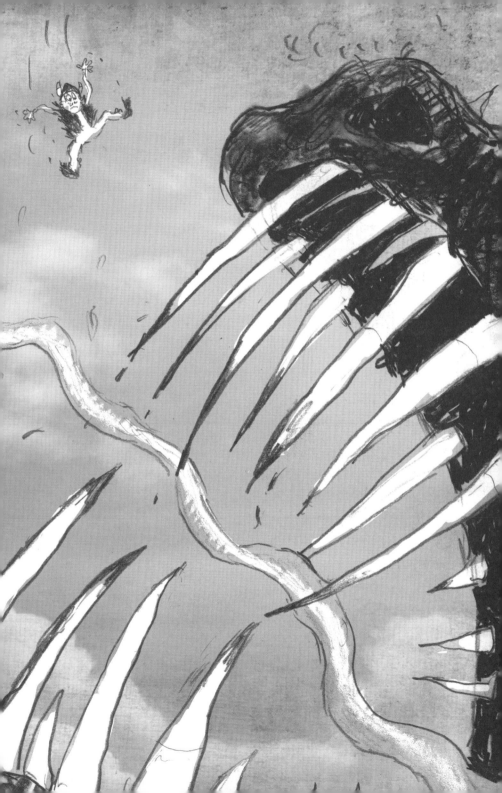

Old Wrinkly

'There's no such thing as im-POSSIBLE, Hiccup,' snorted Old Wrinkly, 'only im-PROBABLE. The only thing that limits us are the limits to our imaginations.'

NOT THE SETTLING KIND

An Old Viking
Archipelago song

I have never cared for castles
or a crown that grips too tight,
Let the night sky be my starry roof,
and the moon my only light.

My Heart was born a Hero,
my storm-bound sword won't rest,
I left the Harbour long ago
on a Never-ending Quest.

I am off to the horizon
where the wild wind blows the foam
Come get lost with me, Love,
and the sea shall be our Home.

take this ruby as a token, I promise you....

I will return, of my love

TRUE LOVE

My one True Love vanished,

and my heart broke that day,

But once you've loved Truly,

Thor, then you know the way!

Once I loved Truly, Thor,

and my heart paid the price,

Let me love Truly, Thor,

let me love **TWICE!**

'We listened hard, for what mothers say to their babies when they are about to be parted – well, that is worth listening to.'

'And as small and quiet and unimportant as our fighting may look, perhaps we might all work together… and break out of the prisons of our own making. Perhaps we might be able to keep this fierce and beautiful world of ours as free for all of us as it seemed to be on that blue afternoon of my childhood.'

Snotface
Snotlout

(Hiccup's
unpleasant
cousin)

'Hiccup will not be leading
this group because HE is
not a leader. I am.'

Does this look like the sort of dragon who would poo in a helmet?

Toothless doing a poo in Alvin's helmet

Conversations with Toothless

Dinner Time...

Toothless: Issa yuck-yuck.
This is disgusting.

Toothless: Me na likeit di stinkfish. Issa yuck-yuck.
Issa poo-poo. Issa doubly doubly yuck-yuck.
*I don't like haddock. It's revolting. It's gross. It's really
revolting.*

You: Okey dokey so questa yow eaty?
Alright then, so what will you eat?

Toothless: Me eaty di miaowla...
I want to eat the cat...

You: (you can raise your voice now) NA EATY
DI BUM-SUPPORT, NA EATY DI SLEEPY-SLAB PLUS
DOUBLY DOUBLY NA EATY DI MIAOWLA!
*Don't eat the chair, don't eat the bed and definitely don't
eat the cat!*

Bath Time. . .

When a dragon has spent the whole day in a mud wallow and they then want to curl up in your bed you have no option. YOU HAVE TO GIVE THEM A BATH. Good luck.

Toothless: Me na wash di bum. Me na wash di face. Me na wash di claws. Me na splishy oo di splashy ATALL.
I do not want a bath.

You are going to have to be cunning and use PSYCHOLOGY.

You: Na bathtime ever never ever never.
Me repeeti. Na bathtime EVER NEVER.
On no account are you to get in the bath.

Toothless (whining): Me wanti splishy splashy.
I want a bath.

You: Okey dokey just wun time.
All right just this once.

Hoody drunken di bath juice?
*Who has drunk up the
bath water?*

SUMMER BOILINGS

'Humungously Hotshot the Hero was as cool as a cat twirling his whiskers on a freshly frozen iceberg…'

And spare
a thought
for those

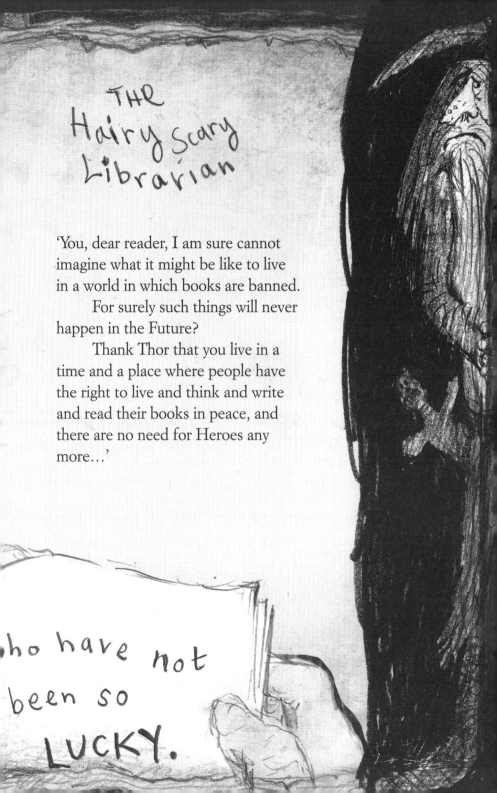

THE Hairy Scary Librarian

'You, dear reader, I am sure cannot imagine what it might be like to live in a world in which books are banned.

For surely such things will never happen in the Future?

Thank Thor that you live in a time and a place where people have the right to live and think and write and read their books in peace, and there are no need for Heroes any more...'

...ho have not been so LUCKY.

SOME MORE FIERY DRAGON JOKES:

Q: What has six eyes, six arms, six legs, three heads, and a very short life?
A: Three people about to be eaten by a Tongue-Twister.

Q: How do you know if there is an Eight-legged Battlegore in your refrigerator?
A: The door won't shut!

Q: What's the nickname for someone who put their right hand in the mouth of a Dark Breather?
A: Lefty.

Q: How do you best raise a baby dragon?
A: With a crane.

Q: Why did the Raptortongue cross the road?
A: To eat the chickens on the other side.

Q: What game does the Giant Bee-Eater like to play with humans?
A: Squash.

Q: What is the best thing to do if you see an Exterminator Dragon?
A: Pray that it doesn't see you.

Q: Where did the teacher send the Viking when he got sick in class?
A: To the school Norse.

Q: Why was the greedy person like a Viking?
A: Because he ate like a Norse!

Q: Why can't Vikings play cards on their longboats?
A: Because they're always sitting on the deck.

Q: What do you get if you cross a Stink Dragon with a flower?
A: I don't know but I'm sure not going to smell it.

Q: How does a Pricklepine play leapfrog?
A: Very carefully!

the slavemark

'Maybe all Kings should bear the Slavemark, to remind them that they should be slaves to their people, rather than the other way around.'

Song of the

NANODRAGON

(while licking off honey)

O Human Fatness who tried to eat me
Great Wobbling Vomit of Repulsive Man-Flesh
I cannot kill you NOW
Though I would like to
But you will regret this, Blubber-Man
You will regret this in the quiet darkness of the night-tim
For I have friends
I have friends who will itch you into nightmares
Their feet will plough your skin into rashes
And you will sleep no more, o Stomach-with-a-Head-on-it
You will sleep no more

O Balloon of Lard who tried to eat me
Man Uglier than an Exploded Jellyfish
I cannot kill you NOW
Though I would like to
But I can wait, Flesh-Dangler
I can wait, ticking in the corner like Fate
And I have friends
I have friends who will crawl with me into your coffin
Where you are lying, hoping for the quiet sleep of Death
And we will eat YOU, o Sad Lump of Man Meat
We will eat you

EMPERORS

Watch out
O Romans with your Empires
and your Stinking Breath
Watch out for the smaller things of this world
For we are going to get you... one day
You live your lives up in the skies
Building your aqueducts and your coliseums
And you never think of US
Ticking away in the grasses
But we see you
And if you bend your ear you just might hear
The steady beat of countless feet that come to eat
The wall that curls a hundred miles across a continent
That temple built with the tears of millions of slaves
And all your most mighty and splendid creations
Shall turn to dust in our mouths
So watch out
O Caesars with Fat Bottoms and Hard Hearts
Watch out

WE WILL
FIGHT THEM
ON THE BEACHES!

WE WILL FIGHT
THEM IN THE BRACKEN!

WE WILL FIGHT THEM

IN THOSE BOGGY
MARSHY BITS THAT
ARE SO DIFFICULT TO

WALK THROUGH WITHOUT

LOSING YOUR SHOES!

WE WILL

NEVER
SURRENDER!

East

West

for Alvin and the Witch

for Hiccup and the Dragonmark

Which way would Snotlout Go?

'THE QUEST WAS OVER.'

Conversations with Toothless

In the Middle of the Night...

I am very hungry

Me has b-b-buckets di belly-scream.
I am very hungry.

Me isna burped si ISSA middling o di zuzztime.
I don't care if it IS the middle of the night.

Me needy di grubbings SNIP-SNAP!
I want food RIGHT NOW!

Oo mes'll do di yowlyshreekers too fortissimo theys'll earwig me indi BigManGaff.
Or I'll scream so loudly they'll hear me in Valhalla.

Me needy di S-S-S-S-SALTSICKS.
I want OYSTERS.

Yow g-g-grabba di saltsicks low indi Landscoop. Sna staraway.
You can get oysters from the Harbour. It's not far.

M-M-Me gogo ta yowlshreck...
I'm starting to scream...

(Three quarters of an hour later)

Yow me p-p-peepers undo!
You woke me up!

Wah is DA?
What is THAT?

Da na goggle com s-s-saltsicks...
That doesn't look like oysters...

DA goggle com sniffersludge...
THAT looks like bogeys...

THAT looks like bogeys

Sniffersludge p-p-plus di squidink tiddles...
Bogeys with black bits in them...

Me no likeit di squidink tiddles. Issa y-y-yuck-yuck.
I don't like black bits. They're disgusting.

Watever, me is tow zuzzready por di scrumming.
Anyway, I'm too tired to eat.

Mes'll zip di peepers.
I'm going to sleep.

'Old Wrinkly named it "Endeavour". He said the name was important, because "to endeavour" means trying to do something even when you know you might be beaten before you even start.'

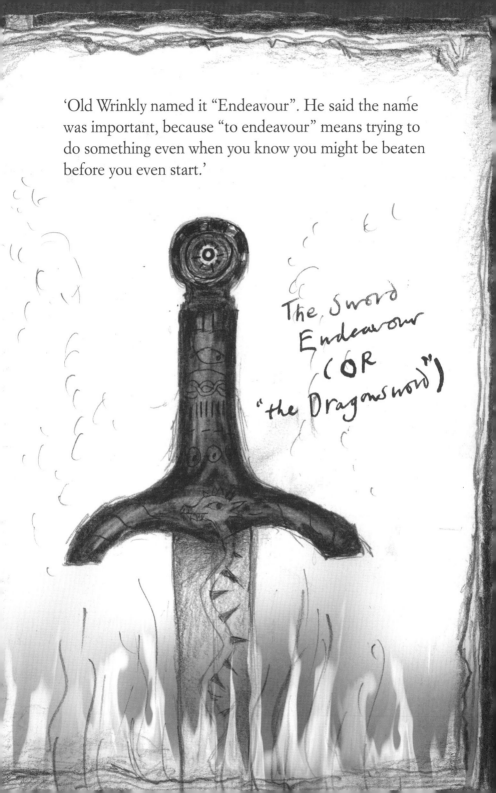

The Sword
Endeavour
(OR
"the Dragonsword")

Watch and learn,
my boy. Watch
and learn.

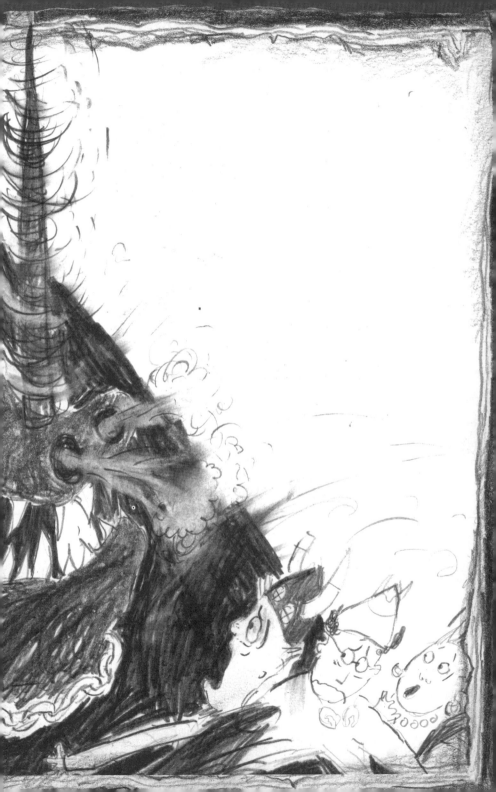

'You do not have to accept the hand that Fate has dealt you. Look at me, the skinniest, most unlikely Viking ever, now known as this great Hero all around the world.'

the
DARK SIDE of THE AXE
(a moving little lullaby)

Come and dance the Deathwalk
Beneath the grinning moon...
We'll do the dance together
In the dying afternoon....

The Deathwalk looks so tricky,
But I think you'll learn it quick,
Just step into my Axe's arms,
She'll teach you in a t...

See the jolly skeletons
A dancing on the seal
They haven't got no cares how
Not like you and me...
They went and did the
DEATHWALK
That crazy night-time
beat...

And now they partner ghosts and whales
On bony pearly feet...

'Now all those who had laughed had watched him as he swam, entirely unaided, up the whole depth of the bay. Even though he was so tired he could barely put one foot in front of another, his back was straight, his head held high.'

A proud moment for Fishlegs.

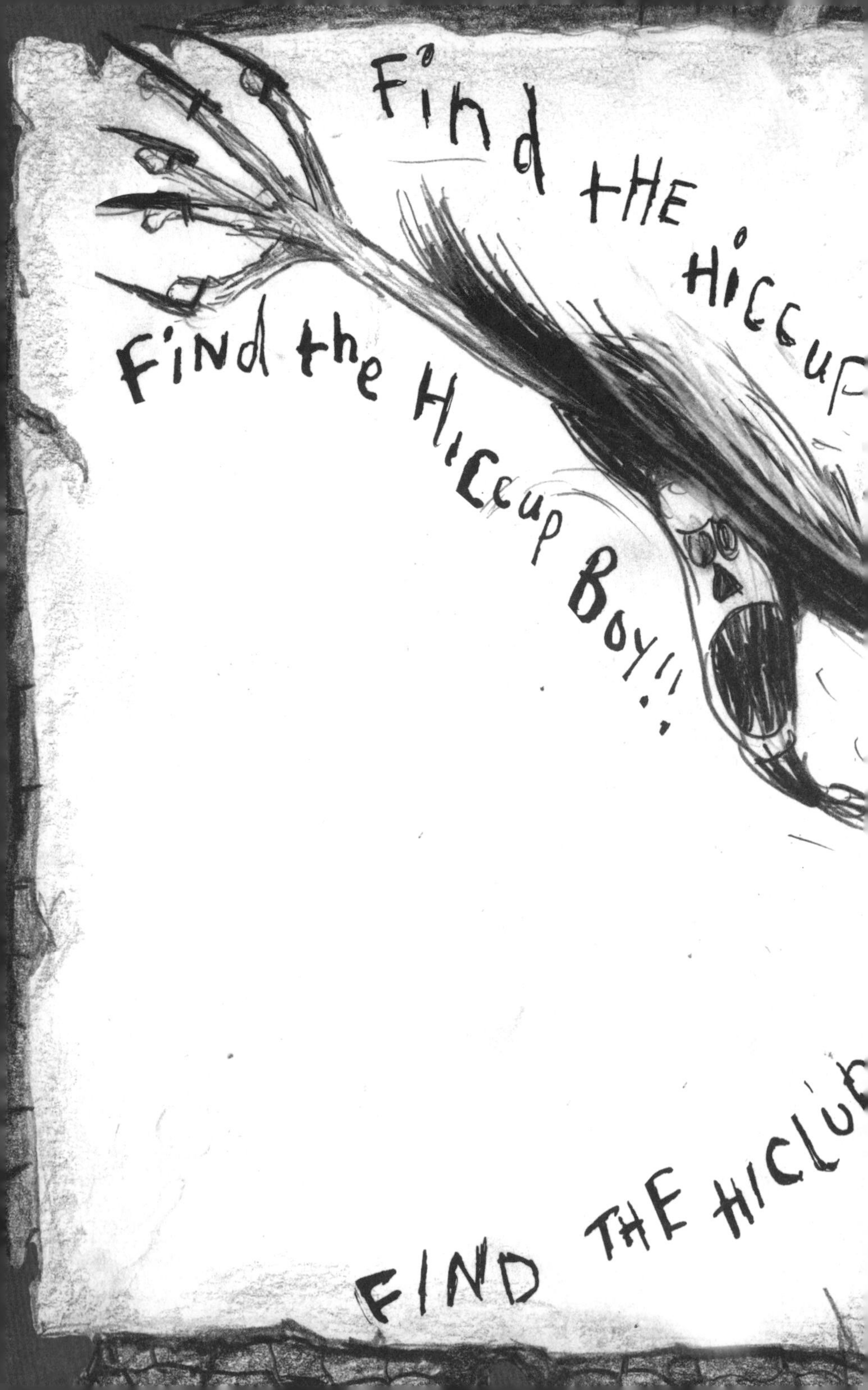
Find the Hiccup
Find the Hiccup Boy!!
FIND THE HICCU

The Witch Excellinor
a particularly unpleasant
and Scary witch

You can't keep a BOG-BURGLAR UNDER LOCK AND KEY!

Conversations with Toothless

Toilet Training...

You: Toothless, ta COGLET me wantee ta cack-cack in ði
greenclaw crapspot...
Toothless, you KNOW I want you to poo in the dragon toilets...

Toothless: O yessee yessee, me coglet...
Yes, yes, I know...

You: (pointing at large poo in the
middle of Stoick's bed) Erg... questa SA?
So what, then, is THIS?

PAUSE

Toothless (hopefully): Ummm...
un chocklush snik-snak?
Er... a chocolate biscuit?

You: Snotta chocklush snik-snak, issa CACK-CACK, issa cack-
cack ði, Toothless, NA in ði greenclaw crapspot, may oopla bang
splosh in ði middling ði sleepy-slab ði pappa.
*This isn't a chocolate biscuit, it's a POO, it's one of YOUR
poos, Toothless, and it ISN'T in the dragon toilets, it's right
bang splat in the middle of my father's bed.*

YET MORE FIERY DRAGON JOKES:

Q: What's big, heavy, dangerous and has sixteen wheels?
A: A Riproarer on roller-skates.

Q: Where does a three ton dragon sit?
A: Anywhere it likes.

A policeman stopped a man who was walking along with a Driller-dragon and ordered him to take it to the zoo at once.
The next day the policeman saw the same man, still with the Driller-dragon.
'I thought I told you to take that dragon to the zoo,' he said.
'I did,' said the man, 'and now I'm taking him to the cinema.'

Q: What steps do you take if a Triple-headed Rageblast is coming towards you?
A: Big ones!

Q: What do you get if you cross a Glow-worm with a python?
A: A fifteen-foot strip light that will strangle you to death!

Q: What time did the Sabre-Tooth Driver Dragon go to the dentist?
A: Tooth hurty.

Q: What do you call a dragon that is good at ryhming?
A: A rap-tile.

Q: What do you say to a lazy Gronckle?
A: Stop dragon your tail!

FUNNY!
F-F-funny

funny!

Q: What do dragons do on their birthday?
A: They have to blow on their cake to light the candles.

Q: How was the Viking able to afford such an expensive ship?
A: It was on sail!

Q: What dragon can jump higher than the Great Hall?
A: Great Halls can't jump!

AUTUMN FALLINGS

'Hiccup's mother is a great Hero who is often away questing.'

THRee cheers FOR ValHallarama!

THE DRAGON BRACELET

'It is a constant reminder to me of the human ability to create something beautiful even when things are at their darkest.

I have worn that bracelet every day of my life.'

I DIDN'T MEAN TO COME HERE

The Hooligan Tribal Anthem, composed by Hiccup's ancestor, Great Hairybottom

I didn't mean to come here…

And I didn't mean to stay…

It's just where the sea wind blew me

One acci-dental day…

I was on my way to America

But I took a left turn at the Pole

And I lost my shoe in a rainy bog

Where my heart got stuck in the hole…

It wasn't where I meant to be,

And it wasn't where I had my start,

But now I'll never leave these rain-soaked bogs

Because Berk is where I left my heart!

"I DIDN'T MEAN TO COME HE-ERE...
NO I DIDN'T MEAN TO STA-A-AY...
BUT I LOST MY HEART TO THESE RAINY BOGS
AND I'LL NE-E-E-VER GO AW-A-AY!!"

I didn't mean to come here,
And I didn't mean to STAY;
It's just where the sea
wind BLEW ME
ONE ACCIDENTAL DAY.

WHAT A HERO!!

ropes for climbing and swinging on

knapsack for burgled items

lots of secret pockets

sword

things for picking locks

protective goggles

tiny dagger for emergencies

spiked shoes for extra GRIP

Camicazi's Burglary Equipment

ADVANCED BURGLARY TIPS from CAMICAZI

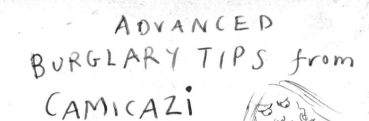

Burgling from Grabbit the Grim.

fig 1.

Gently remove his helmet, approaching from above.

A steady hand is essential for all Burglary Exercises. Quick wits are as important as nimble fingers, as demonstrated HERE

fig 2.

Softly remove swords and sandals, approaching from below

f you get caught
SHEEP-RUSTLING:
ACT SURPRISED.

'Oh, my goodness! You're
right, there IS a sheep on my
head! Well, I have ABSOLUTELY
NO IDEA how *that* could have
got there...'

fig 3. Your victim
realises he has been
BURGLED.

A quick getaway is
ALWAYS a good idea...

EVEN MORE DRAGON JOKES:

A race is about to start. Gobber shouts
'1...2...3...GO!' and blows the whistle. Everybody
except Clueless runs.
GOBBER: Clueless! Why aren't you running?
CLUELESS: Because my number is 4!

Q: Where do Viking warriors keep their armies?
A: Up their sleevies!

Q: What do Seadragonus Giganticus Maximus eat?
A: Fish and Ships.

Q: Why does Hiccup take a pencil to bed?
A: So he can draw the curtains.

Q: Why did the Rhinoback cross the road?
A: Because it was the chicken's day off.

Q: What do you find in the middle of dragons?
A: The letter g!

'Sometimes it is only a True Friend who knows what we mean when we try to speak. Somebody who has spent a lot of time with us, and listens carefully to what we are trying to say, and tries to understand.

Fishlegs understood.'

We must
be STRONG
Fishlegs, we
must hope
for the
BEST!

He would be strong
He would hope
for the best.

'Sometimes time cannot tick backwards.
Sometimes you cannot put a dragon back in a forest,
nor a witch back in a tree-trunk, nor the breath back
into a friend when all the breath has gone.
War really does have terrible consequences.'

'A Hero is Forever.'

Conversations with Toothless

Toothless's Guide to Being P-P-Polite...

Moo-lady, yow snoddly sniffer is giganticus plus warticus, plus, warra eye-pleezee, fur-sprouty hug-dangles!

Madam, you have a very large and lovely spotty nose, and what beautiful hairy arms!

Toothless issa griefspotty me misschance f-f-flicka-flame ta gob-sprout. Twassa bigtime hiccup.

I am so sorry that I accidentally set fire to your beard, it was a total mistake.

WHOOPS! T-t-toothless didn't mean to step in a Goredragon poo and tread it all over your floor...

Toothless mak ta me m-m-most speshally griefspotties. Toothless's runners pop in a cack-cack di Goredragon, plus me pressit muchwide ondi floorsheet.

I make you my most heartfelt apologies. I seem to have stepped in Goredragon poo and trodden it all over your carpet.

T-t-toothless goggla ta struggla wi munch-munch di saltsicks lonelywise. Teggly me adda.

I can see you are having trouble eating all those oysters on your own. Let me help you.

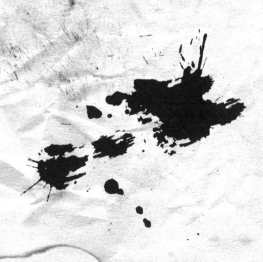

Ne-ah, Toothless na s-s-sporta da sprouty-warm. Ta maka me inta un girly-goo, plus me preffa ma flame-shootys coldover and me flip-flaps lendinta forkfreezies.
Thankee par ta warmwishes.

No, I will NOT wear that furry coat. It makes me look like a sissy and I would rather my fire-holes froze up and my wings turned into ice-lollies. Thank you for your concern.

The Murderous Tribe did not often receive visitors

HEROIC SWORDFIGHTING TIPS

HEROIC SWORDFIGHTING TIPS

The Flash-kick
with-thrust
~~thingummy~~

Do be
careful of
your BACK
Remember:
you are not as
young as you were.

'Of course humans and dragons can live together!' said Hiccup
fiercely. 'Some of my best friends are dragons! It's just that
things have gone wrong somehow… The dragons have become
enslaved when they ought to be free. But you HAVE to believe
that people and dragons can be better. You HAVE to believe in
a better world…'

Song of the Singing Supper

Watch me, Great Destroyer,
as I settle down to lunch,
Killer whales are tasty 'cos they've
got a lot of crunch.

Great white sharks are scrumptious,
but here's a little tip:
Those teeny weeny pointy teeth can
give a nasty nip…

Humans can be bland,
but if you have some salt to hand,
A little bit of brine,
will make them taste div-I-I-I-ne…

I tell the mighty Big Blue Whale,
his life is over soon,
With one swish of this armoured tail
I put out the sun and moon…

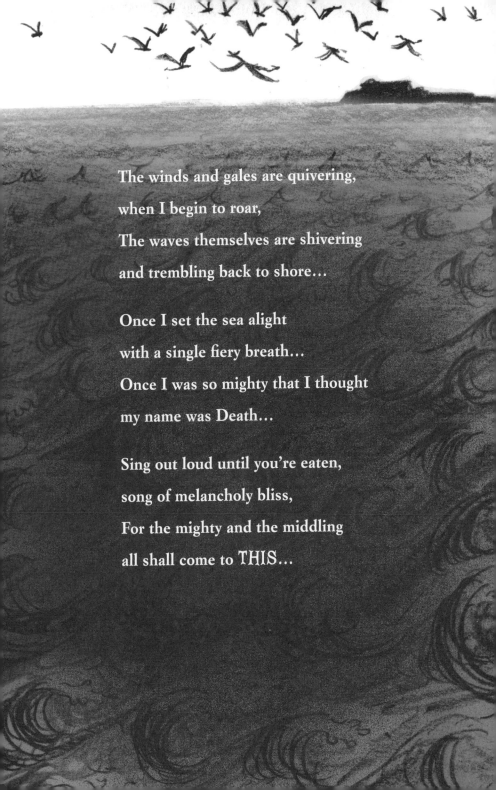

The winds and gales are quivering,

when I begin to roar,

The waves themselves are shivering

and trembling back to shore…

Once I set the sea alight

with a single fiery breath…

Once I was so mighty that I thought

my name was Death…

Sing out loud until you're eaten,

song of melancholy bliss,

For the mighty and the middling

all shall come to THIS…

'You see, it was not only Hiccup who was growing up, it was the entire world around him – and when whole worlds grow up, that can be painful and difficult.'

'Trust me, if you train your dragon the Hard Way, you will develop an unshakeable and lifelong bond… Eventually.'

STILL MORE DRAGON JOKES:

Q: Why did Hiccup's music teacher need a ladder?
A: To reach the high notes.

'Mum, can we have a dragon for Christmas?'
'Certainly not, you'll have turkey like everybody else.'

Q: How do you get down off a dragon?
A: You don't. You get down off a duck.

Q: What did the policeman say to the Triple-Header Rageblaster?
A: Hello, Hello, Hello.

Q: What do you get if you cross a Raptortongue with a dog?
A: A very nervous postman.

Q: Why don't Vampire Dragons have many friends?
A: Because they're a pain in the neck.

Q: Why was the Glow-Worm unhappy?
A: Because her children were not very bright.

Teacher: How do you spell Electricsquirm?
Dogsbreath the Duhbrain: E-L-E-K-T-R-I-K-S-K-W-O-R-M
Teacher: That's not how the dictionary spells it!
Dogsbreath the Duhbrain: You didn't ask me how the dictionary spelt it!

T-T-Tell
Toothless
another one
please
please
please

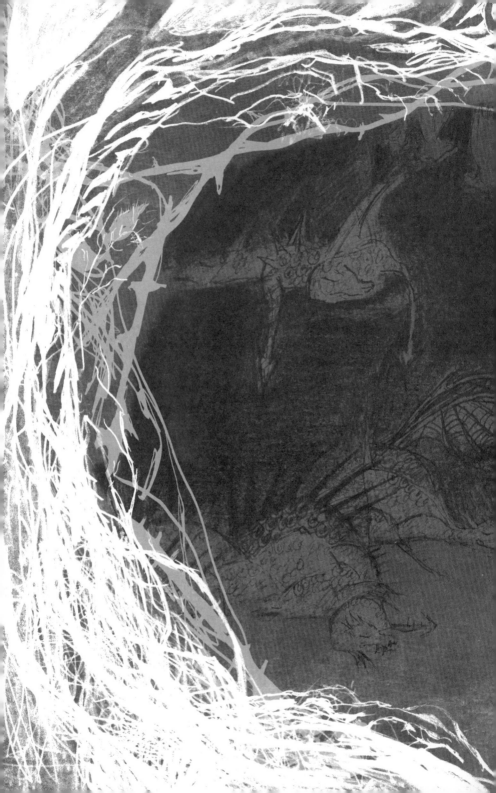

WINTER
FREEZINGS

Dragon Hibernation

Most dragons hibernate in the winter. Big ones go in a cave but smaller ones dig themselves a hole to sleep in, and the deeper the hole, the colder the winter will be.

← A Common-or-Garden dragon hibernating for the winter.

Some dragons, like Saber-Tooth Driver dragons, do not hibernate at all, and they are called evergreens, and this is a funny name for them because Saber Tooth Driver dragons are always white.

A promise
is a promise,
if it is made
in BLOOD...

"The Hero cares not for a WILD
Winter's STORM
For it CARRIES HIM SWIFT
ON THE BACK OF THE STORM
ALL MAY BE LOST AND
OUR HEARTS MAY BE WORN
BUT
A HERO FIGHTS FOREVER!"

'UP with your SWORD and STRIKE at the GALE,
RIDE the rough SEAS for those WAVES are your HOM
WIN-TERS MAY FREEZE but our HEARTS do not FAIL,
..HOOLIGAN..HEARTS.. FOREVER!!! '

♪ 'STRONG are the BREASTS that CRUSH WITHOUT FEAR,
MIGHTY the PLAITS that can STRANGLE the WIND,
NIM-BLE THE FINGERS that BUR-GLE the BOG,
BOG-BURGLARS...STAND...TOGETHER!!!'

I say
NO!
Dragons
and humans
should
be FREE!

'Most of us are lucky not to be Kings and Heroes,
because we do not have to make the choices Kings
and Heroes have to make.'

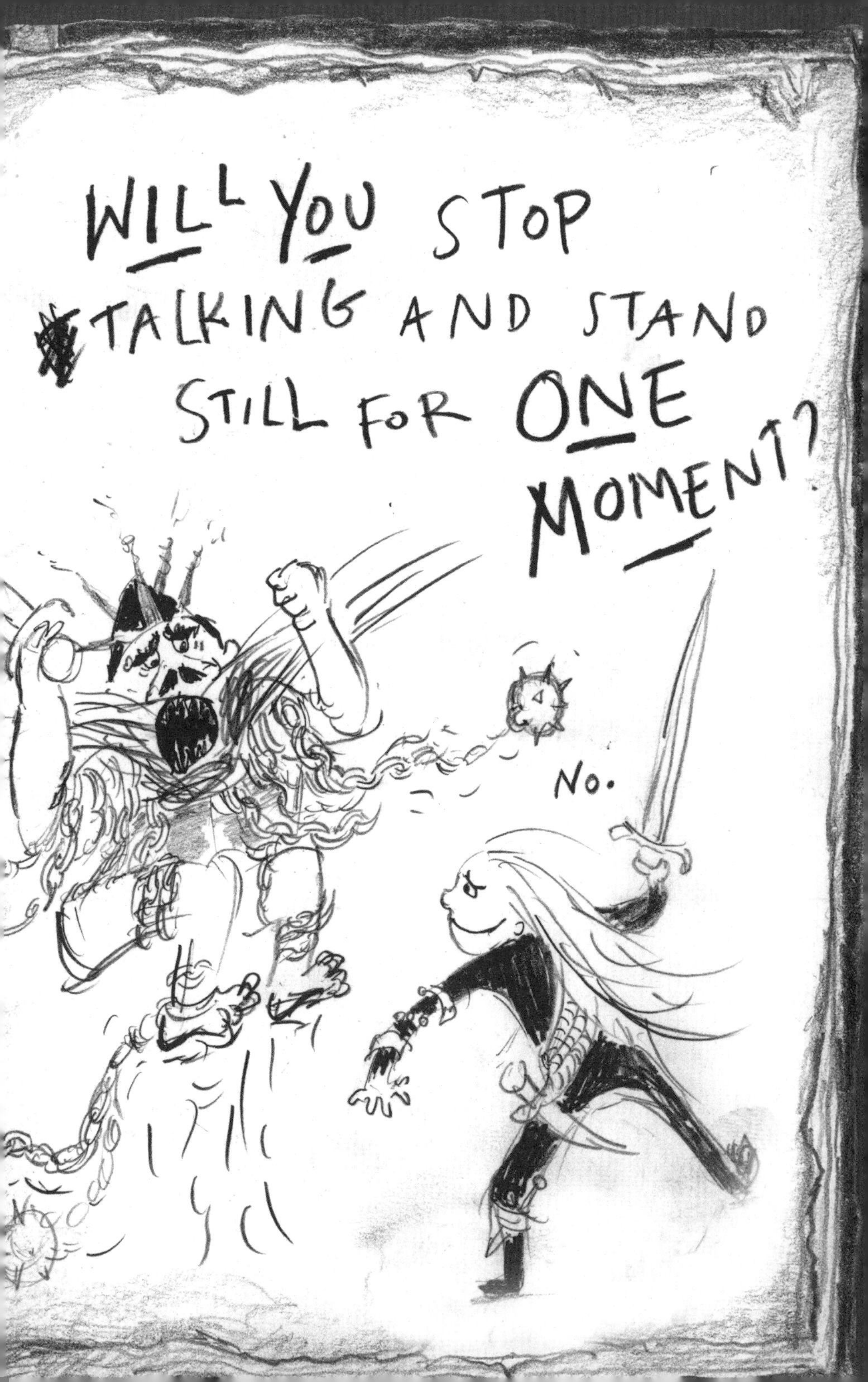
WILL YOU STOP TALKING AND STAND STILL FOR ONE MOMENT?
No.

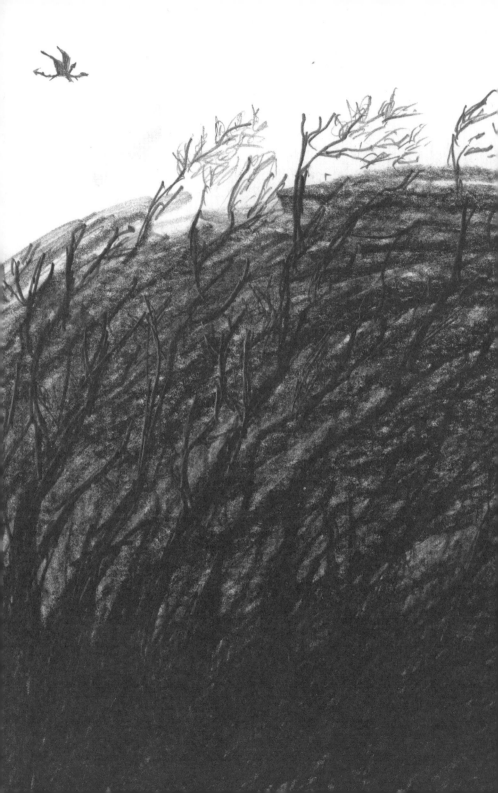

'However small we are, we should all fight for what we believe to be right. And I don't mean fight with the power of our fists or the power of our swords…
I mean the power of our brains and our thoughts and our dreams.'

FISHLEGS'S GUIDE ON HOW NOT TO SKI

Fig 3.
Fall over.

Fig 4.
It is
VERY IMPORTANT

to learn how
to STOP.

'A beautiful little island, all lit up under a canopy of stars. Maybe it was a little rainier on Berk than you might wish for. Perhaps it was a trifle on the windy, boggy, rocky and heathery side. No doubt there were lands with bluer skies and richer soils, somewhere over the horizon. But Berk was the Hooligan's home, and perhaps that is what really matters, after all.'

Conversations with Toothless

Dragon Rivalry...

Your dragon can feel a little threatened when a new dragon enters the household. Be patient and he will get over it. Hopefully...

Toothless: Hogfly ne-ah com sweetie-giggly com T-T-Toothless. *The Hogfly is NOT as cute as Toothless.*

You: Simple ne-ah, Toothless. TOOTHLESS si la Mos Xcellent Oos. May noos ava he keendlee a di fella.
Of course not, Toothless. TOOTHLESS is the Best One. But we have to be nice to him.

Toothless: Simply, simply. Toothless willa be B-B-BIGTIME keendlee a di stupidissimo lacksmart greenblood.
Of course, of course. Toothless will be VERY nice.

Pause.

Toothless to Hogfly: H-H-Hogfly, pishyou, yow goggle com un squealmunch plus yow est plusdim com un snot-trailer.

Hogfly, please, you look like a pig, and you are more stupid than a snail.

You: TOOTHLESS!
TOOTHLESS!

Toothless (whining): May Toothless speekee pishyou!
But Toothless said please!

Another pause.

Toothless: Hogfly, yow wantee a play Hidey-plus-Looky? Y-y-yow hide oppsthere wi di keendlee ickle Wettingsgreenblood, undi Noddle-Scratchers, plus me adda a ponder o marvels und cum opps und loc yow...
*Hogfly, do you want to play Hide-and-Seek?
You hide out there and play with the sweet
little Seadragon and the Brainpickers, and I'll
count to a hundred million and then I'll come
out and find you...*

Hogfly (tail wagging happily): Woof!
Woof!

H-H-Hogfly
NOT as
cute
as
Toothless

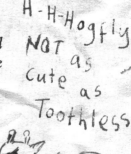

Time cannot
be fought.

'There is nothing more painful than
watching an old lion lose a fight,
particularly to his own son.'

This Quest is now
witHin our grasp.

'Was it all worth
the Archipelago in
flames? I do not
know, you decide.'

"JOIN the Red-RAGE and REBEL,
MaKE red your claws with human blood,
Obliterate the Human Filth . . .
Torch the HUMANs like a wood . . .
The Rebellion is Coming."

. . . .

"JOIN tHE Red-rAGE and Rebel,
 Brother-DRAGons, rebel!"

"Slake your thirst with human fears,"
 Do not spare the human child,
 Incinerate the human pest,
 The Dragontime is Coming."

THE LAST FEW DRAGON JOKES:

Q: Why did Gobber throw butter out of the window?
A: Because he wanted to see butter fly.

Q: Where do tough dragons come from?
A: Hard-boiled eggs.

Q: How do you know if you've had a dragon in your fridge?
A: Footprints in the butter.

Q: Why don't Vikings like long fairy tales?
A: They tend to dragon.

Q: Why did the dragon spit out the clown?
A: Because he tasted funny.

Q: What is green, has four legs and two trunks?
A: Two seasick tourists!

Q: How do Vampire-Dragons keep their breath smelling nice?
A: They use extractor-fangs!

Q: Where do you find Nanodragons?
A: It depends where you lost them.

A Viking went into a cafe with a Doomfang. They ordered lots and lots of food and drink and were stuffing their faces. This went on for about two hours when suddenly the Doomfang fell over dead on the floor. The Viking put his coat and helmet on, left some money on the table and started to walk out. 'Hey' said the cafe owner, 'You can't leave that lying there.'
'It's not a Lion it's a Doomfang,' said the Viking.

Wodensfang

I have to trust in the boy, and hope for the best.

I have to hope for the best.

'Perhaps I am a foolish, fond old dragon, who never learns from my mistakes. But I have to believe that the humans and dragons are capable of living together.'

'The fight goes on
for the Heroes of
the Future…'

HOW TO TRAIN YOUR DRAGON

Collect the
whole series...

1: 978 0 340 99907 3

2: 978 0 340 99908 0

How to Speak Dragonese
3: 978 0 340 99909 7

How to Cheat a Dragon's Curse
4: 978 0 340 99910 3

How to Twist a Dragon's Tale
5: 978 0 340 99911 0

A Hero's Guide to Deadly Dragons
6: 978 0 340 99913 4

How to Ride a Dragon's Storm
7: 978 0 340 99912 7

How to Break a Dragon's Heart
8: 978 0 340 99692 8

How to Steal a Dragon's Sword
9: 978 1 444 90094 1

How to Seize a Dragon's Jewel
10: 978 1 444 90879 4

How to Betray a Dragon's Hero
11: 978 1 444 91398 9

Hodder Children's Books
a division of Hachette Children's Books
338 Euston Road, London NW1 3BH
An Hachette UK company
www.hachette.co.uk

ART AND FREEDOM OF SPEECH

ART AND FREEDOM
OF SPEECH

RANDALL P. BEZANSON

UNIVERSITY OF ILLINOIS PRESS

Urbana and Chicago

Library of Congress Cataloging-in-Publication Data

Bezanson, Randall P.

Art and freedom of speech / Randall P. Bezanson.

p. cm.

Includes bibliographical references and index.

ISBN 978-0-252-03443-5 (cloth : alk. paper)

1. Freedom of expression—United States—Cases.

2. Freedom of expression. I. Title.

KF4770.B487   2009

342.7308'5—dc22   2009009440

For Elaine

The author wishes to acknowledge
the invaluable assistance provided by Susan Troyer,
Andrew Finkelman, and Matt Shaw.

CONTENTS

ART AND FREEDOM OF SPEECH

INTRODUCTION

Art and aesthetics are the forbidden fruit of the First Amendment. They enjoy a tortured history in the annals of constitutional law. And things have not changed much, even today. U.S. Supreme Court Justice Oliver Wendell Holmes Jr. thought judging the worth of art a "dangerous undertaking for persons trained only in the law."[1] Justice Antonin Scalia was characteristically more explicit: "Just as there is no use arguing about taste, there is no use litigating about it. For the law courts to decide 'What is beauty' is a novelty even by today's standards."[2]

The sentiment is deeply ingrained, but its consequences have been far from uniform. From the earliest stages of First Amendment jurisprudence, artistic expression has often been excluded from constitutional protection. And with newly emerging aural and visual technologies, the U.S. Supreme Court has most often declined to apply the full force of constitutional protection, at least for a time, proceeding cautiously and in small steps with the mediums of radio, television, and film, and, most recently, electronic forms of communication. The Court's caution has been particularly evident with the more artistic and emotionally powerful genres of expression such as dance, film, or video. Ideas about freedom of speech have been shaped by the cool, detached, and reasoned medium of print. They are poor fits for the emotional, involved, sensory mediums spawned by twentieth-century technologies.

The reasons for the Supreme Court's caution are many. The roots of free speech and freedom of expression were grounded in religious freedom and political participation. Religion was the home of the aesthetic and ineffable. Speech was an instrument of freedom of belief and of the exchange of information and opinion upon which a new republic was forming. Its point was distinctly cognitive and utilitarian, not emotional and sensory: free speech calmed conflict and enabled self-government. This practical focus remained dominant through the revolution and the founding of the republic, the religious controversies of the eighteenth and nineteenth centuries, the Civil War, the world wars of the twentieth century, and the struggle for civil rights.

Against this background, the claim that the emotionally evocative and reality-transforming roles of art needed equal constitutional protection may have seemed trivial. The more basic commodities of freedom to worship, freedom of belief, freedom to start a life, freedom from want and inequality and war occupied center stage. The role of law was order, organization, predictability, and safety—the critical and mean tasks of process and legitimacy and reason. It was a time for a law of rules.

Claims grounded in artistic or aesthetic expression were ineffable, resting on private judgments of taste and personal exercises of imagination. This was not the stuff that judges "trained only in the law" should or could—or need—decide. Art was a private affair and could be left there. And the public art that did occur was a distinctly public affair, reinforcing collective social and political values in the emerging nation. Buildings, especially public buildings, were symbols of strength and reminders of great Greek and Roman civilizations. The fine arts of painting and theater were instruments of public values produced with the determined support of private patrons and public institutions. Dante's *Inferno* was not welcomed in America. When the artist was an agent of public and private patronage, the patron shaped the artist. In such a domesticated and controlled environment, there was little need for the law to worry about art and its freedom.

Today, art is an autonomous enterprise. The artist is a free agent operating in a robust, open, and competitive market for artistic goods and services. The patron is more an investor in the artist's work than a director of artistic content. The art market is the controlling force: it is decentralized, broad in range of art and genre, and truly democratized. Art is no longer the province of the rich, the educated, the elite, or even the critic. Its forms have blossomed from painting, music, poetry, and sculpture to dance, video, photography, and electronic and multimedia genres. It is not only representational but abstract; not modern even but postmodern. Art, in short, is ubiquitous. Art cannot be avoided by the law. The intersections of art and law are fast expanding, from contract and ownership issues to a new complex of artistic rights of control through copyright and other moral-rights claims, liability for physical and emotional and reputational harm, plagiarism and fair dealing, and provenance and stolen art, to name but a few examples.

The aim in this book, however, is not to address all of the issues concerning art and aesthetic expression but instead to focus on the fundamental questions that underlie any meaningful discussion of the role and status of art as free speech protected by the First Amendment to the United States Constitution.

Thus, the cases discussed and the issues they raise will focus on a limited set of questions: What are the boundaries of art? How does art differ from other, say political, expression? How does artistic expression occur (in the mind of the artist or the mind of the beholder)? What are the limits on the government's role as supporter and "patron" of the arts? Can art be so dangerous, so disruptive and unsettling that it may be prohibited? What, if any, role may core social values of decency, respect, equality, and the like play in limiting the production or distribution of art?

We begin with the *Finley* case, which is used to explore the meaning and nature of art, the standards and processes by which it might be judged, and the government's role as supporter of the arts. The lines that might be drawn between art and politics, art and public values, and art and emotion are the focus in both the *Finley* case and in *Barnes v. Glenn Theatres*, a nude-dancing case. They turn on the nature of artistic and aesthetic expression and the ways it may become manifest (particularly in contrast with political speech). Next we examine the nature and origins of expression in two fundamentally important cases, *Boy Scouts v. Dale*, involving the firing of a gay scoutmaster, and *Hurley v. Irish-American Gay, Lesbian and Bisexual Coalition of Boston*, in which the exclusion of a gay group from the Saint Patrick's Day Parade was challenged on free speech grounds. In both cases, the speech, its origin, and its meaning seem frankly mysterious.

We next turn to cases involving questions of transformation of meaning in art through genre (the *2 Live Crew* case) and community values (*Jenkins v. Georgia*). How does transformation occur, what does it signify, and what if anything can government do about it? A different kind of transformation is next, beginning with the *Virginia v. Black* cross-burning case—aesthetic transformation of a hateful or threatening idea into a real fear that justifies suppression—and then turning to other examples of "dangerous" art. These will include Edouard Manet's *Olympia*, Giovanni Boccaccio's *Decameron*, Roberto Rossellini's film *The Miracle*, and more recent examples.

Finally, we will draw these strands together and look candidly at the central issue that Holmes and Scalia disavowed for courts and judges "trained only in the law": the quality of art and its possible distinction from craft. This book's example—the only main case not decided by the Supreme Court—involves currency art by J. S. G. Boggs, perhaps its highest practitioner, and the crime of counterfeiting. The *Boggs* case forces one to confront the hardest question of all: Should courts judge the quality of a work of art? If so, how, and if not, with what consequences?

Many scholars and experts more knowledgeable than I have tried to define art and the aesthetic. They range from Plato to Hegel to modern scholars like Alison Young and Karol Berger. Most have failed in their ultimate goal, but a great debt is owed them for the effort and the insight they have brought to the subject of artistic expression. Happily, my purpose is a safer and more limited one. It is to open up the questions of the meaning, nature, and role of art and aesthetic expression under the First Amendment and to reveal the underlying issues and questions and the many ways in which those questions might be approached. I supply no fixed answers, but I hope that the reader will come away equipped to supply his or her own and to disagree with some that I offer. If I succeed, the reader will understand that the issues raised by artistic expression are complex and fascinating and, most important, not given to easy or absolute formulas or credos.

These issues' intractability is the most likely reason the Supreme Court has avoided the questions in the past. But the Court can't even hope to avoid them in the future.

PART 1

ART AND THE AESTHETIC

This first section explores in an introductory way the nature and meaning of art and aesthetics. Two interesting and lively cases delve into these subjects, the first involving the lewd and raucous and political performance artist Karen Finley, who got swept up in a firestorm after the National Endowment for the Arts funded an exhibit including the work *Piss Christ* by Andres Serrano. The second case involves nude barroom dancing and its claim to protection as aesthetic and artistic under the First Amendment.

These cases force one to confront the meaning of art and the role of the aesthetic in its production and performance. They also offer an example of the government's claimed role in funding art and in restricting it directly. These are the fundamental questions that are then explored in greater detail in the later chapters.

PERFORMANCE ART

National Endowment for the Arts v. Finley

524 U.S. 569 (1998)

KAREN FINLEY CLAIMS to be an artist. A performance artist.

Not everyone agrees.

Finley's art is who she is. She grew up in a Chicago suburb and was educated at the San Francisco Art Institute.[1] She describes herself as the child of a "not white" mother and a "manic-depressive jazz musician father who eventually committed suicide. . . . I have used that information in my art-making I think very well. I had to get out that emotion somewhere."[2]

Her most infamous performance was described in the *Harvard Gazette* in an article following a public lecture she gave at Harvard in 2002. The title is *We Keep Our Victims Ready*.

> She took her inspiration from Tawana Brawley, the 16-year-old who was found alive in a Hefty bag covered with feces near her home in upstate New York. Finley was moved when Brawley was accused of perpetrating this act herself. "Was this the best choice? What was the worst choice? What was the other choice?" she said of Brawley's apparent desperation. "All of us have that moment where putting the shit on us is the best choice we have."
>
> At the end of the piece, after smearing herself with the feces-symbolic chocolate, Finley covers herself with tinsel because, she said, "no matter how bad a woman is treated, she still knows how to get dressed for dinner."[3]

The *Gazette* article described other, thematically related works. One is "The Body as Rorschach Test."

> [It] showed Finley at work in a studio, surrounded by paintbrushes and other tools. Instead of using them, however, she pulls her breast out from

1. Karen Finley, photograph by Timothy Greenfield-Sanders.

behind her apron and "paints" on a black page with her breast milk, growing increasingly animated and ultimately using both breasts.

Another piece features large, close-up photographs of her daughter's birth surrounded by Post-it Notes of quotes by the practitioners who assisted the drug-free delivery of her 9-pound baby. "I couldn't believe that people were telling me to relax," she said. "This was the most dismissive piece of crap I ever heard."[4]

Finley discussed some of her more overtly political work in an interview in the *Nation* with Bryan Farrell.[5]

QUESTION: "George & Martha" [one of her performances about George Bush and Martha Stewart] had a brief theatrical run in 2004, in which you played the Martha character. Was it difficult to perform such an intense yet insidious psychosexual relationship? Did the audience react the way you expected?

FINLEY: Well, I did perform it nude. And I did diaper Bush. That was a lot of fun. . . . There was a reaction because I created it right after the Republican convention, and I think New Yorkers were so disgusted to have our city taken over by the Republicans and have them use the backdrop of Ground Zero as their platform for George Bush. This happened two weeks afterward, and that feeling was still in the air.

I think we also have to look at our national narratives. We have to be seeing that with Reagan, who was the child of an alcoholic. And when Clinton had his acceptance speech, he was talking about standing up to his father. We vote in a national narrative that we relate to. That's why I was wondering . . . how did this guy get in? What is it that he's reaching? Even if the vote was stolen, there's a national narrative that goes on that people are relating to, and people are relating to his character flaws, his trajectory, his dynamic.

I started to wonder, Why is he so simple? Why does he act so stupid? I think it's to make himself stay like a child. . . . Even Laura is like his mom. She's a librarian. It's like marrying the teacher. His relationship with God is also very grotesque. I think the people of this generation . . . are not doing as well as their parents. People feel like they can't match up to their parents' desires. The expectations we have on our kids are ridiculous. No child left behind? He's no child left behind. . . . I think everyone likes the fact that he's the black sheep. . . . Everyone thought he was the dumb kid. And he showed them. That's one reason I'm against inherited wealth. The playing field would have been even, so he could have just started on his own resources and self-generated what he was doing rather than what he was afforded by the family dynasty. I think he could have had a great bar in Houston.

Finley is by no means alone in seeing her work as art. The critic C. Carr described his reaction in a *Village Voice* review.[6]

When I first saw Finley performing in the clubs in 1985, she was doing scabrous trance-rap monologues that seemed to burst right from the id.

First she'd walk out in some godforsaken prom dress or polyester glad rag, presenting herself as the shy and vulnerable good girl. Then the deluge. While the pieces were heart-stopping in their sexual explicitness, they were never about sex so much as "the pathos," as she called it, the damage and longing in everyone that triggers both desire and rage. She could take a subject like incest and push it to surreal extremes. Above all, she would address it without euphemism. For me, these performances were cathartic, amazing.

But not everyone agreed that Finley was an artist and that her performances were art. As controversy exploded in 1989 over the National Endowment for the Arts (NEA) grant funding to support the exhibition of Robert Mapplethorpe's homoerotic photographs and Andres Serrano's work *Piss Christ*, Karen Finley got caught in the aftershocks. Her request for NEA support for her performance art was rejected by the NEA after consideration of "general standards of decency and respect for the diverse beliefs and values of the American public." Prior to 1990, the NEA funded art based on its artistic merit as art. After 1990, Congress required that grant decisions of the NEA also take into account "general standards of decency and respect." Finley's work was judged indecent and disrespectful, a conclusion not only supported but also widely voiced by such personages as Senator Jesse Helms of North Carolina, who led the fight to enact and thus impose the decency-and-respect requirement on the judgments of artistic merit made by artistic panels of the National Endowment.

Having "painted herself with chocolate, painted with her own breast milk, put Winnie the Pooh in S&M gear, and locked horns with conservative Sen. Jesse Helms,"[7] Finley was subjected to criticism not only from the political and religious right but also from gallery owners and from the National Organization for Women (NOW), which objected to Finley's "Virgin Mary Is Pro-Choice" design for a T-shirt.[8] She claims to have been blindsided by the opposition to her work and the resulting political conflagration: "When I finally realized that Jesse Helms was actually having a public sexually abusive relationship with me and I [became a free speech advocate and symbol], I changed the relationship and I think that I've been healthier ever since."[9]

Performance, not diplomacy, it appears, is her forte.

Finley ultimately joined other artists in a lawsuit seeking to prohibit the NEA from considering decency and respect as part of its grant-funding decisions. As the lawsuit wound its way through the federal courts, she at first lost and then won, finally arriving on the doorstep of the United States Supreme Court where, at shortly after 10:00 A.M. on Tuesday, March 31, 1998, the justices turned their attention to the oral argument in the *Finley* case. To describe her case as much-watched and much-argued would be a colossal understatement.

• • •

Before turning to the *Finley* case, two important matters need to be touched upon. The first is the focus with which to explore Finley's claim. The interest here is with the central questions of art, aesthetics, and how, when, why, and if government should ever intrude into the artistic and aesthetic realms when regulating expression. Are these ineffable or simply prohibited domains for government? Were Finley's performances "art"; if so, what accounts for that conclusion; and what consequence should the conclusion have for art's protection from government regulation under the First Amendment? Finley's claim is that her work is art. Is the stripper's work in a bar art? What if the stripper covers her nude body with chocolate, as does Finley? Or shouts obscenities? Or intends by her work not just to titillate but to symbolize the desperate role of women in a conventional and male society? Does a cognitive "message" strengthen the claim that something is art, or is its effect exactly the opposite?

The Oxford English Dictionary (OED) defines *art* by employing many layers of potential meaning. The term's most ordinary usage is, according to the OED, "Skill; its display or application" or "learning of the schools," as in the liberal arts. The more fitting definitions for purposes here are, again according to the OED, "the application of skill to subjects of taste, as poetry, music, dancing, the drama, oratory, literary composition, and the like.... Skill displaying itself in perfection of workmanship, perfection of execution *as an object in itself.*"[10] Similarly, art is "the application of skill to the arts of imitation and design ...; the skillful production of the beautiful in visible forms."

From these definitions, one might conclude that art has to do with skill as to form in itself, as in perfection of form and execution, and as to the beautiful, in matters of taste. Beauty and taste, moreover, go not only (or not so much) to a message conveyed (cognition) but also to perception itself, as in beauty, pleasure, comfort, or evoked emotion. Art rests on emotion or aesthetic perception rather than cognition or rational understanding. *Aesthetic*, in turn, according to the OED, means "of or pertaining to sensuous perception, received by the senses" or "of or pertaining to the appreciation or criticism of the beautiful." And *aesthetics* is "the science which treats of the conditions of sensuous perception" and "the philosophy or theory of taste or of the perception of the beautiful in nature and art."

Classical and traditional philosophers from Plato to Kant have linked aesthetics to ideas of beauty *and ugliness*, to perceptions of pleasure or disgust, growing out of form and structure itself in a largely sensuous sense.[11] A competing and more "modern" school of philosophers rejects the very idea "that an artwork might be good because it is pleasurable, as opposed to cognitively, morally or politically beneficial."[12] It is the "message" of a work of art, not its form and sensory perception, that counts. Clear signs of this conflict between art as beauty (or ugliness) and art as politics are seen in the *Finley* case. Is a work that appeals in a powerful sensory way but lacks "redeeming social value," as the Supreme Court's definition of obscenity once put it, thereby not *art?*

A third view of art is more utilitarian: What function does art perform, how does it operate, and what does it do that is distinct from other forms of expression? As Karol Berger puts it in his wonderful book *A Theory of Art*, "[E]ver since Plato philosophers have been much exercised by the question of what art is . . . , of getting art's ontological status right, of finding a way to distinguish art from other entities. . . . [But] even if we grant this [defined] object the status of art, we still do not know whether and why we should bother ourselves with it." We should bother ourselves, Berger suggests, "because of art's ability to evoke imaginary worlds, and not representation in the strict and narrow sense. . . . In an act of cognition whereby we get to know an object, the . . . powers of imagination . . . and understanding . . . are engaged like two gear wheels. But in an act of aesthetic contemplation, the two wheels spin without engaging and the cognitive mechanism runs on idle. . . . Aesthetic pleasure is 'in the harmony of the cognitive faculties,' in 'the quickening of both faculties (imagination and understanding) to an indefinite, and yet, thanks to the given representation, harmonious activity.'" Art spurs imagination and re-representation of the objective; it is, perhaps, intrinsic to creativity.

How does one choose among these definitions (and other ones that will come up along the way)? Must one choose? And one must grapple with another and related concept: emotion. As Justice John Marshall Harlan said in 1971 in the famous *Cohen v. California* case involving a jacket with the words "Fuck the Draft" on the back,

> much linguistic expression serves a dual communicative function: it conveys not only ideas capable of relatively precise, detached explication, but otherwise inexpressible emotions as well. Words are often chosen as much

for their emotive as their cognitive force. We cannot sanction the view that the Constitution, while solicitous of the cognitive content of individual speech, has little or no regard for that emotive function which, practically speaking, may often be the more important element of the overall message sought to be communicated.

Emotion, or force or feeling embodied or evoked in an expression, may be part of the connecting fiber between art and politics. Can the same be said of art in the form of dancing, painting, acting, and the like?

These are the questions that will only begin to be explored in Karen Finley's case.

But first, however, a further bit of groundwork should be laid. It may come as a surprise to some readers that the Supreme Court rarely addresses such questions as the meaning of art and the role of aesthetics in expression under the First Amendment, and when it does so, the Court does not delve deeply. Instead, the Court relies on technical or procedural—lawyerly, one might say—standards of decision. These standards should be briefly catalogued so that they can be recognized.

First are concerns about a law's overbreadth or underinclusiveness, a feature of speech regulations that sweep too broadly or narrowly and thus should be stricken and rewritten more carefully so as to aim only at that speech that can be restricted, leaving other speech free. Government might wish to prohibit camping in protest on the Washington, D.C., Mall, but it can't do so by prohibiting camping—for protest or otherwise—everywhere or by banning only antiwar protestors from camping on the Mall, for the very narrow (or overbroad) application of the restriction suggests that its purpose is to censor an idea, not to alleviate a traffic problem.

A second standard is vagueness. The First Amendment requires precision in the language used by the government to restrict speech. Vague terms are potentially too broad and leave too much discretion to the law interpreter or law enforcer. Imagine, for example, that a town enacts a law prohibiting its residents from using insulting words. Because of the sheer number of possible words and settings in which they might be used and the ambiguity of terms such as *insulting*, such a law would likely be unconstitutionally vague. But a defamation—a knowing falsehood about another that harms them in their reputation or business—could be prohibited because *knowing*, *falsity*, and provable harm place fairly exacting and judicially enforceable limits on the kinds of verbal exchanges being regulated.

The third standard involves the capacity in which the government is acting when it selectively restricts or funds speech. Is the government acting as
a censor? An educator? A protector of the rules of order by which others are
also permitted to express themselves? A manager or owner of an enterprise?
In the last instance, for example, government can surely acquire art for the
walls of government buildings, and in doing so, government can make aesthetic choices and exercise artistic preferences. Can public schools exercise
no judgment about art that is appropriate for children or suitable to the educational mission of the school in which it would be displayed? This is tricky
and very important business under the First Amendment.

These three standards, and others that will be noted along the way, are
themselves very important matters to explore. But not yet. They are employed by the law in order to avoid having to answer the underlying questions: the meaning of art; the role played by aesthetic communication; the
value of expression, and more. The purpose here is to focus on the central
question—whether Karen Finley's acts are art, and what is the government's
power to restrict it.

• • •

The justices who gathered in the marble courtroom of the Supreme Court
building on the morning of Tuesday, March 31, 1998, were a singularly disputatious and deeply fractured group. The Chief Justice was William Rehnquist, originally appointed by President Richard M. Nixon in 1972 and then
appointed Chief in 1986 by President Ronald Reagan. As the Chief Justice,
Rehnquist was widely liked as an individual, widely respected for his sheer intelligence, and widely regarded as conservative. Joining him in the conservative quarter of the Court were Justices Anthony M. Kennedy, Antonin Scalia,
and Clarence Thomas. Kennedy was often unpredictable. Scalia was brilliant
and arrogant and acerbic. Thomas was radical in his eagerness to reexamine
long-settled assumptions underlying constitutional doctrine. On the more
liberal side of the ledger were Justices John Paul Stevens, the most senior
justice, Stephen Breyer, a former Harvard professor, Ruth Bader Ginsburg,
a former Columbia professor, and David Souter, formerly a judge in New
Hampshire. Stevens tended to write the most creative, activist, and ambiguous opinions, Breyer and Ginsburg tended to write careful and craftsman-like
opinions consistent with a more limited idea of the judicial role, and Souter
tended to the intellectual and complex, if not arduous, form of discourse when
explaining himself. Finally, Sandra Day O'Connor, appointed by President

Reagan in 1981, sat squarely in the middle and wrote opinions reflecting that analytically untidy posture.

The lawyers charged with constructing and defending an argument before this divided group of justices were Seth Waxman, the Solicitor General of the United States, who defended the NEA's denial of grant funding to Karen Finley, and David Cole, a professor of law at Georgetown University, who argued that the denial violated the First Amendment guarantee of free speech.

The Chief Justice called the case, entitled *National Endowment for the Arts v. Karen Finley*, and invited the Solicitor General to begin.[13]

GENERAL WAXMAN: Mr. Chief Justice, and may it please the Court: Since 1965, the National Endowment for the Arts has selectively provided public funding to arts projects on the basis of aesthetic judgments in order to enrich the lives of all Americans and to expand public appreciation of art.

The question presented in this case is whether although it thus expands the opportunities for artistic expression, Congress violated the First Amendment—that is, made a law abridging the freedom of speech—by directing that the NEA ensure "that artistic excellence and artistic merit are the standards by which applications are judged, taking into consideration general standards of decency and respect for the diverse beliefs and values of the American public."

The way the NEA did this was a bit peculiar, as will be seen from the oral argument exchanges. The NEA traditionally made grant selections through a tiered process. Proposals or applications were first considered by advisory panels, consisting heavily of artists and people involved in the arts. The panels made recommendations based on artistic excellence and merit to the arts council, the final decision maker, passing the recommendations first to the chairperson, who reviewed them and forwarded his or her recommendation to the council along with the panel's.

In the case of the "decency and respect" amendment added by Congress to the NEA statute, the process was modified. The amendment, often referred to here as Section 954(d) and indicated in italics below, provides that:

No payment shall be made under this section except upon application therefor which is submitted to the National Endowment for the Arts in accordance with regulations issued and procedures established by the Chairperson. In establishing such regulations and procedures, the Chairperson shall ensure that—

(1) artistic excellence and artistic merit are the criteria by which applications are judged, *taking into consideration general standards of decency and respect for the diverse beliefs and values of the American public*; and

(2) applications are consistent with the purposes of this section. Such regulations and procedures shall clearly indicate that obscenity is without artistic merit, is not protected speech, and shall not be funded.

In light of Congress's addition of the decency-and-respect criteria, the NEA decided that instead of requiring panel members and the council to expressly judge a proposal's "decency and respect," the chairperson would reconstitute the panels to assure that their memberships consisted of persons who would likely reflect those values in their judgment of artistic merit without any need for instruction or for specific attention to "decency and respect" in their decision. The chairperson might then, as he did in Karen Finley's case, review the panel's recommendation to assure that "decency and respect" were, in fact, reflected in the panel's decision, and if he was uncertain, he would send the recommendation back to the panel for reconsideration in light of his concerns. In Finley's case, the panel reconsidered and forwarded a positive recommendation once again. The recommendation then went to the council, where the "decency and respect" criteria could be judged independently, and the panel recommendation for funding was disapproved by a majority of the council.

The NEA's response to the "decency and respect" amendment, in other words, was to bury it in the panel selection criteria, and hope for the best.

QUESTION: How do you take into account standards of decency in selecting the panel?

GENERAL WAXMAN: In the process of deciding which proposals will be granted on the basis of merit and excellence, and here's how the NEA has construed the statute to work. The NEA Chair thus far has concluded that whatever factors an individual takes into consideration in deciding whether something is art, not to mention artistically excellent and artistically meritorious, may be considerations of the mode and form of expression in the case [as distinguished from the message or point of view expressed].

It's not dispositive, but if it includes a mode or form of communication, the NEA [has] concluded that many, if not most, if not all, certainly at least some people in deciding whether something is really artistically excellent or meritorious or how much it is, will at least think about the mode or form of the presentation that the artist is using.

We will see many references to "mode" of communication (its time and place and its genre [performance art, painting, or drama, for example], as well as the manner of presentation [nudity, profanity, and violent or nonviolent]), as opposed to the substantive message, the point of view expressed (women are abused), or the content of the message, which is a bit more general category of message (the subordinate role of women in society), or the subject matter of the message (equality). Under the First Amendment, restrictions on speech because of its specific point of view (don't say women are abused) are highly disfavored, and restrictions based on content and subject matter (no discussion of inequality and women, respectively) are less disfavored and require application of a less-strict or rigorous scrutiny of the government's justification and the narrowness of the means used to achieve it. Finally, restrictions based on the mode or manner of speech (no lewd words or pictures when discussing sex discrimination in a classroom) are subjected to a fairly light scrutiny testing only the "reasonableness" of the government's purposes and legislative means.

Laws that are imperfect in their overbreadth yet represent a reasonable and good faith effort to achieve a goal are often valid. This is why the Solicitor General seeks to characterize the "decency and respect" amendment as a law focused on mode or manner of expression, not subject or content and particularly not point of view. The "decency and respect" amendment is embodied in the NEA's choice of means. The NEA's decision to embody the decency-and-respect aims in the panel-composition determination clearly qualifies as an imperfect, if not downright messy, means of carrying out Congress's purposes, but it might just pass the lightest form of First Amendment scrutiny.

Two related matters should be noted at this point. First, the inconvenient fact that it was the council, not the expert panel, that rejected the favorable recommendation in Finley's case, undercuts the Solicitor General's panel-composition argument, which is that "decency and respect" are not expressly judged and are reflected only in terms of "mode."

Second, and more fundamentally, the Solicitor General's argument assumes that there is a clear distinction in artistic expression between mode and message, and that for purposes of the First Amendment, message is the most important of the two when it comes to art. This is a doubtful proposition. If art and aesthetics go to beauty (or ugliness) in form and sensual perception quite independent of any "message," indeed of the *need for any* cognitive "message," then with art "mode" and "manner" *are* the message. The First Amendment rule that point-of-view regulations of a message are most forbidden, which is based on a cognitive model of expression, simply doesn't fit purely emotional and sensory expression. What is the point of view of a Picasso painting? Karen Finley's performance had a cognitive message, but does her claim that it is art depend on that? Or does it depend on the skill and the aesthetic and emotional force contributed by the performance itself—the mode or manner of the message's communication?

If art relates to manner of presentation and noncognitive perception by an audience, then traditional First Amendment rules that mainly protect cognitive messages and prohibit point of view restrictions will sweep much art into a category that receives minimal, if any, First Amendment protection.

QUESTION: Are you saying, General Waxman, that if the law is as you say it is, then nobody is being hurt because these words are largely hortatory, is that essentially your position?

GENERAL WAXMAN: Well, that's—that's the essence. . . .

QUESTION: General Waxman, are you trying to persuade us that even after the statute was passed, Andres Serrano would have the same chance of getting a grant as he did before?

GENERAL WAXMAN: Well, we don't think actually that he would have a lesser chance. Congress rejected a provision that would have denied funding to the *Merchant of Venice* or *Rigoletto*, or D. W. Griffith's *Birth of a Nation*. It wanted those to be funded. It just wanted to make sure that in the process of deciding what is the most excellent art in a program which is designed to benefit the American people and expose people, including young people and people in rural areas, to the benefits of artistic expression, that [decency and respect] were taken into account.

The agency's view, Justice Stevens, is that many people—I know it would be true of me—who go into an evaluative process as to whether something is art, or excellent art, or meritorious art, or art that's—that the Congress can spend taxpayer's money to fund, one of the things you think about is the mode of expression. It can either add to or detract from the merit of the proposal, but it's not irrelevant.

QUESTION: It seems to me you're going to have a hard time persuading me the statute's essentially meaningless, which is basically what you're arguing.

QUESTION: I have the same problem. Suppose the statute said that each and every grant must meet the following standard, and then it set forth the statutory standard, and that each panel member will certify that as to each particular artist whose work has been approved, that this statute has been met, is your position the same?

GENERAL WAXMAN: Our position would be twofold. One, because we think that … general standards of decency and respect for diverse values can be defined in a manner that does not take account of viewpoint, that [standard] is not viewpoint discriminatory, [and] for that reason the provision would be constitutional.

As a fallback, if you thought that it was absolutely unreasonable for the agency to conclude that those provisions couldn't be defined without reference to viewpoint, we would have to then address the very difficult question that Congress thought in passing this compromise you wouldn't have to address. That is, do we have a statute that establishes independent funding prohibitions that can't be viewed other than as viewpoint discriminatory, and we do acknowledge that that would pose additional First Amendment concerns, but they were concerns that Congress didn't intend that this Court address.

QUESTION: I would think that most artists would say that they're interested primarily in mode of expression. Did Picasso have a viewpoint? I think he was more, much more interested in mode of expression. It seems to me ultimately that's an unstable line you're drawing.

GENERAL WAXMAN: Well, I do respectfully disagree to this extent, Justice Kennedy. There is no doubt that in considering the content of a work of art, you consider the subject matter, the medium, the mode of expression, and the viewpoint expressed if it's a kind of art that is expressing a viewpoint or could be interpreted as expressing a viewpoint.

This Court has recognized on several occasions that decency … is distinct from viewpoint. Yes, use of indecent speech or controversial speech may very, very well add to or subtract from the force of the message, but it's not the same as viewpoint.

We are now in the land of mode versus viewpoint, or manner versus message, with message meaning a cognitive, reasoned message, not a sensuous or aesthetic one. Where does "force" fit in? Is it emotional and sensory, going to questions of taste on matters of beauty or ugliness, as the definitions of art and aesthetics imply? Or is it part of a cognitive message, altering or reframing the propositional meaning of a work of art? In the *Cohen* case, involving a jacket with "Fuck the Draft" on the back, Justice Harlan said that emotion was an important part of expression—"Fuck the Draft" versus "I Detest the Draft"—that contributed inextricably to the message's meaning and force. But Harlan was dealing with a cognitively grounded free speech claim— the message was against the draft. Much art has a cognitive message; much doesn't. Much art does no more than "express" feelings and evoke emotional response in the viewer or listener. Does a Bach cello solo performed by Yo-Yo Ma communicate a cognitive message to me, like "the woods are dark and mysterious" or "a storm's coming"? Or does the music express only emotional and perceptual feelings—feelings in Bach's case wound up in such things as perfection, beauty, symmetry? And Yo-Yo Ma's performance of Bach? Isn't it attractive to me because it is so skillful that it evokes feelings of awe and sublime satisfaction? To attach either Bach or Yo-Yo Ma to a rational message would be to utterly disrespect their art.

The justices return to this deep enigma of mode versus message presented in Karen Finley's case—is her performance covering her nude body with chocolate and then with tinsel while speaking and swearing and writhing to be judged by its skill and force and emotional power or instead as but one instrumental means by which to communicate a cognitive message to the audience (women are objects or a message something even stronger than that)? Even if the answer is "both," as in *Cohen*, the latter measure of judging seems fundamentally wanting.

For the moment, however, the questions turn to another puzzle: In what capacity was the government (NEA) acting when it judged Karen Finley's performances, and should that matter under the First Amendment?

QUESTION: Well, will you help me with [a] basic inquiry? If the federal government wants to buy artwork to put in the Capitol, I assume it can go out and select works of art that its committee thinks are decent and represent diversity, and can spend the federal money for that kind of art, and it isn't open to challenge, is that right?

GENERAL WAXMAN: Assuredly right.

QUESTION: Now, if the Government wants to educate children, or people, and chooses to speak by way of paying for certain kind of artistic expression as a means of the Government speaking and educating, and insists on decency and diversity, it can do that.

GENERAL WAXMAN: We believe that it can.

QUESTION: All right. Here, it has a limited amount of money to give away. Now, what is it that makes it impossible for the Government to give a limited amount of money away on the same standards? Is the Government not speaking? I mean, what do we have here?

GENERAL WAXMAN: I will state the obvious and suggest that the question probably would be better answered then by my friend Professor Cole, because we don't think that there is any constitutional problem here with this provision.

This answer is really no answer. The Solicitor General wants very much to avoid the subject altogether because there is a newly emerging First Amendment doctrine of "government speech" that applies when the government itself is speaking, not when the government is restricting or regulating the speech of other private persons. Conversation in a democracy must be two-way, from people to government and vice versa. Thus government can sponsor TV ads favoring sexual abstinence or opposing smoking; it can select speakers who will speak at a public university or a graduation; it can buy art for its buildings; it can select the artists and performances for its theaters and museums. In these capacities, the government is not subject to the normal viewpoint/content/subject matter First Amendment rules, for the act of speaking necessarily implies choices about subject, content, and point of view. The Constitution does not require a government speaking against smoking to also speak for it.

The question being raised by the justice is whether the NEA's selection of art and artists to support is an instance of government speaking—expressing its own preferences—and thus not subject to First Amendment scrutiny at all. This turned out to be a hotly debated topic in the oral argument and among the justices. A few problems with the government speech theory are worth pointing out at the beginning. First, few if any persons seeing or hearing art that has been supported by an NEA artist grant are aware of the funding, much less where it came from. Second, the decision to support an artist with a NEA grant does not mean that the government endorses or sponsors the resulting art; it simply means that need for support and artistic quality have been determined by expert panels. By analogy, a faculty member who gives a student an A for a paper should not be understood to agree with the paper or to endorse its views through the rewarding of a high grade.

When government speaks, the argument goes, it must mean to do so and be understood to do so. So when the University of Virginia establishes a student-activity fund that supports, among other things, student newspapers of all stripes but then refuses to fund religious newspapers, the university as government should not be able to claim its own right to speak by discriminating against religious papers, because there is no evidence that the university intended to speak a message against religion, and in any event no reasonable person would understand the university as an arm of government to be speaking. Universities tend to distance themselves as far a possible from signaling any support or endorsement of the student groups that are supported. Instead of speaking, the university has opened up a forum for all student newspapers, and having done so, its act of disqualifying religious student newspapers can only be seen as an act of government regulation of speech, not as government itself speaking.[14]

Against that background, the justices bore in pretty hard on the Solicitor General.

QUESTION: General Waxman, may I suggest that maybe there is something different? Maybe if a faithful executive is trying to carry out the legislative will, the message that comes from the whole history of this is, don't fund Serrano or Mapplethorpe. I think that that's the concern—that, if I am an executive who is trying to be faithful to the legislative will, I know what prompted this, so why don't I say, well, that's my marching orders. I know what the legislature didn't want.

GENERAL WAXMAN: Well, I guess I have a couple of answers. First, a chairperson could have done that. Chairpersons, as the other side points out, were highly cognizant of political concerns without the enactment of this rather innocuous amendment. Second, what the 1990 legislative debate shows is exactly the opposite. The view that certain art that is viewpoint discriminatory or denigrates religion or races won't be funded was rejected.

And the legislative history is shot through and through with the fact that what Congress wanted . . . is that you change the procedures, you do not employ specific content or viewpoint prohibitions, and to the extent you want things like decency to be considered, they should be embedded in the subjective, aesthetic judgments about what's meritorious and excellent.

The Solicitor General's argument is a good one—to a point. Decency and respect are different from racist content. But are they different in degree or kind? One is a message in a work of art about race; the other (decency and respect) is the way in which any message is conveyed—its force, for example. But what about the message that is conveyed in a racist way, thus transforming the message of the art to a racist one? The two are hard to separate, perhaps because they are really part of the same thing. Can it be that "decency and respect" aren't a message if they alter the intended message by their presence? If Cohen had worn "The Draft Is Unwise, Vote for an All-Volunteer Army," the message would have been quite different from "Fuck the Draft," both in manner and, as a consequence, in meaning.

Justice Scalia doesn't like the muddy distinction, so he characteristically and with enthusiasm enters the fray.

QUESTION [JUSTICE SCALIA]: General Waxman, I thought your first response to Justice Ginsburg's question was going to be, so what? I thought that what you responded to Justice O'Connor was, the government doesn't have to buy Mapplethorpe pictures to hang up itself, and so also when it funds the arts, it doesn't have to fund Mapplethorpe, and it can say we don't like Mapplethorpe.

GENERAL WAXMAN: I knew that that would—I knew you would support—

QUESTION: You knew I was going to say that. (Laughter.)

GENERAL WAXMAN: Well, if you're talking about—if we're talking about whether Congress can say, okay, the NEA is going to apply the following standards but it's not going to fund Robert Mapplethorpe, that raises many different constitutional concerns that don't have—in other words, going to single out one particular person, at that point may violate—it would have to be scrutinized.

QUESTION: Well, is it constitutionally principled for the Government to do this by a wink-wink, nudge-nudge—

GENERAL WAXMAN: That's—that is not—that's not, Justice Kennedy, what we're suggesting was done here.

The Solicitor General seems a little taken aback in this exchange, but his caution may be understandable. If he agrees that the government could not simply (or with a wink and a nod) exclude Mapplethorpe, he's leading himself down a slippery slope: Why not Mapplethorpe? Because that would be point-of-view discrimination? Is that because of his message, which is homoeroticism? No, speech with that message wouldn't be excluded. Is it because he communicates that message in an indecent and nonrespectful way? It must be (though the stunning, aesthetic beauty of his photographs can't be denied). So it's the mode and manner that really count, and thus content- or point-of-view-based discrimination, which he acknowledges happened in *Finley*, is unconstitutional? Oops.

On the other hand, the Solicitor General doesn't really want to get on the bandwagon of government speech, which he is being invited to argue as a justification for point-of-view discrimination against Mapplethorpe. Why? Because the government isn't really the speaker; it's providing support to the speech of private artists, hardly a sufficient connection to transform the artist's speech into the government's message. And the government isn't buying speech for its own use or for its expression by another expressly on the government's behalf. Instead, the government-speech argument would have to be that the government is acting as a patron of the arts through its selective support for private artists and art it likes, while keeping its patronage tastes pretty well to itself. The only message (emotional or cognitive) is the art, and the art isn't the government's but the private artist's, who controls it in the private market. The idea of patronage as speech is thus something new—a policy or preference unarticulated and inchoate that may affect expression but does not itself express anything. It's like setting the price of admission for a government-owned hall: the price may affect the type of speech that occurs there, and thus affect expression, but of itself the price is not expression.

Thus, making the government-speech argument on the arts-patron theory would be to tread on entirely new and highly controversial ground. It would open up the possibility that Congress or the executive branch could impose lots of general and specific limits on the NEA's funding in the name of aesthetic preferences and could change them with each new administration or Congress.

But Justice Scalia won't let the Solicitor General off the hook so easily.

QUESTION: But you assume that that's unconstitutional. What if Congress doesn't name names? It just says, no crucifixes in urine. Can it say that?

GENERAL WAXMAN: I—Justice Scalia, I—

QUESTION: Can it say that? It doesn't name any names.

GENERAL WAXMAN: Justice Scalia, I am not assuming—I'm not standing up here arguing that it would be unconstitutional. I think it may well be that in the unique circumstances of public arts funding . . ., viewpoint distinctions may be constitutionally defensible.

QUESTION: So you in effect are saying, I'm not going to rest my argument on the claim that the Government is hiring anyone to speak here, or that what it's doing bears an analogy to that, or that in fact the Government is buying art, or that it bears an analogy to that. You're really saying there's a third rule, the Government as distributor of largesse to the arts, and that, that's a third rule, but you're not saying that the Government is either the speaker or the buyer, is that correct?

GENERAL WAXMAN: Well, I think the Government is the buyer.

QUESTION: What's it buying? What does it own after the grant?

GENERAL WAXMAN: I think this is a distinction without a difference to our argument, but in fact it's behaving as Governments and sovereigns as arts patrons always have. When the Medicis—

QUESTION: Yes, but the King ended up with the picture. The Government is not ending up with the picture.

GENERAL WAXMAN: The King did not necessarily end up with the picture. The Medicis, for example, funded art that was placed all over their realm. The same people who funded and allowed to flourish the great university, that forum, that community where free and uninhibited expression of debate and views occurred, were also arts patrons, and they bought and funded what they liked.

QUESTION: Okay, then you are saying there is an art-patrons rule. I take it you're not hitching your argument either to the claim that the Government is buying, or the claim that the Government is itself the speaker.

GENERAL WAXMAN: Yes. If you're asking whether we're suggesting that there is something unique, particularly unique about the Government funding of the arts for First Amendment purposes, the answer is yes, and for a variety of reasons.

For one thing, and most critically, this is an area in which Government decision makers are expected and required to make precisely the kind of aesthetic judgments which are subjective and may take content and viewpoint into account, and which the Government is ordinarily prohibited from doing.

QUESTION: Why is the Government required, when the Government is not required, in fact, to fund the arts at all? Where does the requirement come from?

GENERAL WAXMAN: Unless, Justice Souter, the NEA is simply disestablished because of a belief that the First Amendment wouldn't permit funding of the arts, or unless you can set up a program where, you know, the proposals that were on the thickest paper, or the ones that came in first were granted, inevitably the decision maker is going to be making the kind of aesthetic judgments that it has made here.

Thank you.

CHIEF JUSTICE REHNQUIST: Thank you, General Waxman.

Well! The foundations of the Solicitor General's argument were pretty shaky—mode versus message; manner versus point of view; panel composition versus speech restriction—and the edifice built on them was pretty ugly, but he made it through alive. The fact of the matter is that shaky foundations, judged by logic and internal consistency, are more common in the Supreme Court than one might expect. The reason is that the lawyers have to calibrate their arguments not only to the prior cases and settled doctrine but also to the multiple schools of thought that exist within the present Court. One has to get five votes to prevail in a case, and this means, on the Court hearing the Finley case, that at least two different views of the Constitution must often be brought together to form a majority. That makes for compromise and untidiness and also great care in taking positions. It's not very aesthetically pleasing.

The argument now turns to Karen Finley's side.

CHIEF JUSTICE REHNQUIST: Mr. Cole, we'll hear from you.

MR. COLE: Mr. Chief Justice, and may it please the Court: As the Government concedes, this is not a case about Government speech. It's not a case about the Government hiring artists to express a Government message. Rather, it's a case about the Government selectively subsidizing private speakers speaking for themselves.

This distinction is the key to Cole's argument. The NEA program is not an instance of government speech for which the normal strict rules of the First Amendment would be suspended. It is not whether the government, as the author of its own message, would be able to choose its own point of view, as any speaker must. It will be recalled that in the Court's decision in the 1995 case *Rosenberger v. University of Virginia*, the University of Virginia set up a program to subsidize, among other things, all student newspapers that served the educational and social purposes of the University, but then it excluded religious newspapers even though they met the qualifications. In setting up the general subsidy program, the University was not expressing any views; it was simply trying to encourage an active and engaged student culture. Thus, excluding religious newspapers represented a content-based restriction of speech—some justices said point-of-view, but the excluded papers could have related to any religion and indeed could have been antireligious papers, so content is the better term. The exclusion was therefore stricken down under the First Amendment for lack of any compelling justification.

Cole must characterize the NEA subsidy program in similar terms. The program provides funding for art judged meritorious, based on decisions by the art panels and the council. Congress then added by amendment the additional requirements that the art be decent and respectful of American values. The decency and respect criteria are not relevant to artistic merit, just like the exclusion of religious newspapers in *Rosenberger* could not be justified by the general educational goals of the student-activities subsidy. The exclusion of indecent and disrespectful art was thus a content or point-of-view restriction on speech—even in the form of a subsidy rather than a direct ban—prohibited by the First Amendment unless the purpose of the decency-and-respect exclusion was compelling, unrelated to restricting expression itself, and narrowly tailored to exclude only speech that threatened the compelling interest, no more and no less. Promoting decency and respect in art may be valid interests, but they are not likely compelling, especially when the exclusion's purpose is to limit speech that while perhaps upsetting to many, is nevertheless fully protected. And the means used to achieve the government's "higher" standard of taste in subsidized art were grossly overbroad and underinclusive. Some offensive (though not indecent) art—for example, art with a racial undertone or nudity in the play *Hair*—is not excluded, and vice versa. This is a necessary byproduct of the vague contours of "taking into consideration general standards of decency and respect for the diverse beliefs and values of the American public."

Professor Cole must hold tightly to this line of argument, or he will lose the case.

MR. COLE, CONTINUING: [When the government established a program in which it selectively subsidizes private speakers who are speaking for themselves,] two fundamental First Amendment principles apply, and the decency and respect clause violates both. First, the Government subsidies must be viewpoint neutral. This Court has held that in *Rosenberger*.

QUESTION: *Rosenberger* was quite different from this, Mr. Cole. Everybody was going to get something in *Rosenberger* except the people who wanted to do something religious. Here, the Government doesn't purport to say we're going to give grants to everybody that wants it. There's a definite degree of selectivity involved.

MR. COLE: There is a degree of selectivity involved here but there was also, Chief Justice Rehnquist, a degree of selectivity in *Rosenberger*. Approximately 9 of 10 applicants were funded in *Rosenberger*. Approximately 2 of 7 applicants to the NEA are granted.

QUESTION: Yes, but I think the Chief Justice is correct in making the distinction. There were no aesthetic judgments to be made. There were no subjective judgments to be made. If you were a student newspaper, you fell within the program. That was it.

And I think your statistical analysis is misleading, because NEA statistics are that they have only so many funds, and they base it on aesthetics. The only reason there were rejections in *Rosenberger* was [that overtly religious newspapers] weren't the kind of newspapers that [qualified] under the program. So I think the Chief Justice is correct in the distinction he makes.

MR. COLE: Well, I'm not sure, Justice Kennedy, whether there's a distinction between a Government agency which makes judgments about educational purpose and allocates funds selectively on that basis, or academic merit, which is what public universities do in hiring, and the NEA, which makes judgments base on artistic merit. All of those programs are selective. They take into account content, but what this Court has said is that when subsidizing private speakers, when the Government is not speaking itself, you cannot engage in viewpoint bias.

QUESTION: Mr. Cole, may I suggest that one is a prize or an award, and there really is a difference between a student activity fund that if you're not social and you're engaged in some respectable student activity, you get it, and an award, a prize, a grant that is highly selective, and so I quite agree, and I don't think that you can maintain that this is just like *Rosenberger*, just like a bulletin board, anybody can put up their names or draw from that pot except certain people.

The distinction being suggested by the justices is between a highly individualized determination of quality or merit or even decency and respect, as in the NEA case, and a more categorical exclusion, such as whether a newspaper is predominantly a religious publication, whatever its specific articles say and whether it is a good or bad newspaper qualitatively. The distinction is real, though slippery.

Assuming the distinction is correct, however, should it be relevant to the First Amendment question? Which is more dangerous from a First Amendment perspective: government making an individualized qualitative judgment about a specific, known work of art or government determining whether the art fits into a general category, such as postmodern or Native American paintings? Are particularized judgments about quality better than judgments about subject? The latter restrict more speech, the former less, but the potential for abuse (hidden, political censorship, for example) runs the other way. And are judgments about decency and respect individual ones, like merit, or more categorical ones, like religious newspapers? Are judgments about merit different from decency and respect, in the sense that merit is more relevant to "art," more inescapable with "art," and less focused on the message or meaning that might be drawn from a work of art? Does *merit* as the NEA statute employs the term, and as applied to the art panels, more neatly focus attention on the aesthetic dimension of the art—color, tone, skill, emotional force, beauty or ugliness—and not on messages or politics or contemporary moral values?

MR. COLE: Okay. Well, Justice Ginsburg, I don't think that the *Rosenberger* case would have come out differently if the University of Virginia had a limited pot of funds, and it said, based on that limited pot of funds, we're going to give funding to those groups which best further the educational purpose of the university, and they—it turned out they gave them out to two of seven applicants, but they excluded religious groups, groups with religious perspectives.

That would still be an exclusion based upon viewpoint, which would be impermissible, and I don't think the case would have come out differently if it [only gave money to] two of seven. The Court in *Rosenberger* said scarcity is not a justification for viewpoint discrimination.

QUESTION: You're a better predictor than I am. I'm not at all sure it wouldn't have come out differently.

The attempted distinction between the NEA program and *Rosenberger* is getting muddled. The argument is not delving into the deeper issue of individual aesthetic judgments versus categorical subject matter or form judgments. Why isn't the individual aesthetic-quality judgment more dangerous in government hands because it is highly discretionary and incapable of being subjected to external, judicially enforceable, standards? Decency can be explained, examined, and judicially superintended. The judicial branch has been doing so for many years—indecency in television, for example. Judgments of quality or perfection of form or emotional and aesthetic power can't be well overseen.

But if this is so, how can the NEA's judgments about artistic merit be justified under the First Amendment? The answer, at this point, seems to be that such judgments are made by the panels that consist of artists and professionals in the art world, people knowledgeable and experienced in judging art and its quality. To take another example, judgments about academic tenure at a state university are based on scholarly quality of published work and the quality of teaching, both of which are essentially subjective and, in a sense, aesthetic. Is the government's involvement in such judgments less dangerous if they are placed, in significant measure, in the hands of an independent professional group, say a faculty-tenure committee, and checked by that group's judgments?

Are decency and respect analogous criteria? Would a "professional" panel of experts in moral precepts and American values be different and thus no justification for government speech restrictions based on the group's judgments? If so, is this because the criteria are intrinsically different—merit versus values—or because one is more social and political than the other and thus smacks of censorship? If so, the NEA's solution of putting people whose antennae are sensitive to decency (moral and social tolerances) and American values would hardly be acceptable for purposes of the First Amendment.

And, finally, is it altogether clear that there is no room in "merit" for judgments about values and decency? If merit has to do with taste, then whose taste is applied? The critics'? The community's? In a democratic government, with respect to democratically funded art, perhaps the values should be those of the democratic majority or perhaps some common denominator of its taste and value. Must the standard of taste—of what is acceptable—be the same in Peoria as it is in Times Square?

More might be said, but the point is that the arguments never dig this deep beneath the surface. They are trapped in the straightjacket of conventional First Amendment analysis, which deals with messages, not aesthetics, and such categories as point-of-view, content, subject matter, and manner (time, place) discrimination.

MR. COLE: There's a very big difference between the Government speaking for itself, where it can make viewpoint decisions, and where the Government is facilitating private expression.

Why is that an important distinction? I think that's an important distinction because there's a very big difference between the Government participating in the marketplace with the power of its ideas on the one hand and the Government engaging in a kind of deceptive ventriloquism in which it says it's funding a broad range of private expression, but then it uses viewpoint-based criteria to exclude—

QUESTION: Well, I'm not sure that decency or indecency is viewpoint based. I'm not sure that respect is a viewpoint-based thing, or diversity. I don't even know what this is.

MR. COLE: Well, I'll answer your questions in turn, Justice O'Connor. First, decency and respect are inherently, as they are used in this statute, viewpoint based. Its common definition of decency is conformity to accepted standards of morality. That's what this Court has said in [other cases dealing with indecency]. Whether something conforms or not is a viewpoint distinction. The same subject matter, if it's treated in a way that conforms to accepted standards of morality, is permitted. If it's treated through a viewpoint that does not, it is not.

The same with respect. The respect clause requires respect of American beliefs and values. If you are disrespectful of American beliefs and values, you are disadvantaged. If you are respectful, you are advantaged.

This is a good argument, but does it work with art? If the question is one's freedom to place the words "Fuck the Draft" on his jacket and wear it in public, one can argue that saying "I Detest the Draft" instead conveys a similar message, just more politely. But with art, the standard of judgment isn't focused on *The Draft* but on the power and emotion in the word *Fuck*. So excising the disrespectful part excises the heart of the art. Even more to the point, the Supreme Court in the "Fuck the Draft" case, *Cohen v. California*, struck down the law prohibiting offensive words. Professor Cole may therefore not have to dwell on the evanescent distinction between viewpoint and subject, manner and force. The *Cohen* case seems to support him even if "decency" isn't viewpoint but is instead an element of the emotional impact of the message. Karen Finley's message about the place of women would be less powerful if she didn't smear herself with chocolate, just like *Fuck* makes objection to the draft more powerful.

QUESTION: I think I would agree with you if the agency here were applying the law the way you interpret it and the way the lower courts interpret it, but I do find it strange that where you have a law which, however unrealistic the interpretation may be, the agency says, we're interpreting it in such a way that we will fund Mapplethorpe and everything else. Why did that hurt you?

MR. COLE: Well, it hurts us for the following reason, Justice Scalia. The Government has been quite ambiguous about its statutory construction, and what it has said is that the statutory construction it is advancing to this Court today is the same statutory construction that they applied for the year-and-a-half before the statute was declared unconstitutional, so let's look at what they did for the year-and-a-half before the Court struck it down.

They instructed each panelist to bring [his and her] own standards of decency to the table in making these decisions.

They went to each panel, they read them the statute, they said the statute says that you must consider artistic excellence and artistic merit, taking into consideration general standards of decency. . . .

Chairman Frohnmayer testified before Congress [and] was asked, how do you take into consideration general standards of decency? He said, no one individual is wise enough to be able to consider general standards of decency and the diverse beliefs and values of the American public all by his- or herself. These are group decisions. They are made by the National Council on the Arts as well as the panelists.

Now, if the chair was making decisions about decency in selecting panels, he wouldn't say these are group decisions made by the Council on the Arts as well as the panelists. He was then asked, well, what would you do—are you abdicating your responsibility in applying this statute? What would you do if something came up to you and it was indecent or disrespectful? He said, I would send it back to the panels and the council if I thought they made a mistake. So he's saying, I'll look at decency to make sure that they've not made a mistake.

The next Chair, who was also enforcing the statute before it was struck down, Ms. Radice, testified in Congress that she would be happy to and would apply decency to the grant-making process.

So I think you have to look . . . at how the agency has in fact applied the statute. There's no dispute about it. And they're quite vague, actually, in this Court in what they say. What's problematic about this statute is, it singles out art precisely because it has a nonconforming or disrespectful viewpoint and, as this Court has said, even when the Government is allocating sub- sidies, if it's doing it to private speakers, it can't skew the marketplace by attempting to impose that kind of ideological screen.

QUESTION: Now, is it the case [that] . . . if, in fact, the NEA wants to give a grant for somebody to produce something that's public work, and suppose what they do is a white supremacist group, and they want to have racial epithets all over the picture—the most horrible ones you can possibly think of, and the person gets up there, and he says, I'm a member of the Ku Klux Klan, or whatever, and this is my point of view—and the NEA says we think that's an inappropriate use of this money, is it your view that the Constitu- tion requires the NEA to fund that, that particular applicant?

MR. COLE: Right.

QUESTION: Tough. [Assuming that] everything you say is correct, and then we get to this point, and the panel's sitting there and saying, you know, I grant you it's as good a work of art as anything else, purely artistically, but I don't think that this particular work of art is appropriate for a school, for a public place, for a television program.

MR. COLE: If it's a program for a school, I think it's appropriate to consider what is suitable for children. I don't think it's appropriate to use viewpoint as a proxy for suitability for children. In the school setting, this Court has recognized that there's a legitimate inculcative role that the school board plays and can therefore make all kinds of viewpoint [judgments related to education] because it is engaged in Government speech. But the NEA—this is not—this is a—the breadth of this statute I think distinguishes it from anything like that.

QUESTION: Well then, I take it that you would say that if general standards of decency were left out of the statute so the statute read, "NEA must take into consideration respect for the diverse beliefs and values of the American people," same problem, unconstitutional viewpoint?

MR. COLE: On your hypothetical—on your hypothetical, Justice Kennedy, if what it means is that it is favoring those artistic expressions which are—

QUESTION: But that's the problem, what it means. And the Government tells us, this is what it means, and you say no, it can't mean that, and two courts have said it can't mean that.

And yet the Government is saying, here were words *decent* and *respect*. They can be interpreted different ways, and usually I thought it was the obligation of a Government officer to give words a meaning that renders them consistent, not inconsistent with constitutional limitations, and yet you're insisting that Government officers take the position with respect to these two words that they interpret them in the way that would be most offensive to the Constitution.

MR. COLE: Well, I'm just saying what they did, and I'm saying that the suggestion that decency and respect might be considered simply through picking diverse panels and no more and not taking decency and respect even into account in choosing the panels is completely inconsistent with the statute. Congress in the statute said decency and respect are the criteria by which applications are to be judged.

QUESTION: No, they're funding artists but artists who just portray particular topics that they've designated.

MR. COLE: Right. Topics—there's no problem with topics. The Court has held that repeatedly. It's viewpoint discrimination which is impermissible, and it's when you take one side or another on a given subject matter.

Under this statute, if an artist presents a nude which is disrespectful or indecent, that viewpoint is disadvantaged. If it's respectful or decent, it's advantaged. That is viewpoint discrimination.

At the risk of repetition, it is worth emphasizing that all of this viewpoint, content, subject-matter business applies to speech whose value is a cognitive message. Art seems different: it is noncognitive, it goes to perceptions and emotion and feeling related to beauty, perfection of form, perception, and the like. The viewpoint and like categories don't easily seem to fit judgments based on the quality or nature of art.

QUESTION: Why is it that the word *decency* or *respect* is somehow more vague than the words *artistic excellence?*

MR. COLE: Well, for two reasons, Justice Breyer. First, artistic merit has been applied by a profession so that there is a set of people, the people who are—

QUESTION: You mean, people who are professionals know more about what's artistically good than the average person? I would have thought there's a strong view, isn't there, that what is good and beautiful is accessible to everyone?

Aha! Justice Breyer is a Kantian! Kant argued that true aesthetic standards of taste are universal.

MR. COLE: Well, I think there's a strong view, Your Honor, that artistic merit, like academic merit, and like character and fitness—

QUESTION: Oh, my goodness! But if the Government says what we want is that which ordinary people believe is beautiful, doesn't the Government have a right to fund that kind of program?

MR. COLE: I think what the Government does not have the right to do is to exclude viewpoints.

CHIEF JUSTICE REHNQUIST: Thank you, Mr. Cole. The case is submitted.

• • •

On that note, Professor Cole ended just where he began. He hadn't budged an inch. And having planted his feet firmly in the soil of conventional First Amendment doctrine, he couldn't afford to budge. It should be said that the Solicitor General's feet were also planted there. Thus, the entire oral argument came down to a disagreement about whether "decency and respect" are viewpoint criteria or content, subject matter, or manner criteria—not whether they have anything to do with art and aesthetics. Such an argument would be pretty boring if only so much didn't turn on it.

The Supreme Court's decision came at the very end of the Term, on June 25, 1998. The Court was not deeply divided on the result in the case. Eight of the justices voted to uphold the decency-and-respect provision. Only Justice Souter dissented. But there the apparent near-unanimity came to a halt, for the justices disagreed quite sharply on the reasons supporting the result. Justice O'Connor wrote the majority opinion upholding the decency and respect requirements.

Justice O'Connor delivered the opinion of the Court.

The "decency and respect" criteria do not silence speakers by expressly "threaten[ing] censorship of ideas." Thus, we do not perceive a realistic danger that § 954(d)(1) will compromise First Amendment values. As respondents' own arguments demonstrate, the considerations that the provision introduces, by their nature, do not engender the kind of directed viewpoint discrimination that would prompt this Court to invalidate a statute on its face. Respondents assert, for example, that "[o]ne would be hard-pressed to find two people in the United States who could agree on what the 'diverse beliefs and values of the American public' are, much less on whether a particular work of art 'respects' them"; and they claim that "'[d]ecency' is likely to mean something very different to a septuagenarian in Tuscaloosa and a teenager in Las Vegas." The NEA likewise views the considerations enumerated in the decency and respect provision as susceptible to multiple interpretations. Accordingly, the provision does not introduce considerations that, in practice, would effectively preclude or punish the expression of particular views. Indeed, one could hardly anticipate how "decency" or "respect" would bear on grant applications in categories such as funding for symphony orchestras.

Respondents' claim that the provision is facially unconstitutional may be reduced to the argument that the criteria . . . are sufficiently subjective that the agency could utilize them to engage in viewpoint discrimination. Given the varied interpretations of the criteria and the vague exhortation to "take them into consideration," it seems unlikely that this provision will introduce any greater element of selectivity than the determination of "artistic excellence" itself. And we are reluctant, in any event, to invalidate legislation "on the basis of its hypothetical application to situations not before the Court."

Permissible applications of the mandate to consider "respect for the diverse beliefs and values of the American public" are also apparent. In setting forth the purposes of the NEA, Congress explained that "[i]t is vital to a democracy to honor and preserve its multicultural artistic heritage." The agency expressly takes diversity into account, giving special consideration to "projects and productions . . . that reach, or reflect the culture of, a minority, inner city, rural, or tribal community," as well as projects that generally emphasize "cultural diversity." Respondents do not contend that the criteria are impermissibly applied when they may be justified, as the statute contemplates, with respect to a project's intended audience.

We recognize, of course, that reference to these permissible applications would not alone be sufficient to sustain the statute against respondents' First Amendment challenge. But neither are we persuaded that, in other applications, the language itself will give rise to the suppression of protected expression. Any content-based considerations that may be taken into account in the grant-making process are a consequence of the nature of arts funding. The NEA has limited resources, and it must deny the majority of the grant applications that it receives, including many that propose "artistically excellent" projects. The agency may decide to fund particular projects for a wide variety of reasons, "such as the technical proficiency of the artist, the creativity of the work, the anticipated public interest in or appreciation of the work, the work's contemporary relevance, its educational value, its suitability for or appeal to special audiences (such as children or the disabled), its service to a rural or isolated community, or even simply that the work could increase public knowledge of an art form." As the dissent below noted, it would be "impossible to have a highly selective grant program without denying money to a large amount of constitutionally protected expression. The "very assumption" of the NEA is that grants will be awarded according to the "artistic worth of competing applicants," and absolute neutrality is simply "inconceivable."

In the context of arts funding, in contrast to many other subsidies, the Government does not indiscriminately "encourage a diversity of views from private speakers." The NEA's mandate is to make esthetic judgments, and the inherently content-based "excellence" threshold for NEA support sets it apart from the subsidy at issue in *Rosenberger*—which was available to all student organizations that were "related to the educational purpose of the University," and from comparably objective decisions on allocating public benefits, such as access to a school auditorium or a municipal theater, or the second class mailing privileges available to "all newspapers and other periodical publications."

We recognize, as a practical matter, that artists may conform their speech to what they believe to be the decision-making criteria in order to acquire funding. But when the Government is acting as patron rather than as sovereign, the consequences of imprecision are not constitutionally severe.

It is so ordered.

Justice O'Connor's majority opinion, both wide ranging and analytically ungainly, garnered the full votes of four other justices: Chief Justice Rehnquist and Justices Stevens, Kennedy, and Breyer, a diverse group, each of whom must have found enough to their liking in the grabbaggish menu of rationales that Justice O'Connor included in her opinion. She says the decency-and-respect clause doesn't necessarily mean what it says; if it does, it doesn't cut very deep because the grant judgments still would be based on mode and manner, not point of view; there may be instances of unconstitutional grant decision-making, but the Court need not worry about them here, where the government must choose because of limited funds, so it must have some room to operate; and in any event the government plays the historic role of a great patron of the arts, like the Medicis. Government is therefore not regulating or even limiting speech and art; it is facilitating and broadening it. Government is a patron speaker.

Justice O'Connor also obtained the limited agreement of Justice Ginsburg, who found much to her liking in the majority opinion but objected to one of the rationales on the menu (Justice O'Connor's broad description of Congress's power to subsidize speech based on its point of view).

Justices Scalia and Thomas agreed with the result but rejected the menu altogether and explained their views on the basis of quite different reasons than those offered up by Justice O'Connor.

> Justice Scalia, with whom Justice Thomas joins, concurring in the judgment.
>
> "The operation was a success, but the patient died." What such a procedure is to medicine, the Court's opinion in this case is to law. It sustains the constitutionality of 20 U.S.C. § 954(d)(1) by gutting it. The most avid congressional opponents of the provision could not have asked for more. By its terms, [the decency-and-respect requirements] establish content- and viewpoint-based criteria upon which grant applications are to be evaluated. And that is perfectly constitutional.
>
> The phrase "taking into consideration general standards of decency and respect for the diverse beliefs and values of the American public" is what my grammar-school teacher would have condemned as a dangling modifier: There is no noun to which the participle is attached (unless one jumps out of paragraph (1) to press "Chairperson" into service). Even so, it is clear enough that the phrase is meant to apply to those who do the judging. The application reviewers must take into account "general standards of decency" and "respect for the diverse beliefs and values of the American public" when evaluating artistic excellence and merit.
>
> One can regard this as either suggesting that decency and respect are elements of what Congress regards as artistic excellence and merit, or as suggesting that decency and respect are factors to be taken into account *in*

addition to artistic excellence and merit. But either way, it is entirely, 100% clear that decency and respect are to be taken into account in evaluating applications.

This unquestionably constitutes viewpoint discrimination. That conclusion is not altered by the fact that the statute does not "compe[l]" the denial of funding, any more than a provision imposing a five-point handicap on all black applicants for civil service jobs is saved from being race discrimination by the fact that it does not compel the rejection of black applicants.

The First Amendment reads: "Congress shall make no law . . . *abridging* the freedom of speech." To abridge is "to contract, to diminish; to deprive of." T. Sheridan, *A Complete Dictionary of the English Language* (6th ed., 1796). With the enactment [of the decency-and-respect provision], Congress did not *abridge* the speech of those who disdain the beliefs and values of the American public, nor did it *abridge* indecent speech. Those who wish to create indecent and disrespectful art are as unconstrained now as they were before the enactment of this statute. *Avant-garde artistes* such as respondents remain entirely free to *epater les bourgeois;* they are merely deprived of the additional satisfaction of having the bourgeoisie taxed to pay for it. It is preposterous to equate the denial of taxpayer subsidy with measures "'aimed at the *suppression* of dangerous ideas.'"

One might contend, I suppose, that a threat of rejection by the only available source of free money would constitute coercion and hence "abridgment" within the meaning of the First Amendment. But even if one accepts the contention, it would have no application here. The NEA is far from the sole source of funding for art—even indecent, disrespectful, or just plain bad art. Accordingly, the Government may earmark NEA funds for projects it deems to be in the public interest without thereby abridging speech.

[The decency-and-respect requirement] is no more discriminatory, and no less constitutional, than virtually every other piece of funding legislation enacted by Congress. "The Government can, without violating the Constitution, selectively fund a program to encourage certain activities it believes to be in the public interest, without at the same time funding an alternative program. . . ." When Congress chose to establish the National Endowment for Democracy, it was not constitutionally required to fund programs encouraging competing philosophies of government—an example of funding discrimination that cuts much closer than this one to the core of *political* speech which is the primary concern of the First Amendment. It takes a particularly high degree of chutzpah for the NEA to contradict this proposition, since the agency itself discriminates—and is required by law to discriminate—in favor of artistic (as opposed to scientific, or political, or theological) expression. Not all the common folk, or even all great minds, for that matter, think that is a good idea. In 1800, when John Marshall told John Adams that a recent immigration of Frenchmen would include talented artists, "Adams denounced all Frenchmen, but most especially 'schoolmasters, painters, poets, & C.' He warned Marshall that the fine arts were like germs that infected healthy constitutions." J. Ellis, *After the Revolution: Profiles of Early American Culture* 36 (1979). Surely the NEA itself is nothing less than an institutionalized discrimination against that point of view. Nonetheless, it is constitutional, as is the congressional determination to favor decency and respect for beliefs and values over the opposite because such favoritism does not "abridge" anyone's freedom of speech.

Respondents ... argue that viewpoint-based discrimination is impermissible unless the government is the speaker or the government is "disburs[ing] public funds to private entities to convey a governmental message." It is impossible to imagine why that should be so; one would think that directly involving the government itself in the viewpoint discrimination (if it is unconstitutional) would make the situation even worse. Respondents are mistaken. It is the very business of government to favor and disfavor points of view on (in modern times, at least) innumerable subjects—which is the main reason we have decided to elect those who run the government, rather than save money by making their posts hereditary. And it makes not a bit of difference, insofar as either common sense or the Constitution is concerned, whether these officials further their (and, in a democracy, our) favored point of view by achieving it directly (having government-employed artists paint pictures, for example, or government-employed doctors perform abortions); or by advocating it officially (establishing an Office of Art Appreciation, for example, or an Office of Voluntary Population Control); or by giving money to others who achieve or advocate it (funding private art classes, for example, or Planned Parenthood). None of this has anything to do with abridging anyone's speech.

The nub of the difference between me and the Court is that I regard the distinction between "abridging" speech and funding it as a fundamental divide, on this side of which the First Amendment is inapplicable. The Court, by contrast, seems to believe that the First Amendment, despite its words, has some ineffable effect upon funding, imposing constraints of an indeterminate nature which it announces (without troubling to enunciate any particular test) are not violated by the statute here—or, more accurately, are not violated by the quite different, emasculated statute that it imagines. "[T]he Government," it says, "may allocate competitive funding according to criteria that would be impermissible were direct regulation of speech or a criminal penalty at stake." The Government, *I* think, may allocate both competitive and noncompetitive funding *ad libitum,* insofar as the First Amendment is concerned.

In its laudatory description of the accomplishments of the NEA, the Court notes with satisfaction that "only a handful of the agency's roughly 100,000 awards have generated formal complaints." The Congress that felt it necessary to enact [the decency-and-respect criteria] evidently thought it much *more* noteworthy that *any* money exacted from American taxpayers had been used to produce a crucifix immersed in urine or a display of homoerotic photographs. It is no secret that the provision was prompted by, and directed at, the funding of such offensive productions. Instead of banning the funding of such productions absolutely, which I think would have been entirely constitutional, Congress took the lesser step of requiring them to be disfavored in the evaluation of grant applications. The Court's opinion today renders even that lesser step a nullity. For that reason, I concur only in the judgment.

Justice Scalia's opinion can only be described as acerbically dismissive of Justice O'Connor's opinion. For Scalia, the statute means what it says— no indecent and disrespectful art should receive grants. If viewpoint versus content or manner discrimination were relevant, which it isn't, this is indisputably viewpoint discrimination. But the fact is that government, as the representative of the people in a democratic society, can spend its money any way it chooses. As long as it isn't regulating or prohibiting speech but just giving money, the First Amendment poses no obstacle. Congress can fund the expression of prodemocracy ideas and not socialist, monarchist, or communist ideas—a clear point-of-view preference. Karen Finley's speech isn't being restricted or abridged or prohibited. It's just not getting support from the government. It will have to seek support from other, true patrons, public or private, or else make it on its own by attracting a paying audience or otherwise competing in the private marketplace.

Justice Souter was alone in dissent, accompanied only by a classical view of the First Amendment and virtually all of the Supreme Court's prior decisions. Strange and lonely spot, that.

Justice Souter, dissenting.

One need do nothing more than read the text of the statute to conclude that Congress's purpose in imposing the decency and respect criteria was to prevent the funding of art that conveys an offensive message; the decency and respect provision on its face is quintessentially viewpoint based, and quotations from the Congressional Record merely confirm the obvious legislative purpose. In the words of a cosponsor of the bill that enacted the proviso, "[w]orks which deeply offend the sensibilities of significant portions of the public ought not to be supported with public funds." Another supporter of the bill observed that "the Endowment's support for artists like Robert Mapplethorpe and Andre[s] Serrano has offended and angered many citizens," behooving "Congress . . . to listen to these complaints about the NEA and make sure that exhibits like [these] are not funded again." Indeed, if there were any question at all about what Congress had in mind, a definitive answer comes in the succinctly accurate remark of the proviso's author, that the bill "add[s] to the criteria of artistic excellence and artistic merit, a shell, a screen, a viewpoint that must be constantly taken into account."

The Government's . . . suggestion that the NEA's decency standards restrict only the "form, mode, or style" of artistic expression, not the underlying viewpoint or message, may be a tempting abstraction. But here it suffices to realize that "form, mode, or style" are not subject to abstraction from artistic viewpoint, and to quote from an opinion just two years old: "In artistic . . . settings, indecency may have strong communicative content, protesting conventional norms or giving an edge to a work by conveying otherwise inexpressible emotions. . . . Indecency often is inseparable from the ideas and viewpoints conveyed, or separable only with loss of truth or expressive power."

The government may act on the basis of viewpoint "when the State is the speaker" or when the State "disburses public funds to private entities to convey a governmental message." But we explained that the government may not act on viewpoint when it "does not itself speak or subsidize transmittal of a message it favors but instead expends funds to encourage a diversity of views from private speakers." When the government acts as patron, subsidizing the expression of others, it may not prefer one lawfully stated view over another.

The NEA is a subsidy scheme created to encourage expression of a diversity of views from private speakers. Congress brought the NEA into being to help all Americans "achieve a better understanding of the past, a better analysis of the present, and a better view of the future." The NEA's purpose is to "support new ideas" and "to help create and sustain . . . a climate encouraging freedom of thought, imagination, and inquiry." Given this congressional choice to sustain freedom of expression, *Rosenberger* teaches that the First Amendment forbids decisions based on viewpoint popularity. So long as Congress chooses to subsidize expressive endeavors at large, it has no business requiring the NEA to turn down funding applications of artists and exhibitors who devote their "freedom of thought, imagination, and inquiry" to defying our tastes, our beliefs, or our values. It may not use the NEA's purse to "suppres[s] . . . dangerous ideas."

While criteria of "artistic excellence and artistic merit" may raise intractable issues about the identification of artistic worth, and could no doubt be used covertly to filter out unwanted ideas, there is nothing inherently viewpoint discriminatory about such merit-based criteria. We have noted before that an esthetic government goal is perfectly legitimate. Decency and respect, on the other hand, are inherently and facially viewpoint based and serve no legitimate and permissible end. The Court's assertion that the mere fact that grants must be awarded according to artistic merit precludes "absolute neutrality" on the part of the NEA is therefore misdirected. It is not to the point that the Government necessarily makes choices among competing applications, or even that its judgments about artistic quality may be branded as subjective to some greater or lesser degree; the question here is whether the Government may apply patently viewpoint-based criteria in making those choices.[15]

Dissenting all alone, Justice Souter plies the narrow channel of conventional First Amendment doctrine, built as it is on a speech model resting on a cognitive message. Souter agrees with Scalia about the purpose and meaning of the amendment. He agrees also that the decency-and-respect criteria, applied to a work of art, are point of view based. Therefore, he concludes, the law is unconstitutional, unless the NEA program is government speech, which it isn't because it affects only private speech by private artists who speak for themselves. Tight logic wrapped up in a pretty bow, but it is unsatisfying because it seems to have so little to do with Karen Finley and the issue of judging art as a distinct form of expression.

With this, Karen Finley's legal fate came to an ignominious end.

• • •

There are many things to think about in the *Finley* case. We will focus on just a few, leaving others to later cases. The main points are Karen Finley's art, the criteria by which art and aesthetics can be judged, and the Supreme Court's treatment of aesthetic-speech claims under the First Amendment. We will take them in reverse order.

One can't help but come away from the Supreme Court oral argument and opinions with a sense of cold, intellectual, abstraction. Nowhere was Finley's performance art or that of the other plaintiffs mentioned. It's not that the Court assumed that her performances were art. The justices and the lawyers simply didn't want to get into the subject at all. Instead, the Court sought procedural and structural ways around the issue. And in doing so, they made two potential errors. First, they assumed that an artist's free speech claim could be treated under the same rules as the soapbox orator—that is, by the content or message of the speech and the government's possible interest in restricting that message in a given place or at a given time or when delivered in a given manner. But the message of the artist isn't necessarily cognitive or exclusively so. It is aesthetic, going to the perfection of technique and the emotional power of performance, quite apart from any cognitive message. Such matters can't be reduced to questions of process alone: Was the NEA's panel process suitable for questions of decency and respect; could the comfort of a group decision be trusted to confine and contain the discretion implied in such a standard; and are decency and respect valid limitations to be placed on art selection? The answers might be that they are not valid criteria, because they have nothing to do with *artistic* quality.

Second, the Court wrongly assumed that decency can be judged by the message of the art, when the message can't be reduced to reason or logic. Therefore, it might be concluded, while decency and respect might be (and are in some settings) perfectly valid legislative concerns, they cannot effectively be lodged in a judgment of artistic merit, and therefore they are constitutionally inapt for the NEA. There is a way to reach such a First Amendment conclusion, but the Court did not take it. Instead, the Court and the lawyers devoted all of their energies to the ineffable question of whether "decency and respect" were point-of-view limitations, in which case they would be unconstitutional; or whether they were subject or manner limitations, in which case they might not be; or whether instead of that the government should be best conceived as acting not as a regulator of speech but as a patron of the arts and therefore freed of all First Amendment limits.

This borders on sophistry. No one can know for certain whether decency and respect are point-of-view criteria or not. The distinction, coherent in the abstract, is far too slippery to apply consistently in *Finley* and like cases. And to define the government's role, as the majority opinion did, as patron of the arts is to allow the government to exceed the more benign role of patron—judging only the artist's technique, emotion, power, and beauty—and to consider instead the reasons a regulator, not a patron, would use, reasons of morals or majoritarian preference having nothing to do with aesthetics. Before the NEA amendment, perhaps the government (NEA) could be accurately seen as a relatively benign patron (a category that rarely if ever existed in the history of art).[16] The amendment stopped all of that by injecting criteria unrelated to artistic merit.

Justice O'Connor's opinion, by this reasoning, was fatally flawed. Even if the NEA was right in thinking it could lodge decency and respect in the composition of the panels, decency and respect didn't belong there, where artistic quality was the standard and where the members, no matter how selected, had to have experience in judging art as art. And the conclusion that prohibiting indecent and disrespectful art from support "doesn't threaten censorship of ideas [or aesthetic feelings]," or compromise First Amendment values is simply declared, not explained. The only real explanation, unsatisfactory as it is for reasons given above, is that the government is not acting as a regulator but as a patron of the arts and thus is entitled to make judgments on the basis of *its* own tastes. But who is the "it"? Any old government employee, the NEA, the panels, the council, the Congress, the president, the secretary of art? Here the indisputable maker of judgments was the Congress, led by Jesse Helms and a host of others whose actions and explanations defy the definition of acting as a patron rather than a regulator.

Finley's work is boisterous, profane, sexual, funny, tragic, and political, among other things. Apart from its message, it evokes humor, revulsion, disgust, sensuality, irony, and deep emotional feelings of hopelessness, sadness, and anger. It addresses such issues as self-loathing, incest, sexualization of women, and AIDS, to name a few. Her work is forceful and powerful, drawing directly on emotions and feelings to inscribe her messages in the audience's minds. And if technique and skill are a function, at least in part, of effectiveness in communicating or evoking feelings of passion or beauty or ugliness through sensuous perception, Karen Finley is indeed skilled. She has a large and admiring following in venues in which she performs, and she is respected widely in the arts community.

Her problem, if it qualifies as that, is that she is "in your face," including in the face of her detractors. She is fond of saying, "When I finally realized that Jesse Helms was actually having a public sexually abusive relationship with me, ... I changed the relationship, and I think that I've been healthier ever since." Her work is different and shocking and controversial, and, perhaps most important, it violates many taboos, it challenges established conventions, it is lewd and crass, it breaks rules. One would not use the word *beauty* to describe it. But *art* and *aesthetics* are not so restricted.

Alison Young, the author of *Judging the Image: Art, Value, Law*,[17] describes the effect on the viewer of Serrano's *Piss Christ*, a photograph of the crucified Christ immersed in a vat of the artist's urine.

> The picture on the gallery wall does not literally touch the spectator; however, the visceral response to artworks such as *Piss Christ* . . . can be interpreted as the shudder arising from an image which transcends the cushioning effect of the fact of representation and threatens metaphorically to touch the spectator. . . .
>
> This is the dynamic of "aesthetic vertigo." Rather than provoking a simple "disgusted" response, artworks such as . . . *Piss Christ* . . . make the spectator dizzy, teetering on the verge of a representational abyss. . . . The desire to judge these artworks not only as disgusting but also as indecent, or obscene or blasphemous, is a desire for the reinstatement of the law (of community, of religion, of representation) and a continued segregation of images into the sanctioned and the unwarranted.

Piss Christ was one of the works that spawned the NEA controversy and the resulting decency and respect amendment and that subsequently caught Karen Finley in its conflagration. Like Finley's performance art, it was confrontational and subverting, representationally transforming the meaning of the image from objective and dispassionate disgust to a subjective and personal "shudder arising from an image which transcends the cushioning effect of the fact of representation and threatens . . . to touch the spectator."

If we recognize the aesthetic power and the skill with which Karen Finley's performance is created as art, or at least that it is not different in kind from the transformative emotions evoked by Bach, or by the objectively ugly and frightening Nazi paintings by Maurice Lasansky or by the surrealists, and if we acknowledge the many descriptions of Karen Finley's work as evoking similar emotion and perception, we are left with three essential questions. First, how, if at all, can the law define art? Second, if something is art, can the law determine its quality? Third, where do decency and respect (or similar criteria) fit in? These are large questions that will be touched upon in a relative brief and introductory way here and pursued further in later chapters.

• • •

In 1903, Justice Oliver Wendell Holmes Jr. wrote:

> It would be a dangerous undertaking for persons trained only to the law to constitute themselves final judges of the worth of pictorial illustrations, outside of the narrowest and most obvious limits.[18]

Justice Scalia voiced similar views in 1987:

[W]e would be better advised to adopt as a legal maxim what has long been the wisdom of mankind: *De gustibus non est disputandum.* Just as there is no use arguing about taste, there is no use litigating about it. For the law courts to decide "What is Beauty" is a novelty even by today's standards.[19]

The gist of these statements is that the law should not undertake to define what is art. But is it really that easy? With Karen Finley, it may be: just take her at her word, based on what she does and claims, and proceed to the next question (decency and respect). In many cases, this will work, for the matter at issue can make a colorable claim to looking like art, at least in form and technique.

But what do we do with other examples? How about the nude dancer in a bar? She certainly evokes emotion. Is it simply not the right kind? How about the cigarette advertisement with the Marlboro Man? At first it was just an effective ad, appealing to emotions but directed to selling a product. Today, the Marlboro Man picture is an artistic icon, much like the Campbell's soup can in the hands of Andy Warhol. To be sure, Warhol himself transformed the can. In the case of the Marlboro Man, time did the work. But why should the agent of transformation matter if it is now considered art? What about a burning cross, an image of great emotional power and transformative meaning, transformed by the hand of the Ku Klux Klan? Is it art? Is it disqualified as art because of its hateful and frightening power over the viewer, its disgusting and violent nature? Can the Court just assume that these are all art, accepting the word of the dancer, the tobacco company, the KKK?

Perhaps we can't escape the definitional question of *art*. If not, courts will at least have to set some wide boundaries—broad but still useful. And in doing so, courts will have to keep questions of illegality or harm or decency and respect separate from questions of art. These questions are looked at in detail in the later chapters about nude dancing, the burning cross, and currency art.

Even if the government and the courts can in some measure judge something as "art," can they take the next step and judge the quality of the art? This, of course, is precisely what the NEA is charged with doing in making grants to artists, exhibitions, and programs. Many think the government ought not to do this at all—indeed, that it should be unconstitutional for the government to judge and support art. Their reasoning, at base, is that the government ought not to be in the business of regulating or selectively supporting art by making qualitative judgments, for in doing so the government will tend to protect its own interests (including avoiding controversy) and, in the long run, will effectively domesticate art. Art is a medium that by its own definition cannot be domesticated, for the point is to challenge, change, evoke responses, even morally revolutionary ones. Art is therefore a private matter for the private sector.

This is a respectable, even very strong, argument. In First Amendment language, a judgment by government of the quality of a work of art is, inherently, based on point of view and thus essentially prohibited. Could the government prohibit a political speaker because of his or her diction or grammar? Because his or her ideas are simply bizarre? The very purposes of the First Amendment would be defeated by such a measure.

Setting aside the decency-and-respect question for the moment, the NEA sought to avoid the problem of government judging quality by delegating the qualitative judgments to panels of private citizens who are artists or expert in judging the arts. These people, of course, are still acting for, *and as*, the government, but they are also independent of the formal bureaucratic mechanisms of government and have no formal allegiances to particular parties or government policies. This delegation to private individuals acting as a group is not, of course, an answer to those who worry that any system, even a delegated one, will have the effect of domesticating art and instilling incentives to perpetuate current ideas about art and discourage radical change, like surrealism.

But practicality also plays an important role. Public university faculties make tenure decisions in much the same fashion as the NEA panels, and those decisions are explicitly focused on the quality of published scholarship (including art or music or dance) and the quality of (the art of?) teaching. The justification is that leaving the qualitative judgments to deans or administrators would be worse, as it could directly discourage and threaten the freedom to explore ideas in the academy; and that failing to make any judgment whatever would be even worse. So a delegated process of choice by experts is perhaps the only process, imperfect and often self-interested as it is, by which the academic purposes of tenure can be achieved. With slight modification, this is the process used in the acquisition process of public libraries—trained acquisition professionals make the judgments, with the qualitative judgments often accompanying that decision, about which books to buy. Teachers give grades, orchestra directors select musicians.

Should necessity and professional delegation be enough to justify the NEA's choices based on artistic merit: Is it art? Is it very good art? Is it consistent with the artistic and programmatic objectives for a specific grant program, such as native American art, modern dance, or performance art? The argument favoring the constitutionality of the NEA selections may well rest on an affirmative answer to this question, for without the artistic screen provided by the panels, the chair of the NEA and the council might possess too much discretion to pass First Amendment scrutiny. They could favor "art" that they personally liked; and they could reject "art" that they disliked. Panel judgments partially constrain such choices.

Or is the NEA differently situated than librarians or faculties in the sense that governmental arts funding—government patronage in the Court's language—is not a practical necessity in the way that selecting books for a library or deciding upon job security for teachers and scholars is? As Justice Scalia says, without the NEA, there would still be a large market in private patronage to which artists might appeal. And without the NEA grant, an artist could still produce her or his art. The existence of the arts is thus not dependent on government subsidy in the way that the existence of a library or a university is dependent on choices based upon artistic or aesthetic or scholarly merit.

And even if the NEA's merit-based grant programs are constitutional, does the addition of decency and respect change the equation? Decency and respect are not criteria that go to artistic merit. They are different, too, from NEA decisions to sponsor Native American art or children's art. Decency and respect are broad social and political goals having little if anything to do with the intrinsic status and merits of art; and they do not lie within the field or genres of good art like the programmatic subcategories of Native American art. Decent and respectful Native American art is not a subcategory of good art but rather a standard for exclusion of good art within the subcategory of Native American art.

If the NEA's mission is principally to judge art and good art, injecting decency and respect reshapes that mission into two parts: judging art as art and judging social and moral and religious preferences about what good art should be excluded for social policy and political reasons. These are two fundamentally different undertakings. The NEA seems unsuited to the latter judgment *because* it is suited to the former. This fact, it might be argued, is a better and clearer reason for the unconstitutionality of the decency and respect amendment than the conclusion that decency and respect are point-of-view criteria, as Souter, Scalia, and Thomas all claim and as the majority disclaims, at least in part. Would we expect the faculty tenure decision to turn on scholarly and teaching merit and also on whether a candidate was suitably religious or spiritual or had the right values of decency and respect in his or her private life?

But if decency and respect are misfits for the NEA, do they have no valid place in the government's selection decisions? Here the argument is between Justice Souter, who has little sympathy for such open and political standards, and Justice Scalia, who says that when the government is not regulating private activity but just choosing how to spend its money, it can make virtually any choices it wants, for the government needs such discretion, and the disappointed applicant is not placed in a worse situation than if they hadn't applied at all—that is, they are on their own in the private market. This is a valid point, because today, unlike at the time of the great patrons like the Medicis, art is an autonomous enterprise, and the market, not the patron, is its standard. But should it make any difference to the First Amendment question? Should the government be able to give me a bonus or award for my own writing because it is more consistent with the official government view than another writer's? What if I write for a newspaper or a magazine?

Ultimately, the Court majority simply avoids Justice Scalia's point, not even deigning to reply, saying instead that decency and respect *might* be valid criteria for government in the arts setting—that is, they aren't necessarily bad all the time, whatever that means—but they might also be quite invalid. We'll have to wait for another case to think about the problem.

This, of course, is hardly an answer. There may be some wisdom in saving the issue for a later day and a better case. Yet, it seems pretty likely that Karen Finley's grant, first recommended by the panel, then reviewed by the chair and returned to the panel to reconsider in light of decency and respect, and then once again recommended by the panel, only to be finally rejected by the council, presents the issue clearly enough if only the Court wanted to delve further into the First Amendment issue based on real facts rather than legal abstractions. That is, it's not that the Court couldn't look further. It's that they chose not to. Why?

THE ARTISTIC TURN?

Barnes v. Glen Theatre Inc.

501 U.S. 560 (1991)

KAREN FINLEY'S PERFORMANCE had been judged to be art—indeed good art—by the NEA. Her "art" was also political, in the sense that she intended to convey a message about social and political matters. The sensual and noncognitive side of "art" was thus inextricably tied to the cognitive message. It was further obscured by the issue of whether decency and respect for American values could rightly be considered part of the "art" question—especially when those factors went to the sensual aspects of her performance, not to the political message. The Supreme Court could therefore limit its focus to the question whether decency and respect were appropriate, content-neutral criteria as applied to a cognitive and political message conveyed through an assumed artistic performance. The distinct question of whether the performance was "art" could be ferreted out and examined, but the Court didn't need to do so.

Such escape from the art question is not possible if the meaning of the performance is only sensual and perceptual, unattended by any cognitive message. How is art to be judged in such a setting? This is precisely the question posed by nude dancing in bars and by general prohibitions on nudity in public. Is nudity itself expression protected by the First Amendment? And if the nudity conveys no cognitive message—political or social, for example—is its purely sensual meaning sufficient to qualify it as art? What about the quite different, performative setting of nude dancing in bars? Is its sensual and perceptual meaning sufficient to qualify it as art, especially when the dancer claims that art was her intention?

These are the questions presented by the *Barnes* case, which involves Indiana's general prohibition on public nudity as well as its application to the nude dancers in the Kitty Kat Bar. Before getting to the issues that *Barnes* presents for art and aesthetic expression, however, we need to better understand the purposes of the First Amendment free speech guarantee. Why is it that art and aesthetic expression have had such an uneasy relationship to freedom of speech?

The Supreme Court's free speech jurisprudence, evolved over nearly a century, rests on general categories of speech. The highest and most protected category is political speech, which includes speech about social, economic, and related issues, conceived broadly.[1] The next and more modestly protected category is "indecent" speech, which often does not touch on the protected category of political speech but instead on sex, violence, and the like. If the indecent speech does touch on politics, it is usually fully protected. But not always. Some political speech may still be deemed indecent because the manner in which it is expressed is indecent (intimidation and hate speech, for example) or the speech is inappropriate for the audience to which it is addressed (children, for example). Indecency is speech protected by the First Amendment, but its low value warrants only modest protection. The third category of speech contains certain types of "speech" that do not qualify at all as speech protected by the First Amendment. These types include, for example, "fighting words," words that produce immediate violent response, and "obscenity," depictions of sexual conduct that are offensive to community values, appeal to prurient interests, and lack serious artistic, political, literary or scientific value. With such "speech," government may prohibit or regulate it freely as if it were simply conduct, like speeding or jaywalking.

These categories are reflections of the central purposes of the free speech guarantee. Those purposes, in turn, reflect the widely held views of the Court, other judges, lawyers, scholars, and most students of the First Amendment. Broadly speaking, four purposes predominate. The first is the *search* for truth (truth, itself, being ultimately transient, fixed to time and place). As Justice Oliver Wendell Holmes Jr. said in 1919, "[W]hen men have realized that time has upset many fighting faiths, they may come to believe even more than they believe the very foundations of their own conduct that the ultimate good desired is better reached by free trade in ideas—that the best test of truth is the power of the thought to get itself accepted in the competition of the market, and that truth is the only ground upon which their wishes safely can be carried out."[2]

The second purpose of the free speech guarantee is enabling self-governance or a free, democratic society. Alexander Meiklejohn, an influential thinker on the subject of free speech, wrote, "The First Amendment, then, is not the guardian of unregulated talkativeness. . . . [T]he vital point, as stated negatively, is that no suggestion of policy shall be denied a hearing because it is on one side of the issue rather than another. [Citizens] may not be barred because their views are thought to be false or dangerous. . . . When men govern themselves, it is they—and no one else—who must pass judgment upon unwisdom and unfairness and danger. [Just] so far as, at any point, the citizens who are to decide an issue are denied acquaintance with information or opinion . . . relevant to that issue, just so far the result must be ill-conceived. . . . The principle of the freedom of speech . . . is a deduction from the basic American agreement that public issues shall be decided by universal suffrage."[3] Free speech serves free democratic elections and choices.

The third purpose of the freedom of speech is individual self-fulfillment and autonomy. David Richards, a widely respected constitutional theorist, argues that people cannot be "constrained to communicate or not to communicate, to believe or not to believe, to associate or not to associate. . . . [T]he value of free expression . . . rests on its deep relation to self-respect arising from autonomous self-determination without which the life of the spirit is meager and slavish."[4] The fourth purpose is peaceful resolution of differences and peaceable change. Thomas Emerson, perhaps the most influential scholar of the First Amendment in the latter half of the twentieth century, said, "[Freedom] of expression is a method of achieving a more adaptable and hence more stable [community]. This follows because suppression of discussion makes rational judgment impossible, substituting force for reason; because suppression promotes inflexibility and [prevents] society from adjusting to changing circumstances. . . . [People] are more ready to accept decisions that go against them if they have a part in the decision-making process. [With freedom of expression,] conflict necessary to the progress of a society can take place without destroying the society."[5]

Although there are many variations on these four basic purposes, they nicely encapsulate the main, broad goals ascribed to the free speech guarantee of the First Amendment. For the present purposes, the important thing to note about them is that, with but one possible exception, the goals all rest on a process of reasoned discussion and cognitive speech. This is understandable given the underlying premise that speech serves and preserves self-government and democracy as well as peaceful change, two structural attributes of the form of government the Constitution establishes. The only exception may be the self-fulfillment and autonomy values, which sweep more broadly than service of democratic governance, and to other realms of individual self-identity. Yet, in most of its articulations, self-fulfillment and autonomy, too, focus on rational thought and belief or cognitive expression even about matters of faith. What is being protected, after all, is speech to others, not personal freedom to hold beliefs, and in serving to shape identity and belief, speech partakes of the cognitive or reasoned explication, not self-gratification alone, even if communicated.

If these are fair representations of the general purposes of freedom of speech, it is not surprising that art and aesthetic expression have had a hard time finding a home in the First Amendment. In Karen Finley's case, the difficulty was solved easily because her claimed artistic expression served as a means of communicating a cognitive political message. Her performance may be art, but it is also speech that qualifies under most of the truth-seeking, self-governance, autonomy, and peaceful change purposes of the First Amendment. Robert Bork argued that the purely sensual and sensory aspects of art and aesthetic expression make it hard to distinguish art from endless other forms of conduct serving only personal self-gratification. Perhaps such conduct and self-gratification should be constitutionally protected, he says, but it is not speech for purposes of the free speech guarantee of the First Amendment.

Is art then no different, as speech, from obscenity? Is it excluded from the First Amendment? The fact that the question can even be asked underlines the Supreme Court's historical uncertainty about the status of art under the First Amendment and reveals the challenges faced by artistic and aesthetic expression when they claim protection as free speech. These are the very challenges faced by the Supreme Court in the *Barnes* case.

• • •

The Kitty Kat Lounge was located in an old and bleak commercial and industrial area on South Michigan Street in South Bend, Indiana, an area populated by other bars and establishments, including the Glo Worm and Quarterback Lounges and the Teasers strip bar. By 2006, the city had bought all of these properties and scheduled them for demolition. "This is a great step forward for the community," said Sharon Kendall, the director of Community and Economic Development, about the Kitty Kat demolition. "We look forward to new investment that will complement the new commercial growth on the south side and help to enhance the quality of life for our residents."

The Kitty Kat had a storied history. Over the years, there had been at least two shootings at the bar. In May of 2000, three customers apparently confronted a bar bouncer who was accompanying a dancer to her car after the bar closed. A fight ensued, and one of the customers was shot and then killed when run over by the other, fleeing customers. The owner of the bar, Arthur T. Ford, was charged in 2003 with six counts of promoting prostitution at the Kitty Kat. On June 1, 2004, he pleaded guilty to three counts and was sentenced to four years in prison. On June 22, 2004, the Alcohol and Tobacco Commission suspended the Kitty Kat's liquor license because "Arthur T. Ford and the management of the permit premises have failed to maintain themselves as persons of integrity and high repute sufficient to continue to hold a ... permit."

The Barnes litigation arose when, in July of 1985, the Kitty Kat Lounge and its owner and employees were threatened with arrest and prosecution under Indiana's public indecency law if nude dancing was not stopped. The Kitty Kat had, earlier, offered only semi-nude dancing, but Ford wished to offer nude dancing. He began to do so, anticipating that the South Bend police would order him to stop and the prosecutor, Michael Barnes, would threaten prosecution, at which point Ford could bring a suit in federal court challenging the constitutionality of the public-indecency law, which prohibited nudity in any public place, including bars. On October 18, 1985, Ford brought his lawsuit against Barnes in the name of the Kitty Kat Lounge and Darlene Miller, one of the Kitty Kat dancers. He claimed that the nudity ban was an unconstitutional restriction on free speech and asked the court to enjoin Barnes from prosecuting him under the law.

The Kitty Kat case was joined on appeal in the federal court with another very similar case brought a few months earlier by Glen Theatre Inc., also of South Bend, and Gayle Ann Marie Sutro and Carla Johnson, two performers who appeared at the Chippewa Bookstore, owned by Glen Theatre. The Chippewa Bookstore neither sold nor permitted alcoholic beverages. It sold sexually oriented publications and materials and offered live nude and semi-nude performances that could be viewed through glass panels. It also offered private booths for individual customers who wished to watch live nude dancers and sold a premium package for those who wished to speak to the dancer while watching her through a glass panel.

There had apparently been no arrests or prosecutions for obscenity, soliciting prostitution, or engaging in prostitution at the Chippewa Bookstore. There had, however, been about eleven arrests of performers between 1983 and 1985 for violating the public-decency law, followed by raids on March 27, 1985, which forced the Chippewa to discontinue live nude entertainment.

Following the series of arrests and the March 1985 raid, Glen Theatre Inc. with Gayle Ann Marie Sutro and Carla Johnson brought suit challenging the public-nudity provision of the decency law.

Two of the dancers/performers who joined the lawsuits filed unchallenged affidavits. The first was Darlene Miller, who performed at the Kitty Kat Lounge. Her affidavit was brief, describing what she did as engaging "in live nude and semi-nude entertainment." Carla Johnson did not file an affidavit but was described in the complaint in the lawsuit as "an entertainer who has performed on the stage of various theatres throughout the State of Indiana [including the Chippewa and] has engaged in live nude dancing as part of her performance."

Gayle Ann Marie Sutro, however, was more expansive in describing her work as a dancer at the Chippewa. In her affidavit, she stated that she has "performed professionally in live theatrical productions and live stage shows . . . throughout the United States, and I have as an integral part of my dance removed my clothes and danced nude in an art form I consider to be artistic." She described her "nude dance performances [as] appropriately choreographed and . . . an attempt to communicate as well as to entertain." She listed "degrees from West Valley College in Saratoga, California (1975), San Jose State College (1978), the Los Gatos Academy of Dance, and the Marne Jones Modeling School in San Jose, California." She "studied acting, dance (including ballet, jazz, tap, and exotic dance), and speech and languages." She had performed in "movies, including Night Shift, Blues Brothers, and several adult films, . . . [and] performances on several prime-time network television programs," including *Love Boat* and *Magnum P.I.* She also "modeled for photographs in such magazines as Penthouse, Shape, Fitness, and New Body." In sum, Sutro described herself as a "professional actress, stunt woman, and ecdysiast." For those who wonder what an ecdysiast is, the *Oxford English Dictionary* defines it as "a stripteaser" and assigns the origin of the word to H. L. Mencken, who likened it to the "zoological process of molting."

The Kitty Kat Lounge and Glen Theatre cases were at first successful in the district court, where Indiana's nudity law was held to be an unconstitutional infringement of the dancers' First Amendment rights. On appeal, the case was reversed and sent back to the district court, which thereafter *upheld* the law as applied to the dancers, on the ground that the nude dancing "was not protected by the First Amendment." The district court described Darlene Miller, who was paid only by a commission on the drink sales during her performances, as a dancer whose "avowed purpose . . . is to try to get customers to like her so that they will buy more drinks, . . . [and as a person who] wants to dance nude because she believes she would make more money doing so." The cases were again appealed to the United States Court of Appeals, which decided the case en banc (with all of the judges participating, rather than deciding by a panel of three judges). That court held, though not without dissent, that the nude dancing involved in the cases was expression protected by the First Amendment, and thus the Indiana law was unconstitutional as applied to the nude dancing and performances at the Kitty Kat Lounge and the Chippewa Bookstore. This time it was the State of Indiana that appealed to the United States Supreme Court, which granted review and set the case for oral argument on January 8, 1991.

• • •

The Court that heard the *Barnes* case was not too much different from the Court that would hear the *Finley* case seven years later. William Rehnquist was the Chief Justice, and with him on the conservative side of the Court were Justices White, Kennedy, and Scalia. In the middle was Justice O'Connor. On the liberal side were Justices Marshall, Blackmun, Stevens, and Souter. By the time of the *Finley* case in 1998, Justices Marshall, Blackmun, and White would be replaced by Justices Thomas (a conservative), Breyer, and Ginsburg (both moderate to liberal). The names had changed some, but the alignment on the Court was about the same—two blocks, one in the conservative corner and one in the liberal corner, with Justice O'Connor (and sometimes Justice Kennedy) in the middle. It would be a hard Court to argue before, given its divisions and the key votes the lawyers would need to attract from the middle. As it turned out, however, the conventional public and press preconceptions about the justices didn't play out in *Barnes,* as is often the case.

Chief Justice Rehnquist called the Court to order. Wayne E. Uhl, deputy attorney general of Indiana, began his argument supporting the Indiana law's constitutionality.

MR. UHL: Thank you, Mr. Chief Justice, and may it please the Court: Under Indiana's law a person cannot leave his home naked and walk down the street. He cannot give a political speech in a park without—
QUESTION: Without being in trouble.
MR. UHL: That's correct.
(Laughter.)
QUESTION: He can evidently sing in an opera without his clothes on.

A brief aside is needed here. The Indiana law prohibits nudity anywhere, in opera or on the beach. But in upholding the law, the Indiana courts said that if nudity in opera, for example, or the play *Hair*, is protected by the First Amendment because the nudity is artistic and expressive, the law would not prohibit it because it could not constitutionally do so. For our purposes, then, there are two basic questions presented in the case: first, is nudity "expressive" and thus protected by the First Amendment, and second, if only "artistic" nudity is protected, how can it be distinguished from the nudity in barroom dancing?

MR. UHL: The Indiana Supreme Court, in order to avoid an overbreadth challenge, has held that the statute does not affect activity which cannot be restricted by the First Amendment. And the term that the court used in that case was "a larger form of expression."

QUESTION: Which includes opera but not go-go dancing? [Is it] the good-taste clause of the Constitution? How does one draw that line between Salome and the Kitty Cat Lounge?

MR. UHL: The line is drawn the same way the line is drawn anytime conduct is involved, and that is whether or not the conduct communicates. If the conduct communicates, then the conduct is speech. If the conduct does not communicate, then the conduct is not speech.

It's not quite so simple as Mr. Uhl would have us believe. He's right that if conduct does not communicate, it is not speech under the First Amendment. But how do we know when conduct communicates, for some conduct surely does? Flag burning does, at least if the circumstances suggest a message or meaning (as opposed to using the flag to start a campfire). And what must conduct communicate to be speech? A message? An intended message? A message interpreted by a viewer or audience? A feeling, like rage or like lust and sensuality? Is murder committed in apparent rage communicating the feelings of the murderer and, thus, protected speech?

And, of course, what about artistic and aesthetic expression, which some would distinguish from other speech because it evokes in the audience an entirely new, cognitive, or sensual message or meaning?

QUESTION: Communicates what? An idea?

MR. UHL: Communicates a particularized message or an idea.

QUESTION: What about a particularized message and an idea of sensuality?

MR. UHL: That could be communicated. However, the plaintiffs in this case did not carry their burden of proving that that was the particularized message that they were sending by their dancing.

QUESTION: Well, could a dance communicate that?

MR. UHL: Yes, a dance could communicate that.

QUESTION: But this one didn't?

MR. UHL: These dances did not.

QUESTION: Because they were not good enough dancers?

MR. UHL: No, Your Honor, it wasn't the quality of the dancing. Go-go dancing can be good or bad, but in either instance it's [not] speech.

Mr. Uhl, of course, wants to stay away from pure quality judgments. Go-go
dancing, good or bad, is not expressive. But he can't really escape quality so
easily. Can a nude woman evoking feelings of sexual pleasure when dancing
in a nude bar be distinguished from a nude woman evoking the same feelings
in an opera? Is the difference simply that opera is more "hoity-toity" and elite
than the workingman's pleasure experienced in a bar? If so, by what standard
is that distinction to be judged? If Mr. Uhl refuses to draw a distinction, he
will likely lose the case.

QUESTION: Well, Mr. Uhl, are you conceding that if conduct does communicate, then it can't be regulated at all under the First Amendment?

MR. UHL: No, Your Honor, our second argument in the case is that even if this
dance is speech, then it can be restricted under the First Amendment. Our
statute is a general criminal prohibition on public nudity that applies—
that is not directed at speech and is content neutral in the sense that it is
irrelevant what message might be sent by the conduct.

QUESTION: But in light of the decisions of your State's courts, it does seem
that what's left is not content neutral in all respects.

MR. UHL: Your Honor, I think the respondents have overconstrued [the cases
when they say that the Indiana courts have] created some kind of a speech
exception.

This is a legally technical point but a very important one. Mr. Uhl's position
is that the Indiana law is a flat ban on all nudity, everywhere in public. Therefore, it bans only the conduct of appearing nude in the interest of general
morals and has nothing whatever to do with speech. The First Amendment
doesn't come into play any more than it would in a prosecution for murder—
even an expressive murder. Mr. Uhl would therefore bite the bullet and say
that the nudity law could be applied to the beach, the bar, *and* the opera.

Two problems confront him in making this argument. First, the Indiana
courts had carved an exception in the law for opera or the play *Hair,* if (but

only if) the First Amendment required one. Mr. Uhl will argue that this is nothing but a tautology, for what the Constitution might require can't be overridden by a statute of the Indiana legislature, and the courts' acknowledgment of a possible exception does not mean they think it is necessary constitutionally. Second, once having made this point, Mr. Uhl must be prepared to argue that the flat ban on conduct only would and could be applied to the opera or to *Hair*. Can he sell that argument?

QUESTION: Then you're saying it would be permissible to pass a statute prohibiting tap dancing?

MR. UHL: Unless tap dancing were shown to be speech under the First Amendment, that's correct.

QUESTION: Well, but under your view, it doesn't convey any particular message so you could prohibit it.

MR. UHL: That's correct, Your Honor.

QUESTION: Could the State prohibit rock music?

MR. UHL: Your Honor, this Court found in the Ward case, [where it upheld the application of a noise ordinance to rock music,] that rock music is speech under the First Amendment, so no, it could not. But—

QUESTION: Well, how is it that music is protected but dance is not?

MR. UHL: Music is different from dance in that the very nature of the medium is communicative. But by the definition of dance that's been submitted by the respondents—

Well . . . Mr. Uhl has to be careful here. How is dance by its nature less communicative than music? Both are generally perceived as expressive; both have deep cultural and expressive roots. Music is moving the mouth or playing an instrument, appealing initially to auditory senses, dance is moving the feet or body and appealing initially to visual senses. But seeing both is an interpretive experience, at least for the audience that, in art, may give new meaning to either. It is dangerous to conflate medium with meaning or message, for at some point everything can collapse into speech under such reasoning.

The Court pursues the point in the questions. And Mr. Uhl tries to tough it out.

QUESTION: Do you think some of the rock music played in the *Ward* case conveyed a message?

MR. UHL: An artistic message. Yes, Your Honor. Whereas not all dance conveys an artistic message.

QUESTION: Well, I suggest not all music does either.

MR. UHL: That may be a case-by-case determination, and this Court hasn't addressed that except in *Ward* to say that music in general is communicative and therefore is speech under the First Amendment.

QUESTION: Well, dance in general might be communicative under that test, might it not?

MR. UHL: We would resist that, Your Honor, because dance can be so broadly defined as to include perhaps what I'm doing here today.

QUESTION: Song and dance.

(Laughter.)

MR. UHL: Well, not that kind of song and dance.

(Laughter.)

MR. UHL: The respondents have suggested that a production in which nudes simply stand nude on a stage would be dance—rhythm is not important to the definition of a dance. Improvisation can be dance, according to the respondents. Any movement can be defined as dance. And if this Court were to hold that all dance as it's defined there is speech, then the First Amendment would be trivialized to include any kind of movement or motion that expresses some kind of emotion.

And our second argument assumes arguendo that the dance is speech and argues that even if it is speech that we can protect under the statute because the statute doesn't ban dancing. It doesn't ban performances. It simply requires that anytime a person in Indiana appears in public that vital areas of the body be covered. And for that reason this is the type of general criminal prohibition that this Court has held can be applied consistently with the First Amendment, notwithstanding a claim that the conduct at issue is protected—is speech under the First Amendment.

We are now getting down to the core questions about speech and dancing and art. Is nudity speech protected by the First Amendment? If so, when and why? Is it so if, as the Indiana Supreme Court suggested, the nudity is part of a "greater message," such as that in an opera in which nudity occurs? But why should nudity as speech have to rely upon something else? Karen Finley didn't. Was her chocolate-covered nudity not speech? Or is nudity speech when it conveys any message, even a message about sexual excitement only? And how about emotion, the stuff of art and aesthetics? Emotion, it turns out, is the subject the Court next tries to explore.

QUESTION: If we were to find that an emotional communication as opposed to a particularized message were protectable, what would you then say to the argument on the other side that they simply cannot communicate the message in any other way except by nude dancing? I think what they're saying in effect is some kind of a medium-is-the-message argument.

MR. UHL: If the medium is the message, Your Honor, then it's our contention that the nudity is not an essential part of that particular medium. The dance can be communicated just as effectively, or almost as effectively, with pasties and g-strings covering the vital parts of the body that are at issue under the statute. And it's our contention that alternative means of communication are open to these plaintiffs and that the mere requirement that certain parts of the body be covered is not essential to their communication.

QUESTION: So you're saying they cannot define their activity by saying the medium and the message are identical and thereby evade the possibility of otherwise permissible First Amendment regulation?

MR. UHL: That's correct, Your Honor. In one sense their claim that nudity is an inherent part of their dance is no different than someone who might be putting on a play and decide that the use of marijuana during the play is also protected because it's connected with this protected play. I think the Court would immediately reject that argument out of hand, that that kind of criminal conduct, even though it's in the context of a protected production, can be criminalized by a State.

This is a good question and a good answer by Mr. Uhl. If the medium is the message, everything collapses into or out of speech depending on some criterion of when a medium is itself communicative of a message. Art, we might say, is more than medium. Medium can be part of its message or evoked meaning but not all of it.

QUESTION: These particular dancers have never claimed or indicated that they had any such message to deliver, I gather.

MR. UHL: That's correct. One of the respondents in this case submitted an affidavit where she said that she intended to communicate and to entertain, and then she stopped and didn't tell us what she intended to communicate or entertain. And that respondent, respondent Sutro, also failed to submit any other evidence of the type of dancing that she wanted to perform. She did not submit a videotape, as did some of the respondents, nor did she even just submit to the court a verbal or written description of the dancing that she wished to perform.

QUESTION: Would the case really be different if the dancer had a sign up at—

on the stage that said she was a member of a nudist colony and she believed it healthy for people to attend nudist colonies and some message with it and then said, "I'll illustrate to you how nice it is to be nude" or something like that? Would that be a different case?

MR. UHL: No, Your Honor, that would be no different than the case in Florida of the sunbathers who claimed that they wanted to bathe out on the beach and show—

QUESTION: But it's different in the sense that you have a particularized message, and the dance is suppose to dramatize this message that she's also got a sign stating it.

MR. UHL: In terms of the particularized message, then it would be a different case.

Why is this so? Is it just because of the dancer's stated intent to speak—and to speak a message? And if no one hears the message intended? How about the "text" of the message or speech—her performative act, or the audience's understanding (or not) of her message or, indeed, any message, or general cultural understandings of the significance of her nudity, expressively intended or not? Is a beggar holding out a tin cup on the streets of New York really expressing a message of social failure and cultural despair? Or is he just seeking a dime? If the passerby sees the former, has he expressively transformed the beggar's act into one of free speech, whether the beggar likes it or not?

If we stick to this narrow set of questions, what do we do with art and aesthetic expression? Can the First Amendment demand an intended and accomplished particularized message of art in order for it to command constitutional status as speech? Surely not, if art consists in important if not essential part in material that evokes feelings and cognitive ideas that transcend the picture or dance or music in the mind and imagination of the audience members, whose transcendence will hardly be uniform. Must the message be cognitive—reasoned or rational? Would Karen Finley qualify under such a standard? And what about sensual or reality-changing interpretive experiences, like impressionism or, in the latter instance, like a Picasso painting that allows the viewer to perceive a new reality?

QUESTION: So if the particularized message distinction is not upheld, then you have no way of drawing the line between the higher and lower form.

MR. UHL: That very well may be true. I would like to reserve the balance of my time for rebuttal, Mr. Chief Justice.

QUESTION: Very well, Mr. Uhl.

The oral argument by Mr. Uhl was interesting and lively but ultimately unrewarding—perhaps as much because of the Court's failure to delve deeply into the issues raised by the nude dancing in the Kitty Kat Lounge: Why is dancing expressive? What is the difference between aesthetic and cognitive expression? What role, if any, do intent and audience interpretation play? That's too bad, because the Court will not likely be able to avoid those issues in its decision in the case.

Mr. Uhl did have two clear tracks to his argument. First, nudity is conduct, not speech, and that's the end of the matter. Second, even if nudity (in dance, for example) is expressive, its value under the First Amendment is low, and, furthermore, it is indecent, so it should be seen only as a manner of speech, not a message, and, thus, only modestly protected. They are both reasonable arguments, but they require that he (and the Court if it agrees) bite the bullet of *Hair* or the opera and then swallow it.

After Mr. Uhl returns to his seat, Bruce Ennis, one of the most highly respected First Amendment lawyers in the country, takes the podium and immediately bores in on the unanswered questions that the Court and Mr. Uhl left in their wake.

MR. ENNIS: Mr. Chief Justice, and may it please the Court: Nude dancing is sufficiently expressive to at least trigger First Amendment analysis for two independent reasons. First, nude dancing is expressive because performance dance is inherently expressive of emotions and ideas, and, second, because nude dancing communicates a particularized message of sensuality and eroticism.

Performance dance, like music, is one of the oldest forms of human communication and is inherently expressive of emotions and ideas. In *Ward* [involving the noise limit for rock music], this Court found that music is expressive without bothering to determine whether the music at issue did or did not communicate a particularized message. A particularized-message test applies only to conduct that is not ordinarily expressive, such as flag burning. Even that kind of conduct can be found expressive if in context it communicates a particularized message. But the Court has never used that test to determine whether marching or picketing or other traditional expressive forms of activity are expressive or not.

The Court's decisions made clear that if conduct is otherwise expressive and protected by the First Amendment, the fact that the conduct involves nudity does not shed that protection.

Mr. Ennis has packed a lot of stuff into his opening statement: particular messages, emotional meaning, pure conduct versus inherently expressive conduct, such as picketing or marching. We'll see the latter in the *Hurley* case. But the statement also reveals, in its many and undefined standards, that the question is not so easy, maybe. And *Hurley* will show us that, too.

Is dance "inherently expressive," therefore needing no further particularized message? If so, why? Can the same be said about music? If "inherently expressive" means that no further inquiry is needed, does that also mean that a child banging on the piano keys indiscriminately is making music? Is a person jumping for joy dancing? If not, then the hard questions remain but only shift to the definitions of music or dance and require the Court to answer whether writhing around a pole nude in a bar is dance. Mr. Ennis's argument just takes us full circle back to the beginning.

QUESTION: Mr. Ennis, would you concede that a State ban on nudity on public thoroughfares and sidewalks is constitutional?

MR. ENNIS: The State could probably prohibit it because of the captive audience problem or exposure to children.

QUESTION: You began by using a term—was it dance performance?

MR. ENNIS: Performance dance. By that I mean dance which is intended as a performance in front of an audience, to distinguish that from recreational dance or dancing at home in your own room.

There are clear shades of the *Finley* problem here. What is performance dance? Mr. Ennis says it is dance intended as a performance in front of an audience. The definition is not only tautological—what's intended is done, though we don't know why intent should matter—but it is also vacuous. It falls away once pressed at all.

With this, Justice Scalia can no longer contain himself. He jumps in on "performance dance." When he jumps in, the experience is usually not a pleasant one for the lawyer arguing the case.

QUESTION: Mr. Ennis, nobody is stopping her from dancing. Suppose you win this point: dancing is expression. They have not stopped her from dancing. They have stopped her from going about nude, whether dancing or doing anything else, just as I suppose they have murder laws in Indiana which prevent people from killing people, whether in the course of dancing or not.

Now, would one have to analyze the Indiana murder law as a—as valid or invalid under First Amendment if the murder happens to be performed in the course of a public performance dance? Would we have to consider that a First Amendment case?

MR. ENNIS: Well, let me turn directly to that, Justice Scalia. That depends on the State's justifications, assuming this is expressive activity. This statute cannot—

QUESTION: So your answer to my last question is yes, it does turn on the State's justifications?

MR. ENNIS: It does—

QUESTION: That's a First Amendment case, if you kill somebody in the course of dancing?

MR. ENNIS: If someone uses peyote or commits a murder for the purpose of communicating or expressive activity, that would trigger First Amendment analysis. But the State could nevertheless prohibit it. [But the Indiana law is different,] and here's why, Your Honor. This statute is not content neutral. The statute as construed [by the Indiana courts] exempts other expressive activity precisely because of its artistic or expressive content or value and thus cannot be deemed a content-neutral statute.

QUESTION: The statute here, Mr. Ennis, isn't addressed to dancing at all. It's addressed to public nudity. It's not nude dancing. It's not dancing. It's nudity, period.

MR. ENNIS: Justice Scalia, the Court's opinions in all the flag-burning cases uses the same analysis. It says the State must justify the application of an otherwise content-neutral statute to expressive activity for reasons unrelated to expression. In this case, you can look at the State's briefs. The State has acknowledged its fear that nude dancing is, quote, "likely to inspire patrons to solicit sex from performers or contemplate rape or adultery." The State has admitted it has concerns about the effect of nude dancing on attitudes toward women and has argued that it should be free to ban nude dancing because it "encourages activities which break down family structure and advocates adultery, licentiousness, prostitution, and crime."

These justifications are related to expression because they focus on the direct impact of speech on its audience, and they are concerned with listeners' reactions. Therefore, this cannot be considered a content-neutral statute—

QUESTION: Well, what if the dancer wanted to do kind of an Annie Oakley dance in the course of which she fired off a revolver at various targets around the room, and the State says that's a violation of our law. You can't fire a revolver without a permit. You can't do it in this kind of a place. And the dancer says, well, I can't really get across the Annie Oakley message without firing off the gun. But the State then says, well, we have real fears that if you do it in a crowded adult bookstore, you might hurt somebody. That's certainly talking about the application right there to the bookstore.

MR. ENNIS: But it does not depend upon the listeners' reactions to the speech. That's like setting a fire. Perhaps burning a flag in an enclosed public building might be bannable because of the State's independent interest in fire safety. It is unrelated to expression. The State has an interest in applying that statute to this expressive activity that is completely unrelated to the expressive activity.

QUESTION: Well, let's assume that the State has said hypothetically, we don't care what are the audiences' reactions. We just don't think public nudity anywhere is a good idea.

MR. ENNIS: Well, Your Honor, that would be a different case. That is—

Mr. Ennis is getting into very tricky waters here. The State says it cares about nudity and nothing else—just conduct. The Indiana Supreme Court decision exempting nudity protected by the United States Supreme Court from the ban isn't relevant, for if the State's argument in this case prevails and all nudity can be banned as conduct, then the exemption (which was theoretical only) goes away. Mr. Ennis argues, in the alternative, that nudity—all of it—is expressive, so the State was nevertheless clearly interested in expression when it passed the statute. But that's a hard argument to make. The slippery slope leading to the conclusion that all conduct is expression is both greased and very steep.

QUESTION: So the State didn't advance quite the right justification here?

MR. ENNIS: No, that's not my position, Justice Rehnquist. The State did advance reasons, and the reasons it advances are related to expression.

QUESTION: What about a noise statute? Is that related to expression?

MR. ENNIS: I think the noise point, for example, in your opinion for the Court in *Ward*, the Court found that controlling volume there was unrelated to the expression because it applied—no matter who was expressing the message and regardless of the State's agreement or disagreement with the views or the listeners' reaction to that.

QUESTION: Well, why couldn't you say the same thing about nudity? Do you think there's any difference between, say, opera and the dancing in this case, in terms of the effect on the audience?

MR. ENNIS: The State seems to feel there is. The State seems to feel that if nude dancing is artistic, it has one effect on the audience and does not incite the audience to prostitution, rape, or adultery, but that if nude dancing is not artistic, it does have that effect on the audience.

QUESTION: I suppose there are some things the State can prohibit even if— just because it has an effect on the audience. What about shouting fire in a crowded room?

MR. ENNIS: Your Honor, I think that there are—the distinction is that here what the State is concerned about is that the consenting adults in the audience will agree with this message, will follow what they take the message to be and will go out and have bad attitudes about women or commit prostitution, rape, or adultery. It depends upon the listeners' reactions of being persuaded by the message that the State wants to suppress. That is not true in the shouting-fire-in-the-theater context. It doesn't matter whether the people in the theater think there's really a fire or not. There's a stampede, and people get hurt. That's a very different case.

There is more trouble here for Mr. Ennis—trouble he may not be able to avoid. Shouting "Fire!" has a particularized message and evokes an emotional interpretation and response. Isn't it therefore just the same as nudity is about speaking sex and evoking sexual emotions and urges? To be sure, as Mr. Ennis says, the likelihood of the harms—being trampled in the theater versus being raped by a member of the audience—is very different, but that difference goes to harm, not whether that which produced the harm is speech. Mr. Ennis's argument is that the difference goes to the existence of speech itself.

This is not to say that the two instances of claimed speech are not different but rather to say that the likelihood of harm can't really be the defining factor, at least without some additional explanation. Maybe intent. Maybe cultural understanding. Maybe taste.

Mr. Ennis is saved the task of probing the issue more deeply. That is unfortunate, for he is a very well-respected constitutional lawyer, and he likely would have had something insightful and perhaps useful to say. But the Court proceeded to get hung up in a legal technicality and never emerged from it until the end of the argument. So Mr. Ennis had no opportunity to advance his argument further, and he may have paid for that.

CHIEF JUSTICE REHNQUIST: The case is submitted.

• • •

The Supreme Court did not hand down its opinion in the *Barnes* case until June 22, 1991, almost six months after the oral argument and at the very end of the Term. The Court was divided 5-4 on the outcome. It was even more divided on its reasoning. The Chief Justice wrote a plurality opinion representing the views of only three justices, the Chief, Justice O'Connor, and Justice Kennedy. Justices Scalia and Souter wrote separate opinions and concurred only in the result, not the reasoning, of the plurality opinion. Justices White, Marshall, Blackmun, and Stevens dissented in an opinion written by Justice White. Not only was the outcome closely decided but the alignment of the justices was a bit peculiar, with Justice Souter, who tends to be liberal on free speech issues, joining the otherwise-conservative group, and with Justice White, who was generally conservative, joining the dissenters and writing the dissenting opinion.

> Chief Justice Rehnquist delivered the opinion of the Court.
> Several of our cases contain language suggesting that nude dancing of the kind involved here is expressive conduct protected by the First Amendment. We have previously said: "[A]lthough the customary 'barroom' type of nude dancing may involve only the barest minimum of protected expression . . ., this form of entertainment might be entitled to First and Fourteenth Amendment protection under some circumstances. [We have also] said that 'nude dancing is not without its First Amendment protections from official regulation.'" These statements support the conclusion of the Court of Appeals that nude dancing of the kind sought to be performed here is expressive conduct within the outer perimeters of the First Amendment, though we view it as only marginally so.
> The public indecency statute furthers a substantial government interest in protecting order and morality. This interest is unrelated to the suppression of free expression. It can be argued, of course, that almost limitless types of conduct—including appearing in the nude in public—are "expressive," and in one sense of the word this is true. People who go about in the nude in public may be expressing something about themselves by so doing. But the court rejected this expansive notion of "expressive conduct" in *O'Brien* [the draft-card-burning case], saying: "We cannot accept the view that an apparently limitless variety of conduct can be labeled 'speech' whenever the person engaging in the conduct intends thereby to express an idea." And [in another recent case involving ballroom dancing,] we further observed: "It is possible to find some kernel of expression in almost every activity a person undertakes—for example, walking down the street or

meeting one's friends at a shopping mall—but such a kernel is not sufficient to bring the activity within the protection of the First Amendment. We think the activity of these dance-hall patrons coming together to engage in recreational dancing—is not protected by the First Amendment."

We do not think that when Indiana applies its statute to the nude dancing in these nightclubs, it is proscribing nudity because of the erotic message conveyed by the dancers. Presumably numerous other erotic performances are presented at these establishments and similar clubs without any interference from the State, so long as the performers wear a scant amount of clothing. Likewise, the requirement that the dancers don pasties and G-strings does not deprive the dance of whatever erotic message it conveys; it simply makes the message slightly less graphic. The perceived evil that Indiana seeks to address is not erotic dancing, but public nudity. The appearance of people of all shapes, sizes and ages in the nude at a beach, for example, would convey little if any erotic message, yet the State still seeks to prevent it. Public nudity is the evil the State seeks to prevent, whether or not it is combined with expressive activity.

The judgment of the Court of Appeals accordingly is *Reversed.*

Chief Justice Rehnquist's opinion is a little bit of this and a little bit of that. Barroom nude dancing is sufficiently expressive to fall "within the outer perimeters of the First Amendment" but "only marginally so." But it doesn't tell us why this is so or what "marginally" means. It appears to be a hold-your-nose kind of speech. But the opinion also suggests that barroom dancing isn't really protected expression. It's really no different than simply "appearing nude in public," which can be regulated because, like "walking down the street or meeting one's friends at a shopping mall . . ., such a kernel [of expression] is not sufficient to bring the activity within the protection of the First Amendment."

Which is it: speech protected only marginally or conduct not protected by the First Amendment? Or is it a little bit of both: speech protected so marginally that it is not protected at all?

Justice Scalia, concurring in the judgment.

I agree that the judgment of the Court of Appeals must be reversed. In my view, however, the challenged regulation must be upheld, not because it survives some lower level of First Amendment scrutiny, but because, as a general law regulating conduct and not specifically directed at expression, it is not subject to First Amendment scrutiny at all.

As Judge Easterbrook put it in his dissent below: "Indiana does not regulate dancing. It regulates public nudity. . . . Almost the entire domain of

Indiana's statute is unrelated to expression, unless we view nude beaches and topless hot dog vendors as speech." The intent to convey a "message of eroticism" (or any other message) is not a necessary element of the statutory offense of public indecency; nor does one commit that statutory offense by conveying the most explicit "message of eroticism," so long as he does not commit any of the four specified acts in the process.

The dissent confidently asserts that the purpose of restricting nudity in public places in general is to protect nonconsenting parties from offense and argues that since only consenting, admission-paying patrons see respondents dance, that purpose cannot apply, and the only remaining purpose must relate to the communicative elements of the performance. Perhaps the dissenters believe that "offense to others" *ought* to be the only reason for restricting nudity in public places generally, but there is no basis for thinking that our society has ever shared that Thoreauvian "you-may-do-what-you-like-so-long-as-it-does-not-injure-someone-else" beau ideal—much less for thinking that it was written into the Constitution. The purpose of Indiana's nudity law would be violated, I think, if 60,000 fully consenting adults crowded into the Hoosier Dome to display their genitals to one another, even if there were not an offended innocent in the crowd. Our society prohibits, and all human societies have prohibited, certain activities not because they harm others but because they are considered, in the traditional phrase, "*contra bonos mores,*" *i.e.*, immoral.

Indiana may constitutionally enforce its prohibition of public nudity even against those who choose to use public nudity as a means of communication. The State is regulating conduct, not expression, and those who choose to employ conduct as a means of expression must make sure that the conduct they select is not generally forbidden. For these reasons, I agree that the judgment should be reversed.

Justice Scalia's opinion is characteristically clear and to the point. Barroom dancing is not speech. And even if it were, that doesn't matter because the Indiana law is a general regulation of conduct—appearing nude in public—having nothing to do with regulating expression, even if it does hit expression within its conduct aim. Must a law barring spitting on a public sidewalk contain an exception for someone whose act of spitting expresses a meaning to others or is intended by the spitter to convey his or her distaste about something? For Scalia, the answer is clear: find another way of expressing distaste if spitting is illegal, even if the law banning spitting is enacted for purely moral or decency reasons or instead, perhaps, for reasons of public health.

But what about the civil rights marches, which violated flat prohibitions on people walking on the pubic streets?

Justice Souter, concurring in the judgment.

Not all dancing is entitled to First Amendment protection as expressive activity. This Court has previously categorized ballroom dancing as beyond the Amendment's protection, and dancing as aerobic exercise would likewise be outside the First Amendment's concern. But dancing as a performance directed to an actual or hypothetical audience gives expression at least to generalized emotion or feeling, and where the dancer is nude or nearly so, the feeling expressed, in the absence of some contrary clue, is eroticism, carrying an endorsement of erotic experience. Such is the expressive content of the dances described in the record.

Although such performance dancing is inherently expressive, nudity *per se* is not. It is a condition, not an activity, and the voluntary assumption of that condition, without more, apparently expresses nothing beyond the view that the condition is somehow appropriate to the circumstances. But every voluntary act implies some such idea, and the implication is thus so common and minimal that calling all voluntary activity expressive would reduce the concept of expression to the point of the meaningless. A search for some expression beyond the minimal in the choice to go nude will often yield nothing: a person may choose nudity, for example, for maximum sunbathing. But when nudity is combined with expressive activity, its stimulative and attractive value certainly can enhance the force of expression, and a dancer's acts in going from clothed to nude, as in a striptease, are integrated into the dance and its expressive function. Thus I agree with the plurality and the dissent that an interest in freely engaging in the nude dancing at issue here is subject to a degree of First Amendment protection.

I nonetheless write separately to rest my [judgment] not on the possible sufficiency of society's moral views to justify the limitations at issue, but on the State's substantial interest in combating the secondary effects [such as crime and sexual assault] of adult entertainment establishments of the sort typified by [these] establishments.

Accordingly, I . . . concur in the judgment.

Justice Souter agrees with the dissenters that barroom dancing is protected expression under the First Amendment. He doesn't agree with Justice Scalia that the law is a general, morally based regulation of conduct unrelated to the suppression of expression. Instead, he views the law as specifically directed at the Kitty Kat Lounges of the world, and thus it is directed at suppressing expression. But the secondary effects of such a law—limiting crime, sexual assault, and the like in the areas where such establishments are located—make the State's effort to curb crime and sexual violence through the law a reasonable, if highly imperfect, measure and thus a constitutional one.

This is a perfectly coherent view. It allows the State to bar nude barroom dancing but not the nude dancing in *Hair* or other more conventional (more proper?) places. But there are also substantial problems with Justice Souter's have-your-cake-and-eat-it-too approach. The first is that there is absolutely no evidence that deterring crime and sexual assault were the State's purpose. Indeed, the State denied that these were its purposes. The law applied to all nudity, not just nude dancing or nudity in places where crime might be fostered by it. So Justice Souter has effectively rewritten Indiana's law, though without providing a narrower, substitute law that would accomplish his objectives. Second, there is no evidence that the location or activities in the Kitty Kat Lounge or the Chippewa are related in fact to higher rates of crime or sexual violence, and there is certainly no substantial and systematic evidence connecting either of them specifically with any crime by its patrons (two deaths, prostitution, and a burglary at the Kitty Kat hardly make a general pattern for such places, and the Chippewa had no record of criminal activity related to nude dancing). Finally, there is no way to determine from Souter's approach whether other locations for nudity—say a nude beach, or a public street, or a nude hot dog vendor, or even a theater showing *Hair*—might likewise be susceptible to crime and sexual violence, thus justifying application of the ban to them. If the theater showing *Hair* is downtown and surrounded by bars and near a college campus, might the possible increase in date rape, for example, be enough to ban *Hair* there?

We do know, however, that the only reason the law is valid as applied to a bar, and not, presumably, a legitimate theater, is the resulting threat of violence and crime. In either location, the status of the nude dancing under the First Amendment is the same—it is expression and thus speech protected by the Constitution, and it is art or aesthetic expression. Justice Souter thus creates one mess—how to know whether the crime-and-violence rationale applies—in order to avoid another—what is art, and is the nude dancing in *Hair* differently artistic from the writhing, nude dancing in the Kitty Kat Lounge?

Souter's neat solution works (if only because he says so) in the *Barnes* case. But it won't in many others. Indeed, Justice Souter quite explicitly says in his opinion that "ballroom dancing . . . and dancing as aerobic exercise . . . [are]

outside the First Amendment's concern," but barroom dancing is protected by the First Amendment—even, we must assume, if both are done in the nude. There must be some expressive distinction between dancing nude in a ballroom—with many others joining in or watching—and nude dancing in a bar. He doesn't tell us what it is. He says only that barroom dancing is "performance directed to an actual or hypothetical audience that gives expression at least to generalized emotion or feeling [like] eroticism, carrying an endorsement of erotic experience." But wouldn't this also be true if a couple performed their ballroom dance in the nude? Hypothetically?

Justice White, with whom Justice Marshall, Justice Blackmun, and Justice Stevens join, dissenting.

The first question presented to us in this case is whether nonobscene nude dancing performed as entertainment is expressive conduct protected by the First Amendment. The Court of Appeals held that it is, observing that our prior decisions permit no other conclusion. Not surprisingly, then, the plurality now concedes that "nude dancing of the kind sought to be performed here is expressive conduct within the outer perimeters of the First Amendment. . . ." This is no more than recognizing, as the Seventh Circuit observed, that dancing is an ancient art form and "inherently embodies the expression and communication of ideas and emotions."

[The following paragraph appears at this point as a footnote to the opinion.] Justice Scalia suggests that performance dancing is not inherently expressive activity, but the Court of Appeals has the better view: "Dance has been defined as 'the art of moving the body in a rhythmical way, usually to music, to express an emotion or idea, to narrate a story, or simply to take delight in the movement itself.' 16 *The New Encyclopedia Britannica* 935 (1989). Inherently, it is the communication of emotion or ideas. At the root of all '[t]he varied manifestations of dancing . . . lies the common impulse to resort to movement to externalize states which we cannot externalize by rational means. This is basic dance.' Martin, J., *Introduction to the Dance* (1939). Aristotle recognized in *Poetics* that the purpose of dance is 'to represent men's character as well as what they do and suffer.' The raw communicative power of dance was noted by the French poet Stéphane Mallarmé, who declared that the dancer 'writing with her body . . . *suggests* things which the written work could express only in several paragraphs of dialogue or descriptive prose.'"

In arriving at its conclusion, the plurality concedes that nude dancing conveys an erotic message and concedes that the message would be muted if the dancers wore pasties and G-strings. Indeed, the emotional or erotic impact of the dance is intensified by the nudity of the performers. As Judge Posner argued in his thoughtful concurring opinion in the Court of Appeals, the nudity of the dancer is an integral part of the emotions and thoughts that a nude dancing performance evokes. The sight of a fully clothed, or even a partially clothed, dancer generally will have a far different impact on a spectator than that of a nude dancer, even if the same dance is performed. The nudity is itself an expressive component of the dance, not merely incidental "conduct." We have previously pointed out that "'[n]udity alone' does not place otherwise protected material outside the mantle of the First Amendment."

This being the case, it cannot be that the statutory prohibition is unrelated to expressive conduct. Since the State permits the dancers to perform if they wear pasties and G-strings but forbids nude dancing, it is precisely because of the distinctive, expressive content of the nude dancing performances at issue in this case that the State seeks to apply the statutory prohibition. It is only because nude dancing performances may generate emotions and feelings of eroticism and sensuality among the spectators that the State seeks to regulate such expressive activity, apparently on the assumption that creating or emphasizing such thoughts and ideas in the minds of the spectators may lead to increased prostitution and the degradation of women. But generating thoughts, ideas, and emotions is the essence of communication. The nudity element of nude dancing performances cannot be neatly pigeonholed as mere "conduct" independent of any expressive component of the dance.

That the performances in the Kitty Kat Lounge may not be high art, to say the least, and may not appeal to the Court, is hardly an excuse for distorting and ignoring settled doctrine. The Court's assessment of the artistic merits of nude dancing performances should not be the determining factor in deciding this case. In the words of Justice Harlan: "[I]t is largely because governmental officials cannot make principled decisions in this area that the Constitution leaves matters of taste and style so largely to the individual." "[W]hile the entertainment afforded by a nude ballet at Lincoln Center to those who can pay the price may differ vastly in content (as viewed by judges) or in quality (as viewed by critics), it may not differ in substance from the dance viewed by the person who . . . wants some 'entertainment' with his beer or shot of rye."

As I see it, our cases require us to affirm absent a compelling state interest supporting the statute. Neither the plurality nor the State suggest that the statute could withstand scrutiny under that standard.

Accordingly, I would affirm the judgment of the Court of Appeals, and dissent from this Court's judgment.

The dissenters' view is clear and coherent. Nude dancing in a bar is fully protected speech, communicating sensual feelings and meanings often incapable of expression through words. Indeed, barroom dancing is "art," and the quality of it as art—likely not "high art," they imply—is a matter of taste for the individual, not the government. There being no compelling interest supporting Indiana's law, the law is invalid, at least as applied to this form of art.

While analytically clear, the opinion raises a few important questions. If barroom dancing is art, why is that so? Is the fact that the dancing "generate[s] emotions and feelings of eroticism and sensuality" enough to make it art? Can no distinction be made between what happens at the Kitty Kat Lounge and on the stage in the play *Hair*? And if the Indiana law is stricken only when applied to barroom dancing or *Hair* and not to other forms of nudity like, perhaps, topless hot-dog vendors, why is that so? Is the State's interest differently compelling in the two cases? If the State's purpose is good enough for hot-dog vendors, why not for barroom dancers (whose audience may be different only in its degree of inebriation)? Or is the interest the same, but the value of art overrides it in the case of barroom dancing?

• • •

What should we make of the *Barnes* case and, particularly, the Court's opinions, on the interrelated questions of expression and art under the First Amendment? A number of things can be said with some confidence at the outset. First, a full majority of the Court (Souter and the dissenters and more modestly the plurality of Rehnquist, O'Connor, and Kennedy) stated that the nude barroom dancing in the case was expression protected by the First Amendment. Five justices (Souter and the dissenters) said that it was fully protected expression. But here a difference emerges. The dissenters treat nude dancing as "pure speech" subject to protection identical to that afforded political speech. Justice Souter considers it speech for First Amendment purposes, but speech arising from conduct and thus less protected by the First Amendment. Souter's view may be peculiar to this case only (as discussed earlier), however, for he, like the dissenters, treats the expression as inherent in the speech itself and thus unambiguous: dance is expression, in other words, just like hitting the keys on a piano is inherently an act of expression, and just like moving a pen with the hand to create words is an act of expression, not separable from conduct that is treated with less respect under the First Amendment. It is thus unlike the act of burning a draft card, which becomes expressive only if intended to convey a specific message that the audience actually finds in the act and thus is subject to a more modest degree of protection as speech given its ambiguity as an act of speech or expression.

Second, the same five justices explicitly held that the dancing was expression in the form of the evocation of emotion or feeling, such as eroticism, without any attendant cognitive message. Moreover, the five justices impose no requirement of intent by the dancer to evoke more than a sensual feeling and no requirement that most of the audience perceive such a feeling. Disgust, beauty, eroticism, sexual passion all seem to be qualifying feelings, and those feelings may be held distinctly by various members of the audience. Justice Souter adds, though descriptively and not, it seems, by way of requirement, that the evoked eroticism in *Barnes* "carries an endorsement of erotic experience." Were this a requirement, it would be largely tautological. And were one's reaction disgust, it would likely flow from a reaction to the eroticism contained in the dance. The dissenters simply and forthrightly declare that "nude dancing performed as entertainment is expressive conduct protected by the First Amendment." This statement of the matter may, as we will see later, introduce a certain level of intent or knowledge on the part of the nude dancer, but it hardly disqualifies nude dancing unless it is political or satire or expressing a person's cognitive beliefs. It is instead a description of the facts of the case before the Court, and little more.

Third, and finally, the four dissenters quite expressly view the nude barroom dance as artistic expression—the dancer's act is "writing with her body . . . suggest[ing] things which the written work could express only in several paragraphs of dialogue or descriptive prose." She is "externaliz[ing] states which we cannot externalize by rational means." Justice Souter's emphasis on emotion, feeling, and eroticism—or aesthetic expression—seems to follow the same analytical line of reasoning, but he does not use the word *art*. This makes his position on the expression-versus-art question somewhat ambiguous. *Art* seems an unlikely description for the plurality's view, which treats nude dancing grudgingly as expression of a marginal sort. And Justice Scalia rejects either view, treating the nude barroom dancing as conduct pure and simple—at least under a law broadly prohibiting nudity in public.

Against this background, the interesting question is where things stand on the questions of the meaning of art, the value of aesthetic (emotional) and artistic expression under the First Amendment, the bases upon which expression can be distinguished from nonexpressive acts, and whether the purposes of the First Amendment can be reconciled with the noncognitive mediums of aesthetic and artistic expression through dance and, more broadly, through music, photographs, painting, and on and on. This large quest only begins in the *Barnes* case.

We can start by saying that all of the justices agreed that protected expression need not take cognitive, or reasoned, form and need not have a cognitive message. The plurality was perhaps a bit more grudging on this point than the dissenters and Justice Souter, and Justice Scalia was skeptical about accepting aesthetic or emotional expression as a class under the First Amendment, but even Justice Scalia seemed to accept the proposition that purely aesthetic or emotional expression *could be* protected speech.

At many points in the opinions and in oral argument, the question of intent, or purpose, of the dancer came up. The issue arose in two ways: first, in terms of the dance being performed before and for an audience, and, second, in terms of the dancer's intent to convey an artistic or aesthetic feeling or perception to an audience. At first glance, these elements of intent or knowledge on the dancer's part make sense. Do we want to credit with a "right to speak" someone who dances for, and before, herself or himself only? Without a recipient of the expression, there is no speaking, if speech means, at least, communication to another. And do we want to credit a dancer under the First Amendment for a message (cognitive or aesthetic) that he or she does not intend to convey and even intends not to convey?

But these questions are more complicated than they at first appear. Just as a tree falling in the woods is known or communicated only if someone sees it, so also a dance or its message is known and communicated only if someone sees it, regardless of the dancer's knowledge or intent. Did the person who created the Marlboro Man know that it would be later seen as an artistic cultural icon? Did the person who designed the Campbell's soup can know that in the hands of Andy Warhol, it would be transformed, though representationally unchanged, into art? Drawing on these examples, we might say communication, especially aesthetic communication, is for First Amendment purposes *a fact*, not simply a product of intent or foreknowledge. And the expressive significance given to an act or thing is also a fact, indeed a transient fact that can change over time or with circumstance or even audience. The barroom dancer might mean to communicate only to men drinking in a bar and to communicate only the grunts and moans of physical gratification or the message "Buy another drink." But a different audience (or audience member) might see her intentionally crude dance in terms, as Justice Souter put it, of sensuousness and eroticism or, as the dissenters put it, as expressive of feelings that can't be put in words. One of the dancers in the *Barnes* case said she was simply dancing nude for money. Another said her dancing was intended to be expressive and artistic. If we believe them both, should only one be credited with protection under the First Amendment? Perhaps, perhaps not.

But if we reject a decisive role for intent, yet hold to the need for there to be communication between *people* (as opposed to the flower that conveys aesthetic beauty), we are left only with the audience. Looking at the problem this way has its own challenges. How do we identify the audience—those who see the dance in a bar or those who see it elsewhere or see it in a bar but interpret it differently than most customers, or those who see it (as the soup can) twenty-five years from now? And which audience interpretation of the dance counts—the ordinary bar customers', the few who saw the dance as erotic and transformative, those who see it ten years later in altogether different social and cultural circumstances? If any single person's aesthetic and artistic interpretations are determinative of the dance's quality as expressive and artistic, then, as Justice Souter observed, everything becomes expression and, potentially, art. This would require, as a practical matter, that the First Amendment be so watered down as to be meaningless or that the First Amendment be seen as creating a state of freedom that exceeds even the most ardent libertarian's ideal. No wonder the Court's reasoning in *Barnes* is, to put it lightly, opaque. The next chapters wrestle further with these issues.

Does the Court's crediting as protected expression messages that are purely aesthetic or emotional and sensual mean that such expressions are art? Surely not. If I kick my dog in a rage in the company of a few friends, have I performed art? Perhaps we can say, for present purposes, that some aesthetic and sensual expression is art, and some is not, just like some cognitive expression is art (Lincoln's Gettysburg Address? Karen Finley's performances?), and some is not. The question, of course, is, How do we know? And does it matter if noncognitive and sensory expressions are protected speech?

As to noncognitive expression (barroom dancing, ballet) always being speech, we can first say that a majority of the justices (indeed, perhaps all) would not paint with such a broad brush. For the plurality, nude barroom dancing as speech doesn't count for much, if anything. For Justice Scalia, it counts for nothing. It counts for a lot for Justice Souter.

The dissent's view, however, is sharply limited. For the dissent, the erotic dancing counts as protected speech because—and perhaps only because—it fits the historical and contemporary forms or genre of dance as an expressive medium. If I kicked my dog in anger in the course of a dance, presumably that wouldn't count as speech, much less dance. So genre or characteristics of the artistic medium (painting, music, dance, poetry) may matter a lot for the dissenters.

The dissenters' approach may reflect a broader approach, too. (1) All non-cognitive, or sensory, expression can count as protected speech, but it may not count for much at all. (2) But dancing, including erotic and sensual dancing, fits into a category of expression (genre) that by historical and contemporary standards counts as expression and, though its aesthetic or sensual meaning is ascribed by the audience, qualifies as fully protected speech. This might also be a way to think about the pesky question of art versus entertainment, addressed in oral argument. The dichotomy is false: there is nothing wrong with art being entertainment (like Karen Finley's performances), but art need not be entertaining. And vice versa. Whether something is art, evoking re-representation and aesthetic/sensory responses, is influenced instead by whether it fits into the genres of expression that are artistic themselves.

This is a sensible way to view the problem of art, but as with all approaches, it has its problems. Chief among them is the need to accept new or changing genres into the artistic domain over time. A historically grounded approach to art and its forms would exclude new forms such as rap music, Dada, im-pressionism, modernism, cubism, and now postmodernism. Is the concept of form or genre flexible enough to encompass change as it is first happening, yet concrete enough to provide meaningful distinctions?

Finally, how can the sensual and erotic meanings that a majority of the justices saw in barroom dancing in *Barnes* be fit into the purposes of the First Amendment discussed earlier: self-government, truth, self-determination and autonomy, and reasoned, peaceful change? The most obvious purpose that might explain the importance of noncognitive aesthetic and sensual expres-sion is self-determination and autonomy. But how does the grimy business of barroom dancing—nude or not, perhaps—serve these purposes? In thinking back to the definitions of aesthetic and artistic expression discussed in the *Finley* case, we might conclude that noncognitive expression that is transfor-mative or re-representational of the reality before us, leading the audience to imagine or conceive something altogether new or different in perspective from that which logic or mere description can reveal, fosters free will, indi-vidual autonomy, and creativity. These qualities (among others) are what is essential to the functioning of a truly free government and a truly free social and political and economic order. In this way, art and aesthetic expression serve the utilitarian purposes of the First Amendment and foster the bedrock assumption of free will upon which free speech necessarily rests.

But barroom dancing? Is its function of "giving expression at least to generalized emotion or feeling" the same as fostering free will, autonomy, and creativity? One can easily argue that it is not. The essence of nude barroom dancing is lust and animal desire, hardly the higher order and freedom-fostering forms of creativity and self-identification. For the dissenters, the established form or genre of dance justifies the conclusion that nude barroom dancing is expression—perhaps art, though not "high art"—and from this conclusion the justices, heeding Holmes, decide that nothing more can be said.

But on this issue, the plurality and Justice Scalia may have the better argument. Nude barroom dancing, no matter the dancer's intent, is expressive in the most minimal ways, if at all, because it does not serve the self-governing, truth-seeking, and individual autonomy goals of the First Amendment. Karen Finley is one thing—an accepted genre, skill in performance, provocation of thought and reflection in the audience, widespread recognition as an artist. But however intentioned, Darlene Miller's dance in the Kitty Kat Lounge and Gayle Ann Marie Sutro's nude dances behind a window in the Glen Theatre just don't get the aesthetic and artistic job done.

The problem, however, is that this approach, like all of the Court's approaches, is at base culturally elitist—indeed, it views art and aesthetics as elite forces beyond the reach of the lower classes. Yet, reflection, creativity, re-representation of reality may look different for the highly educated classes than for the working classes. For many, stopping at the bar to see nude dancing may provide just as much escape, room for reflection on reality, sensual perception and pleasure, as does an opera for the hoity-toity in New York. Self-determination and autonomy and free will, after all, aren't limited to questions of high philosophy, metaphysics, culture, equality, business, or war and peace. The meaning of life takes many forms. Watching nude barroom dancing with friends after work on the assembly line is just as important and may serve similar, though for many less-lofty, goals of individuality and escape from reality.

But a few beers without the dancing will do that, too. And beer isn't art.

So we are at a standstill, perhaps, with the nature and value of aesthetic and artistic expression still up in the air. The Supreme Court said only as much as it needed to say to decide the case, and even on that the justices disagreed. It's hard to blame them, really.

But they didn't go far enough for us.

"WHAT MATTER WHO'S SPEAKING?"

Samuel Beckett's famous question, "'What matter who's speaking,' someone said, 'what matter who's speaking?'"[1] captures perhaps the central question in much art and aesthetic expression: Who speaks, and why should we care? If art is in the mind of the beholder, as it is often said, and the aesthetic consists of often-idiosyncratic sensory and emotional reaction, then understanding art, which involves the aesthetic, requires that we explore the origin of artistic meaning and the role of an audience in the artistic communication process. It requires, in other words, that we come to grips with the nature of the communicative process in a deeper way.

The ambiguity of communication and its relationship to free speech is a problem that the Supreme Court has only recently confronted—and has not confronted well, in the minds of many observers. Free speech has historically been premised on a linear process beginning with a speaker who *intends* to express a *message*, which message is in turn *understood* by an audience. Can art and aesthetic communication be so confined, restricted to a cognitive and reasoned expression of a view? If not, how must the First Amendment handle it? These questions will not arise in the Supreme Court in the setting of art. Instead, they will arise in the setting of the Boy Scouts dismissing a scout leader because he is gay, and in the context of Boston's St. Patrick's Day Parade and its exclusion of a group wishing to march in celebration of gay members of the community.

The mysteries these two cases present are: Who is the speaker, and what is the source of meaning of the "speech"? In short, "What matter who's speaking?"

SOURCES OF EXPRESSION

Boy Scouts of America v. Dale

530 U.S. 640 (2000)

SINCE AGE EIGHT, James Dale had been a Scout in his hometown of Monmouth, New Jersey. He began scouting as a Cub Scout, then advanced to Boy Scouts. By 1988, when he finished as a youth Scout on his eighteenth birthday, he had earned twenty-five merit badges and had become an Eagle Scout, one of the highest honors in Scouting. The next year, he applied for and was accepted as an assistant Scoutmaster of Troop 73 in Monmouth. About six months later, he left for college at Rutgers University in New Jersey; he also remained an assistant Scoutmaster for Troop 73. James Dale had been an exemplary Scout and was a fine assistant Scoutmaster.

He was also gay. He was gay as a Boy Scout and as an assistant Scoutmaster. He had not been open about it, and it didn't affect his stellar performance as a Boy Scout or his performance as an assistant Scoutmaster. "I think what the Scouting program teaches is self-reliance and leadership," Dale said. "Giving your best to society. Leaving things better than you found them. Standing up for what's right. That's one of the tragic ironies of this whole story—that when they found out that I was gay, suddenly I wasn't good enough anymore." Dale had found the Boy Scouts "much less homophobic than the norm of society. I think the Boy Scouts allows for the human factor a lot more than other organizations. It was a more supportive environment."[1]

Dale "came out" at nineteen, when he was attending Rutgers. He had met many other gay students—students who, like him, were positive role models—and he became comfortable with the idea of being publicly known to be gay. In his second year at Rutgers, he became involved with the lesbian and gay organization at the university, and shortly thereafter, he was elected by the Lesbian and Gay Alliance to fill the open position of president. He became active in the gay community. "It was [in] the summer between my sophomore and junior years that I was speaking at a conference for social workers. Shortly thereafter, an article ran" in the *New Jersey Star Ledger*.[2] The story was about the seminar and Dale. A photograph of Dale was prominently displayed, with the caption "Co-President of the Rutgers University Lesbian/ Gay Alliance."[3]

"About a week later I got a letter from the Boy Scouts that said I no longer meet its standards for leadership. I didn't even know what it was about. So I sent them a letter, and then I got a second letter back from them, and that said avowed homosexuals are not permitted in the Boy Scouts of America. When I heard that, I felt really devastated and betrayed. This is a program that I spent my weekends and time after school focusing on, helping out at nursing homes and cleaning parks. I had given so much to the program so freely and happily."[4]

Dale sought to appeal the decision but to no avail. He was dismissed from his position as assistant Scoutmaster, and his adult membership in the Scouts was revoked. Left with no further recourse within Scouting, he sued, claiming that the Scouts' decision was illegal under the terms of the New Jersey public accommodations law, which prohibited discrimination on the basis of "affectional or sexual orientation" in any "place of public accommodation," which included the Boy Scouts. Dale's lawsuit was brought in the New Jersey courts, where he lost at the trial-court level but ultimately prevailed in the New Jersey Supreme Court.

The Boy Scouts then appealed the case to the United States Supreme Court. In order to get to the Supreme Court, the Scouts had to argue that the New Jersey law could not constitutionally be applied to the Boy Scouts. The Scouts rested just such a claim on its First Amendment right of free speech, on the theory that a legal requirement that "avowed" or open homosexuals be free to serve as Scoutmasters would interfere with the Scouting organization's ability to express its own message that homosexuality was not "morally straight" or "clean," as the terms are used in the Scout Oath and the Scout Law.

If the Scouts' claims of free speech and associational speech (i.e., by and on behalf of the members of an organization or association) sound confusing, that's because they are confusing. The Scouts' claim rested on James Dale "coming out" and the publicity that attended his speech to the social workers' conference. The public knowledge and the Scouts' knowledge of Dale's homosexuality had the effect, the Scouts would argue, of making the Scouts appear to approve of homosexuality. Without the publicity given Dale by the *New Jersey Star Ledger*, it is possible that no one on Monmouth nor in the troop would have known of Dale's homosexuality, and therefore the Scouts wouldn't have had a progay sentiment attached to them by Dale's presence as an assistant Scoutmaster.

This is a peculiar speech claim and a peculiar First Amendment theory. It is a claim, in effect, that the Scouts are being forced to speak an unwanted message by the New Jersey law's requirement that they continue to employ Dale as an assistant Scoutmaster, given that Dale has publicly (whether willingly or not) become known to be gay and associated with gay rights. It doesn't matter whether James Dale wanted or sought the publicity; it only matters that he got it. Because the Scouts don't have to be actually, physically, speaking to anyone, young Scouts or the public at large, to make their own free speech claim, and because Dale doesn't himself have to intend to speak or even say anything about the Scouts, the argument before the Supreme Court will reflect a good deal of confusion on the part of the justices. Exactly what is the speech that the First Amendment protects? And exactly who is doing the speaking—if anyone? We know what the message of the "speech" is: The Boy Scouts are progay. We just have to figure out where it is coming from.

If the speech comes from no one but simply emerges from the circumstances, we might call the progay message asserted by the Scouts to be nothing more than an artifact—something that has no knowable source but that nevertheless exists in fact. Perhaps like the meaning a viewer gives to a work of art, especially one like a soup can or, forty years later, the Marlboro Man. Or Dada, art in the form of purposely deconstructed, indecipherable, meaningless objects or sounds or "text." Such "speech" is much different than the speech historically associated with the First Amendment. Traditionally, the speech guarantee applies to the known message of a speaker to an audience intended to inform or convince or influence—most often in a cognitive way. Such speech might be called structural or liberty-based, as it grows out of the First Amendment's purpose of protecting the liberty of individuals to hold political and other beliefs and to express them purposefully to others in order to spawn an open and free marketplace of ideas. Only intentional human speech that is understood by an audience serves these constitutional purposes. Indeed, the structuralist nature of protected speech is the reason that art, obscenity, and related forms of largely emotional and aesthetic expression have found uncertain protection under the First Amendment.

So Dale's case can be thought of as something like a pacifist driving a car with the license plate motto "Live Free or Die" (New Hampshire), which leads other drivers to believe that he believes in war. And one can think of the Scouts as an organization that stands for moral straightness but whose ability to do so is frustrated by the emergence of a new message accepting homosexuality that is now attributed to it. Is the pacifist forced to speak a message with which he wishes not to be associated? Is the license plate speaking such a message, forcing it on him?[5] Is speech an artifact of communicated meaning, or is it instead a manifestation of communicative intention? Can a speaker and a message be dispensed with, leaving only an audience that constructs its own meaning out of one's failure to speak (as with the Scouts)? These questions go to the core of what is meant by freedom of speech and the protection of art.

The *Dale* case involves a conflict between artifact—the fact of communication—and intention. It involves the absence of a speaker or author. The message in *Dale* was constructed by bystanders and attributed to the Boy Scouts (absent Dale's discharge). An unwanted message "by" the Scouts was therefore actually communicated to an audience. But the Boy Scouts did not intend to speak any message whatever. Is the fact of a message alone sufficient to qualify an act as speech under the First Amendment, or must intention by an author or creator *also* accompany a message in order for it to amount to a First Amendment claim of the messenger?[6]

• • •

The justices who would hear oral argument on this confusing and largely unprecedented First Amendment claim were the same justices who had decided the *Finley* case. They were a pretty deeply divided group in terms of the judicial role (constrained or creative) and ideology (conservatives, who claimed to be bound tightly to the text and original meaning, versus liberals, who saw the Constitution as a charter whose purposes could evolve over time). The former group was led by William Rehnquist, the Chief Justice. The latter group was led by John Paul Stevens.

The lawyers arguing before the Court were George Davidson of New York, representing the Boy Scouts, and Evan Wolfson of New York City, representing James Dale. The lawyers had their job cut out for them, as the justices came armed with plenty of difficult questions.

At shortly after 10:00 A.M. on Wednesday, April 26, 2000, the Chief Justice called the case.

CHIEF JUSTICE REHNQUIST: We'll hear argument now in Number 99-699, Boy Scouts of America and Monmouth Council v. James Dale. Mr. Davidson.

MR. DAVIDSON: Mr. Chief Justice, and may it please the Court. This case is about the freedom of a voluntary association to choose its own leaders. The New Jersey Supreme Court has held that the State and not Boy Scouting may decide who will wear the Scout leader's uniform and act as a role model of Scouting's values for a group of 10 to 15 boys in a Scout troop.

Far from a business networking organization, Boy Scouting is so closely identified with traditional moral values that the phrase, he's a real Boy Scout, has entered the language.

QUESTION: Do we take this case as one in which Dale was terminated because of the reasonable likelihood that he would use his position to advocate for his cause?

The question goes to the exact definition of the issue in the case. Is the claim that Dale will advocate homosexuality and its legitimacy to the Scouts or instead that knowledge of Dale's sexual orientation by Scouts would influence them in some way? Neither is the case. There was no evidence in the record that Dale had promoted or discussed sexual orientation with Scouts, and there was no claim that Dale retaining his position would harm or influence the Scouts. Instead, the claim is that Dale's official position would convey a message by the Boy Scouts as an organization about its views of homosexuality. The questions that follow show the justices agonizing over the precise definition of the issue presented in the case and the harm claimed by the Boy Scouts of America.

MR. DAVIDSON: Your Honor, Mr. Dale had created a reputation for himself by the newspaper article which appeared, and the reputation would have carried into the troop meeting and affected his ability to be a role model to the youths in his troop.

QUESTION: If a troop leader simply said to other officials, not to the newspapers, not in any public forum anywhere, I am a homosexual, would he be excluded from his leadership position for that alone?

MR. DAVIDSON: That precise question hasn't come up. I believe that there would be the right to do that.

Mr. Davidson is doing a little evading of the question here. He doesn't want to say that the Scouts could not exclude a homosexual (Scout or troop leader, presumably), but that's not the question here. Yet, he seems a bit uncomfortable about saying that the issue in this case is strictly limited to the Scouts' "institutional" right to express their views free from the inferences people might draw from their failure to fire Dale when his sexual orientation becomes known—even though the Scouts' firing of Dale was simply an act, not intended as expression, and even though the New Jersey nondiscrimination law applied only to acts, not speech. It's tricky business for Mr. Davidson.

QUESTION: But you're defending an expressive policy, and that's one of the things that's confusing. Are you saying the policy is don't ask, don't tell, or is the policy, if you are gay, you are not welcome in the Boy Scouts? Which is it?

MR. DAVIDSON: The policy is not to inquire. The policy is to exclude those who are open . . . being openly homosexual in [the sense that he] communicates the concept that this is okay. This is an alright lifestyle to pursue.

Now we're getting down to brass tacks. The problem isn't that Dale is homosexual. The problem isn't the Dale is acting it; his actions are private. It's just that he is being open about it by communicating (not to the Scouts specifically—or even at all) who he is.

QUESTION: All right. Now, clarify for me, because I—it is not clear to me yet. A heterosexual male adult who wants to be a Scout leader who openly espouses the view that homosexuality is not immoral, and that it is consistent with Scout law and oath, is that person qualified for membership as a troop leader?

MR. DAVIDSON: That person could take that position in Scouting Councils to urge that a change be made, but if that person were to take that position to the youth in the program and urge it on the youth in the program, that person would not be able to continue as a Scout leader.

QUESTION: How about if he just made speeches about this in the community as a whole? Did anything happen here, other than what's in the complaint, which I take it was that Mr. Dale, sometime in the past, was a member of the Gay Alliance at a university, gave some seminars, was interviewed then, and it was in the newspaper. Then he received a letter of termination.

MR. DAVIDSON: I have no information as to how that situation would be resolved. I would observe that it would be open to the Scouts to conclude that somebody who is himself presenting a personal example, as well as advocating, might be more unacceptable than somebody who was merely advocating.

QUESTION: All right. How are we supposed to know—and this is genuinely bothering me—how are we supposed to know whether the basic principle that the Scouts is operating on is thinking that this is very, very bad conduct, or is simply being quite concerned about public reaction? I mean, if it were very, very bad conduct, it's surprising you don't look into it, but if what you're concerned about is public reaction, it all makes quite a lot of sense.

That is, why don't the Scouts not only prohibit openly gay leaders but also those who are not gay but support gay rights in public or in Scouts? For purposes of the First Amendment argument, after all, it is the public perception and message, not the fact of homosexuality itself. This is a hard question for Davidson.

QUESTION: I ask the question in terms of the expressive association claim. The problem is that we're not at the point where anyone is using the Boy Scouts, or proposing to use the Boy Scouts, for expression. Mr. Dale has not, in effect, asked to carry a banner. He's saying, I'm not going to carry a banner, I'm not going to get into it. . . .

The point of the question has to do with intent to speak. Generally, in a First Amendment case, the person claiming a free speech right has to intend to speak a message and convey it to an audience. Inadvertence is not enough, and mere intended conduct others might see as "expressive" of a view—say, racism by not hiring minorities—doesn't count at all. Why shouldn't the same be true of claims by a white-supremacist organization or association to speak collectively for its members?

MR. DAVIDSON: Justice Souter, he [Dale] put a banner around his neck when he got himself into the newspaper, and Scout leaders throughout Monmouth Council sent the article in to headquarters. He created a reputation. This is a place he goes once a week, a camping trip once a month, summer camp for a week. These are people that see him all the time. He can't take that banner off. He put it on himself, and, indeed, he has continued to put it on himself in this week's *Time Magazine,* the *Out 100,* the *New York Times*—

QUESTION: But in effect—I understand what you're saying, but you're saying he has created a kind of public persona for himself and therefore simply for him to be in the Scouts in that position does carry a message.

MR. DAVIDSON: Well, it requires Boy Scouting to identify with that message that Mr. Dale has created. Mr. Chief Justice, I would like to reserve a bit of time for rebuttal.

Mr. Davidson finally got to the heart of the case but only at the very end. Most of the argument was spent trying to clarify what the exact question presented in the case—a free speech case, not a nondiscrimination case—

was. But perhaps this was best for Davidson, as greater attention to the free speech/association claim would have delved more deeply into the center of the free speech claim: Why should people's reaction to the Boy Scouts be seen as forced or garbled speech by the Scouts?

An example might reveal the peculiarity of the claim. In the law of libel, a person whose reputation in the community is harmed by another's false but allegedly factual claim about him or her can sue for damages for the harm. But to recover, the harmed person must overcome the libeler's (speaker's) claim that imposing liability and damages on the libeler would violate his or her free speech. The harmed person's right is to their reputation as protected in common law or statutory law; the libeler's protection is the First Amendment. In *Dale*, the Scouts are turning the tables. If Dale is a speaker whose message harmed the reputation of the Scouts, he would be the libeler and have the protection of the First Amendment. But the Scouts are arguing that Dale's speech is subordinate or irrelevant to the case, except to the extent that it forced a false image on the Scouts, effectively libeling them. They don't claim a right to reputation and damages. The Scouts instead claim a right to free speech that protects them against liability to Dale, the speaker, through the New Jersey law. Why should this be the result even though the Scouts didn't intend to say anything?

Yet, before dismissing the Scouts' argument that they were forced to speak a message because of the audience's own interpretation of an act, we need to think a bit about art and aesthetics. Is the message of art the cognitive message (if any) that an artist intends to convey? Or is the message lodged largely in the audience through the artist's depiction of a person or thing that inspires an altogether different message—one based on emotion and impression and imagination supplied by the audience or viewer? Much can be said for the latter view. But it can also be taken too far, as the remainder of the oral argument shows, for potentially all acts and messages can be seen metaphorically and, arguably, aesthetically, and protecting art can't be allowed to start the law down a slippery slope at the end of which all conduct is convertible into free speech. So what are possible limits? Do the aesthetic perceptions that count have to be shared in common by all or most or many people? Must the impressions be "artistic" and "aesthetic" in nature? Must they satisfy some standard of quality and taste and skill—even intention? Can we escape an operative definition of art (though no one has ever really succeeded in giving one)?

These are the important questions raised by the *Dale* case and the act of speaking. The Court didn't get to them in the first half of the oral argument. And even if it could have, there is also the question of whether it should ever get to them. The National Endowment for the Arts (NEA) is probably a better judge of art and aesthetics—even decent art—than nine cognitively skillful lawyer-justices without experience in such matters.

CHIEF JUSTICE REHNQUIST: Mr. Wolfson, we'll hear from you.

MR. WOLFSON: Mr. Chief Justice, and may it please the Court. The State of New Jersey has a neutral civil rights law of general applicability that is aimed at discriminatory practices, not expression. The law protects gay and nongay people within New Jersey against discrimination based on their sexual orientation.

QUESTION: You seem to suppose a dichotomy between an entity that's a public accommodation and an entity that has expressive rights. Surely there can be both.

MR. WOLFSON: Oh, absolutely, Your Honor.

QUESTION: If that's so, then in your view, a Catholic organization has to admit Jews, a Jewish organization has to admit Catholics. That's your view of the constitutional law?

MR. WOLFSON: The constitutional question that would be before the Court in that case, as in this case, is whether the organization has borne its heavy burden of winning an excuse from compliance with the law based on its ability to show a specific expressive purpose that brings its members together that is being significantly burdened by the exercise—

Wolfson can't win the case by arguing that discrimination against gays, as such, is the issue or that discrimination against gays is higher or lower on some nonconstitutional pecking order than race and gender or religion and national origin. He's got to argue a First Amendment case, and he has some very good arguments to make but not these. Where is the speech? Why should it count for much, when the Scouts didn't even intend to say anything? If the speech claim, which the Court wants and intends to address, is weak, then Wolfson wins because the State can define a large range of persons and groups against whom to prohibit discrimination. If, instead, Wolfson effectively concedes that the speech claim is a real and important one—even by his failure to contest it—he will likely lose.

QUESTION: Well, suppose that it says this is basically a Jewish organization, or this is basically a Catholic organization. And it is. Suppose it is. Then what?

MR. WOLFSON: Well, that may very well be the kind of criterion that would have taken it out of being a public—

QUESTION: Fine. If that's so, if that's what we're supposed to do, then how are we supposed to determine, in your opinion, whether or not the relationship of the anti-gay to the Boy Scouts is or is not fundamental, or core, in the way that I've just described in respect to other organizations?

MR. WOLFSON: The Court, Justice Breyer, looks for that specific expressive purpose that brings the members together, not simply the views that some may happen to hold and not simply a policy or a practice of discrimination.

QUESTION: Why doesn't that exist here? That's what I don't understand. I mean, is there any doubt that one of the purposes of the Boy Scouts, if not its primary purpose, is moral formation, the Scout's oath, and all that good stuff? Isn't that what you say—he's a Boy Scout, as you say.

MR. WOLFSON: Right. That's correct, Your Honor, and—

QUESTION: Okay. So moral formation is. You concede that. And they say, and I don't know why we have any power to question it if the leadership of the organization says so, that one of the elements of that moral formation is that they think that homosexuality is immoral. Now, how does that not make it an essential part of Scouting's purpose?

MR. WOLFSON: What New Jersey has prohibited, Justice Scalia, is identity-based discrimination in its membership practices. It has not limited what Boy Scouts may say. It has not limited its ability to express whatever message it wishes to express. It has not limited its ability to require that members—

Mr. Wolfson keeps focusing on identity-based discrimination. The Boy Scouts, however, is not challenging the law's prohibition on discrimination against gay people. It is instead arguing its First Amendment right to free expression—the ability to control its own message. Its claim is not a right to exclude Scoutmasters if they are gay but only if they are avowedly and openly gay in their Scouting capacity. The Court (finally we might add) takes Mr. Wolfson to this distinction.

QUESTION: You think it does not limit the ability of the Boy Scouts to convey its message to require the Boy Scouts to have as a Scout master someone who embodies a contradiction of its message, whether the person wears a sign or not? But if the person is publicly known to be a contradiction of its moral message, how can that not dilute the message?

MR. WOLFSON: Assuming, arguendo for your question, that they have established that is such a message and such a purpose that they wish to convey, Justice Scalia. Nevertheless, a human being such as Mr. Dale is not speech.

A human being is certainly not speech as to a view, or as to a message, other than perhaps the message, I am who I am, I am here, and this Court has taken great—

This has the makings of a good argument. First, the Boy Scouts did not convey the antigay message Justice Scalia seems to be implying, because the message is not antigay, but instead the Scouts wish to disassociate themselves with the message that gay is moral. Second, Dale's identity is not speech; it just is. So how can that be transferred to the Boy Scouts as speech?

QUESTION: I don't know that our law requires that it be speech. I think our law simply prevents the State from diluting or imperiling the message that an organization wants to convey, whether the State does it by speech, or whether the State does it by dropping a bomb. It seems to me that's what's going on here.

MR. WOLFSON: Well, no. What's going on here, with respect, Justice Scalia, is that the BSA bears the obligation of showing that it needs a First Amendment shield to excuse it from this neutral law, content-neutral law.

QUESTION: Well, I think you assume in your answer to Justice Scalia that the Boy Scouts do have a moral message.

MR. WOLFSON: I accepted that for purposes of answering Justice Scalia's question. But what this Court should look to is the record as to what burden is placed on the organization's members' ability to deliver the *specific* expressive purpose for which they come together. That's what the right protects.

QUESTION: Well, are you saying, Mr. Wolfson, that it has to be a definite expressive purpose? I mean, supposing you have some of the kinds of organizations that Justice Breyer hypothesized: we're a Catholic organization and we just feel much more comfortable with Catholics, and we do Catholic work, or a Jewish organization. Now, they don't have any great message of—substantive message. Can they be required under a public accommodations law that is construed as broadly as New Jersey's is, to take on non-Catholics, or non-Jews?

MR. WOLFSON: Well, with respect, Your Honor, I don't believe that that's how the public accommodations law would be interpreted with regard to those organizations, but accepting that arguendo, the question before the Court would be, is there a specific expressive purpose of those organizations that is impaired or infringed, warranting—

The answer is not directly responsive. Is the Boy Scouts' message any less a message than Catholicism or Judaism as referents for the specific beliefs they contain? Specifics are implied in both cases.

QUESTION: Let's get away for a moment, because my question was intended to direct you away from freedom of speech to freedom of association, which is also guaranteed by the First Amendment.

MR. WOLFSON: That's correct, Your Honor, as a right in furtherance of the expression of the members.

QUESTION: And in almost all of your answers it seems to me that you say once there is a public accommodation, that right of expression is somehow secondary, or somehow must be subordinated. You simply cannot find that proposition in our cases.

MR. WOLFSON: I totally agree, Justice Kennedy. I'm certainly not arguing that at all. What I'm saying is that this Court has held that the creation and implementation of public accommodations laws fulfilling those important interests is a legitimate and important exercise of a State's power, and what is at issue here, Justice Kennedy, then is, has this organization shown that for its First Amendment expressive purposes there is a burden on its ability to convey its messages warranting excusal from that law?

Of course, the First Amendment would trump the public accommodations law in such a setting, but this Court has made it very clear that it will not simply allow the mere statement, we don't want to comply with the civil rights law, to be the exception that defeats the civil rights law.

QUESTION: All right. Let's assume, then, that the Boy Scouts tomorrow morning take formal steps to amend all of their official statements of objective, and they say in the Boy Scout manual, the troop leader's manuals and so on, that it is essential to our objective of moral decency that homosexual conduct not be permitted, and that those who avowedly engage in it or believe, indeed, that it is appropriate, may not be members of the organization. Would your case, on your view, then be different?

MR. WOLFSON: That's correct, Your Honor, but if I understood the hypothetical you were giving, there were two elements in it. One was this establishment of a specific expressive purpose that has in fact not been shown here, with the additional point that the organization is actually requiring that it be conveyed to members and others.

QUESTION: Does the case, then, turn on the sufficiency of the Boy Scouts' statement of its position as essential to its message? Does it turn, then, on how well they have made their message known?

MR. WOLFSON: No, Justice Souter. Even were you to assume that they have the implicit moral they say they have, what they have failed to show is that their expressive messages, that their activities are burdened—

QUESTION: Why so? Implicit messages are still messages. What about divinity of Jesus? The infallibility of the Pope? Both can be said to be implied in a message of Christianity or Catholicism.

QUESTION: Yes, but doesn't it follow that if their message is clear, the burden upon the message, by putting an avowedly homosexual person in a leadership position, would be [clear]?

MR. WOLFSON: Well, that's correct up as far as it goes, but it doesn't mean it shows the significant burden that then gets to—

QUESTION: But it shows a more significant burden than you believe they are entitled to be given credit for now?

MR. WOLFSON: That's correct, but—

QUESTION: So if this is the basis on which you prevail, what you will have succeeded in doing is inducing the Boy Scouts of America to be more openly and avowedly opposed to homosexual conduct in all of its publications. Is that what this case is all about?

Whoa! This question smacks of unfairness, but it is a full court press to get Wolfson to the point of the case, too. Wolfson should probably just say yes, in the sense that the message should be a clear one in order for the State's regulation to rise to the level of a violation of the right of free speech of the Scouts. Instead, Wolfson descends into pure speculation of the Scouts' real motives—speculation that has no basis whatever in the record in the case.

MR. WOLFSON: Actually, Justice Scalia, there is most likely a reason why they have not—why they in fact concede in their own brief that they are not an antigay organization, and they do not require members and sponsors and Scout masters to inveigh against homosexuality or to teach anything about sexual orientation, and the reason for that, Justice Scalia, is not so much that they're afraid of losing the gay people. It's that they are afraid of losing the nongay people who, as Justice O'Connor's question pointed out, do not agree with this policy, whose charter is renewed year after year after year, despite their not sharing this moral view, or having disagreement over this, because that's not why they come into Scouting.

QUESTION: I think there's a distinction between being an antigay organization and having a policy of disapproving of homosexual conduct. You don't have to have as your raison d'etre to oppose homosexuality in order to believe that it is part of your moral code that that conduct is inappropriate, and that's the position that the Boy Scouts have taken. You insist that they go further and make that a prominent part of their promotion.

MR. WOLFSON: It's their burden, Justice Scalia, to show that their specific expressive purposes, not simply views they hold implicitly, but the expressive purposes of conveying any such views, are significantly burdened, and then that those outweigh the State's interest in this neutral law. The State—

QUESTION: How do we do that? That is, I'm back to Justice Scalia's earlier question and the Chief's. Maybe you've answered it. I'm not sure. I think we both agree that a basically Jewish or a basically Catholic organization, expression or not, maybe association, would be immune from New Jersey's law under the First Amendment. B'nai B'rith, Knights of Columbus, et cetera. I mean, you know—don't we agree about that?

This is a hard and good question. Mr. Wolfson's answer should be "Yes, we agree." But instead he dissembles. Why?

MR. WOLFSON: They certainly draw in many other strands, free exercise or other principles that would protect them as well.

QUESTION: You're saying that if a church were a public accommodation, that the church could then deny admission to the church, to non-Catholics, the Catholic Church?

MR. WOLFSON: Well, in the unlikely event that it were a public accommodation, which it would not be, then what we also have operating with religion, and perhaps this goes to your question, Justice Breyer, is that that's addressing people on the basis of views. It's addressing people on the basis of message and expression. It is not the identity-based discrimination.

QUESTION: My question was—maybe we don't agree on the assumption— that if there are some groups, say religiously oriented groups that could keep out people of the other religion—

MR. WOLFSON: Yes.

QUESTION: —that on the other hand if you take these basic organizing principles and push them to the periphery, so that now they're only a peripheral principle, and you accept that, you could submerge all civil rights laws? You said that at one point. In other words, if you take what is a basic principle, and say the same law applies if it's just a secondary or tertiary or sort of peripheral principle, if we accept that as an excuse, there will be no civil rights laws left.

MR. WOLFSON: Certainly, if—

QUESTION: All right. Fine. [S]o I thought we were agreeing about those two things, and then I wanted to know what the Court is supposed to do to figure out when an association claims that a principle is very important, whether it is really central, or whether it is one of these things that you call peripheral, or tertiary, that it would submerge the civil rights laws. Are we supposed to—how are we supposed to find that out?

MR. WOLFSON: With respect, Justice Breyer, I don't know that it turns on centrality so much as it turns on specific expressive purpose. The Scouts do not require any Scout master or sponsoring entity or whatever to convey that to youth, and in that case it's an easy determination for this Court to see that there's no burden on this conveying of an expressive message— central, specific or otherwise—because they themselves do not convey it. They themselves don't do it, and therefore these—

QUESTION: Mr. Wolfson, there seems to be some conflict on that point, because I believe counsel for the Boy Scouts told us that one troop's charter was continued only when it agreed that it was going to adhere to this policy, and that it wasn't going to advocate gays are okay.

MR. WOLFSON: But Mr. Dale is not here to advocate that he be allowed to advocate that gays are okay within Scouting, nor does New Jersey tell the Boy Scouts what they can or can't say within Scouting, nor does it tell them that they can't limit what is said within Scouting. What it tells them is, identity-based discrimination, the equation of a human being with forced speech, or a speech, or an assumed message, is off the table.

Ah! Identity-based discrimination is unrelated to the free speech argument the State must make, but the speech argument needn't be made because Dale did not speak with the Scouts. This is a good point (too late, though) that needs to be driven home. The issue in the case is what is "speech" protected by the First Amendment. Dale did not want to profess his beliefs to the Scouts. The Scouts didn't want to speak on the question. So where is the "speech" for purposes of the First Amendment?

QUESTION: But, of course, they're saying that it's not merely identity-based discrimination. They're saying it's advocacy-based, that by making the public statements that he has made, he in effect has put himself in a position of being identified, understood by people as an advocate, and therefore if he's in a leadership position in the Scouts, by that very fact he's going to carry sort of the aura of the advocacy with him. How do you respond to that?

MR. WOLFSON: Well, in this specific case, Your Honor, Mr. Dale was expelled for taking part in a seminar outside of Scouting, in which he made no connection to Scouting, in which he asserted a view that, as questions have indicated, had nongay people asserted them, would have been perfectly fine.

QUESTION: Well, your opposing counsel I think gave us an example of nongays who were taking that position who were challenged by the Scouts and backed down, so I don't know whether the differential treatment is as clear as I thought when I came in here.

This is a very good point. The heterosexual progay man is equally not allowed to speak in public. So it's not about gays or homophobia by the Scouts but about keeping issues off the moral agenda of the Scouts' educational activities. We're back to the beginning of the oral argument. And if so, this case is about speech or at least avoidance of speech about a belief, not about discrimination against gay versus nongay, and it's therefore not about identity-based discrimination under New Jersey law.

The oral argument, unfortunately, ends with this critical point hanging. Wolfson must have been as intent upon avoiding the speech issues in the case as was Davidson.

CHIEF JUSTICE REHNQUIST: Thank you, Mr. Wolfson. The case is submitted.

• • •

The oral argument in *Dale* was, frankly, disappointing. On both lawyers' parts, it seemed an exercise in avoidance. For its part, the Court was trying mightily to pin the lawyers down, clarify the exact issue and the posture in which the case presented it, and then engage the lawyers in grappling with it. But it just didn't work out. So the Court had to do it on its own. With such fundamental questions as were presented in the *Dale* case—questions going to the construction of meaning and the act of speaking, which are deeply relevant to art and aesthetics—doing it on one's own can be dangerous business.

The Court's opinion in the case was issued at the very end of the Court's Term, a fate virtually guaranteed by the difficult First Amendment questions raised by the case. The decision was 5-4 in favor of the Boy Scouts, with Justices Rehnquist, O'Connor, Scalia, Kennedy, and Thomas in the majority, and

Justices Stevens, Souter, Ginsburg, and Breyer in dissent. The majority opinion represents a very broad and important—*and creative*—expansion in the reach of the First Amendment. The dissenters stuck to the hallowed and well-trodden ground of traditional free speech law. So much for the conservatives being constrained in the exercise of judicial power and the liberals being creative.

Chief Justice Rehnquist delivered the opinion of the Court.

To determine whether a group is protected by the First Amendment's expressive associational right, we must determine whether the group engages in "expressive association." The First Amendment's protection of expressive association is not reserved for advocacy groups. But to come within its ambit, a group must engage in some form of expression, whether it be public or private.

The Boy Scouts asserts that it "teach[es] that homosexual conduct is not morally straight," and that it does "not want to promote homosexual conduct as a legitimate form of behavior." We accept the Boy Scouts' assertion.

We must then determine whether Dale's presence as an assistant Scoutmaster would significantly burden the Boy Scouts' desire to not "promote homosexual conduct as a legitimate form of behavior." As we give deference to an association's assertions regarding the nature of its expression, we must also give deference to an association's view of what would impair its expression. That is not to say that an expressive association can erect a shield against antidiscrimination laws simply by asserting that mere acceptance of a member from a particular group would impair its message. But here Dale, by his own admission, is one of a group of gay Scouts who have "become leaders in their community and are open and honest about their sexual orientation." Dale was the copresident of a gay and lesbian organization at college and remains a gay-rights activist. Dale's presence in the Boy Scouts would, at the very least, *force the organization to send a message, both to the youth members and the world, that the Boy Scouts accepts homosexual conduct as a legitimate form of behavior.* [Emphasis supplied.]

Here, we have found that the Boy Scouts believes that homosexual conduct is inconsistent with the values it seeks to instill in its youth members; it will not "promote homosexual conduct as a legitimate form of behavior." [T]he presence of Dale as an assistant Scoutmaster would . . . interfere with the Boy Scouts' choice not to propound a point of view contrary to its beliefs.

The judgment of the New Jersey Supreme Court is reversed, and the case is remanded for further proceedings not inconsistent with this opinion.

It is so ordered.

Justice Stevens, with whom Justice Souter, Justice Ginsburg, and Justice Breyer join, dissenting.

The majority does not rest its conclusion on the claim that Dale will use his position as a bully pulpit. Rather, it contends that Dale's mere presence among the Boy Scouts will itself force the group to convey a message about homosexuality—even if Dale has no intention of doing so. The majority holds that "[t]he presence of an avowed homosexual and gay-rights activist in an assistant Scoutmaster's uniform sends a distinc[t] . . . message," and, accordingly, BSA is entitled to exclude that message. In particular, "Dale's presence in the Boy Scouts would, at the very least, force the organization to send a message, both to the youth members and the world, that the Boy Scouts accepts homosexual conduct as a legitimate form of behavior."

It is true, of course, that some acts are so imbued with symbolic meaning that they qualify as "speech" under the First Amendment. At the same time, however, "[w]e cannot accept the view that an apparently limitless variety of conduct can be labeled 'speech' whenever the person engaging in the conduct intends thereby to express an idea." Though participating in the Scouts could itself conceivably send a message on some level, it is not the kind of act that we have recognized as speech. Indeed, if merely joining a group did constitute symbolic speech; and such speech were attributable to the group being joined; and that group has the right to exclude that speech (and hence, the right to exclude that person from joining), then the right of free speech effectively becomes a limitless right to exclude for every organization, whether or not it engages in any expressive activities. That cannot be, and never has been, the law.

The only apparent explanation for the majority's holding, then, is that homosexuals are simply so different from the rest of society that their presence alone—unlike any other individual's—should be singled out for special First Amendment treatment. Under the majority's reasoning, an openly gay male is irreversibly affixed with the label "homosexual." That label, even though unseen, communicates a message that permits his exclusion wherever he goes. His openness is the sole and sufficient justification for his ostracism. Though unintended, reliance on such a justification is tantamount to a constitutionally prescribed symbol of inferiority. As counsel for BSA remarked, Dale "put a banner around his neck when he . . . got himself into the newspaper. . . . He created a reputation. . . . He can't take that banner off. He put it on himself and, indeed, he has continued to put it on himself."

It is not likely that BSA would be understood to send any message, either to Scouts or to the world, simply by admitting someone as a member. Over the years, BSA has generously welcomed over 87 million young Americans into its ranks. In 1992 over one million adults were active BSA members.

The notion that an organization of that size and enormous prestige implicitly endorses the views that each of those adults may express in a non-Scouting context is simply mind boggling. Indeed, in this case there is no evidence that the young Scouts in Dale's troop, or members of their families, were even aware of his sexual orientation, either before or after his public statements at Rutgers University. It is equally farfetched to assert that Dale's open declaration of his homosexuality, reported in a local newspaper, will effectively force BSA to send a message to anyone simply because it allows Dale to be an Assistant Scoutmaster.

As Justice Brandeis so wisely advised, "we must be ever on our guard, lest we erect our prejudices into legal principles."

If we would guide by the light of reason, we must let our minds be bold. I respectfully dissent.

• • •

The logic of the majority's reasoning in *Dale* was that (1) Dale himself expressed a message legitimizing homosexuality by public awareness of his sexual orientation and political activism on behalf of homosexuals, which took on symbolic meaning; (2) Dale's formal association as a Scoutmaster with the Boy Scouts would cause the public to attribute Dale's message (legitimacy of homosexuality) to the Boy Scouts, becoming, in effect, the Boy Scout's selection and adoption of Dale's message as its own; (3) by having the unwanted and disagreeable message attributed to it, the Boy Scouts would be forced by any legal prohibition on Dale's exclusion to express a message with which they did not concur; and (4) therefore the public accommodation statute denied the Boy Scouts either its First Amendment right not to speak or its right to speak its own message or both. The majority's opinion, in short, is one of attribution on attribution; artifact built upon artifact— attribution to the Boy Scouts of a message constructed by an audience and attributed to Dale.

For us, the *Dale* opinion is important for what it may imply about artistic expression. As Karol Berger says, "In an act of aesthetic contemplation . . . understanding insists on no particular concept and hence the object of contemplation is a pure 'this' with no further definition."[7] Must it be the artist who controls the fact and meaning of cognitive and sensory messages? Or may the artist be treated as incidental only, with meaning and expressive significance arising from the artistic object (or one so understood) itself? If the latter, isn't it the fact of meaning alone that counts, or must meaning at least be traced to ordinary conventions of expression or artistic genre to count as

First Amendment expression? And if the artist is expressively irrelevant, what becomes of the artist's liberty?

• • •

The competing arguments about the meaning of speech in *Dale* boil down, in the end, to a sharp divide. On the one side are those who argue, much like the *Dale* majority did, that the First Amendment should protect the mere transmission of speech—communicative stimuli of human or corporate origin, whether words, acts, images, identities, or even institutional policies and programs that are of communicative significance to the actor or to those who perceive the act.[8] On the other side are those who argue, like Justice Stevens did in his dissent in *Dale*, that speech should consist only of purposeful communicative acts that reflect the speaker's freely formed communicative intention.[9] The first view, which focuses the First Amendment's protection on the stimulus of speech, itself, I will call the artifactual position. The second view, which focuses the First Amendment's protection on expressive acts of individuals, I will call the liberty view. The first centers on speech or the object of art, the second on speaking or the art. The focus here is on speech, and thus also art, as artifacts of meaning.

The artifactual theory of speech extends the Constitution's protection to speech itself. As Justice Harlan put it in the seminal case of *Cohen v. California*, the First Amendment claim rests, in the end, on the "fact of communication." Only if a communicative artifact is *understood as expressive*, as conveying a message or meaning, is it protected speech under this theory. The artifact of speech is protected, as was the unwelcome message in *Dale*, irrespective of the knowledge or intention of the person or thing that produced it. Attaching protection to speech makes questions of origin, authorship, authority, and intention unimportant.

The artifactual theory nicely avoids the complex, even inscrutable, definitional complexities of the alternative liberty view, which protects the human free-willed act of expression. If an instance of speech by a person turns out, upon examination, to be inadvertent, that fact makes no difference under the artifactual theory, for the presence of a communicative fact (and, more important, its meaning) is not dependent on knowledge or intention of a person or thing that originates the speech. Similarly, the fact that speech is originated by an artificial entity such as an organization or even an object is a matter of constitutional indifference. The speech still receives First Amendment protection if it is understood as expressive by others. Indeed, under the artifactual theory, there is no reason to disqualify communicative stimuli produced by a machine or by an inanimate object or even by a different species. After all, a painting is expressive—it conveys meaning to the viewer—even though it is inanimate, and this is especially true when the expressive meaning bears no relation to the original communicative design of its producer.

But if speech is grounded in the fact of communication—the fact of something being *understood* expressively—a host of complications are immediately confronted. What is an expressive understanding? Is it simply the fact that a person has interpreted a stimulus metaphorically—as saying something more than the thing itself: not letters only but words, not words but a new message, not a soup can but a symbol of culture, not a beggar's tin cup but a metaphor of despair, not a parade but a cultural ritual, not Karen Finley covered with chocolate but with feces? Must the understanding be rational and reasoned, or can it be a feeling, a purely sensory experience, such as Yo-Yo Ma playing Bach in the deep woods or love at first sight? The stimulus of fear visited by the cross burning, the stimulus of lust fostered by obscenity (which the Supreme Court implicitly acknowledges to be "speech" in artifactual form by the Court's Herculean efforts to define it out of the Constitution on other grounds), or the stimulus of gay rights arising symbolically from Dale's very existence suggest that both possibilities, and perhaps others, qualify for First Amendment status.

But what about the problem of varying meanings that arise when different persons receiving a stimulus have different expressive understandings? Is the important point the fact of *an* understanding, indeed *any* understanding, or must the understanding be "reasonable"—shared by many or a product traceable to skill or genre—as the Court has sometimes suggested? What if the meaning differs from that intended by the speaker? If Karen Finley intends to convey a qualifying message, such as the banality of sex, but those who witness the stimulus of the speaker understand instead a message of prurience and obscenity, should Finley be just out of luck? Conversely, if the speaker's intention carries no weight, should the speaker get the advantage of speech protection due to the fact of communication even though no communication was intended? This, of course, was what happened in *Dale*, where the Boy Scouts disclaimed any intention to speak the symbolic message attributed to them, yet were granted the status of a speaker—an involuntary one, to be sure, but a speaker nonetheless. If a racist slur is not intended to be communicative but is in fact so understood, is the racist protected by the First Amendment?

The artifactual theory implies that the answer to all of these questions will be affirmative, for the "speech moment" is not the production of a stimulus but its reception. The speaker is instrumental only to the First Amendment's practical enforcement. Indeed, the artifactual theory should not, to be consistent, place the First Amendment claim of "right" in the hands of the speaker at all—not to the council in *Hurley* or to Andy Warhol, who simply transmitted the Campbell's soup can on his canvas. The speech claim belongs, instead, to the audience, which serves as the interpreter, the giver of meaning, and either the beneficiary of liberty lodged in the act of perception or the instrument of a larger social good that grows out of the collective perceptions of millions of persons and millions of meanings.

Some scholars contend that the speech right belongs to the audience. This is the view articulated by the "right to receive ideas" school of First Amendment thought. The purpose of the First Amendment, it is said, is to encourage the dissemination of information and views and communicative stimuli to the audience, the viewers or receivers, or the public: to educate, presumably, and to stimulate. By so doing, exposure to ideas and information communicates new ideas and stimulates mental and emotional activity, thus enhancing the capacity of the individual as a free-willed and thinking human being. In short, the audience-centered view of free speech is based on protecting liberty, but not the liberty of the speaker. Instead, it protects the liberty of the recipient of communicative stimuli. The point is a valid one, as we know that the brain's development is stimulated and expanded by mental activity of all sorts. A cacophony of speech is thus a useful and basic human enterprise.

If the First Amendment seeks primarily to secure intellectual and aesthetic stimulation, then the fact of stimulation is central and meaning is incidental. The fact of stimulation and indeed its manner and subject and object are truly idiosyncratic. I see a Marlboro Man and want a cigarette; my friend sees a cultural icon. I see Dale and feel good about liberty and equality; the Boy Scouts see him and think "morally crooked." A general or reasonable meaning given by an audience need play no part in this scheme; indeed, even as with art, the fact that most people are not stimulated in the least may make no difference. The audience is important only as a universe of persons in whom stimulation might occur (and when it does, those who enjoy it receive constitutional protection in the form of protection of the object as an instrument for their stimulus). The audience, as a collective group, plays no definitional or instrumental role in whether there is a generally understood communication or what meaning it might reasonably be assigned. Indeed, this view so deconstructs communication that one is left to wonder why the Constitution used the word *speech* at all.

Let us, then, remain with the audience as a body that is at once the beneficiary and the locus of definition of "speech." If the audience's liberty is dependent on persons or things producing the needed stimuli but if the producer has no independent freedom to produce but is instead subordinate to the audience—if, that is, the speaker's First Amendment claim is only that of the audience, and the speaker's standing to raise the audience's speech claim is made dependent on the audience's (often unascertainable) expressive understanding—then the fullest realization of the audience's interest cannot be achieved. The problem, in other words, is which comes first: freedom to speak or freedom to hear; free expression by the artist, which audiences then may enjoy though not control; or freedom to receive artistic stimulation, which may thus, if not naturally forthcoming, be compelled or controlled? If speech or art is stimulation, and stimulation is idiosyncratic, how can we know when and how they will occur, with what effect, and to what public or private end? The answer may be that we do not and cannot know, so government cannot manage speech. It must be satisfied with a world of random stimuli.

An alternative justification for the audience-centered view rests on the premise that speech, itself, produces a more informed and educated citizenry better capable of engaging in self-government and better equipped to preserve freedom in a democratic society. It is these ends, not individual liberty, to which the First Amendment is principally directed. The audience's elucidation is thus treated not as an end of the First Amendment but instead simply as a means for achieving other structural ends of democracy and a free civilization.

This view, too, can be described as a "right to receive" theory, but it is of a different ilk. The structural ends of self-government and freedom serve to define the scope and nature of protection accorded the free speech. They serve to justify virtually complete immunity for some speech because its content is deemed central to the business of self-government and freedom, but they also serve to disqualify other speech that does not serve, or even disserves, those ends, not because the other stuff is not speech, artifactually speaking, but because it is not useful speech when judged by the structural purposes of the First Amendment.[10] Directly political speech, even false political speech, is given nearly complete immunity from government regulation, but nonpolitical speech, including false nonpolitical speech, *and much art, is* given markedly less protection.

The arrival of commercial speech on the First Amendment scene also nicely illustrates the point. Commercial speech is protected, the Court says, because of the audience: Commercial speech provides information needed by people when making individual choices in a free economic market. Previously, the Court deemed commercial information less important to the structural ends of the First Amendment, but it is hard to dispute its importance in the late twentieth-century, postindustrial information age. The standard of value, in other words, can change, as can the breadth of the audience's right—need, really—to receive. But the audience's "right to receive" commercial speech depends on its truthfulness and accuracy. These dimensions are evaluated from the perspective of the receiver: Commercial speech must neither be false nor misleading, requirements lodged firmly in the communicative understanding of the recipient.

A few serious problems attend this branch of the artifactualist view. First, when one must regulate speech for structural purposes—impose disclosure or equal time or decency requirements, setting preferences for certain types or subjects of speech—the artifactualists seem to have forgotten their own main premise: that speech is a communicative stimulus whose meaning is lodged in the audience whose understandings are far from uniform (and, it should be added, far from understood). Truth, accuracy, balance, fairness, decency, and equality as regulatory instruments are thus often likely to be incoherent, resting on assumptions that topple like a house of cards.

The second problem is that the democracy-serving view of speech and its meanings, driven to theoretical conception as an instrument of expression in the service of self-government and preservation of a free society, places the definition of structural purposes, the means by which they will be achieved, and their regulatory enforcement against offending speech in the hands of the very government over which people are to have control and from which they are to be free. This is accomplished largely by justifying government action on the skeptical impulse that people are not free agents—at least not interpretive free agents able to discern for themselves—but are instead easily manipulated by artifacts of communication and thus must be protected against them. This is a fundamental premise of campaign-finance and speech restrictions. It is also a premise of "decency and respect" requirements applied to art. Because people cannot discern, government should do the discerning for them, a position that, notably, leaves no room for an intervening liberty to speak or be free from unwanted speech, which the *Dale* case recognized. It is the government, after all, that now defines obscenity for all of us. Indeed, it is the Supreme Court.

At a more basic level, however, the deeply skeptical premise of nondiscernment—whether true or not—is flatly inconsistent with the premise that underlies the structural objectives of self-government and free social and political order. If one tries to preserve freedom by denying its possibility, the remaining game will be only about who holds power. This, as Robert Post has so nicely argued, is precisely what this branch of artifactualist speech theory is all about.[11]

A final problem raised by this view is most interesting. It is, by First Amendment standards, age-old. How does aesthetic expression fit into this purposeful structuralist view of the First Amendment? The problem of assigned meaning is intractable for a structuralist. Art is famously productive of idiosyncratic understandings or audience meanings. Art may deepen the senses and broaden sensory perception, but we do not really know when this happens, nor do we understand whether or how it happens. For art to be privileged, the structuralist must know more, for politics and commerce and voting and judging—the stuff of structuralist purposes—have little to do with aesthetic perception and much more to do with fact and reason and logic and real experience. In an audience-oriented world where the amount of protection accorded various types or instances of speech is made contingent on the closeness of their relationship to self-government and the preservation of freedom, art will not likely come out on top. Witness obscenity law.

Art is easier to value as speech under the straightforward artifactualist view, which rests the First Amendment's protection on the *audience's* freedom to be stimulated, unconditioned by the servicing of other structural constitutional ends. This is because aesthetic perception, sensory stimuli, are arguably as conducive to the development of one's human potential and mental growth as are facts and logic and reason. The mind is not simply a computer driven by logic; it is a complex system of senses and structures. Who we are is a combination of all of our senses, all of our experience, all of our capacity for feeling and insight and reason and language.[12]

The artifactualist thus can claim a theory premised on an appeal to universal "truth": that protecting speech in the interest of the individual's growth and development (and, incidentally, but incidentally only, the capacity for freedom and free-willed choice) is coherent in the abstract. But the artifactualist cannot explain why expressive stimuli are limited to those of human or corporate origin only, as opposed to the wind whistling through the pine trees, or why, if stimulation is the key, "speech" was made the constitutional prerequisite. If speech is a function of "meaning," and if stimulation does not depend on an ascertained or standard "meaning," then stimulation does not seem to have much to do with speech.

The *Dale* case, on reflection, seems a strange combination of artifact and liberty. The "speech" in *Dale*—the message or meaning—arose from Dale as a symbolic artifact of meaning, the meaning lodged not in Dale's intention but in the audience's construction, which was then assigned by the audience as an act of speech to the otherwise-mute Boy Scouts. This is artifactual analysis. Yet, having created the speech by artifact, the Supreme Court extinguished it in the name of liberty—the liberty of the Boy Scouts of America to be free from bearing Dale's message as its own speech. Some might describe this alliance of artifact and intention as unholy. It is, at the very least, messy. Does the artist have a right to control the meaning attached to her art? Can Karen Finley object to Jesse Helms's view of her performances as smut and trash by claiming a First Amendment right to censor Helms for attributing the wrong message to her performance?

Now that would be interesting ... but hardly consistent with our general conceptions of free speech.

SPEAKING OUT OF THIN AIR

*Hurley v. Irish-American Gay, Lesbian
and Bisexual Group of Boston*

515 U.S. 557 (1995)

THE LAST CHAPTER, the *Dale* case, considered the constitutional status of unintended speech by a speaker (the Scouts) that had no intention to speak. This speech was called speech by attribution—the assignment of speech and meaning by attributing it to the acts or status of a third party. The attribution was accomplished, in a rough-hewn way, by estimating the "audience's" interpretation of an event or person or entity and then giving it cognitive meaning. Attribution is, of course, a central feature of what so far in the current volume has been called art and the aesthetic: the giving of new or altered meaning in the form of perception, emotion, and appreciation (of beauty or ugliness) to an object—dance, painting, and the like—and its creator. Attribution also necessarily implies the identification of an author or creator of an expressive object—a painter or dancer, a painting or dance. For art to be considered free speech, perhaps it needs a message (an aesthetic) and a source (an artist). With both in place, meaning can roam more freely and still claim constitutional protection.

This chapter, centering on the *Hurley* case, pursues the question of speaking and meaning even further, again with an eye to art.[1] What if speech might exist even in the absence of a creator and an expressive object? Can constitutionally recognized speech emerge "out of thin air"? Indeed, with art and the aesthetic, might not much expression emerge from thin air?

An example may help. Dada is a form of art that consists of the ridiculous, the purposefully incomprehensible, and the totally deconstructed. An early Dada stage performance involved:

skits enacted by (African) masked figures dressed in colorful costumes . . . who accompanied themselves with drums, pot covers, and frying pans as they recited poems that sounded like this:

gadji beri bumba
glandridi lauli lonni cadori
gadjama bim beri glassala
glandridi glassala tuffin I zimbrabim
blassa galassasa tuffin I zimbrabim

The noise from the stage was deafening. There was bedlam in the hall-
way. The performers behaved like new recruits simulating mental illness
before a medical commission.[2]

One might say, in this example of Dada, that the expression has speakers
and creators and many individual and collective objects or performances, but
the meaning or message, cognitive or aesthetic, is largely of the audience's
construction.

But now examine another example, that of the Marlboro Man advertisement. When functioning as an advertisement, the Marlboro Man has a
speaker (cigarette company, actor), a message ("Marlboro, a real man's cigarette. Buy some."), and objects of performance and expression (photographer,
subject on horse, etc.). The message works in a clear, cognitive, and linear
way from speaker to viewer, just the way the Supreme Court often describes
speech protected by the First Amendment (whether direct expression or
expressive conduct).

But how is the Marlboro man described fifty years later when it may be
seen as an iconic work of cultural art? From this perspective, all trappings of
the speaker (the advertiser) and the message ("Man's cigarette; buy some.")
have fallen away. The picture in historic context is the icon, whose significance has emerged through the passage of time. The message is not cognitive,
at least in the same way as the original. It is instead evocative, metaphorical,
sensual, seen now as a reflection of skill and talent related to a new meaning.
At least for those who appreciate it as art, its meaning lies at the emotional
level, the level of taste and imagination, perhaps. The picture is itself its own
creator (of the message), the object, and it is the stimulator of a message in
the minds and emotion of the audience. The Marlboro Man, in short, has
transformed himself into art without knowing so, without intending to do
so, without anything to say, really.

Is this very uncommon way in which we might think of speech necessary
to a full appreciation of what is happening with art? Is it necessary to the very
nature of the value of art? If so, a threshold has been crossed, perhaps, in the
conception of freedom. But the new threshold will prove treacherous. How

can the concept of speech out of thin air be limited? Everyone sees meaning in objects, events, memories, acts. Must everything, at least for the meaning giver/receiver (one and the same), become speech: the storm, the blade of grass, the warm bath? Might the feeling of comfort and security and peace evoked by the warm bath on a cold day be described as aesthetic, as the term has been used so far? Do all acts of discrimination directed at others qualify as "speech" acts that those who would see them as metaphors should be free to preserve from government prohibition or regulation?

It is to these questions that the profoundly important, yet often frustrating, *Hurley* case will be considered in the following story. The case presents a great story, and I will indulge the reader a bit with the events and characters. But we must also keep our eye trained on the issues: What is the nature of art and the aesthetic? How does artistic speech occur? Is artistic speech distinct in any useful ways from political or cultural speech, not in subject necessarily, but in process, form, skill? Are the costs—even to the First Amendment freedoms themselves—simply too great to cross the cognitive/aesthetic line without an author, because there can be no principled and practical limit that can be enforced to stop a tumble down the slippery slope?

The *Hurley* case involves the exclusion of an objectionable group with an objectionable view—pro-gay—from the long-standing annual St Patrick's Day Parade in Boston. Is a parade speech? Is a parade an event in the nature of metaphor and viewer construction rather than a linear transmission of a message from a known, intending speaker to an audience that comprehends what the speaker means? Is the selecting of parade participants in the construction of the parade distinguishably expressive from the rejection of one or more participants? Is an orchestra director's selection of instrumentalists for a performance an act of free speech? What if the director deselects a violinist, not on grounds that he is a poor violinist but on grounds that he is black, and the aesthetics of racial diversity is not a message the director wishes to convey?

• • •

The South Boston Allied War Veterans Council is a private association of representatives of veterans' groups that for many, many years has organized and conducted the annual St. Patrick's Day–Evacuation Day Parade in Boston.[3] In the early 1990s, the parade was firmly in the hands of the Veterans Council and its chief marshal, John Hurley. For as long as he could remember, Hurley has been known widely and affectionately in South Boston as "Wacko" Hurley, or better yet, as Wacko. His family calls him Wacko, his friends call him Wacko, virtually everyone he knows calls him Wacko, says Hurley. "Some people find it hard to say. They say 'John,' but that goes right by me. There's a lot of Johns. Sometimes you might be in a bar and someone says, 'Hey Wacko!' and everyone gets nervous. Like 'here we go.'"[4] He obviously cherishes the name.

Hurley's work with the parade began many years back, in 1953, six years after he returned from World War II, in which he served in the U.S. Navy. The Allied War Veterans Council was then a smallish group, and while the parade had been around for many years, it had not yet grown to the size and stature it attained by the 1990s. By 1964, at the age of thirty-three, Wacko Hurley was elected chief marshal, and he never looked back.

As chief marshal, Hurley organized the parade, issued invitations for groups to participate, acted upon applications by new participating groups, and, in the case of controversy or uncertainty, took a questionable application to the full Veterans Council, which made a decision with everyone having one vote. Hurley's job was to put the whole parade together, from start to finish.

By the early 1990s, the parade had many groups and floats and an audience of as many as a hundred thousand people. It received some city support— police, maintaining order, cleaning up afterward, and a relatively small eight thousand dollar contribution for other expenses. But the city's involvement was strictly limited: It played no role in selecting the participants, managing or organizing the parade activities, or even offering advice about themes or groups wishing to participate. It was the transportation department that issued the permit based on traffic-related criteria. The parade had three themes, as Hurley would later testify: traditional family roles and values, honoring St. Patrick, and being Irish. But it was not a parade to make one or even three specific points; it was rather an amalgam of participants and celebrations that were consistent with tradition in the parade and not discordant with the three themes—or what might be better described as values. And the council and Hurley were firmly in charge of the themes.

In 1992 the trouble started. It began with an application by the Irish-American Gay-Lesbian and Bisexual Pride Committee of Boston (the name eventually became the Irish-American Gay, Lesbian and Bisexual Group of Boston, or GLIB) to march in the parade. GLIB members wanted to march as a group behind their banner, which took varying forms over the course of the controversy but in the end simply carried the group's name as a symbol of pride and presence in the community of South Boston. GLIB stated that its members wished to "march in the parade as a way to express pride in their

Irish heritage as openly gay, lesbian, and bisexual individuals, to demonstrate that there are such men and women among those so descended, and to express solidarity with like individuals who sought to march in New York's St. Patrick's Day Parade."[5]

It didn't take long for the Veterans Council to consider and reject the application; nor did it take much time for controversy to swirl in Boston and, soon, on a national level. Accusations swirled, local politics took center stage, and, ultimately, the matter went to court in Massachusetts. GLIB claimed that because its members were gay and its identity pro-gay, its participation had been rejected in violation of Massachusetts nondiscrimination law. The Veterans Council, in other words, was simply homophobic, and in rejecting GLIB's application, the council had denied GLIB's right to free speech in the marketplace of ideas—the parade. But that would be so only if the parade were sponsored and run in significant ways by the city. The Veterans Council insisted that the parade was private, that the messages and themes were the council's, not the city's, and that excluding GLIB had nothing to do with excluding homosexuals from participating in the parade but instead meant only that the Veterans didn't want their parade to carry GLIB's unwelcomed message. The intricacies of these and other legal positions are at the center of the Supreme Court's oral argument.

Over the roughly three-year period from 1992 to 1995, lawsuits were filed and defended by all of the parties involved in the controversy: the Veterans Council, GLIB, Boston's transportation department, the city of Boston, and the mayor, to name some. The litigation engaged repeatedly the attention of every level of the Massachusetts and federal courts, including the United States Supreme Court. The Veterans Council lost virtually every battle until the very end. The council was ordered by the Massachusetts courts to allow GLIB to march in the parade (they obeyed and then the next year cancelled their parade instead of submitting to GLIB's inclusion). They were ordered to pay GLIB's legal fees and costs, as well as other assessments. The council was forced to defend its position on six or seven different legal fronts.

A great deal of legal talent became engaged in the fight, mostly on GLIB's side, and often without any or much cost. The council, however, had to pay its own legal fees and costs and hire its own attorney. This it did in the person of Chester Darling, a solo practitioner in Boston with a small practice. Along the way he had help, but it was he who carried the load from start to finish. It would not be until June 19, 1995, that the case would effectively end with a unanimous decision by the Supreme Court. It was a decision that in many ways went to the heart of our ongoing inquiry: Exactly what form did the speech take? Who was doing the speaking, for constitutional purposes? What were they saying? Should it really matter if no one was speaking, as long as expression emerged "from thin air"?

• • •

The Supreme Court that heard oral argument in the *Hurley* case in April of 1995 was the same in membership and not much different in ideological composition from the Court that would hear Karen Finley's case three years later in 1998. The Chief Justice was William Rehnquist, and with him on the more conservative side of the Court were Justices Scalia, Thomas, O'Connor, and Kennedy. On the liberal side were Justices Stevens, Souter, Ginsburg and Breyer. The lawyers who argued the case were Chester Darling, a local lawyer in his own one-man firm in Boston, who had handled the case from beginning to end, and John Ward, of Boston, who represented GLIB. Ward was relatively new to the case and practiced with an established firm in Boston.

The oral argument was active, engaging, even exciting, according to those fortunate enough to get a seat in the Supreme Court's courtroom. People literally sat on the edges of their seats.

• • •

CHIEF JUSTICE REHNQUIST: We'll hear argument first this morning in Number 94-749, John J. Hurley and the South Boston Allied War Veterans Council v. the Irish-American Gay, Lesbian and Bisexual Group of Boston. Mr. Darling.

MR. DARLING: Mr. Chief Justice, and may it please the Court: The central issue in this case is whether Government can mandate the expression of messages and viewpoints in a privately organized parade over the objections of the private organizers.

After ordering the respondent, the Irish-American Lesbian, Bisexual, and Gay Group of Boston, into the 1992 and 1993 parades, and after a hearing before a trial court, a judgment issued and was affirmed by the supreme judicial court of Massachusetts, and in that judgment the supreme judicial court upheld a statement and declaration by the trial court that a proper celebration of St. Patrick's and Evacuation Day requires diversity and inclusiveness.

The Veterans Council clearly stated what the expressive purpose of their parades were. They announced during trial and prior to their application for a parade permit that they wished to celebrate their traditional religious and social values.

QUESTION: What is the evidence to show that the purpose of this parade was to express any viewpoint?

MR. DARLING: The parade is inherently expressive, Justice—

QUESTION: Well, do you want us to make a finding, then, that a parade is *per se* an expressive activity?

MR. DARLING: Yes, I do, Your Honor, and—

There is a long and deep history here, going back at least to the Court's decisions upholding the right to parade and march in the civil rights era. In those cases, the Court severely restricted the government's ability to condition approval of parades on anything other than speech-neutral criteria such as traffic safety, crowd control, and the like. Mr. Darling's point is that those cases would be in jeopardy if the government in Massachusetts could require the veterans to admit a gay-rights group to the parade when the veterans did not want to express a gay-rights view in or through the parade. The legal and factual issues surrounding this basic claim by the veterans are complex, but the nub of the idea isn't, and it's Mr. Darling's obligation to keep that clear. What would the Court have done in the 1960s had the Ku Klux Klan asked to participate (in robes or with a KKK banner) in a civil rights march led by Dr. Martin Luther King Jr.? Is the march an expressive event protected by the First Amendment? Would the KKK's participation itself be expressive and thus undermine the marchers' point?

Of course, one can argue that the civil rights marches had a clear theme, indeed a clear message, too: racial equality. This message would have been specifically negated by KKK participation. The veterans' parade message was more ambiguous—less cognitive, more aesthetic. GLIB's participation also may have negated part of the theme the council claimed to have in mind for the parade, but with the veterans' parade, it is less clear that the theme and message the council sought to communicate had any real relationship to the message actually disseminated and received by those attending the parade.

QUESTION: Mr. Darling, you've answered, I guess, two questions, and I want to make sure that you stand by the answer in each one, and I want you to comment again on the relevance of each one. First, I think you told Justice Kennedy not only that the parade was expressive in its nature—I guess all parades are in your view—but that that was crucial to your case. You also said that the particular message, the viewpoint, if you will, was generally a celebration of religious and social values of Irish Catholics. Is that viewpoint crucial, the existence of that viewpoint as the expression conveyed by the parade, crucial to your case?

MR. DARLING: I would think not, Justice Souter.

QUESTION: May I just interrupt you and get to another point? You're saying that your viewpoint is essential to your case, and I take it you're saying it's not essential to your case that your parade have any viewpoint at all.

MR. DARLING: That's correct.

QUESTION: But is it essential to your case that the parade be expressive?

MR. DARLING: No, it's not. As far as I'm concerned, if my clients march down a street on a permit that's issued by the City of Boston, whether it's a moving assembly or a group of persons, there will be some people that will make a determination that my clients or that group of people are expressing something.

This view of parades as expressive will need and get much more attention in the argument. The point, however, is worth underlining here. Mr. Darling is saying that the expressiveness of a parade—its character as speech protected by the First Amendment—inheres in the parade itself through the interpretation given the parade event by those who see it. This is a pretty dramatic view of speech, but it is the strongest (though not the only) view upon which Mr. Darling can stand, and he will do his very best to hold the ground.

QUESTION: But let's assume that in fact they are expressing nothing, so that the parade stands on the same footing, let's say, as a public restaurant, would the result be the same in this case?

MR. DARLING: If it was a permitted activity and there was no expression involved, probably not, Justice—

QUESTION: Okay.

QUESTION: Well, I'm not sure. I take it that the whole position of the respondents [GLIB] is that they want to proclaim a message.

MR. DARLING: They do indeed, Justice—

QUESTION: And it seems that your answer would be that even if your parade is nonexpressive in its history and in its tradition, that you have the right to keep it that way.

MR. DARLING: Well, Your Honor—

QUESTION: Or is that your—it seems to me that's a plausible position.

MR. DARLING: We have a judgment that made a finding that it was impossible to discern any specific expressive purpose in my client's First Amendment activity, but this Court has access to the exhibits, and particularly a videotape that demonstrates without question that my clients are engaging in a First Amendment activity with viewpoints and political messages and celebrating their religious values. The judge, the trial judge, acknowledged and identified those very values my clients are expressing.

Mr. Darling is doing his best to limit the scope of the very broad claim of protected expression he has stated, and rightly so. He's saying that it's the *parade* that is expressive—of *what* it is expressive is in part a function of the audience. A permitted restaurant isn't expressive, as such. Would a group of protestors entering the restaurant to challenge one of its policies—themselves expressing their view—somehow convert the restaurant's ordinary business into expression because of the protest? This, of course, is just what happened in the Boy Scouts' case ... and just what makes it frustrating to fathom for many. Mr. Darling, though, would rather not go there. His position is that a parade—and especially his clients' parade—is *itself inherently expressive*, and its protection under the First Amendment doesn't depend on what GLIB had in mind.

QUESTION: Well, just hypothetically, let's assume, following Justice Souter's line of questioning, that this parade was like a picnic or something that had no expressive purpose whatsoever. That may be wrong. Let's assume [it] hypothetically. It seems to me that you still have an argument, and maybe you don't think you do. I should think you still have an argument that even if it is neutral in its custom and in its format, you have the right to say that it cannot be used for some other person's message.

MR. DARLING: Well, I'm sorry if I misspoke, Justice Scalia, but the fact is that no group of people nor any individual can be compelled to speak on behalf of the State or be the courier for the State's message [here, a message of diversity].

QUESTION: Mr. Darling, I understood your brief to say this is your parade and you can do with it what you will, somebody else can do what they will with their parade. That's the essence of your argument. It's your parade to make it do whatever you want it to do.

MR. DARLING: That's correct. My clients define the scope and content of the parade. They vote to include and exclude people and groups with messages that they approve of in their parade that are consistent with the overall theme, a celebration of the patron saint of the Archdiocese of Boston, St. Patrick.

QUESTION: Are there any limitations on that?

MR. DARLING: Yes. The limitations are adjudged on a case-by-case and a group-by-group manner by the veterans. They vote to include and exclude groups, and they vote on the basis of their own personal feelings. Not just Mr. Hurley but the vote of sixty people made the determination to exclude the respondent in this case.

QUESTION: Mr. Darling, I thought you said you couldn't do whatever you wanted with a parade. I thought you conceded that you could not exclude gays, lesbians, and bisexuals from marching in the parade if they want to march, so long as they are not trying to convey a message which you do not want conveyed.

You don't contest that the Massachusetts law is applicable to the parade insofar as the exclusion of someone simply for being a homosexual or lesbian or a bisexual is concerned, right?

MR. DARLING: That's correct, Justice Scalia. The fact that my clients do not have a litmus test so far as sexual orientation is concerned for participation in the parade is very clear from the record. My clients have excluded messages, not the people. The—

QUESTION: What is the message in this case? How would you state the message that GLIB is trying to convey?

MR. DARLING: GLIB had three purposes that were found as expressive during the trial. They were enumerated by the court as first to express its members' pride in their dual identities, second to demonstrate to the Irish-American and the gay, lesbian, and bisexual communities the diversity within those respective communities, and to show support for the Irish-American gay, lesbian, and bisexual men and women in New York City, the ILGO members, who were seeking to participate in the New York St. Patrick's Day parade. They sought to demonstrate and proclaim their diversity on the basis of their sexual orientation in the parade. They also had a political message to support the people that were excluded from the St. Patrick's Day parade in New York.

My clients have messages that they really don't have to explain. They merely have to display them. They—

QUESTION: The message is, it's great to be Irish.

MR. DARLING: That's one of them, Justice Souter.

QUESTION: That's enough, isn't it?

(Laughter.)

MR. DARLING: One of them.

I cannot emphasize enough the fact that for 3½ years I've been explaining the basis for my client's speech and being asked why they wish to express their religious values, what relationship do the Joey's clowns have to St. Patrick, all of the most absurd questions I've heard in my modest career.

What this case revolves around is messages. My clients have their messages. They may be old-fashioned, or they may be traditional messages.

QUESTION: Well, what you're saying, I gather, Mr. Darling, is it isn't just a message it's great to be Irish, but that it's great to be Roman Catholic, too.

MR. DARLING: Your Honor, Mr. Chief Justice, the messages contained in my client's parade are numerous and powerful messages. They include an anti-abortion group. Now, that group had been excluded for several years because they wished to display signs and pictures and shout to the crowd, the spectators, and hand out literature as they passed down the street.

QUESTION: Well, could you answer my question more directly? Is the Roman Catholic religion a part of your message?

MR. DARLING: It certainly is, Mr. Chief Justice. The Ancient Order of Hibernians have been an integral part of the veterans parade for many years. They declined to participate in the parade because of the forced inclusion of [GLIB] in the '92 and '93 parades. My clients wanted that religious component in their parade, the Ancient Order of Hibernians. Because of the forced inclusion of the viewpoint by the courts, the Hibernians did not participate. My client's speech was diminished.

QUESTION: Why do they let the Baptists join the parade if it's a Catholic parade?

MR. DARLING: Well, it's part of their cultural expression, Justice Stevens. They're ecumenical in their Irish—

QUESTION: Up to a point.

(Laughter.)

QUESTION: Well, as I recall, the district court found that St. Patrick would not have excluded the homosexuals, lesbians, and bisexuals, isn't that right, something to that effect. His mission was not just to the straights or something of that sort.

(Laughter.)

QUESTION: Is that a finding of the district court or the lower court here?

MR. DARLING: I believe that was a homily that was added at the end of the judgment in the superior court decision, but clearly the fact that homosexuals and bisexuals and lesbians have marched in my client's parade for years is of no great consequence to my clients, that a gay city councilor who is openly gay marched, and that appears in the record, and he was not disturbed. And Mr. Hurley did not have him excused from the parade, as he did in '93, when the court ordered my clients to include GLIB with their sexual orientation message, and Mr. Hurley ordered the exclusion of a truck with an antigay message on it, and assisted by the police they were thrown out of the parade.

My clients do not care about the sexual orientation or the religious background or the ethnic composition of anyone in their parade. They select groups that are consistent with what they perceive to be their version of a celebration of St. Patrick in their neighborhood, and it has some neighborhood features, and that's why the Baptist Bible trolley is invited, and that's why a number of local organizations are invited.

A great deal has been made about the factual situation relating to people showing up and paying to join in the parade. Well, this is not supported at all in the evidence, not one iota.

QUESTION: So what are we supposed to do—I take it that you concede, or do you not, that if your groups want to—your group cannot discriminate on the basis of race, can it?

MR. DARLING: Justice Breyer, my clients, if they wish to discriminate on the basis of their speech, in their speech they can, but as far as discriminating independently of their speech, that is conduct, and—

Here is where the argument starts sinking into a morass (an instructive one, ultimately), and the questioning gets tedious, yet also challenging. The underlying problem is the slippery slope. Can a person who refuses to hire someone because he or she is black claim that it wasn't race that accounts for the decision but the unwillingness to express a message of approval of equality? To go so far would convert all illegal acts, potentially, into speech. Mr. Darling does not want to get into this area. He wants to stand on the clearer ground of saying that the Veterans were clearly speaking through the parade; gays were not prohibited from participating; it was just the message of GLIB that undermined the Veterans' message and thus would deny the Veterans' freedom of speech. He quite willingly says that, of course, discrimination—acts of discrimination (like the Scouts'?)—are not speech but acts that government can clearly regulate. He would like for that statement to be enough for the moment, given that in his view the parade was speech and therefore the line to be drawn between acts of discrimination, and discriminatory speech need not even arise in the case. But he knows better because he litigated the case from the very beginning, and he is aware of the fact that the Massachusetts courts made some strange fact-findings about why GLIB was excluded and whether the parade was speech. Fact-findings in trial courts are usually binding on appellate courts, including the Supreme Court, whose business is law, not fact. But if the Supreme Court is bound by a finding that the Veterans were not expressing anything in the parade and, more important, if it is bound by the finding that the GLIB march and marchers were excluded because they were gay, not because of the effect their participation would have on the Veterans' speech, Mr. Darling is in very, very deep trouble.

He knows it.

QUESTION: I take it that there's a finding that the parade normally includes everybody, and however they didn't include these people not because they weren't proud to be Irish—they were—but because they didn't like their sexual orientation. Now, are you saying that you do have a right to exclude because of the sexual orientation, or are you saying that wasn't why they were excluded, and if it's the latter, what do we do about the fact-finding?

MR. DARLING: I'm suggesting that the finding of discrimination, Justice Breyer, was made inappropriately on the very basis of the words you have just read. The trial judge equated the sexual orientation with messages and values. In my book, if you combine a message and a value you've got a viewpoint, not a sexual orientation.

QUESTION: But what are we supposed to do, because what we have is that sentence of the supreme judicial court, which I take it is a finding. Are we supposed to say—look into the record and say they're wrong? Are we supposed to remand it for a further factual finding? Are we supposed to take it as a fact? What do you suggest we do?

MR. DARLING: I would suggest, Your Honor, that the Court review the entire record, because I would be very distressed if my clients' rights of free speech were abridged on the basis of one judge's opinion of what message and viewpoint combined to mean.

QUESTION: But one judge always finds the facts. Where the trial judge makes the finding that Justice Breyer has asked about, he says the defendant's final position was that GLIB would be excluded "because of its values and its message, i.e., its members' sexual orientation." That seems to conflate two different concepts. It's quite a confusing finding.

MR. DARLING: Mr. Hurley and the Veterans Council knew nothing about this group when they first approached the Veterans Council to march in their parade. They had no name. They had three people that were forming a group that wanted to march, so naturally, when they finally sent in an application, which is reflected in the exhibits, that described themselves as a social club, they did not have enough information about the group and they were also hearing information in the community about the three participants that wanted to organize the group.

After they found out what the messages of the group were, they took a vote, and they voted to exclude any group with any sexual theme from their parade. They're entitled to do that. They're entitled to define the parade in any form and shape that they wish. That was not pretextual.

If my clients were marching with a group of people that did not have the signs and the messages that are reflected in this record, then there would be no dispute. The fact that the sign, the proclamations on the sign, and their announced messages [were included, means that] my clients can reject [it]. They can include and exclude any messages they wish to.

I reserve the balance of my time if there are no further questions.

Mr. Darling has acquitted himself quite well. He knows the case, knows the record, knows the problems, and has a clear, direct, and forceful theory from which he argues. He holds his ground and tries mightily to stay away from the treacherous shoals of the state courts' fact-findings on whether the Veterans were engaged in speech through the planning, organizing, and executing of the parade; or whether they were just parade planners who intended no message or expression of any note; or whether they were simply engaged in hidden discrimination against gays. Mr. Darling says the parade is an inherently expressive event, and that the planning, organizing, and executing of the parade is a creative act entitled to respect as speech because of the themes it pursues through the parade and because of the meanings the spectators draw from it. This is good but far from firm ground to stand on.

But what if, as the Massachusetts courts implied, the Veterans were just parade planners who intended no message—or more specifically whose in-the-air cultural message was very diffuse and noncognitive? Just a feeling-good-today-in-our-nation-and-community message? Should that be protected speech? Must speech have a message, or at least a fairly coherent, message? Or is asking that much ignoring the sensuous and aesthetic and emotional properties of speech?

And what if the Veterans' parade is protected but very diffuse speech, and it is now competing against GLIB's competing claim to be able to express its own, more specific, more cognitive and pointed view? Why in such a case should the Veterans prevail over a better-defined claim of right to expression? Because the Veterans did all of the work?

And then, finally, there was that nasty fact-finding. What if the Veterans' parade doesn't count at all as speech, for whatever reason (nothing there, too general, not intended to express)? Then, of course, the Veterans would have no shelter in the First Amendment because their rejection of GLIB would look just like a discriminatory act. But what about the Boy Scouts? In the alternative, the Veterans could argue that the government forced them to include GLIB under the nondiscrimination law and by doing so to carry GLIB's message. That would be a case of compelled speech of the Veterans. This argument is there, but Mr. Darling doesn't emphasize it. Why? Because it rests the Veterans' claim on the speech intentions and activities of GLIB: only if GLIB was speaking a clear message would the Veterans be able to say that the government had required the Veterans to carry it and even then only if the spectators saw GLIB's message as being endorsed by the Veterans. Who would believe that?

As shown in the second half of the oral argument, this is indeed messy, fascinating, and really interesting and fundamental stuff the Court and the lawyers are getting into. Do the participants also realize that lots more is at stake—like the constitutional protection for art? Think about a Picasso painting—what he put there, what we see there, what those who would pro-test might assign to it.

CHIEF JUSTICE REHNQUIST: Mr. Ward, we'll hear from you.

MR. WARD: Mr. Chief Justice, and may it please the Court: This is a case about discrimination. The finding of the trial judge in this case was that the council excluded the members of GLIB on the basis of their sexual orientation, that they excluded them for who they were, not what they said.

QUESTION: Well, I assume you concede that your clients wanted to be in the parade because they wanted to proclaim a message.

MR. WARD: Well, I think the term *message* as it's been used in this case really is more confusing than illuminating, Justice Kennedy. My clients wanted to be included in the parade. They wanted to be included in what the trial judge found to be an open recreational event. The trial judge found that they had been discriminated against. He ordered that they be included on the same basis as everybody else. Everybody else self-identified.

QUESTION: Do you think it's a fair conclusion from this record that the plaintiffs had no interest in proclaiming their [GLIB's] message in this event?

MR. WARD: I think that there is a difference between who someone is and what their message is. They did not come in with a sign saying, "Gay is Good."

Mr. Ward must be careful here. Is he saying that there is no message in self-identifying? What about gays who "come out of the closet"? Isn't that all about message? The question here is whether there was expression protected by the First Amendment as speech. The Court is bound and determined to plumb the depths of this question—to get as close to the heart of the matter as possible.

QUESTION: Precisely, but the First Amendment is concerned with the latter, and if messages are the grounds for the exclusion from the parade, it would seem to me that is the end of it.

MR. WARD: The council has the right to exclude on the basis of a viewpoint [expressed in the parade]. What the trial judge found was that they excluded on the basis of sexual orientation. That's discrimination under State law.

QUESTION: To get back to the question of why GLIB wanted to be in the parade, they didn't want to be there to recreate, as was found by the Massachusetts supreme court. GLIB's purposes are to express its members' pride in their dual identities as Irish or Irish-American, to demonstrate to the Irish-American community and to the gay, lesbian, and bisexual community the diversity within those—and to show support. All of those are expressive activities. They were there to express something, weren't they?

MR. WARD: Justice Scalia, I think that when Linda Brown went to school in Little Rock, her going in there was expressing something. For purposes of the discrimination statute, the expression is incidental. When a discriminator excludes someone, that also under some circumstances sends a very powerful message. The—I think that the point here, Justice Scalia, is that one—under the antidiscrimination laws, one cannot be penalized for merely self-identifying any more than the—when a discriminator excludes—

Mr. Ward is getting himself led into a pointless squabble here, and it doesn't supply the makings of a clear argument. Unless explicit, cognitive (logical, not emotional or sensuous) declarative statements are the only things that count at speech (which they aren't according to the Supreme Court—witness flag burning), the fact is that self-identification can, in some circumstances, constitute speech and the expression of a message. The hard questions lie below the surface: When, why, how, who?

QUESTION: Why is that? This isn't a matter of penalizing. It's a matter of not wanting to convey the expressions, the demonstrations, and the showings of support that this group wanted to make in that particular parade. If Massachusetts antidiscrimination law results in forcing parade organizers to allow people with signs and placards that are inconsistent with what the parade says its message is, then it's a problem under the First Amendment, isn't it?

MR. WARD: That is correct, but what I—I think I—

QUESTION: You're saying that didn't happen.

MR. WARD: I'm saying that didn't happen, and I'm saying it for two reasons, Mr. Chief Justice. First of all, there was a State finding also that this was an open recreational event, that there really was—

QUESTION: Well, let's pose it in a different context. Suppose there's a Ringling Brothers Barnum and Bailey Circus in town, and they have a parade, and an animal rights group wants to join the parade with their signs that say, animals shouldn't be used as they are in circuses. Now, do you think they have a right under a public accommodation law to join that parade?

MR. WARD: Justice O'Connor, I see a very clear distinction between viewpoint discrimination and discrimination against people simply for being who they are.

QUESTION: Yes, but a Barnum and Bailey parade doesn't have any viewpoint other than just, gee, the circus is in town and everybody come.

(Laughter.)

MR. WARD: I think that if the issue here—

QUESTION: A public event.

MR. WARD: A public accommodation, right, but what the council is doing is that they're reading a message into the mere presence of a group that's protected under the Massachusetts statute. Discriminators always do that. That's what discrimination—

QUESTION: They're not reading into it. The group said that they wanted to express their pride in their dual identities as Irish and homosexuals. The parade organizers do not believe, whether you agree with it or not, that being homosexual is something to be proud of and therefore do not want that idea to be expressed in their parade. Why is that not simply saying you don't have to have expressed what you do not want to have expressed?

MR. WARD: Because whatever the group had as its expressive notion when it formed, all it said in the parade is, we are Irish-American lesbians, gay men, and bisexuals.

The exchanges remain tendentious, but there is an important point lurking under the surface. It is the slippery-slope argument. If speech isn't objectively or by intention ascertainable, can't virtually all acts be converted into speech, like the act of job discrimination? Mr. Ward will work hard on emphasizing the slipperiness of the slope, in the hopes of getting the Court, when it sees the bottom, to scurry quickly back to the top and draw a clear line. The speech act must be objectively ascertainable by evidence; the message must be clear and coherent (and therefore, perhaps, cognitive). Otherwise, no speech protection. If that's unsatisfactory, the person who wants to speak can simply be clearer about what they are doing and what they want to say. That's not too hard, is it?

Well . . . maybe it's not too hard for a hard-core proponent of a view. But politicians sure have difficulty with it. And artists? Is that kind of clarity even possible—or desirable?

QUESTION: But the point—suppose that were true. You know the case of *Wooley v. Maynard*—the New Hampshire driver's license that said "Live Free or Die" [which the driver had illegally covered up because he disagreed with it and believed that other drivers would think he supported war]?
MR. WARD: Right.
QUESTION: The driver of that car was not engaged in expression. He didn't think about it. But the point was that once somebody told him he had to express a message, the court found that this was State interference, and that this was State-mandated expression, which is contrary to the First Amendment. And the point is that even if the parade were not expressive earlier, and I doubt that, I should think the organizers could say we don't want it turned into an expressive activity, and that this case is much easier than a driver's license case.
MR. WARD: I think, Justice Kennedy, that GLIB is like the numbers, it's not like the sign. In other words, what the council was doing is what discriminators always do. They're conflating identity with some message that they read into it, and—

The justices are getting frustrated, especially with Mr. Ward's continual sliding and ducking around the questions and issues. He needs to get off this ground, for it isn't helping his case, and, more important, it doesn't have the quality of an affirmative argument. The negation of everything is just negation.

QUESTION: Well, can we just get one thing established. You would agree that if the reason for the exclusion of your clients was solely because of their message—solely because of their message—that the exclusion would be within the First Amendment rights of the organizers of a private parade?

MR. WARD: I would agree that the council is free to discriminate on the basis of viewpoint. If my clients came in with a sign saying, "Gay is Good," they could keep it out. However, that's not what happened here. The finding—

QUESTION: Mr. Ward, there is—there are three—there's a statement I think in the court of first instance and in the supreme judicial court of three purposes. They sound like they're expressive. The last one was support for the New York group that was seeking to march in the parade there. Now, would you review those three and tell me why each of them is not conveying a message?

MR. WARD: I don't disagree that each of those purposes is expressive, Justice Ginsburg. My point is that none of those messages was stated in anything that GLIB said in the parade. They simply carried a sign.

QUESTION: Well, none of the parade's messages were, either, and we're talking about that which is kind of reasonably implicit and reasonably conveyed throughout. Are you taking the position that unless you literally have a sign with a declarative statement on it that the rule does not apply?

Mr. Ward is now invited to make the slippery-slope argument or at least tell the Court where it can draw the line. We have some lines: intention of the speaker, objective facts of express speech, cognitive messages. What about emotion? And most importantly for Mr. Ward, *why* is self-identification a good line to draw?

MR. WARD: I'm taking the position that when all other groups in the parade are allowed to simply self-identify, that the act of my client in simply self-identifying, which is all they did, is not the expression of an antithetical message in that sense.

QUESTION: So I guess you're saying that in the absence of an express declarative statement, none of these three purposes to which Justice Ginsburg has alluded and the Massachusetts courts found as your expressive point, is in fact a point being expressed at all.

MR. WARD: I'm saying—no, they certainly *did not find* any expression in the parade.

Now Mr. Ward turns to the fact-finding. It is perhaps his strongest tactic, though it really has nothing to do with the issues. And when the Court gets down to examining the "fact" found—the Veterans were not speaking, they were just discriminating against gays—the justices likely don't believe it any more than Mr. Ward would if asked in confidence. It would also be pretty ugly for Mr. Ward to win the case on the basis of an ambiguous and, frankly, unwise off-handed footnote in a state-court judge's decision, leaving the First Amendment issues hanging.

But there is something to Mr. Ward's tactic, even if one might not ap-plaud it. Appellate courts, like the Supreme Court, are generally bound by fact-findings made in the trial court, which has the advantage of seeing the witness and judging credibility, for example. But there are some exceptions to this rule, and fact-findings on which First Amendment rights turn are among them. There, the Supreme Court can dig into the record more searchingly and is not bound by the lower court's fact-findings.

QUESTION: Well, what did your group's sign say?

MR. WARD: It said simply, Mr. Chief Justice, "Irish-American, Gay, Lesbian and Bisexual Group of Boston," which is the identity of who these people were. It did not say, repeal the sodomy laws. It did not say, we question your traditional values. It did not say anything of that kind.

QUESTION: That is enough to show that you are proud of that fact, which is what their object is to express their pride in those dual identities. That's all you need to show that pride is to hang it up in a sign. How else does one show pride in a certain thing?

MR. WARD: In the same sense that a black person marching in the parade, I take it, would be proud of his or her identity.

QUESTION: That's right, and if that person held up a sign and said, black unity, that would be an expression of pride in blackness.

MR. WARD: Except that generally speaking, lesbians, gay men, and bisexual people are not immediately evident to the—

Oops! If gays are not evident, then they have to send a message. But does black skin do that? To whom, when, why, how? Is it enough if it sends the message to just one person? These are questions of line drawing that can't be escaped. But the Court seems to want no part of Mr. Ward's answer—be explicit. Is his answer too simplistic?

The justices try mightily to probe this fundamental question.

QUESTION: Exactly. I mean, the point at issue is whether there's an expression of anything in their mere marching with a sign saying what they are, and it seems to me you must acknowledge that it is—there is an expression of pride in what they are.

MR. WARD: I would call it self-identifying, just as a Star of David, just as—

QUESTION: So long as you mean, by self-identifying, pride. I'll accept that. (Laughter.)

QUESTION: May I ask you a question, Mr. Ward? It's really remarkable in this case, it seems to me, that both of you seem to agree on the applicable law. They agree they can't exclude you because of who you are, and you agree they can exclude you if you're sending a message. So the real question is, how do you decide which it is, and the point, the question is, for me at least, do you answer that question by looking at your motive, their interpretation of what you look like, or the reasonable neutral person's interpretation of the sign? What is the standard?

MR. WARD: I think it's objective facts. It's an objective question. You look at two things. You look at what kind of event the council has created, what the court found was an open recreational event, and then you look at the impact of the inclusion of the unwanted group on that event.

This Court's cases have suggested that if a group [the parade organizer] is so organized around a discernible specific expressive purpose that the mere inclusion of the unwanted group would seriously disable them from their expressive purposes, then perhaps the group wins. In this case—

QUESTION: Well, I don't know that "seriously disable" is found in any of our cases. I think quite the contrary, that if you have an expressive purpose, you're entitled to maintain the purity of that expression. Newspapers, for instance, can't be required to print retraction articles.

MR. WARD: Exactly. However, what the trial judge found and what the supreme judicial court affirmed was that the relationship of the council to this event was that of standing basically indifferent to the messages, that that's what really happened, and that that—

QUESTION: Well, but I think even if that were so historically, they could change their position when another group wants to have a message.

MR. WARD: Well, I think that clubs often did that when they wanted to exclude black people, and this Court consistently said you can't reorganize around a racist purpose and become thereby a private club. I think the analogy fits here.

Right! Like that increasingly troublesome Boy Scouts' case. The problem here, though, is a different one, and Mr. Ward is testing his credibility. The fact is that notwithstanding the "finding" of discrimination against gays by the Veterans (if finding is the right term for a confused comment in a footnote), there is absolutely no affirmative evidence to support the finding that the Veterans excluded GLIB or anyone else because they were gay. Did they? Who knows. But the responsibility to pin this matter down rests with GLIB's lawyers at the trial level, and they either dropped the ball or couldn't prove it and now want to engineer the claim back into the case through a judge's loose language.

QUESTION: Mr. Ward, can I ask another question, following up on my preceding question? If it's an objective test, and say objectively the neutral observer would say yes, there's an expression going on here, but nevertheless the evidence was very clear that the real motive was that they didn't want you to march with them, which is what [the court] found, that real motive would really not be controlling under the objective test, would it?

MR. WARD: Well, it controls as to the finding of discrimination.

QUESTION: Yes, but it would be permissible discrimination if the objective observer would think that there's a message there they don't like. Now, maybe they would have excluded you whether or not there was a message, but maybe they can get away with it if there's a message.

MR. WARD: I think what that really means, Justice Stevens, is there are some circumstances under which discrimination is incidental. That's the Ku Klux Klan case, for example, where the Ku Klux Klan, which we both cite, the Ku Klux Klan wanted to march through a town of Maryland with members only, and the NAACP wanted to march alongside of them. The trial judge said the mere inclusion of this unwanted group would destroy the message. That's a far cry from this case, where the trial court and the Supreme Judicial Court both found an open recreational event in which the parade organizers, despite what they later said, which was found to be basically pretextual, stood more or less indifferent to the messages.

QUESTION: Well, they didn't. They didn't let everybody else—was that the finding, that no group was ever excluded? They kept out the KKK, didn't they?

MR. WARD: On the basis, Justice Scalia, that they can discriminate on the basis of viewpoint. However, the finding was that that's not what was going on here.

QUESTION: Could they exclude the Ku Klux Klan on the basis of the uniforms they wear or the sheets and so forth?

MR. WARD: Anything they want to, sure.

QUESTION: But why is that different from self-identification?

MR. WARD: Because that goes to the essence; otherwise you would give a discriminator an objector's veto. Every time somebody came along and self-identified, they'd say, we don't object to you. We object to your Jewish surname or to your Star of David or to your—some other feature.

QUESTION: Well, the trial court said the Veterans' position is paradoxical. [It said that] a proper celebration of St. Patrick's and Evacuation Day requires diversity and inclusiveness. I suggest that for a State entity, which is the court, to tell a private speaker how to celebrate St. Patrick's Day is antithetical to First Amendment principles.

MR. WARD: Your Honor, I think that what the trial justice was doing was characterizing their position, not dictating it to them. In the end, this is a case about discrimination. The finding of the two courts below, well-supported in the record, was that the reason, the real reason that GLIB was kept out was its members' sexual orientation and not any message, because there was no message in that sense, and for that reason the judgment of the supreme judicial court should be affirmed.

And with that, Mr. Ward closes his argument. He had a very tough argument to make. He held his ground. But it was not good ground to hold. He needed to but did not effectively craft an argument that there is a limit on the slippery slope and that it can be managed and principled. And the Veterans Council fell below it and thus should have no free speech protection or should have less than the more explicit speech by GLIB.

Mr. Darling now returns for his few reserved minutes, and he hits hard right out of the gate—on the facts.

MR. DARLING: Again, I would urge, Mr. Chief Justice and Your Honors, that any review of the record will reflect that there is absolutely no evidence of discrimination on the basis of sexual orientation by my clients in this record—in the whole enterprise.

My clients discriminated against messages. Historically they have. They included the NAACP, they excluded the KKK, they excluded an antigay group, and they wished to exclude a group—

QUESTION: Mr. Darling, would you comment directly on your opponent's argument that the particular signs they were going to carry, and it's all—forget your motive in letting them out and their motive in doing it, but

just, I want to watch the parade. Now, would I see anything that would be
more than what he describes as self-identification?

MR. DARLING: A sign that stated, Irish-American, Gay, Lesbian, and Bisexual
Group of Boston.

QUESTION: Is that self-identification, or is that message, and if so, what is
the message?

MR. DARLING: It's a message, it's an identification, it's a proclamation, and it
is a message that my clients did not deem appropriate to include in their
expression of their version of a celebration of a St. Patrick's Day parade,
however they designed it.

QUESTION: Suppose that their actual reason was that the sign calls attention
to a fact that makes them feel uncomfortable. Is that a justification?

An interesting question indeed. Is the communication of feelings or the
inducement of feelings in others speech? An artist would certainly say so. And
so does Mr. Darling. But what about the contested field of hate speech, where
the feelings are made "harm" and the speech is prohibited in order to avoid
the harm? In such cases is the explanation for greater government power to
regulate that the epithet, for example, isn't speech? Or that it is speech but the
harm outweighs it? Both answers can be found in the cases. Are the feelings
of disgust expressed by Jesse Helms (and many others) at Karen Finley's act
really any different? And how do we judge those feelings of hurt and disgust
to be any different or less creditable than the black student who is addressed
by an epithet? Both are indecent and disrespectful of American values.

Discomfort, the Court has long told us, is the very nature of speech if it is
free. And art? It is about feelings, perceptions, skills, whether in relation to
the beautiful and sublime or the ugly and shocking, most artists would say.
And they have a point. How about Dante's *Inferno*? Not art?

Oh my, what a mess we seem to be in.

QUESTION: Suppose that what happens is that that just makes them feel uncomfortable, since it's public, and they don't like it. Now, where does that
stand under First Amendment law?

MR. DARLING: My clients can exclude it. They can exclude any message in
any parade that they deem inappropriate.

CHIEF JUSTICE REHNQUIST: Thank you, Mr. Darling. The case is
submitted.

• • •

The Court's opinion came out at the end of the Term. That was not surprising, for the case was very important and very complex and highly political, too. What was surprising, however, was the Court's unanimity, not just in result but also in reasoning. The Court begins with the brave and broad, even stirring sentiment that parades are inherently expressive. From that point on, the case is over, and Mr. Darling, having lost in virtually every lower court over three years of litigation, gets his full victory, as do the war veterans.

But the case is not so simple as that. Speech is a many-faceted thing, and parades aren't all that count. We know about the slippery slope and the absolute need to fix a point to stop the slide. We know about the many problems raised by concepts like cognition versus emotion; sensuality; beauty and ugliness; attribution of expression to conduct; intention; audience interpretation; and on and on. And we know that we need to think very carefully about art and the aesthetic. We will do so once we have digested what the Court, speaking through Justice Souter, is saying.

Souter, J., delivered the opinion for a unanimous Court.

If there were no reason for a group of people to march from here to there except to reach a destination, they could make the trip without expressing any message beyond the fact of the march itself. Some people might call such a procession a parade, but it would not be much of one. Real "[p]arades are public dramas of social relations, and in them performers define who can be a social actor and what subjects and ideas are available for communication and consideration." Hence, we use the word *parade* to indicate marchers who are making some sort of collective point, not just to each other but to bystanders along the way. Indeed, a parade's dependence on watchers is so extreme that nowadays, as with Bishop Berkeley's celebrated tree, "if a parade or demonstration receives no media coverage, it may as well not have happened." Parades are thus a form of expression, not just motion, and the inherent expressiveness of marching to make a point explains our cases involving protest marches.

The protected expression that inheres in a parade is not limited to its banners and songs, however, for the Constitution looks beyond written or spoken words as mediums of expression. Noting that "[s]ymbolism is a primitive but effective way of communicating ideas," our cases have recognized that the First Amendment shields such acts as saluting a flag (and refusing to do so), wearing an armband to protest a war, displaying a red flag, and even "[m]arching, walking or parading" in uniforms displaying the swastika. As some of these examples show, a narrow, succinctly articulable message is not a condition of constitutional protection, which if confined to expressions conveying a "particularized message," would never reach the unquestionably shielded painting of Jackson Pollock, music of Arnold Schöenberg, or "Jabberwocky" verse of Lewis Carroll.

Not many marches, then, are beyond the realm of expressive parades, and the South Boston celebration is not one of them. Spectators line the streets; people march in costumes and uniforms, carrying flags and banners with all sorts of messages (*e.g.*, "England get out of Ireland," "Say no to drugs"); marching bands and pipers play; floats are pulled along; and the whole show is broadcast over Boston television. To be sure, we agree with the state courts that in spite of excluding some applicants, the Council is rather lenient in admitting participants. But a private speaker does not forfeit constitutional protection simply by combining multifarious voices, or by failing to edit their themes to isolate an exact message as the exclusive subject matter of the speech. Nor, under our precedent, does First Amendment protection require a speaker to generate, as an original matter, each item featured in the communication. Cable operators, for example, are engaged in protected speech activities even when they only select programming originally produced by others. For that matter, the presentation of an edited compilation of speech generated by other persons is a staple of most newspapers' opinion pages, which, of course, fall squarely within the core of First Amendment security, as does even the simple selection of a paid noncommercial advertisement for inclusion in a daily paper. The selection of contingents to make a parade is entitled to similar protection.

Respondents' participation as a unit in the parade was equally expressive. GLIB was formed for the very purpose of marching in it, as the trial court found, in order to celebrate its members' identity as openly gay, lesbian, and bisexual descendants of the Irish immigrants, to show that there are such individuals in the community, and to support the like men and women who sought to march in the New York parade. The organization distributed a fact sheet describing the members' intentions, and the record otherwise corroborates the expressive nature of GLIB's participation. In 1993, members of GLIB marched behind a shamrock-strewn banner with the simple inscription "Irish-American Gay, Lesbian and Bisexual Group of Boston." GLIB understandably seeks to communicate its ideas as part of the existing parade, rather than staging one of its own.

• • •

The Massachusetts public accommodations law under which respondents brought suit has a venerable history. . . . After the Civil War, the Commonwealth of Massachusetts was the first State to codify this principle to ensure access to public accommodations regardless of race. The legislature continued to broaden the scope of legislation, to the point that the law today prohibits discrimination on the basis of "race, color, religious creed, national origin, sex, sexual orientation . . . , deafness, blindness or any physical or mental disability or ancestry" in "the admission of any person to, or treatment in any place of public accommodation, resort, or amusement." Provisions like these are well within the State's usual power to enact when a legislature has reason to believe that a given group is the target of discrimination, and they do not, as a general matter, violate the First or Fourteenth Amendments.

In the case before us, however, the Massachusetts law has been applied in a peculiar way. Its enforcement does not address any dispute about the participation of openly gay, lesbian, or bisexual individuals in various units admitted to the parade. Petitioners disclaim any intent to exclude homosexuals as such, and no individual member of GLIB claims to have been excluded from parading as a member of any group that the Council has approved to march. Instead, the disagreement goes to the admission of GLIB as its own parade unit carrying its own banner. Since every participating unit affects the message conveyed by the private organizers, the state courts' application of the statute produced an order essentially requiring petitioners to alter the expressive content of their parade. Although the state courts spoke of the parade as a place of public accommodation, once the expressive character of both the parade and the marching GLIB contingent is understood, it becomes apparent that the state courts' application of the statute had the effect of declaring the sponsors' speech itself to be the public accommodation. Under this approach any contingent of protected individuals with a message would have the right to participate in petitioners' speech, so that the communication produced by the private organizers would be shaped by all those protected by the law who wished to join in with some expressive demonstration of their own. But this use of the State's power violates the fundamental rule of protection under the First Amendment, that a speaker has the autonomy to choose the content of his own message.

"Since *all* speech inherently involves choices of what to say and what to leave unsaid," one important manifestation of the principle of free speech is that one who chooses to speak may also decide "what not to say."

Petitioners' claim to the benefit of this principle of autonomy to control one's own speech is as sound as the South Boston parade is expressive. Rather like a composer, the Council selects the expressive units of the parade from potential participants, and though the score may not produce a particularized message, each contingent's expression in the Council's eyes comports with what merits celebration on that day. Even if this view gives the Council credit for a more considered judgment than it actively made, the Council clearly decided to exclude a message it did not like from the communication it chose to make, and that is enough to invoke its right as a private speaker to shape its expression by speaking on one subject while remaining silent on another. The message it disfavored is not difficult to identify. Although GLIB's point (like the Council's) is not wholly articulate, a contingent marching behind the organization's banner would at least bear witness to the fact that some Irish are gay, lesbian, or bisexual, and the presence of the organized marchers would suggest their view that people of their sexual orientations have as much claim to unqualified social acceptance as heterosexuals and indeed as members of parade units organized around other identifying characteristics. The parade's organizers may not believe these facts about Irish sexuality to be so, or they may object to unqualified social acceptance of gays and lesbians or have some other reason for wishing to keep GLIB's message out of the parade. But whatever the reason, it boils down to the choice of a speaker not to propound a particular point of view, and that choice is presumed to lie beyond the government's power to control.

While the law is free to promote all sorts of conduct in place of harmful behavior, it is not free to interfere with speech for no better reason than promoting an approved message or discouraging a disfavored one, however enlightened either purpose may strike the government.

Our holding today rests not on any particular view about the Council's message but on the Nation's commitment to protect freedom of speech. Disapproval of a private speaker's statement does not legitimize use of the Commonwealth's power to compel the speaker to alter the message by including one more acceptable to others. Accordingly, the judgment of the Supreme Judicial Court is reversed, and the case is remanded for proceedings not inconsistent with this opinion.

It is so ordered.

Mr. Darling, the solo practitioner from Boston who had litigated the case from beginning to end, losing at almost every turn (though not because of any failing as a lawyer), had finally won the case at the nation's highest court, and he had done so with a unanimous decision. His is a truly remarkable story.

The Court's opinion is in many ways an equally remarkable one: long, scholarly, yet bristling with ambiguity at its foundation. Justice Souter concluded for the Court that because the parade was private, the only party that could claim free speech rights was the Veterans Council. The council's job was to construct the parade, a job accomplished by decisions to include and exclude participants, but not to alter or shape the message, if any, that their participation or marching carried. It was a thematic parade, reflecting Irish Pride, the sacrifice of Irish Veterans, the Catholic Church, and the family values of the South Boston community. The themes were broad and, frankly, ambiguous, which is not to say that the council did not shape the parade around its sense of those themes. But the parade's message was at best broad and evocative. It was not like a freedom march led by Dr. King in the south, or a pro-choice or anti-abortion parade or march around the Supreme Court. Yet, the council's parade, the Court says, was something more than, perhaps, a Macy's parade in which discriminating values and images are hardly the point.

Perhaps the simplest and most fitting description of the parade's message is that it was aesthetic, as well, perhaps, as artistic in its construction of floats, colors, marchers, and the like. Its message lies in evoking feelings and images and interpretations in the audience that are generally consistent with the values (family, pride) evoked by aesthetic and artistic representations. As Justice Souter says, "Real 'parades are public drama of social relations, and in them performers define who can be a social actor and what subjects and ideas are available for communication and consideration.'" If this is so, then we have a clearer understanding of what the speech or expression protected by the First Amendment was and the limited role the council played in shaping it. We must know this, for if the parade has no message—no specific (or cognitive) statements or claim, and no evocative (aesthetic) themes—around which the selection choices of the council can be seen as expressive ones, there is no basis for the council's First Amendment claim, and there would be no damage to free speech from a requirement, imposed by the lower courts, that GLIB be allowed in the parade.

If the Boston parade was a means of communicating an aesthetic message, then two very important things can be known about the role of the council as "speaker" and the form in which the "communication of a message" occurred through the parade and its participants. First, the council's speech acts—inclusion and exclusion of participants—did not involve the construction of a cognitive message, but instead they served to construct an aesthetic message. They served more like decisions about the pallet and form of a painting than decisions about the object to be represented. Second, the identity of the specific message being communicated lay in the minds and imaginations of the spectators, not the council and not the individual participants. Much like art, the council and the participants constructed the representation of the parade, and the viewers provided the re-representation of its meaning and message through their individual acts of creativity. There was no specific message of the parade—there were countless messages interpretively constructed from the parade. The council hoped that those messages would be generally similar, at least at the thematic level of pride and family and community values, but it could no more assure that outcome than a novelist can assure that his or her readers will draw the same meaning from the novel as the author holds in his or her own imagination.

Armed with this understanding of the parade, one can explore the most important questions raised by the case, knowing also that these questions in many ways mirror those raised by aesthetic and artistic expression. The central question is: What is the nature of the process of communication upon which the Court rested the protection of the First Amendment? Answering this question is essential, for aesthetic and artistic expressions do not fit the traditional mold of speech protected by the First Amendment: the speaker on a street-corner soapbox trying to convince an audience to his way of thinking about a social or political issue. This speaker, unlike the council in *Hurley* or the poet or painter, is one with a specific, cognitive message and who intends to communicate that message to an identifiable audience, who will receive and understand that specific message, whether they agree with it or not.

In order to undertake this inquiry, four illustrative, and very different, conceptions of what communication involves and how it works will help. The theories are reflected in the work of J. L. Austin, E. D. Hirsch, John Peters, and James Carey. This discussion will only consider the speaker status of the Veterans Council, not GLIB. This is because the Court concluded that government was not significantly involved in the decision to hold the parade and the choices to admit or exclude participants. Without government involvement, the council's decisions did not deny anyone his or her First Amendment rights, because the First Amendment limits only government action, not action of private parties like the council. More important, the status of the council as speaker is the question on which to focus in relation to artistic and aesthetic expression, for the council's speech claim is ultimately an aesthetic one.

SPEECH ACTS

J. L. Austin's speech-act theory introduced a category of language called the *performative*.[6] Performative statements are acts, in and of themselves. When results or consequences are brought about by saying something, then the speaker can be said to use language in the performative sense. The performative statement is qualitatively distinct from a statement that simply reports facts. The latter type of statement, once heard, may change someone's course of action subsequently, but when a performative statement is issued and understood, certain effects immediately obtain. For example, if one articulates a descriptive statement of fact, such as, "It is forty degrees outside,"[7] the receiver of that statement may rely on that information and, thus, choose to put on a coat. But that consequence is not a *necessary* response to or effect of the utterance. The doing of the act is not achieved by the speech.

Statements with a greater degree of illocutionary force and, hence, performative quality, include statements such as, "I promise to pay you five dollars in exchange for your hat." Assuming this statement is uttered in the appropriate context, it constitutes a promise and enacts a legally actionable contract.

Although there is no such thing as a "pure" performative[8]—there are only uses of language with more or less illocutionary force according to the speech situations in which the expression is uttered—the idea of the performative says something important about the nature of language: that sometimes speech and act are so intertwined as to be inextricably intertwined. Put simply, some speech is more powerful—not in its tone or decibels but in its impact on an audience—and thus may deserve greater respect as communication when it competes with other, less-performative, expression.

In *Hurley,* Justice Souter could have used Austin's theory to support the conclusion that GLIB was entitled to little or no constitutional protection. Because the explicitly performative statement has a high degree of force and consequence, it might be said that the individual paraders marching in procession generated no noticeable illocutionary force and thus no speech. The pride, entertainment value, or any other values communicated by the parade were not generated by or intrinsic to a single marching entity. To the extent that the individual parade units engaged in communication with no (or little) illocutionary force, their speech acts approach the legal realm of nonexpressive "conduct," which raises no First Amendment issues. The Court could then conclude that the council's speech selections qualify as conduct attended by substantial (or greater) illocutionary force—like "coming out" perhaps.

In this way, Austin's theory could have supported the Court's conclusion that the Veterans Council has the right to combine multifarious voices and/ or edit their themes according to its private dictates and without regard to speech interests of GLIB, because the council's decisions to include and exclude marchers "spoke" within the meaning of the First Amendment. The council's composition of the parade, which included its particular speech-selection judgments, can qualify as a speech act with great, indeed primary, illocutionary force . . . not unlike an orchestra director's selection of instruments and musicians to play a score. Because the council's announcement of GLIB's disqualification performs the very act that it states and immediately effects the exclusion of GLIB, the council's judgment carries great weight, and the council's speech act can therefore be privileged above GLIB's alleged speech interest.

Justice Souter's opinion, however, did not employ speech-act theory. The opinion viewed the parade as a form of robust expression, not conduct. It characterized parades in general as "public drama[s] of social relations" that make a "*collective* point."[9] It held that parades constitute "a form of expression, not just motion."[10] Characterized this way, the parade itself constitutes speech. The parade itself thus becomes the focus of the Court's analysis, rather than the council's speech-selection judgment (which Austin's theory would have directed the Court to examine as an instance of performative speech).

While the Court's insight about parades may be right, the Court's initial premise—that marching is inherently expressive—would seem to concede the argument that the council's speech-selection judgments do not uniquely cause a collective point to be made; indeed, even absent a permit-granting process—for example, if the parade were run by the city, and everyone could participate—a collective, multifarious message could still be extrapolated from combining the multiple paraders' voices. In other words, the council's decisions are not productive of the thematic message communicated ultimately— that overarching message can't be known in advance. Functionally, all the council can do is control that which is *not* said. It only controls the silences. Under Austin's theory, act and speech are not inextricably intertwined in the council's (de)selection act, so the council's speech-selection judgment has little illocutionary force; its process of denying permits looks more like pure "conduct" than "speech" and should not receive First Amendment protection.

If the Court did, in fact, believe that act and speech were inextricably intertwined in the council's (de)selection act, no evidence of this fact exists in the opinion. Nothing mentioned by the Court would provide support for the conclusion that the council's speech act (i.e., the selection process) qualifies as an explicitly performative statement and, as such, trumps the historically sedimented meaning that inheres in (most forms of) marching as a kind of expressive conduct. If a parade's message is social, dramatic, and thematic, arising from an entrenched historical appreciation for the cultural significance of marching, it seems unlikely that the council's intended message—be it vague or specific—could consist of anything more than its own mental construct, bearing no real significance to the parade. It makes little sense that the council should get credit under Austin's view as the preeminent speaker just because it takes individual paraders' messages and allegedly transforms them, by virtue of granting or denying a permit, into some *later-constructed* "collective" point.

Ultimately, the Court's decision positioned the council as the preeminent message organizer not by virtue of the illocutionary force inherent in speech-selection judgments—like civil rights marches—but, rather, by default. The Court impliedly held that the marchers' specific messages were constitutive of the *council's* message and thus subordinate to it. The council thus received ownership over all the marchers' speech, just like a symphony owns the individual performances—or, perhaps, like the painter owns the painting and its compositional choices even though it takes on a meaning and life of its own once displayed.

AUTHOR INTENT

E. D. Hirsch established the author's intent as the prevailing normative guideline for evaluating the interpretation of (literary) texts.[11] He defined authorial intent as the author or speaker's intended message—an orientation that assumes an identifiable message *and* a singularly or arguably "best" interpretation of a text. Hirsch chose this rubric because, he argued, one must be able to stabilize meaning and then judge it according to systematically reliable principles. Doing so enables the possibility of assessment. Using the notion of intent as one's measuring stick, Hirsch predicted that authorial intent would typically bring readers, interpreters, or other assessors to the most correct understanding of a text, if not to a perfect understanding. Put differently, Hirsch's theory grounded the possibility of determinate meaning in a human's preexisting determinate will to share a largely cognitive message (and trapped the meaning of the message there).

Under Hirsch's theory, the threshold question in *Hurley* must be whether the council intended to speak an identifiable message. The council did, of course, organize the parade and select the participants. But an intent to do these things would not satisfy Hirsch's conception of intent nor qualify the council as a speaker whose claim could subordinate the more clearly intended and specific message of GLIB. To trump GLIB's interests, the council must, at the very least, intend to express some message or express its own disagreement with one (like GLIB's). The fact that a parade is inherently expressive cannot, without more, bootstrap the council into the category of "speaker" under Hirsch's theory. Without more by way of intent and message, the parade is an event, not speech, and the council is an actor, not a speaker.

The *Hurley* Court conferred "speakership" upon the council because (1) the council was a private organizer, (2) a speaker is not required to generate, as an original matter, each item featured in the communication (i.e., republishers may be entitled to First Amendment protection when they only select speech originally produced by others), and (3) the selection of contingents to make a parade is an act of authorship intended to create a collective message.

While the Court offers justifications to explain why it privileges the council as *the* speaker, it does not do this by relying on the traditional doctrine of speaker intent. Instead, the Court begins from the premise that parades and marching constitute speech and implicitly addresses the question of intent:

> To be sure, we agree with the state courts that in spite of excluding some applicants, the Council is rather lenient in admitting participants. But a private speaker does not forfeit constitutional protection simply by combining multifarious voices, or by failing to edit their themes to isolate an exact message as the exclusive subject matter of the speech. Nor . . . does First Amendment protection require a speaker to generate, as an original matter, each item featured in the communication. [Similar to a cable operator or newspaper editor,] [t]he selection of contingents to make a parade is entitled to First Amendment protection.[12]

In answering GLIB's argument that speakers only receive First Amendment protection when their communication contains identifiable messages, the Court elides the question of intent and simply reasserts that speech-selection judgments have been protected under First Amendment precedent. It does not explain why this is so. It simply draws an analogy among cable operators, newspapers, and parade organizers. But later in the opinion, the Court concludes that the council, in fact, is much different than a cable operator, resting its conclusion not on intent but on audience perception:

> Respondents contend . . . that the admission of GLIB to the parade would not threaten the core principle of speaker autonomy because the Council, like a cable operator, is merely "a conduit" for the speech of participants in the parade "rather than itself a speaker." But this metaphor is not apt here, because GLIB's participation would *likely be perceived* [emphasis supplied] as having resulted from the Council's customary determination about a unit admitted to the parade, that its message was worthy of presentation and quite possibly of support as well.[13]

The Court concludes that the council's claim is about autonomy more than anything else. Again skirting the question of why the council deserves speaker status, the Court likens the council to a composer:

> Petitioners' claim to the benefit of this principle of autonomy to control one's own speech is as sound as the South Boston parade is expressive. Rather like a composer, the Council selects the expressive units of the parade from the potential participants, and though the score may not produce a particularized message, each contingent's expression in the Council's eyes comports with what merits celebration on that day.... The Council clearly decided to invoke its right as a private speaker to shape its expression by speaking on one subject while remaining silent on another. ... [I]t boils down to the choice of a speaker not to propound a particular point of view.[14]

The metaphorical alignment between a composer and the council, however, fails to provide a reason why the council's speech-selection judgment is specific enough to cancel out other potential speakers and forms of speech under Hirsh's view. At best, the "composer" metaphor imports an uncritical assumption into the *Hurley* equation: that the council necessarily must have had an intent to speak because a composer always has an intent to compose music. The confusion stems, perhaps, from a failure to appreciate the differences between cognitive speech and sensual, artistic expression, where intent and message are dramatically different.

In short, the Court equates the council's selection judgments with an intent to speak and liberates the council from the requirement of a specific, intended message or even from a requirement of express agreement or endorsement by the council and implies that intention inherently resides in parades (not speakers) even without the possibility of stabilized meaning. It then uses the traditional element of intent to disqualify GLIB as a speaker. The opinion offers no doctrinal reason grounded in intent that explains why, for the purposes of the First Amendment, the council deserves credit as a speaker.

COMMUNICATION AS DISSEMINATION

John Peters discusses a model of communication that views communicative activity through the metaphor of a one-way "broadcast" to which there exists a general access.[15] This communication-as-dissemination model is indifferent to its receivers, which is not to say that receivers are of no relevance. It means that all receivers are equally desirable, and the model relinquishes any investment in (or control over) the meanings that highly diverse audiences may assign to the message. The theory never maintains that audiences receive messages uniformly. Whereas Austin's model locates the creation of meaning within the text itself (as interpreted within a certain context), and Hirsch calibrates the evaluation of meaning using the construct of author intent, the Peters model locates meaning-making primarily within audiences themselves. The conditions of possibility in which the relevant audience(s) circulate determines the degree of intelligibility and, thus, the significance of a message, and the model does not presume that any given message will, in fact, get taken up by those on whom it falls. Ultimately, the dissemination model values the sheer "expenditure" of seeds of communication, because that activity distributes, or plants, the roots for engagement in democratic practices.

Whether the medium is newspaper advertisements, radio broadcasts, price tags, or art, the Court and Peters agree that dissemination of information is a crucial prerequisite to fertile democracy. If Peters's theory is applied to *Hurley*, however, it becomes evident that the value of dissemination itself was not determinative of the Court's decision.

Under the communication-as-dissemination model, the parade arguably constitutes a technology of dissemination because listeners or receivers enjoy a general access to the unidirectional message(s) aired. Viewers of the parade need only stand on the street or perhaps watch the parade on television. Parades are a medium whose historically politicized form and typically public appearance tend to advertise the views expressed. The disseminator's purpose or intention is not the message's source of meaning; neither of these need to be pinned down for speech or a speaker to qualify as a technology of dissemination. That being said, two potential speakers exist in *Hurley*: the individual marchers or entities participating in the parade (GLIB) and the composer (organizer) of the parade (the council).

If the parade itself qualifies as First Amendment speech under Peters's theory, it seems likely that the individual marchers or entities participating in the parade ought to be protected as speakers, if only because one cannot have a parade without paraders. In that sense, the human body functions as a technology of dissemination and ought be protected vigorously even though it presents an instance of "organic" technology. An intended message is not needed to qualify the marchers as a technology of dissemination, only the foreknowledge, perhaps, that their acts will be perceived as communicating some kind of message.

Under the dissemination model, speech-selection decisions in general, like those of the council, might rise to the level of protected speech—even though selection necessarily involves the exclusion of some speech—because selection decisions are a necessary precondition to any forum or medium that must edit the amount of content carried due to spatial constraints or the constraints of a competitive marketplace. However, if the council's attempts to exclude parties such as GLIB can be viewed as exclusionary or akin to soft censorship, then its role qualifies as something less than "sheer" dissemination and perhaps verges on the antidemocratic. More basically, if the council's exclusion is alleged to result from the council's intent to disavow a specific message, then the council's action may no longer qualify as dissemination under Peters's view. The council as censor—a shaper of its specific message at the cost of others' messages—may have no privileged place in a world that regards dissemination so highly.

In reality, however, the Supreme Court adopted a much different approach and did not base its opinion strictly on ideas of dissemination. The Supreme Court argued in *Hurley* that parades, unlike cable lines, operate as *more than* "conduits" for the dissemination of information, which suggests that the Court views the parade as more than a mere technology of dissemination but as an aesthetic expression, perhaps. Rather than derive the First Amendment privilege of a parade purely from its capacity to function as a technology of dissemination, the Court articulated two different grounds for protecting the parade as expression. First, unlike a cable transmission, which involves no substantive message contributed by the cable operator's channel-carriage decisions, a parade constitutes speech because it makes a "point" or communicates a new message tailored by the council's selection choices. Second, the Court emphasized that the parade deserved protection because it did not threaten the very survival of certain speakers. GLIB could hold its own parade.

The Court's attempt to distinguish the council from cable operators and newspapers makes little sense considering its reliance on an analogy among the three earlier in the opinion, where it reasoned that the council exercised editorial judgment similar to that of a cable operator and/or a newspaper editor. In order to argue that the *parade* constitutes speech, the Court has to say that the council is totally *different* from the cable operator or newspaper editor. Yet, in order to argue that the council's *speech-selection judgment* constitutes protected speech, the Court has to say that the council is *highly similar* to the cable operator or newspaper editor. As such, the Court refuses to characterize the parade as a technology of dissemination, yet likens the parade to those figures (newspaper editors or cable operators) who receive First Amendment protection due, in large part, to their position as critical disseminators of communication.

COMMUNICATION AS CULTURE

The key feature of James Carey's communication theory is its cultural perspective. Carey contends that, historically, Americans conceived of communication "in the idea of transmission: communication is a process whereby messages are transmitted and distributed in space for the control of distance and people."[16] But in Carey's view, to reduce communication to a mode of transmission is unduly and artificially to narrow the realm of activity that can be said to have communicative significance and to deceive oneself into believing that humans only communicate for the purpose of sharing information or getting things done. That is to say, the transmission model treats communication like an instrument—a tool for getting things done.

Carey claims instead that "media of communication are not merely instruments of will and purpose but definite forms of life: organisms, so to say, that reproduce in miniature the contradictions in our thought, action, and social relations,"[17] including those contradictions housed within the symbol of the First Amendment itself. In defining communication as "culture," Carey widens the very definition of what qualifies as communication beyond notions of intent or purpose. Instead, he contends that "communication is a symbolic process whereby reality is produced, maintained, repaired, and transformed."[18]

Thus, Carey's model, unlike Hirsch's model, accepts the premise that meaning is socially constructed. Though humans trade in the currency of words,

> words are not the names for things but, . . . things are the signs of words. Reality is not given, not humanly existent, independent of language and toward which language stands as a pale refraction. Rather, reality is brought into existence, is produced, by communication—by, in short, the construction, apprehension, and utilization of symbolic forms. Reality, while not a mere function of symbolic forms, is produced by terministic systems—or by humans who produce such systems—that focus its existence in specific terms.[19]

In other words, humans can identify semi-stabilized meaning—shared meaning—through ritualized communication practices, but stabilized meanings and their structures of reference gain force through human, ritualistic repetition, and they act back on us with the power of "truth" in a manner that is always culturally and historically informed.

Carey's shift from a transmission model to a cultural one entails several implications. First, because humans live in a symbolically mediated and constructed reality, communication is valuable for different reasons than might be assumed under, say, Peters's dissemination model. Communication becomes "the primary phenomena of experience" and warrants more (and different) attention than it receives historically. It includes not only "relations of property, production, and trade—an economic order"[20] but also, more important, "the sharing of aesthetic experience, religious ideas, personal values and sentiments, and intellectual notions—a ritual order."[21] Art and speech are inseparably linked.

Second, Carey's shift means that thought is

predominantly public and social. It occurs primarily on blackboards, in dances, and in recited poems. The capacity of private thought is a derived and secondary talent, one that appears biographically later in the person and historically later in the species. Thought is public because it depends on a publicly available stock of symbols.[22]

Thus, Carey troubles the notion and the very possibility of a "private" speaker. Third, because thought is a priori derived from a publicly shared stock of symbols, "problems of communication are linked to problems of community."[23] Because *habits* of communication entail a participatory process necessarily derived from the republic, communicative practices are both sources of and resources for maintaining and changing the democratic order.

In short, a cultural, ritualistic theory of communication values expressive activity for the kind of comment it makes about the relationships between culture and society or between expressive forms. It values the ways in which "experience is worked into understanding and then disseminated and celebrated."[24]

Carey's theory opens up two distinct understandings in *Hurley*. The first is that if the paraders as a whole effect a collective expression that captures, in miniature, the council's idyllic ritual order, then the parade ought to function as a political comment on the council's beliefs about the status of social relations. The council, as "conductor," is an entity that holds certain ideas; the parade is the dramatic embodiment of the idealized ritual order that the council imagines. Ostensibly, the council's ideal world would exclude GLIB as outside the boundaries of a virtuous civic life. Irrespective of the fact that many people today would find this message reprehensible, the council possesses the permit for the entire parade, which is one historically common procedure for entering into and participating in the (re)construction of social structures. Because, for Carey, symbolic enactment is something in which all humans engage, his model of communication might dictate that civic participation in the form of parading or marching is inherently ritualistic, symbolic, and therefore inherently human. For these reasons, it ought to qualify as speech under the First Amendment. Hence, forcing a privately organized parade to grant a permit to objectionable messages presumptively usurps a basic right. This is, of course, what the Court ultimately decided.

Although this view explains why the parade itself ought be protected as First Amendment speech, it provides little ground for characterizing the parade as the *council's* speech. Because the origin of communication takes on a radically "public" character in Carey's theory (and Carey does not explain whether one can ever "own" words), it is difficult for the council to find much basis for asserting preeminent speaker status. The council may hold a permit to conduct the parade, but that does not provide us with a First Amendment–based rationale as to why the council should be granted dominion over other communicators. Carey's broad definition of communication would likely encompass the council's speech-selection judgments as inherently expressive, but it would undoubtedly extend the same to the parade itself and to the individual marching units.

In a competition for primary-speaker status between the council and GLIB, Carey's theory would arguably preference GLIB. To the extent that the council's conception of itself as *the* speaker is grounded in a transmission model—that is, as the council claimed, it sought to control the transmission of traditional religious and social values and people's ability to express sexual themes—Carey's theory might reject the council's post hoc rationalization as less important than the individual marchers' ability to engage in expression. If meaning in a public parade is indeterminate—only later constructed by audiences—there seems little First Amendment justification for privileging the council's exclusion of GLIB. Communication is the name Carey extends to experiencing, disseminating, and celebrating phenomena, not the name for the practice "of controlling space and people."[25]

Moreover, under Carey's view, meaning is socially constructed and constitutive of reality. This premise has a couple of implications, each of which favors GLIB. First, in order to make an educated guess about the council's claim that GLIB marching would be seen as an endorsement by the council or would cause a different message to be communicated, the Court would have to consider the sociopolitical context in which the audiences viewed the parade and would have to engage in a cultural analysis to determine whether GLIB's participation in the annual parade would arguably hold symbolic significance for the relevant community. This would necessarily entail a study of popular reactions to or anxieties expressed after GLIB's participation in the parade the previous year. The Court might need to consider cultural artifacts—such as newspaper stories, transcripts from town-hall debates, or other cultural clues—and perform a rhetorical, cultural analysis to decipher whether GLIB's participation really had the anticipated effects that the council claimed it would (i.e., misattribution and dampening of the council's proffered traditional values). Given the variety of audience reactions to any single message—particularly cultural dramas unaccompanied by explicit, preexisting statements of intent or purpose, such as the meaning of the Boy Scouts retaining Dale as a Scout leader—such an analysis would not be one the council could reliably prove. It is extraordinarily difficult to predict causation or audience reaction. What neither the government nor the council can regulate under a cultural theory of communication, such as Carey's, is audience response.

Carey's radically "public" theory of communication suggests that communication is always public because it relies on a publicly shared stock of symbols. Private thought is a derived and secondary capability. This distinction inserts something of a gap between public performances, like parades, and the private thoughts that follow (e.g., a bystander's impressions of GLIB's participation or the significance and meaning of the parade), and it suggests that the relationships between the two are decidedly *not* governed by the council's intentions but rather by the ritual order(s) prevalent in the observers' minds. If Carey is right, then the state courts may have been correct when they declared the council's speech itself to be a "public" site, subject to the Massachusetts public accommodation law prohibiting discrimination against homosexuals. Of course, this is a radical departure from the traditional view of speakers under First Amendment jurisprudence, and it unravels many of the fundamental assumptions about the feasibility of owning speech. And it has troubling implications for the rights of artists and the public role of art.

What happened in the actual *Hurley* opinion? The Court recognized implicitly the ritualistic power of parading. It recounted in detail the historic nature and significance of the St. Patrick's Day Parade in Boston. It characterized parades as public dramas of inherent symbolic and communicative worth. As an initial premise, then, the Court agreed with Carey's notion that ritualistic human practices become imbued, over time, with great cultural significance that reveals social actors' relationship to the broader American culture.

The Court ultimately held that the council's parade could not be declared "public." Doing so would have shocking results, according to the Court:

> Under this approach, any contingent of protected individuals with a message would have the right to participate in petitioners' speech, so that the communication produced by the private organizers would be shaped by all those protected by the law who wished to join in with some expressive demonstration of their own. But this use of the State's power violates the fundamental rule of protection under the First Amendment, that a speaker has the autonomy to choose the content of *[its] own message.*[26]

Thus, the Court departs from Carey's theory and instead justifies its decision by naming the council the preeminent speaker and the parade the private expressive instrument of the council.

SPEAKING OUT OF THIN AIR

The First Amendment was born within a political image that presumed the existence of an individual human speaker, standing on a street-corner soapbox (i.e., in a public forum), speaking his or her mind to those who choose to listen. The First Amendment's protections have long been tethered to that explicitly verbal, vocal conception of speech and to its concomitant public address mode of delivery.

Hurley changes that in dramatic ways. The Court's theory of communication is new, yet ambiguous. The decision in *Hurley* does not fit nicely into any single view of communication. Indeed, the Court at various points seems to rely on all versions of communication discussed here. It agrees with Austin that certain kinds of acts, including parades and marching, have undeniable communicative force and are therefore inherently expressive speech acts. The Court also seems to argue, as Hirsch would, that intent or purpose is relevant to discerning the meaning of the message behind a speech-selection judgment. At other times, the *Hurley* opinion also relies heavily on audience construction of a message, as Peters's dissemination model would, to determine the value of the disseminated expression at issue. Finally, the opinion also resonates with Carey's idea that communication is cultural and ritualistic. But all four theories cannot coexist—at least not coherently.

More important, some versions of the Court's communication theories are radically at odds with the traditional assumptions of the First Amendment: that speaking is an intentional act; that messages are a function of a speaker, a meaning, and an intent; and that speech is a liberty of the speaker, not the audience. *Hurley's* result resonates only momentarily with the assumptions about intention and stable meaning that underlie Hirsch's conceptions; the same can be said for the notion of illocutionary force articulated by Austin or for Peters's view of communication as dissemination. *Hurley* is perhaps most easily squared with Carey's view of communication as culture. The Court's language is clearly most sympathetic with Carey's cultural and constructed conception of communication.

While *Hurley* in this sense may be an attractive mélange of communication theory to some, it may serve poorly as a basis for law. Carey or Peters may be quite right about how communicative phenomena work and quite content with the idea that meaning is a social phenomena. But their models may be deeply flawed once institutionalized in the legal realm as a basis for *First Amendment speech*, sedimented in precedent and enforced by the formal powers of the government.

The larger implications of these models, as law, may give pause because the Court's reasoning subordinated the speech interests of the people literally speaking and performing (the paraders) to the council's speech interest in an arguably unidentifiable message, unaccompanied by a clear speaker. Justice Souter's reasoning, like Carey's, thus threatens to cast off, for First Amendment purposes, much of the protection the law traditionally grants to individual speakers or, for that matter, individual artists. The Court effectively loses meaning "out of thin air," tethering the determination of Constitutional rights to the vagaries of audience perception. Even if audience interpretation is that crucial to determining the meaning and effect of a message within a given cultural matrix, it would be a mistake to further consolidate that power by immortalizing—in positive law—the interpretation of a speakerless expressive act. To decipher this genre of "speech act," one must always rely on context, which means the *legal* result will shift as frequently as the *speech situation* does. Another way of saying this is that the answer to the definitional question— whether a speech-selection judgment will qualify as "speech" within the First Amendment—will shift as often as the speech situation does.

The implications of viewing free speech as disseminated cultural metaphors and images are vast. Such a view would privilege as free speech the inadvertent as well as—indeed perhaps more than—the advertent. It would formally disconnect speakers from speech. It would also countenance an active role by government in judging and managing speech in light of its social and democratic value and benefits. Carey's theory of communication as culture would convert a broad range of acts now deemed conduct into speech and vice versa.

Yet, with art, all of this seems much truer and much more fitting. Art has no single speaker. It need have no predetermined or even intended message. Its expressive significance lies in its capacity to enable an audience, over time, to transcend the text or image or movements, supplying new shape and meaning. Its speaker is, indeed, the interpreter, the audience. It must be able to speak for itself, and its meaning must often come out of thin air. Art is the opposite in most ways of the paradigm of a speaker intentionally expressing his or her own view to an audience that receives the speaker's message, not its own.

In light of *Hurley* and its implications for First Amendment protection of art, the prevalence and complexities of what speech is cannot be ignored. Should the complicated and new forms of speech growing out of new or different performative and technological conditions be allowed to override or distort the hallmark speech situation that first animated the right of free speech? Though the realities of contemporary speech complicate the idyllic picture of a single orator delivering a political speech, shouldn't the rights of the intentional, *speaking individual* be afforded the greatest degree of privilege under the First Amendment? Even if the cost of doing so is limiting the First Amendment's protection for art?

Or should the United States Supreme Court limit the application of the *Dale-Hurley* conception of First Amendment speech just to aesthetic and artistic expression? Perhaps so. But that takes us back to where we began: What is art and how do we define it?

PART 3

TRANSFORMATION

Art, it is said, involves transformation, a sensory or aesthetic quality that leads to the construction of new meaning by the audience. The object depicted in a painting, for example, is thus re-represented through an aesthetically inspired act of imagination and new perception or understanding. The following cases explore what this thing called transformation is all about, what its source is, and the extent, if any, that historical or cultural perceptions play a legitimate role in the giving of transformative meaning to a work of art. Do community values, even prejudices, effect the process of giving meaning, and even the likelihood that new, transformative meaning will occur? Are values epistemological—that is, do they reflect what we know and don't know and thus what we see and don't see? If a community sees nothing but prurience and lust in a movie, should the fact that something else is seen by people in another culture or time or place matter on the question of transformative art?

Similarly, what role do genres—categories or types—of expression play in artistic judgment? Is something history and therefore not literature; rap music and not rock? Do genres channel and limit the process of transformation of meaning? What if a song, say a rock-music song, is performed in rap instead? Should the change in genre itself qualify as artistic transformation or, instead, nothing more than theft in the form of copyright infringement?

Finally, what should government do about dangerous art or aesthetic expression, like the burning cross of the Ku Klux Klan? Is harm from art time- and culture-bound—defined by the forbidden domains of the dominant ethos—and thus, being culturally set and belief mediated, never a sufficient ground for government censorship?

Exploration here of these important and controversial questions involves the movie *Carnal Knowledge* in Albany, Georgia, 2 Live Crew's rap rendition of *Oh, Pretty Woman*, and the symbol of the burning cross, as well as a brief historical survey of art that produces intimidation, blasphemy, uncertainty, and fear.

POLITICS AND COMMUNITY

Jenkins v. Georgia

418 U.S. 153 (1974)

DO WE SEE what we choose to see, or do we also see only what we know? Are seeing and interpreting what we see conscious and political acts, or may they instead be an epistemological act reflecting only what we can see and not what we can't? This is a question Plato considered long ago.[1]

Plato, *The Myth of the Cave*

And now, I said, let me show in a figure how far our nature is enlightened or unenlightened:—Behold! Human beings living in an underground den, which has a mouth open toward the light and reaching all along the den; here they have been from their childhood, and have their legs and necks chained so that they cannot move, and can only see before them, being prevented by the chains from turning round their heads. Above and behind them a fire is blazing at a distance, and between the fire and the prisoners there is a raised way; and you will see, if you look, a low wall built along the way, like the screen which marionette players have in front of them, over which they show the puppets.

I see.

And do you see, I said, men passing along the wall carrying all sorts of vessels, and statues and figures of animals made of wood and stone and various materials, which appear over the wall?

You have shown me a strange image, and they are strange prisoners.

Like ourselves, I replied; and they [the prisoners] see only their own shadows or the shadows of one another, which the fire throws on the opposite wall of the cave?

True, he said; how could they see anything but the shadows if they were never allowed to move their heads?

And of the objects which are being carried in like manner they would only see the shadows?

Yes, he said.

And if they were able to converse with one another, would they not suppose that they were naming what was actually before them?

Very true.

To them, I said, the truth would be literally nothing but the shadows of
the images.

Plato's allegory is about meaning, about how the meaning of what we see is
a function of what we know. Our story is also about meaning: the meaning
of speech and, more specifically, the meaning of movies about sex. Is sexual
intercourse portrayed in a movie the true image, or is it instead a shadow of
another image, such as liberty and freedom, hopelessness and despair, lust
and immorality, love and intimacy?

Drawing on Plato's allegory, the question of a film's meaning is, at one level,
one of epistemology, the "theory of the nature and grounds of knowledge."

What we know is a result of what we perceive, and perception, as Plato
understood, is a subtle and complicated thing. "The eye and brain," according to Ulric Neisser, "do not act as a camera or a recording instrument. In
perceiving, complex patterns are extracted from that input and fed into the
constructive process of vision."[2] What we perceive, in other words, is not the
image before us but rather what our neurological filtering systems make of
the fragments of color and texture as they are first deconstructed and then
reconstructed in light of our experience, language, culture, and social relationships. "The perceptual object," Christian Metz said, "is a constructed
unity, *socially constructed*, and also (to some extent) a linguistic unity."[3]

The meaning of an act of sexual intercourse depicted on film, then, is a
product of the viewer's act of perception. If the viewer sees prurience but not
despair—just as a listener hearing a chirp would see a bird and not a car—can
one describe the perceptual act of ascribing that meaning as a *chosen* one, as a
self-conscious social, even political, act in which the viewer perceives a range
of possible meanings but elects only one based on personal preferences and
values and prejudices?

Or might the act of giving meaning instead be a deeply imbedded process
reflecting learned patterns of culture, language, and experience, revealing to
the viewer only the image that passes through the filtering lens of perception?
Is meaning, as Plato suggested in *The Myth of the Cave*, a shadow only, the only
thing one can see through a template that shapes the image one perceives?

The story here involves the distinction between epistemological ignorance,
on the one hand, and political preference, on the other. Which of these, igno-

rance or politics, explains a southern town's failure to perceive racism in the early 1960s? Which of these explains the same southern town's failure to perceive the art in sexual intercourse a decade later? And which of these explains a northern town's failure to perceive parody in sexual bestiality in 1995?

Should a community whose ignorance is borne of epistemology—of failure to see because the lens through which the community "saw" prevented the other meaning from being perceived, much as a template placed upon an image changes it into something else—be able to preserve its ignorance, *its* template, much as the Amish struggle to protect their children from knowledge of the outside world? Can a community be conscious of its blindness (though unaware of what it cannot see) *and* wish to preserve it? Is such an act a political act? Or is it instead a benign act entitled to respect as interpretation, the political act consisting instead in the acts of those who would force others to see that which the others cannot see?

Not always, as it turns out. But to find out when and why, one must turn to the beginning of the story, to the deep south in the civil rights era and to the mysteries of obscenity law.

CARNAL KNOWLEDGE

In 1972, the movie *Carnal Knowledge* opened in Albany, Georgia.

The theater was the Broad Avenue Cinema, located in downtown Albany. It could have been the kind of theater that many Americans then had frequented in their youth, with Saturday matinees for the children, movies that families could attend, and, of course, popcorn, soft drinks, and candy. The theater manager was Billy Jenkins, a businessman who managed the Broad Avenue Cinema for Martin Theaters, an Atlanta chain. *Carnal Knowledge* was playing in Albany and on Main Street in theaters across the country, to an audience of nearly twenty million people.

Albany was a town that believed in law and order, with an emphasis on "order." Just a few years earlier, Martin Luther King Jr. had been jailed there four times, each without incident. The civil rights movement had come to Albany, beginning in the bus depot and spreading thereafter through protest and resistance to all quarters of the community. But the police chief's unyielding demand for law *and* order had left the civil rights movement stillborn in Albany and forced to move on to other venues. And in the court of public opinion, King was humbled, and the chief was made a national hero.

The citizens of Albany, Georgia, were for the most part decent people. The community had values, and while its values can be criticized for the selectivity with which they were applied, once adopted they were fiercely embraced. Principal among Albany's values was the characteristically southern convention of courtesy and propriety in one's public demeanor. *Obscenity* was thus a dirty word, and it was given broad definition.

In 1972, Albany, Georgia, was a town possessed of its own history, its own culture, its own values. *Carnal Knowledge* was not welcome there.

Albany lies about one hundred miles south of Macon, well beyond the grasp of Atlanta's "new south" orbit. Tuscaloosa, Alabama, lies two hundred miles west, over occasionally rolling but dominantly flat southern-pine country. This is the deep south, hot and steamy in the summer but green and lush, too. Albany sits just east of the low, rolling foothills of the Piedmont Mountains' southern extreme.

The name of the town seems discordant to a northerner, who associates it with the capital of New York. Perhaps, so as not to confuse Albany, Georgia, with its northern namesake, the name is pronounced with the accent on the second *a*, which is mounted high and with a muted twang. The city's location in southern Georgia plants an image of a small, rural, steamy, racially divided southern town. But with a 1972 population of sixty thousand, forty percent of whom were African American, Albany did not fit the classic stereotype of the small, backwater, southern town whose racial divisions were enforced by a brutal sheriff and a well-placed railroad track.

Not that Albany had no racial divide. It did, and like most towns in the deep south, the divide was deeply ingrained in the culture. In Albany's case, however, the railroad track was redundant, for the racial divide was enforced not by one but by two officers of the law: a brutal sheriff *and* a hard-nosed, astute, take-all-prisoners, law-and-order police chief. During the "time of racial unrest," the brutality was provided by Sheriff Cull Campbell, an unreconstructed man given to using force to solve problems. The law and order was astutely provided by Police Chief Laurie Pritchett, described in a *Newsweek* story as "a red-haired, red-faced former paratrooper" who, by comparison with Campbell, was fairness incarnate. Howard Zinn commented, "Campbell would beat somebody bloody and Pritchett would call for an ambulance."

Albany has a notable, if not always commendable, history. President Jimmy Carter's childhood nanny, Annie Mae Rhodes, lived there, and starting in the 1930s, she traveled twenty-one miles north on Route 19 and nine miles west on Route 280 to Plains, Georgia, where she worked in the Carter home.

There, beginning at age sixteen, she supplied young Jimmy with sweet-potato pie and peanut bread ... and a lifelong friendship. When, in 1994, Annie Mae's Albany home was destroyed in a flood, President Carter turned his attention from nuclear arms in North Korea and reinstalling President Jean-Bertrand Aristide in Haiti to helping "Mrs. Annie Mae" get back on her feet with a new house from Carter's Habitat for Humanity.

Albany is also the Quail Capital of the World. Each year, the town hosts a celebrity quail hunt attended by famous sports, movie, television, and entertainment VIPs, who have included General H. Norman Schwartzkopf and test pilot Chuck Yeager. The city also bore the less-notable distinction, in 1994, as the city with the nation's highest percentage of single-parent households, just ahead of New York City.

But Albany's most notable claim to fame traces back to 1961 and 1962, in the early, grim days of the civil rights movement. It was in Albany that the fates of Reverend Martin Luther King Jr., Sheriff Cull Campbell, and Chief Laurie Pritchett were drawn together with jarring and improbable results. It all began in late 1961 in the wake of the Montgomery, Alabama, bus boycott. Three young civil rights activists, Charles Sherrod, Cordell Reagan, and Charles Jones, of the Student Nonviolent Coordinating Committee (SNCC), who were later joined in what would be known as the Albany Movement by a coalition of groups including the National Association for the Advancement of Colored People (NAACP), Congress of Racial Equality (CORE), Southern Christian Leadership Conference (SCLC), and the Baptist Ministers' Alliance, selected Albany as the first step in a coordinated effort to bring full-scale integration to cities throughout the south. Beginning with the then-segregated Albany bus depot and train station, SNCC organized sit-ins, marches, protests, and voter-registration drives to integrate Albany from top to bottom, from City Hall to department stores, restaurants to schools, bus transportation, theaters, and churches. It was nothing less than an attempt to transform the city's soul.

In the short run, at least, the city's soul resisted. But the city's reputation didn't. The *New Republic* described it in March of 1962:

> This sprightly, but mannerly and basically well-meaning south Georgia city has lately attained an undesired and at least partially undeserved national reputation as the prototype of all the relics of the Middle Ages that are stubbornly refusing to surrender to the 20th Century. This is the result of the arrests of 700 Negroes, including the Rev. Martin Luther King, on the technical charge of parading without a license in a demonstration

against segregated seating on the city bus lines. But the reputation is fantastically wrong. Albany is simply a community that has a wolf by the ears and cannot discover any safe way of letting go.

A conflict that cannot be escaped or resolved must at least be managed. Here Chief Pritchett shone through. Law and order was his theme, and he pursued it relentlessly, arresting and jailing 50 people here, 170 there, 15 people elsewhere, and so on, including on one occasion in 1962 a group consisting of Reverend King and 69 priests, ministers, and rabbis. Chief Pritchett's distinction was not to be found in his skills of arrest and prosecution (which were possessed in equal measure by many police chiefs in the south) but rather in the evenhandedness with which he applied the medicine. His answer was simply to arrest everyone, young and old, black and white, northerner and southerner, saved and sinner.

Chief Pritchett's medicine was generously doled out for every breach of the law, distributed in a matter-of-fact, nonjudgmental, and orderly way. And he did this with an eye to quelling any eruption of passion and violence, often removing the most notable of the arrestees to "living quarters" in other counties. Chief Pritchett is reported to have arrested King four times but in each instance to have released him from custody quickly enough to avoid his being made a martyr. *Everyone* who distributed handbills in violation of the Albany ordinances was arrested, whatever the message, a policy described by the *New Republic* as a "mockery of the Bill of Rights [made] thus . . . very precise, being limited principally to ideas."

For this, Chief Pritchett achieved not ignominy but fame. He was invited to a symposium sponsored by the Ford Foundation, where he shared his skills and tactics with other police chiefs. He was widely praised in the media for maintaining law and order (and, not coincidentally, segregation) in Albany. He "earned this praise from the establishment press," according to Zinn, "by simply putting into prison ('nonviolently,' as he boasted) every man, woman, and child in the city of Albany who tried to exercise their constitutional rights of free speech and assembly."

Sherrod, Reagan, Jones, and all of the others came to transform Albany's soul by lifting its shadowed veil of ignorance—wresting it away, in fact. But Albany, for the moment at least, could not be made to see so easily. It resisted being led from the cave into the light.

• • •

One gets the distinct impression upon reading about Albany, Georgia, at the time of the civil rights protests and ten years later when *Carnal Knowledge* played at the Broad Avenue Cinema that not much had changed between 1962 and 1972. To be sure, the characters were new, as was the surface appearance of the town. But the soul was still intact—a soul that consisted not only of racial division but also of small-town southern values of mannerliness, religiosity, and (always) law and order. There was, it seems, a coherence of values, a belief in limits, an old-fashioned idea of propriety in one's public conduct and, importantly, in matters related to sex.

Or so it could have seemed in early 1971 as the sheriff, in concert with the district attorney, launched a program of investigation and seizure of allegedly obscene films that were playing in Albany's movie houses. The enterprise was a systematic and relentless one intended to purge Albany of obscenity. In July and August of 1971, for example, as many as forty-three films were investigated by the sheriff's deputies. Six months later, in January of 1972, *Carnal Knowledge* got caught in the trap.

On an afternoon in early January, Lynn Stout was among the patrons who walked up to the ticket booth at the Broad Avenue Cinema. He purchased a ticket and then proceeded inside to see the movie that was playing. The movie was *Carnal Knowledge*. Stout thus joined roughly twenty million other Americans who watched a critically acclaimed film depicting the experiences of two young men whose lives were centered unrepentantly and unfulfilling on sex. The film dwelled on their sexual activities and on their conversations, which likewise were dominated, with increasing emptiness and despair, on sex. By today's standards, the film was not explicit, at least in the graphic sense to which we have become accustomed; it could best be described, instead, as sexual and sensual, representational but not explicit.

After the film was over, Stout rose from his seat and walked out of the theater with all of the other patrons who had seen *Carnal Knowledge* that afternoon. The dinner hour was fast approaching, and most of the patrons probably headed for home. But home was not Stout's destination. He headed, instead, for the district attorney's office.

On January 13, 1972, Stout returned to the Broad Avenue Cinema, this time in his official capacity as chief investigator for the Dougherty County Sheriff's Office, and he was armed with a search warrant. With 150 or so people watching *Carnal Knowledge* at the time, Stout proceeded to serve the warrant on Billy Jenkins, the manager, and seize the film. As Stout later testified, Jenkins "is the man that I served the warrant on. He's the man that gave all the orders to rewind the film and to have the people leave the theater and etcetera."

Carnal Knowledge, as it turned out, achieved a special distinction in Albany, Georgia. In the days following Stout's visits to the Broad Avenue Cinema, *Carnal Knowledge* was seized three more times in other Albany theaters. Albany, it seems, took sex seriously.

On March 6, 1972, a warrant was issued for Jenkins's arrest on a charge of distributing obscene material, a violation of Georgia's criminal code. In a remarkable example of justice's swiftness, Billy Jenkins's trial was held just fourteen days later, on March 20.

The trial itself was unexceptional as obscenity trials go. Characteristically for Albany, it was orderly, efficient, and short. Apart from testimony about the time and circumstances of the seizure and arrest, the location and admission policy of the theater (the film was R rated), and testimony about other dirty films and magazines that had not (yet, one suspects) been seized in Albany by the sheriff's officers, the only direct evidence of the film's obscenity was the film itself, which the jury, after its lunch break, was taken to view in the same Broad Avenue Cinema from which it had originally been seized.

There was nothing untoward about this rather spare proceeding, as the United States Supreme Court's decisions had said that a jury could decide on a film's obscenity based on the jury's viewing of the film, alone, without any testimony about its meaning or value. And for a lawyer defending an obscenity case in a small, rural, southern town, bringing fancy movie critics or academic types into the courtroom to lecture the jury about the "proper" standards of taste and aesthetic judgment could be risky business, indeed. After all, the citizens of Albany, Georgia, are capable of making their own aesthetic judgments.

More notable than the brevity of Billy Jenkins's trial, however, is the fact that it occurred not once, but twice. The first trial, on March 20–21 of 1972, ended in a mistrial, as one member of the twelve-person jury held out for acquittal and hung the jury. The trial judge thereupon dismissed the jury and set the matter for retrial the next day. After a second, similarly short-and-sweet trial, followed by a matinee showing at the movie house, the case was once again submitted to the jury on March 22.

The State prevailed the second time around, but not without difficulty. On the afternoon of March 22, the judge charged the second jury, and the jurors retired to the jury room for deliberations. The jury returned to the courtroom late that afternoon to report on its deliberations. The transcript reveals the following events:

THE COURT: Mr. Foreman, have you been able to reach a verdict yet?

THE FOREMAN: No, sir, we haven't.

THE COURT: Do not tell me how you stand for acquittal or conviction; tell me simply how you stand numerically.

THE FOREMAN: Well, Judge, we have had one vote, and I would say that it would be about five and ten, and that would not be for sure because some said that they were not committing themselves.

THE COURT: Well, we have this problem. Under the law, you are required to stay together, and experience has shown that if you go to a hotel to eat, that it will take about an hour and a half or something like that.

I was just wondering . . . if you would like to deliberate until around 7:30, and then we will arrange for you to be set up over at the hotel, and you can make your arrangements to spend the night and have your meal and resume your deliberations in the morning. Does that sound reasonable to you?

THE FOREMAN: Well, it will take awhile for them to set up at the hotel, and suppose we just wait in the Jury Room until they set up at the hotel, and we can just use that time to deliberate.

THE COURT: All right, we will do that. If you haven't reached a verdict at that time, then we will just let you make arrangements to spend the night and to get your meal and to resume deliberations in the morning.

THE FOREMAN: Can I ask you this? I think that a dictionary would be of some help if it were available to us.

THE COURT: Ordinarily not. There is no dictionary which has been introduced into evidence, and you can resume your deliberations, and we will let you know when arrangements are made.

Later that afternoon, the jury returned to the courtroom.

THE COURT: Mr. Foreman, are you still unable to make a verdict?

THE FOREMAN: We haven't reached a verdict or close to it.

THE COURT: You are not close to it?

THE FOREMAN: No, sir.

THE COURT: All right, arrangements have been made for whatever you want to have to eat at the hotel, and arrangements have been made for rooms.

Now, if you will, be back in the morning after having your breakfast over there and be here in the Courtroom in this box over here at 9:00 o'clock in the morning.

• • •

THE COURT [FOLLOWING A DISCUSSION WITH COUNSEL OFF THE RECORD]: If any of you should want to pick up a magazine, is there a magazine counter over there? Is there any objection to them getting a newspaper from out of town? Does anybody have any objection to that?

There being no objection, the hearing was then recessed, and the jury went to the hotel. The next morning, March 23, 1972, the jury returned to the courtroom.

THE COURT: All right, Gentlemen, if you will, go to your Jury Box and resume your deliberations.

After a period of deliberations in the jury room, the jury returned to the courtroom.

THE COURT: Mr. Foreman, do you have any communications that you would like to make?

THE FOREMAN: Well, I think we have just finally reached it, Judge. I don't know if we stayed there 'til the 4th of July that we would get much further.

THE COURT: Has there been any change?

THE FOREMAN: Yes, sir, it's 11 to 1.

THE COURT: Well, some jury is going to have to pass on this case.

THE FOREMAN: We have tried very diligently to reach a decision, and it just looks like that it is impossible. We will be glad to do whatever you wish us to do.

THE COURT: Well, try it a while longer, and if you then find that you can't do it, we will have to re-evaluate it. At this time, I—would like to reiterate that I am not trying to force a verdict, but unless somebody has some deep abiding conviction that he cannot give up through reason and thinking, a verdict should be made because both the State and the Defendant want this Jury to pass on this question.

THE FOREMAN: I can't say that it would help any, but if it could be done, if you could—could you read the charge? It might help some; I don't know.

THE COURT: Is there any particular part that you are interested in?

THE FOREMAN: I don't believe that it would be any particular part. We have tried to ascertain the particular question and haven't been able to get one.

THE COURT: I will be glad to do that if you think it would be helpful.

THE FOREMAN: I don't know whether that would be in order or not. I thought that I would ask it.

THE COURT: Do you have copies of the code section that you have requested?

THE FOREMAN: That's correct, sir.

THE COURT: I can give you the whole charge again, but I don't know that that will help because—why don't you go back to your Jury Room and discuss any specific questions that you want to ask about the charge or whatever the law may be and then write out your request, and I will tell if we can answer it.

THE FOREMAN: All right.

Following further deliberations, the jury returned to the courtroom.

THE COURT: Mr. Foreman, have you been able to reach a verdict?

THE FOREMAN: We have, Your Honor.

THE COURT: All right, Mrs. Gable, receive the verdict and publish it, please.

THE CLERK: State versus Billy Jenkins. We, the Jury, find the Defendant guilty, this 23rd day of March, William M. Dorsey, Foreman.

Following the reading of the verdict, the judge promptly dismissed the jury. With little further ado, the judge then sentenced Billy Jenkins to twelve-months' probation and fined him $750.00.

A dinner and a good night's sleep at the local hotel, combined with a gentle, last-minute nudge from the judge, appeared to have done the job.

Jenkins appealed his conviction to the Georgia Supreme Court, claiming that the jury's determination that *Carnal Knowledge* was obscene was unsupported by the evidence, and that the Georgia obscenity law violated the First Amendment. In an opinion issued on July 2, 1973, the Georgia Supreme Court, over the dissent of three of its members, held that the evidence supported the verdict of guilty, that the Georgia obscenity law was constitutional, and that Jenkins's conviction would stand.

Jenkins then sought to have his conviction reviewed by the United States Supreme Court. In the fall of 1973, the Supreme Court agreed to hear Jenkins's appeal and set his case down for oral argument on April 15, 1974. The case, formally entitled *Billy Jenkins v. Georgia*, would soon become known as the *Carnal Knowledge* case.

• • •

It is hard to imagine a less-enlightening Supreme Court oral argument than that which occurred in the *Carnal Knowledge* case. Louis Nizer, a famous and extraordinarily skilled lawyer from New York City, argued on behalf of

Jenkins. But no lawyer who is experienced at oral argument before the Court, as Nizer surely was, would expect, much less be prepared for, utter—indeed virtually dumb—silence from the bench. That is what Nizer got.

The lawyer who argued for the State of Georgia, Tony Hight, was the executive director of the District Attorneys' Association of Georgia in Atlanta. His experience was similarly strange. His oral argument was marked by long periods of silence, perhaps even indifference, from the justices, only occasionally punctuated by questions focusing almost exclusively on technical, even arcane, procedural aspects of the Georgia jury and appellate procedure. On the constitutional issues, Hight, like Nizer, was left to a monologue that, for him, too, seems to have had no audience.

The explanation for this seems clear enough. *Carnal Knowledge* was not, after all, just *any* dirty movie. It was not *Sex Kittens*, one of those anonymous stag films that inhabit seedy and decrepit theaters located on the wrong side of town. *Carnal Knowledge* played in five thousand theaters on Main Streets of virtually every American town to a huge national audience. It received national attention and critical acclaim: reviewed by Vincent Canby in the *New York Times*, written about by Studs Terkel in the *Chicago Daily News* and George F. Will in the *Washington Post*, and nominated for an Academy Award. Its actors were not the nameless and invisible denizens of the pornography trade. They were instead Jack Nicholson, Candice Bergen, Art Garfunkel, Ann-Margret—famous actors and, more to the point, serious and accomplished artists.

Carnal Knowledge may not have been the full film equivalent of *Ulysses*, but it surely wasn't the equivalent of *Sex Kittens*. It was not a movie *of* sex but one *about* sex: about the emptiness and ultimate destitution and self-destructiveness of sex as sex, about moral despair and decay.

One can safely assume that the justices knew much of this even as they gathered to vote on accepting the case for review, and one can be certain of it when, following oral argument, they gathered in their private conference room to discuss the case and cast their votes on Billy Jenkins's fate. They had been repeatedly—indeed relentlessly—reminded of the film's stature in the briefs presented to them in the case. The Author's League of America, which was only one of the organizations that filed briefs *amicus curiae* (briefs submitted by interested groups that would be affected by the decision, as "friends of the Court"), quoted from a review of *Carnal Knowledge* that appeared on July 3, 1971, in the *Saturday Review:* "Not only is the film, overall, the best acted in years; it is also the most mature of all those American films that have attempted to deal with the subject of sex in these ultra-liberated cinematic times." "[A]ll of the reviewers" of the film, the brief declared, "considered, and evaluated, *Carnal Knowledge* as a film of serious literary and artistic value." Another *amicus* brief was more direct, declaring it "inconceivable that a movie such as this—which many critics found to be one of the ten best of the year; which had a star [Ann-Margret] nominated for an Academy Award; and which scores of reviewers analyzed on a sophisticated level, debating the ideas and values which it contained—could be found to be without serious literary, artistic or political value." Yet another brief simply announced, "Twelve jurors bring no greater aesthetic expertise to *Carnal Knowledge* than they would to *Ulysses, Waiting for Godot,* or *Les Demoiselles D'Avignon.*"

Nizer, however, left no room for misunderstanding about the film's stature and quality, even at the late date of oral argument. And he didn't mince words in doing so.

MR. NIZER: Indeed, your honors, . . . it is unthinkable that this picture should be confused with hardcore pornography.

The film depicts two college students over a span of about 30 years. They grow older but they don't grow up. They are preoccupied with sex. But the picture is not. It does not involve the senses with erotica, driving out all other ideas, which is the typical characteristic of hardcore pornography.

On the contrary, it depicts the failure of the boys' lives, though they are successful in their professional careers, because they cannot establish meaningful relationships, and they are ultimately crushed by boredom, loneliness and impotency.

The film deals with the human predicament resulting from the enthronement of impersonal detachment, the inability to love, and the sequelli of cruelty and psychic illness. And this artistic treatment of this problem which besets this decade has evoked many social and philosophical studies, has been the subject of plays from Strindberg to Tennessee Williams, and . . . is why the *New York Times* reviewer called it "profound" . . . and the *Catholic Film Newsletter,* despite some reservations, called it "a perceptive and brilliant put-down of a certain lifestyle." . . . [T]he many critics throughout the country who have heaped similar praise upon this picture certainly could not have been fantasizing.

The story in *Carnal Knowledge* predominates over any visual presentation. The greatest care was lavished on sets, lighting, camera effects, musical score, brilliant ensemble acting, all under the direction of [Mike]

Nichols, acclaimed among the most gifted of cinema techratic artists who synthesized the ancient arts of painting, writing, composing, acting in a new universal medium and the resulting dominant effect of the picture as a whole is a sincere and earnest effort to create a literary and artistic work. *And to confuse that result with pornographic imbecility is cultural illiteracy* [emphasis added].

To confuse *Carnal Knowledge* with obscenity, *as the jury had*, "is cultural illiteracy." These are strong words, indeed. And they are no doubt true, too . . . depending, of course, on one's perspective—or one's culture.

But to confuse such baldly political sentiments with the makings of a Supreme Court opinion justifying the First Amendment's protection for *Carnal Knowledge*, while denying it to *Sex Kittens*, is an altogether different matter. For *Sex Kittens* could likewise be characterized as a reflection on the moral destitution of sex "for its own sake" or the centrality of sexuality to life, even in a post-Victorian but still-repressive social order. To be sure, *Sex Kittens* did not play on Main Street, it was not seen by twenty million people, its actors were not famous, its director was not acclaimed, its budget was not over three million dollars, and it was certainly not seriously reviewed in all of the right places.

But can the size of the audience or the fame of the actors or the views of critics be employed as the indicia of "quality" for purposes of the First Amendment? Can we afford to let them be so? *Sex Kittens* might have had a huge (though demographically different) audience, too. Its stars may be household names to millions of people. It, too, may have met with critical acclaim in its own critical quarters.

To rest judgments of art and quality on such factors is not to choose among films but among cultures. This is the dilemma in which the law of obscenity finds itself, even today.

• • •

After years of huddling together in a small viewing room deep in the recesses of the Supreme Court Building, watching allegedly obscene movies whose legal fate had been left to the final, unreviewable aesthetic and cultural standards of nine old men, the United States Supreme Court had at last managed, just a year before the *Carnal Knowledge* case, to delegate questions of "value" and community standards of taste in obscenity cases to the lowest reaches of the polity—to put the definition of culture squarely in the hands of the citizens who inhabit cities, towns, and communities.

The delegation was accomplished in a 1973 Supreme Court decision in the case of *Miller v. California*. The *Miller* case involved the unsolicited mass mailing by Miller of advertising brochures containing pictures of men and women engaged in group sexual activities. Miller was convicted under California's obscenity law and appealed his conviction to the Supreme Court, claiming that the pictorial advertising brochures constituted speech protected by the First Amendment.

The Supreme Court's prior obscenity decisions had said that materials falling within the legal definition of "obscenity" did not qualify as speech and were therefore not protected by the First Amendment. But those earlier decisions had also left the Court, not the jury, with the ultimate responsibility in each case to determine whether the materials were, in fact, obscene. It was this ultimate responsibility that had obliged the justices to watch the dirty movies, read the dirty books, view the dirty magazines, and, in Miller's case, to review the dirty, unsolicited, advertising brochures. By so doing, each justice was exercising his solemn constitutional duty to supervise the quality of aesthetic and political judgments rendered by juries throughout the United States.

As it turned out, the facts of the *Miller* case were not terribly important to the Court's decision in the case. This was because the Court had something very specific in mind when it decided to accept the case for review. The Court's interest lay not in Miller's sleazy brochures but instead in announcing new rules for distinguishing obscenity from expression protected under the First Amendment, rules that would limit—indeed eliminate—the Court's obligation to supervise the jury's *qualitative* judgment by delegating virtually complete authority to the jury.

To this end, the Court's opinion in *Miller* announced a new definition of obscenity. Juries were, thenceforth, instructed by the Supreme Court to base their decisions on three questions:

(1) whether, to the average person, applying *contemporary community standards*, the work taken as a whole appeals to the prurient interest;
(2) whether the work depicts or describes, *in a patently offensive way*, sexual conduct specifically defined by the applicable state law; and
(3) whether the work, taken as a whole, lacks *serious* literary, artistic, political or scientific value.

The jury would be required to answer each of these questions. And it could do so, as it did in Billy Jenkins's case, on the basis of no more evidence than the film itself. Thus, for the Albany, Georgia, jury the question was whether, "to the average person applying contemporary community standards" of Albany, *Carnal Knowledge* appealed to the prurient interest; whether, to those citizens of Albany, Georgia, who were serving on the jury, it depicted sexual conduct in a patently offensive way; and whether, taken as a whole, the jurors in Albany judged it to lack serious literary, artistic, political, or scientific value. If the Albany jurors satisfied their constitutional obligation to answer these questions and rested their judgment about the movie's obscenity on those answers, that should be the end of the matter.

So the Court thought, at least. With the value conundrum thus disposed of, the jury could be trusted to administer justice wisely, judging not "value" itself but its "lack" of seriousness. And the justices would thus be able to extricate themselves from their unseemly judicial gatherings before a small screen in the darkened basement room of the majestic Supreme Court Building, judging what they saw by their collective judicial sense of value. The small viewing room in the Supreme Court had been put out of business forever.

The difficulty posed by the *Carnal Knowledge* case was that the Court had only a narrow frame in which to judge the film's obscenity. The question was not whether *this* jury had simply reached the wrong qualitative judgment but whether a jury, apprised of sufficient evidence (the film itself, in this case) and applying the three *Miller* standards, *could possibly* conclude that *Carnal Knowledge* lacked serious value. On *this* question, the *Miller* definition had left the Court with no artillery at all, for the Court had not said that the question of value is one of law for the Court to decide; nor had the Court stated *any* criteria, except for the jury's three factual conclusions, by which such a question might be answered.

In view of this very limited and highly abstracted frame for decision, it is not surprising that the lawyers defending the film were so anxious to supply an answer to the "quality" question: it can be found, they said, in the budget, the producer, the actors, the audience, and, most troublingly, the critics. But the Supreme Court knew that to accept this answer was to reject the *Miller* test itself, to substitute the critics for the regular jury, to get itself once again into the obscenity business, this time applying not its own aesthetic judgment but its judgment about the aesthetic judgment of the film critics. To take this step would be to make a bad situation even worse by placing government judgments, troubling as they are under the First Amendment, in private hands.

The *Carnal Knowledge* case had thus "cornered" the Court. The *qualitative* judgment implicit in the Albany jury's decision was essentially unreviewable. This is the reason Justice Rehnquist had such difficulty formulating an opinion for the Court. And this explains why, when Justice Rehnquist did finally issue his opinion, *nothing* was said about "quality" or "value" or even the wrongness of the jury's judgment on these questions.

But the Court could not escape the deeper problem of quality—the one going to the film's *meaning*, not to its goodness or badness—for it was firmly entrenched in the case. Indeed, it was embedded in the very function assigned to the jury in free speech cases, for quality is, fundamentally, a function of meaning, and *meaning* is assigned by the Court's *Miller* standard to the jury. Just as one cannot judge the quality of a photograph without seeing the photographic image itself, as opposed to witnessing the scene the photographer captured; so also one cannot judge the quality of a film without "seeing" it. And "seeing" a film, as opposed to simply viewing it, is an act of interpretation, of extracting meaning, significance, and perception from what is otherwise simply a descriptive and inchoate two-dimensional representation.

The danger presented by the jury's control over the fate of *Carnal Knowledge* was not, really, the jury's ability to decide whether the film was "good" or "bad" theater, but rather the jury's ability to determine its *meaning*. Quality, in the sense of the film's goodness or badness, is utterly dependent on what the film is "seen" to be—its meaning. In Billy Jenkins's case, the jury was required to decide *what the film meant to the community and culture of Albany Georgia.* And the jury served up a direct and unambiguous—*and practically unreviewable*—answer.

QUALITY AS A FUNCTION OF MEANING

To summarize what has been said so far about the *Carnal Knowledge* case, two relatively clear propositions can be stated: (1) Quality is not an admissible factor in the free speech equation. "One man's vulgarity," as Justice Harlan had once said, must be presumed for constitutional purposes to be "another man's lyric." (2) Meaning, however, is an altogether different thing than quality. It relates not to a film's goodness or badness but rather to its very identity, to what is seen or perceived.

Meaning is thus a precondition to the interpretive judgments of quality, for quality can only be judged in terms of the message conveyed, as Plato suggested, and identifying what message is conveyed is a question of *meaning*. Meaning, the Supreme Court implies, is to be judged in the polity, by the jury, and not in the elite sanctuary of the movie critic's review or the judges' chamber.

At first blush, the two propositions about quality and meaning seem logically inconsistent. Quality and meaning, being interdependent, cannot be so
easily isolated from one another. But perhaps on further reflection, the logical
problem can be solved. Quality is, the Court implies, a function of meaning
but not vice versa. Meaning, in other words, can first be assigned, and by so
doing, a smaller universe of possible interpretation is defined within which
questions of quality can be judged (or not, as the case may be).

In some instances, then, "one man's vulgarity" *cannot* be "another man's
lyric." The adage holds true only if both men are reading from the same
script; if, that is, they are both reflecting on the quality of the same message.
If not, the "lyric" stems not from a different interpretation of the "vulgarity's"
quality but from an altogether different message that contains no vulgarity.
In such cases, differences of opinion are not based on different standards of
taste but on the fact that altogether different scripts are being read: one in
shadow, one in light.

This is precisely what happened in the *Carnal Knowledge* case . . . with the
Court's blessing. Upon hearing the evidence and viewing the film, the jury
was instructed, in effect, to "see" the film—to interpret it and give it meaning.
The standard the jury was to bring to this task was that of the "community,"
which one can take to mean either (1) the values, habits, and culture of Albany,
Georgia, or (2) the shared values, habits, and culture of the members of the
jury, drawn from Albany.

The jury was instructed to "see" the film *Carnal Knowledge* through the
standards of the community, to assign it *meaning* by superimposing the
template of Albany's community standards upon the screen, extracting the
message, or meaning, from that which filtered through. The jury's template
might, of course, have allowed a message of despair and meaningless of a life
dominated by sex without love to show through. It might have revealed the
same meaning when applied to *Sex Kittens*, as well.

But a different template of community standards, perhaps the one actually
used by the *Carnal Knowledge* jury, may have been more constricting, allowing much less to be "seen" and thus narrowing the jury's range of possible
interpretation. Such a template might have yielded a very different meaning,
one that revealed little more than the excitement of sexual lust (punctuated,
though without significance, by representations or spoken lines about despair), or one that legitimated sexual promiscuity (even though at the risk of
boredom), or one that contained a message of male domination and female
sexual subordination. This is the template, perhaps, of the community that

had not been lifted from the cave to confront, and thus to "know," the new image revealed by the light of the sun.

With the meaning thus revealed by the template, the *Carnal Knowledge* jury was left to judge, *in light of its assigned meaning,* whether the film, *taken as a whole,* appealed to the prurient interest; whether it depicted in a patently offensive way sexual conduct specifically defined by Georgia law; and whether the film, *taken as a whole,* lacked serious literary, artistic, political, or scientific value. If for the Albany jury that judged *Carnal Knowledge* the template revealed a meaning equivalent to that conveyed by *Sex Kittens,* it is hardly surprising that *Carnal Knowledge* was judged to be obscene. More important, it would be virtually impossible to reverse the jury's decision without the Court once again going into the movie business.

The Supreme Court was able to avoid this result. It reversed Billy Jenkins's conviction only by relying on a technicality. Obscenity, the Court said, must in all cases involve the depiction of sexual conduct, a term that the Court drew from the specific language of the *Miller* test and then took literally. In *Carnal Knowledge,* much and varied sexual conduct was implied. Its concrete imagination could not be escaped. But the act of sexual intercourse, to state but one possible example, was not *literally* and explicitly depicted on the screen. No matter how powerful the film's evocation, how prurient its appeal, how offensive its content, how lacking its value, no film that stops short—just short, as we know from experience—of actual depiction of intercourse, the Court said, is obscene.

This is, surely, a technicality only and an unconvincing one. It bears no sensible relationship to the community's standards or to the presence or absence of serious literary, artistic, political, or scientific value. It yields the incongruous—obscene seems a more fitting word, actually—result that *Sex Kittens,* if craftily filmed to avoid any frames showing the physical act of penetration, must be allowed to play in Albany, but *Carnal Knowledge,* if it contains but one such graphic sequence, need not. This peculiar result flies in the face of the very purpose of the *Miller* test. For this reason, if no other, it is small wonder that Justice Rehnquist had such apparent difficulty crafting the Court's opinion.

But setting the technicality of the *Carnal Knowledge* opinion aside, the more basic questions raised the Court's community standards approach are clearly revealed. Why, we should ask, ought the question of *meaning* be left to the community? Are there no limits that can be practically enforced on the range of meanings that community standard templates reveal?

The first question has many answers. Communities *do* have different standards borne of different cultures, histories, aspirations, and values. Albany, Georgia, is very different from Albany, New York. Times Square is even different from Wall Street. Must the maintenance or destruction of those differences, many of which are valuable, be left only to market forces? Times Square wouldn't sell on Wall Street, which is why the two places are different. But if a foolish entrepreneur wants to try a little Times Square in Wall Street, must we let him do it?

We know from our experience that the same message often means different things in different places and to different people. Thus, a rule that flatly protects all sexually explicit speech, for example, would not, in fact, be equal in its consequences. A rule that prohibited talk of fornication, for example, would affect a religious community differently than it would affect a community devoted to sexual liberation. Likewise, a rule that permitted all uses of a racial epithet would yield uneven results depending on who expressed it, how it was expressed, or whether it was used in a community of white supremacists, in an integrated community, or in the targeted racial community by members of that community toward each other.

No rule, in short, can be crafted in a way that assigns only one meaning or even a range of meanings, unless exceptions to it are allowed. Given this, the issue of the appropriate role of the jury boils down to whether we must simply accept, in the name of the First Amendment, a rule that all speech is absolutely protected notwithstanding the unfortunate but necessary fact that some of its meanings will surely produce harm, or whether room may instead be left for exceptions in light of the certainty of harm flowing from different meanings in different circumstances.

The first alternative, absolute protection for all speech, has never been accepted by the Supreme Court, and it isn't likely to be adopted in the foreseeable future. It is not, after all, a violation of the Constitution to use zoning to keep adult movie theaters from setting up shop in residential neighborhoods, nor is government prohibited from restricting public-school classroom activities to education, or from regulating the time and manner of telemarketing in the interest of preserving our solitude. Even Justice Hugo Black, the First Amendment "Absolutist," left room for government to regulate the speech activities that could take place in public libraries or around courthouses or in courtrooms.

So absent a constitutional revolution, we are left with the second alternative: that some exceptions to the freedom to speak can be made in recognition, among other things, of the differential harms that a given instance of speech may produce in different times or places or communities. And this alternative leads, finally, to the Court's solution in the obscenity arena, for if exceptions can be made in recognition of differences in meaning and harm, we must ask: who will be assigned the task of making them?

The Court's answer in *Miller* was that exceptions should be crafted by the jury and the community, not by the legislature, not by the judges, not by the speakers, not by the invisible hand of the free market, and *certainly not by the critics*. And the common-sense reason for selecting the jury flows naturally from the recognition that harm, like quality, is a function of meaning, that meaning is a product of interpretation, that only that which can be seen can be interpreted, and that interpretation based on shared values is preferable, because it is more restrained, than interpretation at the level of the individual, and in any event interpretation at the community level is but a more finely tuned approximation of the exceptions that would be carved at the legislative, judicial, or executive level.

If this be so—if, in other words, the Albany jury's decision was an epistemological one, concerning what it saw and therefore knew, and not a political one, concerning what it preferred—who but the jury and the community is better situated to judge the questions of meaning from which conclusions about value and harm spring? By what reasoning would we judge the Georgia legislature more able than a jury in Albany to ascertain the consequences *Carnal Knowledge* would produce in Albany, Georgia?

• • •

Surely the Supreme Court would not have reversed Billy Jenkins's conviction on a technicality if an alternative were available to it. But if we accept, as the Court did, the correctness of the jury's role in defining the template through which the film would be seen, we must confront a second question: Is there any ground upon which the jury's range of discretion can be effectively limited?

At one level, of course, we know that there is. If the *Jenkins* case had involved *Ulysses* rather than *Carnal Knowledge*, few would doubt that the case involved something very different than *Sex Kittens* and that a template yielding the same meaning for both is simply, because obviously, wrong, even in Albany, Georgia. This is the very point Nizer was making with his crude but effective charge of "cultural illiteracy." It is also the point Justice Potter Stewart made some years ago when he said, in obvious frustration, "I can't define obscenity, but I know it when I see it"—to which he might have added with respect to *Carnal Knowledge*—and this isn't it!

But knowing that the jury had gone too far, that the template was simply wrong, is an entirely different matter from explaining why that is so. The Supreme Court doesn't simply decide cases. It gives reasons for its decisions, reasons that relate to the purposes and principles of the Constitution, and reasons that provide guidance for the decision of future cases. So mere foot-stomping won't do. .

Some general limits that might be placed on the jury's authority are obvious. One of them is representativeness. If the jury is to make a value- and culture-based judgment for the community, it ought to reflect the community for which it speaks. The jury ought to know, also, whether the template it selects is being applied evenhandedly and thus in pursuit of the community's standards or whether the pattern of prosecution suggests selective enforcement. If the latter, something other than the community's values is at work, and the jury's template, no mater how appropriate, should not serve as a shield for other aims. These are enforceable, practical limits that could be judicially applied to limit the jury's power, but thanks to the example of Police Chief Pritchett in an earlier time, in the *Carnal Knowledge* case (where the second jury was all male but racially diverse and where the law enforcement effort was anything but discriminating or selective), they were of doubtful utility.

Another possibility for limiting the jury's discretion is to require that the jurors hear the judgment of the critics so that, even if they don't accept it, they are aware of the range of possible meanings the film has been given. Here, however, the problems are substantial. If the question is really one of the community's standards, how are the critics' interpretations relevant? If they are relevant only for comparative—for educational—purposes, can the jury's use of them be so limited? The danger, of course, is not that the jury will be swayed to the critics' view but exactly the opposite: that the jury's reaction to their testimony will cause a backlash, reinforcing the jurors' conviction that the everything-goes moral relativism of Times Square should at least be confined to Times Square and certainly not exported to Albany. This, of course, is the very reason that a defense lawyer in a case such as Billy Jenkins's might decide that prudence is the better course. Nothing now prevents the defense from introducing such evidence, but requiring that it do so would be an unprecedented and unwise step.

So we are left with nothing more than "I can't define obscenity, but I know it when I see it . . . and this isn't it." There is precious little intellectual satisfaction in this ending. But it is the end of Billy Jenkins's story. His conviction was reversed, for which we can perhaps be grateful, but little was done in the course of his case about the still-intractable "obscenity problem."

IMAGES

The Supreme Court has worked mightily to extricate itself from the movie business—from the rite of gathering together nine wise and well-educated men and women of the law in the darkened room in the basement of the Supreme Court. In this, at least, they seem to have succeeded, for the moment at least. The *Carnal Knowledge* case left the jury's power intact and virtually unreviewable, a necessary result if closing the Court's theater was the ultimate aim. But we are entitled to ask: at what cost?

Equally important is the obverse question: What are community values, and are they such a bad thing?

Image One: Meaning or Culture

Meaning is a function of culture, values, aspirations, and experience, derived through a process of interpretation. In "Foucault's Pendulum," Umberto Eco quotes Elphias Levi, writing in 1856: "Allegory, mother of all dogmas, is the replacement of the seal by the hallmark, of reality by shadow; it is the falsehood of truth, and the truth of falsehood."

Is there "truth" in the meaning of *Carnal Knowledge*? Is that truth, as the citizens of Albany, Georgia, would have it, moral decay? Or is it, as feminists would have it, "glorification of violence in sex," the normalization of the abnormal, the representation of women and children as dominated sexual objects? Is it the truth of falsehood or the falsehood of truth?

If, in pondering these questions, the conclusion is that the only "truth" *is* allegory and that because there are many possible allegories, there are many truths, must we then also conclude that all allegories must be admitted to the marketplace? Or might we conclude instead that because there is no *real* truth but only allegory, we violate no truth by selecting the preferred allegory and rejecting the others?

The jury's template is its preferred allegory, grounded in the collective preferences and values and aspirations and norms of the community: Albany, Georgia; New York City; intellectuals; parents; feminists. Feminists do not see the pornographic representation of women as dominated sex objects as a political statement. They instead see pornography as an allegory, a template through which the values and aspirations of the audience are shaped, through which the community's preferred norms of family, decency, and equality are wrested from it. The template that reveals women as dominated sex objects is not theirs or the community's. It is instead the knowledge that comes from being forced to see the light. The First Amendment, they argue, should not be read to prohibit the community's insistence on *its own* template, its own allegory. The *political* fight about the rightness of the community's template—are we a community of dominance or peace, equality, or violent submission—can take place in the open, free, and reasoned marketplace of argument. To consign the argument to allegory is unnecessary and, more important, dangerous. Was this what the National Endowment for the Arts' decency and respect for American values fight was all about—not politics but templates, not knowledge but allegory?

For many, the feminists' view—just like Jesse Helms's—is little more than foolishness, an unprecedented division of freedom of speech into separate camps of reason and emotion, argument and allegory, and an unjustified fear of the power of stories to move us, unconsciously and therefore surreptitiously, to adopt attitudes that we would not, under the civilizing influence of reason, consciously embrace.

But for others, the feminists' view has the ring of truth to it: We raise our children on those allegories that teach the right lessons, we distinguish conduct, which is often emotion incarnate, from the more dispassionate and reasoned forms of speech, our institutions—schools, libraries, businesses, governments—are large allegories of civilization. Prohibiting *Carnal Knowledge* in Albany, Georgia, is not an act of censorship but instead one of authority over the preferred allegory, a claim of right to the image seen rather than the image others would force us to see.

Many devotees of the First Amendment, of course, would view the matter very differently. For them, rejection of the Albany jury's verdict is a necessary step in the struggle against ignorance. After all, to borrow from Plato's allegory, wasn't it to *make* them "see the light" that people were forced from the cave? And after they were acclimated to the light and beheld its new wonders—after they saw the objects of which they had formerly seen only the shadows—didn't the people reflect on their fellows who were still in the cave and "pity them," preferring "to endure anything, rather than think as they do and love after their manner"?

But Plato's allegory is neither as simple nor as comforting as this view of the First-Amendment-as-Light would have it, for it turns out that lightness and darkness are epistemologically the same, opposite sides of the same coin, so to speak, neither superior to the other. While revealing new images to the people who emerged from the cave, the light also blinded them to what they had seen before. For Plato, light and dark represent the falsehood of truth and the truth of falsehood, a closed circle revealed at his story's end:

Image Two: Pornography as Politics

> Imagine once more, I said, such a one coming suddenly out of the sun to be replaced in his old situation; would he not be certain to have his eyes full of darkness?
> To be sure, he said.
> And if there were a contest, and he had to compete in measuring the shadows with the prisoners who had never moved out of the den, while his sight was still weak, and before his eyes had become steady (and the time which would be needed to acquire this new habit of sight might be very considerable), would he not be ridiculous? Men would say of him that up he went and down he came without his eyes; and that it was better not even to think of ascending; and if any one tried to loose another and lead him up to the light, let them only catch the offender, and they would put him to death.
> No question, he said.

If we can understand the disturbing allegory of sexual violence and domination and the felt need to block it out, is it such a stretch to understand the allegory of *Sex Kittens* in the jury's interpretation of *Carnal Knowledge*? If the template used by the jury in the *Carnal Knowledge* case is a true reflection of values of mannerliness, propriety, religiosity, and order, can we deny the good-faith intention of the jury in Albany, Georgia, to guard its template from subversion by a competing allegory, the meaning of which its template would distort?

Perhaps not. Perhaps, when it comes to speech, templates should be inadmissible. But even if this is so, we can at least hope that the template used by the Albany jury was truly based on decency, respect, love. For if by 1972 this had become the preferred allegory in Albany, we might conclude that its soul had at last been transformed.

• • •

Carnal Knowledge was not obscene. The Supreme Court said as much even as it left the discretion of the jury intact. *Carnal Knowledge* simply did not lie inside the boundary within which jury discretion based on community tolerance and values could be unreviewably exercised. That is, it did not *explicitly* depict sexual conduct, a definitional precondition to a finding of obscenity.

But the important thing is that within the boundary, the jury serves a constitutionally acceptable role in judging the community's standards of sexual tolerance and aesthetic taste. This was a duty taken seriously by the two Albany juries who were asked to decide Jenkins's fate. The first jury deadlocked. The second jury labored at length in reaching its guilty verdict. The juries' job was to judge (1) whether, to the average person, applying *contemporary community standards*, the work taken as a whole appeals to the prurient interest, (2) whether the work depicts or describes, *in a patently offensive way*, sexual conduct specifically defined by the applicable state law, and (3) whether the work, taken as a whole, lacks *serious* literary, artistic, political, or scientific value. The first two criteria explicitly ask the jury to look to the community's standards of taste. The third factor—serious artistic value, viewed as a whole—does, too, although inferentially. A juror must consider artistic value on his or her own, but in doing so the juror will inevitably draw on the attitudes and tastes common to the community—the community's template, if you will. And while one can read the third criterion as leaving the "artistic value" question, at least in part, to the courts, not to the jury, the Supreme Court has not so applied its own standard. And if it did, the Court would be right back in the movie-viewing business, thus negating the very objective of the *Miller* standard.

So community standards, community templates, community values can and do *and should* make a difference. Local, community-based values are permissible standards of judgment under the First Amendment, even as to art. Does this mean that nude barroom dancing can be deemed different, artistically, from Karen Finley's performances? Do a community's standards of decency and respect play a useful role in making judgments about art? Is a community's tolerance for homoerotic depictions a valid consideration in a work's qualification as speech under the First Amendment? How about depictions of sexual activity that implant attitudes of subordination and inferiority of women? Can a community, acting for itself and imposing its standards on no other community, protect itself against values of homosexuality, of sexual inequality, with which it disagrees?

In thinking about the role that "community" might play in judging art and aesthetics under the First Amendment, a number of questions must be considered. First, is there really any alternative to some form of community in judging whether science, literature, or, in the current case, art and aesthetic expression qualify for protection under the First Amendment? Some people argue that there is an alternative: protect all speech regardless of its type or quality because that is what the First Amendment says and means. Yet, this "absolutist" position is hard to defend. Definitional distinctions can't be avoided in free speech cases. Is the activity at issue "speech" or not? Kicking my dog is presumably not speech, even though it expresses a message to my dog and others witnessing the event. The First Amendment offers precious little help with this question. It doesn't define speech. And those who wrote it clearly didn't intend defamation, or inciting immediate violence, or copyright infringements, or fraud, or obscenity to be speech protected by the free speech guarantee. So distinctions have to be made. The question is simply, "By whom?"

The absolutist position has another serious problem. It treats all forms and kinds of speech equally. Yet, it is pretty clear from the First Amendment's history in the hands of the framers and the Supreme Court that not all constitutionally protected speech is treated the same. Political speech, for example, can lay claim to an unbroken historical record of serving a critical function and therefore occupying a preferred place under the Constitution. Commercial speech, though protected, is given less protection, perhaps because of its private and self-serving nature and the risks of deception. The same is true for "indecent" speech, a type of speech going to its manner of expression, not its substance. Speech by government is important to the operation of the political process, yet it is not considered speech protected by the First Amendment, and the government is not considered a constitutionally protected speaker. And, of course, artistic and aesthetic speech has historically enjoyed a troubled status as speech protected by the First Amendment.

If these and other kinds of definitional and balancing judgments are well established and unavoidable, then the question is not whether distinctions in the meaning of speech or the calibration of its protection can be avoided, for they can't. The question instead is when and how and by whom the distinctions should be crafted and enforced. And this, in turn, means that the true issue is which community—lawyers, judges, critics, sociologists, jurors, nation, state, town, and the like—is best equipped to make the judgments with respect to particular types of speech claims. The *Miller* decision splits the decision, leaving part of it to legislators, part to judges, and the rest to jurors. Should the artistic and aesthetic speech question be treated similarly or placed elsewhere? If so, where and to whom?

At first blush, the most likely place to leave such vexing questions as whether an expression is art and serious art when viewed as a whole (a snippet of Shakespeare won't do) is to the legislative process, the heart of democracy and the best locus of shared values. But the legislative process is unfortunately broad: broadly elected and thus hardly an approximation of a coherent community and broad in the sense that it deals in the abstract, not the specific. Moreover, a critical function of the First Amendment is to serve as a check on the legislative process and product, which can too easily be swayed by immediate passion and concentrated interests. These defects also suggest at best a limited role even for regional and local legislative bodies, like city councils. The legislative branch is well equipped to deal with whether obscenity, for example, ought to be illegal, but the application of that policy to a particular expression is too individuated, too adjudicative, to be left there in its entirety.

Courts, of course, adjudicate specific facts and controversies. Judges are varyingly independent of the legislative process and less susceptible to passions of the moment. Judges are also well trained and smart. But they are trained and experienced in the law, not in art, philosophy, literature, aesthetics. And they represent no real community whose habits, history, and values can be ascertained and applied. For Holmes, judges were perhaps the most ill-suited candidates for decisions about art and aesthetics. They can state the law and instruct a jury but more than that may be well beyond their ken.

Critics are, of course, trained and experienced in art and aesthetics. They make their living judging them. But the critics are not a community, in the sense we are using the term: they often disagree vehemently, their personal judgments are just that, right or wrong. Would it be appropriate in a democracy to turn over such important judgments to individuals who bear no democratic responsibility? Even if we were to create an "Art Court," it is hard to imagine its decisions being consistent and coherent, much less sufficiently explainable to satisfy demands of democratic accountability.

Would it be better to have an art council selected locally, consisting of people who purport to know something about art? Or an art jury? There is an elitist quality to such a body. But more basic is the fact that the identification of local community values and tolerances seems hardly to fall within the expertise of such a group. How but through the community's voice—rich to poor, black to white, Asian or Native American, men to women, parent or not—can appeal to prurient interests or patent offensiveness or even artistic seriousness be judged? In these senses, it is the representative cross-section of the community selected (in theory at least) to serve on a jury that is equipped to make such judgments, and that is limited in its power and its ability to succumb to passions of the moment by a rule that it can only decide by unanimous agreement. Otherwise, the claimed freedom of speech is secure.

There are other serious questions about who should decide, but we will put them aside, because whatever the suggestion, it needs to be subjected to scrutiny not unlike that given above. Instead, we will turn to a final and even more complicated question. What is meant by community? Is it the town from which jurors are selected? Small towns versus large ones or, instead, neighborhoods in the latter case? Is it a group of people who share common values and interests and aspirations, like a religious community, a business community, a community of educators or parents? The Supreme Court hasn't really answered this question. Instead, when questions of art or aesthetics come to court, the default answer is the jurisdiction, typically local, from which juries are drawn.

Many, if not most, such communities don't really have widely held values and standards of tolerance. Few would qualify if near unanimity were required. Was Albany, Georgia, a community that qualified? Was its comparatively small size and shared history and its apparent commitment to good (law-abiding, at least) behavior for all citizens enough to give its jury the benefit of the doubt? What about Bellingham, Washington, whose needed values and standards must not only include prurience and offensiveness and seriousness about art and literature but also shared standards about gender equality and the shaping of people's attitudes? How about a very large city, like Chicago? Or a college town like Iowa City, Iowa, which is as ethnically, racially, internationally, sexually, and ideologically as diverse as almost any other town the size of Albany, Georgia? Perhaps New York City and Iowa City, among many others, are simply disqualified from enforcing community standards on most aesthetic or artistic questions. For them, whether a challenged expression is art or not, prurient or offensive or not, decent and respectful of American values or not has already been decided. If anything goes, then anything is art. But only in New York City and Iowa City. Albany, Georgia, is not stuck with New York City's or Iowa City's values or culture. The First Amendment, for them, does not force them from the cave into the light or vice versa. Not, at least, at the hands of legislatures, lawyers, judges, or critics.

The Supreme Court's solution in *Miller*, like Congress's solution for the NEA, is not perfect.

But if judgments must be made about art and aesthetics, is there a better solution?

GENRE: RAP AND ROCK

Campbell [2 Live Crew] v. Acuff-Rose
510 U.S. 569 (1994)

LUTHER CAMPBELL is a deeply divided soul. To most people, he is one of the famous, disgusting, dirty, dehumanizing pioneers of gangster rap. Under the name Luke Skywalker and with his group 2 Live Crew, he was perhaps the most controversial rap music artist of the late twentieth century. His persistent theme was raw sex, sexism, misogyny, and filthy images and lyrics spoken from and for the black street-gang culture.

Campbell, however, is also a husband and father who now lives in the suburbs and spends a great deal of his time and money on supporting education for African-American youth. He supports after-school football and summer Little League programs in Florida, college scholarships, and gives generously to assist the homeless and AIDS victims. His wife, Tameka, says, "All the nasty words and stuff, that is what he does. It's his product, but I know the person behind that. He is sweet and gentle."[1]

Luke's two souls have not exactly existed side by side. The nastier side was first dominant with his rise to fame in the 1980s with 2 Live Crew. This side of Luke began in a poor, black part of Miami, where he was born, and burst forth with his gang involvement, his growing attachment to music as a youth, and his sudden turn to fame with the release by his small independent label, Skywalker Records, of *Throw the D*, a sexually graphic song described carefully by the *New York Times* as a "propulsive, uptempo dance tune with a monstrous, reggae-style bass line."[2] Then, in 1986, 2 Live Crew released an album named *We Want Some Pussy*, which sold over a half-million copies. The group was on its way. In 1987, *Move Somethin'* was released, with songs like "S & M" and "Head, Booty, and Cock." It sold over a million copies. Fame and fortune followed.

The fame was not always unblemished. In 1989, 2 Live Crew released the album titled *As Nasty as They Wanna Be*, which was laced with oral sex and anal sex and sexual violence against women, accompanied by "Ghetto Bass," as Campbell described its "bottom-heavy sound."[3] Shortly after its release, *As Nasty as They Wanna Be* was judged obscene by a federal judge in Florida. At about the same time, Campbell, along with a black record-store owner and two other members of 2 Live Crew, were prosecuted on obscenity charges. Campbell "launched a media offensive" portraying himself as an honest, hardworking man who was trying to get ahead in the American culture and economy. He told *USA Today*, "I know that in the world today there are a lot of people who just don't want to see a young black man succeed." In Campbell's obscenity trial, Henry Louis Gates, now of Harvard, testified, describing 2 Live Crew as a group engaged in "sexual carnivalesque" whose "off-color nursery rhymes are part of a venerable Western tradition."[4] The federal judge's ruling of obscenity was reversed, and in the criminal prosecution, the jury acquitted Campbell and the other defendants.

The obscenity prosecution had generated attention throughout the nation and, especially, in the black community and the rap community. As Campbell saw the matter, "To get to the record store to pull my record off the shelf, the Broward police had to drive by stores selling X-rated videos, clubs with X-rated live sex shows and stores selling magazines like *Penthouse* and others—but they just singled out my record, produced by a black group with their own independent black company. Now if that's not racism, what is?"[5] Sales of the album soared to over three million copies, and Luke Skywalker Records "became the most successful independent label in the United States."[6]

Yet, *As Nasty as They Wanna Be* led to fame in another and less desirable way. In July of 1989, 2 Live Crew followed it with an album titled *As Clean as They Wanna Be*, a play on the earlier famous *Nasty* album and a comment on the legal travails and ultimate successes it had achieved. A cut titled "Pretty Woman" was included on the album. It was the tenth cut, far from prominently located and hardly noted on the album itself. But it would prove to be real trouble. Luke had written the rap song "Pretty Woman." But not from scratch. It was instead a takeoff of the famous rock ballad "Oh, Pretty Woman," by Roy Orbison and William Dees. Accompanied by the famous guitar riffs, the lyrics of Luke's rap version started the same but soon took a decisive turn.

Pretty Woman
(as recorded by 2 Live Crew)
Pretty woman walkin' down the street
Pretty woman girl you look so sweet

Pretty woman you bring me down to that knee
Pretty woman you make me wanna beg please
Oh, pretty woman

...

Bald headed woman girl your hair won't grow
Bald headed woman you got a teeny weeny afro
Bald headed woman you know your hair could look nice
Bald headed woman first you got to roll it with rice
Bald headed woman here, let me get this hunk of biz for ya
Ya know what I'm saying you look better than rice a roni
Oh bald headed woman[7]

Luke variously described his song "Pretty Woman" as a parody or satire of "Oh, Pretty Woman" and as a comment on the innocent 1960s when the sweet ballad was first released.

The Orbison and Dees song "Oh, Pretty Woman" had been a big hit in 1964. It had helped make Orbison a star, and it set his style and artistic identity in the public mind. No doubt partly because of the tragic death of his wife and two of his children in the late 1960s, Orbison's career peaked soon thereafter, but "Oh, Pretty Woman" remained universally known, and both it and Roy Orbison began a comeback in the 1980s. In the midst of his comeback, in 1988, Orbison died. The copyright owner of "Oh, Pretty Woman" was Acuff-Rose Music, the preeminent Nashville music publisher and Orbison's publisher for virtually all of his career.

Campbell had written the self-described parody or satire of "Oh, Pretty Woman" in early 1989, shortly after Orbison's death. In June or July (the date is disputed), 2 Live Crew notified Acuff-Rose Music that it had written the song and would credit Acuff-Rose, Orbison, and Dees with ownership and authorship and pay a fee for recording and releasing it as their own. Acuff-Rose refused the offer and declined to authorize a parody of the song. Almost simultaneously with (if not before) Acuff-Rose's rejection of the offer, 2 Live Crew released its rap version of the song, titled "Pretty Woman," on the *As Clean as They Wanna Be* album.

Over the next year or so, the album, which contained but did not highlight "Pretty Woman," sold about 250,000 copies—disappointing sales given 2 Live Crew's earlier successes. Toward the end of the album's first year, Acuff-Rose Music sued 2 Live Crew for copyright infringement in federal court in Nashville. Acuff-Rose was unsuccessful in the district court, but on appeal to the circuit court, the decision was reversed in favor of Acuff-Rose and against

Luther Campbell on the ground that 2 Live Crew's "parody" was dominantly motivated by profit, and, thus, "Pretty Woman" was not a fair use permitted under the copyright law, parody or not. Following the circuit court decision, Campbell appealed to the United States Supreme Court. The Court agreed to hear the case and set it down for oral argument on November 19, 1993.

• • •

A note about our forthcoming discussion is warranted at this point. The *Campbell* case, which this story will refer to as the 2 *Live Crew* case, is a copyright case arising under the federal copyright statute. This story, therefore, first will view the protection afforded art and the related concept of genre as it arises under copyright law. Then art and genre will be discussed from the more general First Amendment perspective, drawing on 2 *Live Crew* to ask a broader set of questions about art and aesthetic expression.

As it turns out, this initial focus on copyright is hardly an awkward way to get to the constitutional questions for two important reasons. First, copyright law and principles are, of themselves, of great importance to art and its protection. Understanding copyright will therefore be quite useful. Second, and perhaps even more important, copyright law is now in the early stages of change in light of the sometimes-competing rights under the First Amendment. Copyright law was traditionally seen to be consistent with free speech law because copyrights provide a valuable incentive for the production of new speech. This was largely true when, beginning with the Copyright Act of 1790, copyright protected only writings of an informative nature that the author had registered for copyright protection, and the copyright lasted for a fourteen-year period, renewable for another fourteen years. Today, however, copyright covers a broad expanse of creative activity, including film, painting, sculpture, and other artistic forms of expression, as well as electronic communications. And today, copyright protection is automatic whether applied for or not and extends for a period of seventy years after the death of the author.[8]

The broadening of copyright law's reach has resulted in increasingly obvious clashes with First Amendment values of access to ideas and literary and artistic freedom to build upon prior work of others.[9] To cushion the conflicts, Congress added to the copyright law exceptions for "fair use," allowing limited copying, use, and reproduction for many forms of "criticism, comment, news reporting, teaching . . ., scholarship, or research." In the 2 *Live Crew* case, the question is Campbell's use of "Oh, Pretty Woman" for purposes of criticism through the genre of parody. But "fair use" is proving to be inadequate to reconcile the competing copyright and First Amendment interests, and therefore the Supreme Court is being forced more openly to rely on free speech principles in judging the constitutionality of provisions of the copyright law. Over time, First Amendment protections will increasingly become part and parcel of the interpretation of the copyright law. The discussion here of the 2 *Live Crew* case, therefore, will often rest on principles of free speech.

The focus, of course, is art and aesthetic expression—its definition and protection under the First Amendment. More specifically, with the 2 *Live Crew* case, inquiry will focus on *genre*, a term that includes such diverse categories as rap, rock, parody, satire, and irony. What, precisely, does *genre* mean? Is *genre* a synonym for *transformation*—the creation of meaning beyond mere representation to new sensory or cognitive meaning? Or is genre a descriptive but not substantive term that simply draws a line between new expression versus outright theft and no more? Can genre, as employed in 2 *Live Crew*, help one judge a work or performance as art, as with a distinction between Karen Finley's performance art, viewed as a genre, and barroom dancing as a distinct genre in *Barnes?* Or is genre, while perhaps analytically useful, also a dangerous criterion when applied to art, because art is constantly changing and in flux, and genre categories imposed on it therefore risk ossification of art itself?

In the end, one may conclude that genre provides a neutral concept that is of some but limited usefulness in identifying and judging artistic and aesthetic expression. On the other hand, one may find that a different standard, like sensory and representational transformation, is a purer and better approach and that genre is little more than a cultural form or habit without useful intrinsic qualities of its own.

• • •

The justices who would hear *Luther R. Campbell v. Acuff-Rose Music*, or the 2 *Live Crew* case, were a mixture of new and old. William Rehnquist was the Chief Justice, a widely liked and effective Chief. He had been appointed to the Court in 1972 and confirmed as Chief Justice in 1986. Harry Blackmun was the most senior justice, having been appointed in 1970. He would retire at the end of the Term in 1994, just four or so months after the case was decided. The other two "old hands" on the Court were John Paul Stevens, appointed in 1975 and a liberal justice, and Sandra Day O'Connor, appointed in 1981 as the first woman justice and, over time, a most influential one who often cast the deciding vote in close cases. The less-senior justices were Antonin Scalia, Anthony Kennedy, David Souter, Clarence Thomas, and Ruth Bader Ginsburg. Justices Scalia and Thomas were generally seen as conservatives, Justices Souter and Ginsburg as liberals, and Justice Kennedy as a moderate who joined Justice O'Connor in the middle of the Court. The justices were an experienced and talented group, but as the membership had changed over the prior ten or fifteen years, the justices had become more self-centered and committed to their individual judicial philosophies. The Court was less collegial and more argumentative and disputatious in its opinions, even when differences among the justices really didn't have anything to do with the outcome of cases. Perhaps as a result of this, oral argument before the Court became more animated and exciting, though the lawyers standing before the high bench representing their clients would not have described oral argument as really enjoyable. It often took on the character of an intellectual jousting match.

The two lawyers appearing before the Court in the 2 *Live Crew* case were able and experienced. Luther Campbell, a.k.a. Luke Skywalker, was represented by Bruce Rogow of Ft. Lauderdale, Florida. The copyright holder of the "Oh, Pretty Woman" song was Acuff-Rose Music Inc., represented by Sidney S. Rosdeitcher of New York, New York. The lawyers faced a challenging Court and a challenging argument, for the 2 *Live Crew* case raised many altogether new questions that the justices would have to resolve. Very shortly after 10:00 A.M. on Tuesday, November 9, 1993, the case was called by the Chief Justice.

CHIEF JUSTICE REHNQUIST: We'll hear argument first this morning in No. 92-1292, Luther R. Campbell v. Acuff-Rose Music, Inc. Mr. Rogow.

MR. ROGOW: Mr. Chief Justice, and may it please the Court: Since the statute of Anne in 1709 through the Copyright Clause of our Constitution, through the copyright statute and until today, the purpose of copyright has been to encourage creativity. Parody is a creative force in our society and has historically been a creative force, and parody should be encouraged.

The decision of the Sixth Circuit discouraged parody, and we ask the Court today to reverse [its] decision. The rule that we suggest is that parody is a fair use unless it materially impairs the market for the original, and material impairment of the market for the original means supplant the original.

The 2 *Live Crew* case involves the use of part of the music and lyrics of "Oh, Pretty Woman" in what is asserted to be a parody of the original, performed in Rap music. The genre question, for purposes of fair use, is largely restricted to whether 2 Live Crew's use of the song constitutes "parody," a genre that we will see the Court struggling mightily with. The question of "Rap" as a genre is largely kept in the background, and for the moment we will keep it there too. One genre is enough.

Our principal focus will be on what "genre" is—a mode or form of expression distinct from others—and whether it is a concept with useful meaning and application to claims of artistic and aesthetic expression. More specifically, can the genre of parody be used as an instrument for judging the existence of unique and new speech, its value, and its consequences? Mr. Rogow says "yes." Parody is itself a fair use, without more. It is an infringement of the original only in the rare case that it supplants the market for the original without justification. This is a very muscular claim.

2 Live Crew claimed that its "Pretty Woman" was a critical commentary on the original song and on more general social themes, and that it was thus itself original as parody of the original song, transforming its meaning and significance into something new that should not be protected by the copyright to "Oh, Pretty Woman" owned by Acuff-Rose Music Company. Is parody always transformative of the original? Does it possess new sensual or cognitive meaning that makes it different, artistically or aesthetically, from a mere copy of a song? Can the meaning of parody be sufficiently contained that it can serve as an effective tool in understanding and judging art, or is it often just a fancy name for stealing for profit, its essence not aesthetic or artistic, but simply skillful, even crafty?

QUESTION: How do you define parody?

MR. ROGOW: A parody imitates and ridicules. It pokes fun at the original.

QUESTION: So it has to poke fun at the original work.

MR. ROGOW: Not necessarily. It can poke fun at the original, or it can poke fun at something else using the original work. There are two aspects of the criticism. One would be criticism of the original work, the other would be criticism of society using the original work as a means of conveying that criticism.

QUESTION: So that any time someone takes a melodic line and substitutes new lyrics, that is permitted so long as it is making fun of something else in society.

MR. ROGOW: As long as—yes, Justice Kennedy, as long as it is making fun of something else in society or the original, because that is the purpose of parody.

QUESTION: Well, Mr. Rogow, that's a little broader than it needs to be, isn't it, for this case? Don't we have a situation here where it's making fun of the original?

MR. ROGOW: We do, Justice O'Connor.

QUESTION: And I would have thought that maybe the *Harper & Row* case we [decided] a few years ago [involving *Nation* magazine publishing a limited number of quotes about President Gerald Ford's pardon of President Richard M. Nixon before publication of Ford's memoir] refused to recognize a fair use exception even for political commentary. So I think your position that a parody should have some kind of all-encompassing provision as being a fair use, even if it's directed at something other than the original work, is a pretty big step to take.

MR. ROGOW: Justice O'Connor, it is true that the parody in this case only poked fun at the original. And one could limit this case to just those facts and that would be quite fine.

QUESTION: So it's your position that a parody should be found to be a fair use when it—when the lyrics poke fun at the original, but the music is the same?

MR. ROGOW: Yes. One needs to use the music from the original in order to evoke the image of the original . . . because that is the purpose of parody, to borrow from the original and then to imitate and ridicule the original, which is what happened in this case.

The Court is getting into something of a definitional circle here. The use by 2 Live Crew is a parody because it meets the definition, but nothing is said about whether the dictionary definition is one that appropriately balances the free speech interests. That is a question of constitutional law, not of dictionary definition. And more basically, what are the nature and value of parody? If it criticizes society, not just the original, is it less valuable? Is satire less valuable and thus not presumptively a fair use?

QUESTION: Mr. Rogow, could you explain to me why criticism either of the original song or, as your position states, of almost anything using the original song, is to be encouraged more than, let's say, patriotism? Why shouldn't I be able to use any song that anyone's ever written in order to set patriotic lyrics to it? Isn't that something that's to be encouraged?

MR. ROGOW: It is, although one can encourage patriotism without necessarily borrowing the music from another tune, although historically we have borrowed from other tunes to have patriotic songs.

QUESTION: Well, but one can criticize other things without borrowing the music from a tune. Unless you're willing to limit your proposition as much as Justice O'Connor just suggested, your argument doesn't hold.

MR. ROGOW: For this case I can limit it to exactly these facts.

This is a wise concession by Mr. Rogow. If one can take another's music or lyrics or text to make a political or social point that is completely unrelated to the original, the possibilities seem potentially endless. And what about the breadth of the term *social*? Isn't most everything social in some sense?

QUESTION: But let's assume the more general proposition that you were trying to establish. What's your answer to my question for that?

MR. ROGOW: That as long as the parody is commenting critically upon society, be it cultural, be it social, be it political, the use of the tune would still fall within the definition of criticism, which has to have some breathing room.

QUESTION: But you can make fun of society—you can criticize society—in a lot of different ways. Why do you have to take my tune to do it?

MR. ROGOW: Because sometimes taking that tune conveys to the listener something extra.

Transformation enters the picture here. Using parody to criticize society, not the original work, clearly "conveys to the listener something extra." But on reflection this is a mere tautology: because it does not focus criticism on the taken work, it by definition conveys something extra and therefore proves its value. But doesn't transformation have to mean something different than this—at least in the context of art or aesthetics, where new perception comes from the work itself?

Justice Scalia strikes.

QUESTION: My tune is very effective. You like my tune. It's catchy. People remember it. But a lot of people would want to use it for that reason, probably.

MR. ROGOW: But the tune—Justice Scalia, the tune can go with the parody. For example, there is a video that the Court has in this case where the "Beverly Hillbillies" is used, but the parody is called "Capitol Hillbillies." Now, using the "Beverly Hillbillies" evokes a certain image, and then the criticism that is conveyed by "Capitol Hillbillies," the parody, is useful.

I think that's a threshold issue here. Is parody useful? Is criticism useful? And the copyright law does say that criticism is useful and should be encouraged.

QUESTION: Is patriotism useful?

MR. ROGOW: Yes, it is useful, but pure patriotism without making the political comment, critical comment, is not embraced within [fair use], although I'm not saying it isn't something worthwhile of protection. Obviously, it is. But we're in this narrow copyright area where we have on one side the private interest of the copyright holder versus the public interest and the historical interest of promoting creativity. Parody is a creative force in our society. Historically it is.

QUESTION: Mr. Rogow, you're not saying that if it's parody, it is *necessarily* a permissible fair use.

MR. ROGOW: I'm not, Justice Ginsburg.

QUESTION: Since the Sixth Circuit agreed with you that we are dealing here with parody, where did the Sixth Circuit go wrong?

MR. ROGOW: By applying a presumption that if it is a commercial parody, then it is presumptively harmful to the market.

QUESTION: But there's language in our cases that says exactly that. Is it your position that the commercial nature of the use is a factor to be considered, but even if it is found to be for a commercial purpose, that that isn't the end of the inquiry.

MR. ROGOW: That is our position, Justice O'Connor.

QUESTION: Now, what is the market that we should look at? Is it the market for parodies, or do we look at whether it would supplant, somehow, the demand for the original work? What is it we look at?

MR. ROGOW: That is what you look at, Justice O'Connor: would it supplant the demand for the *original* work in many or multiple venues, not just a single venue.

Mr. Rogow speaks of demand for the *original* work (my emphasis here and above). The reader and listener must be careful here. Does "original work" just include the Orbison rock original or also other new variations on that original that are called "derivative works"? These would include a new edition of the song by Orbison, a version by another licensed artist, or even a rap version, for the copyright law gives the copyright holder control over all such derivative works. Does Mr. Rogow mean that Campbell's "Pretty Woman" must supplant demand for the earlier and original Orbison rock version or all other derivative uses that could in the future be allowed, including the rap version?

This is slippery and subtle ground that the Court is trying to navigate. And the slipperiness is also why Mr. Rogow places very heavy weight on 2

Live Crew's version being parody, not just rap, because parody has some claim to being nonderivative and therefore outside the copyright holder's control. Why? Because parody is transformative? More so than a rock-to-rap transformation?

QUESTION: And what were the findings of the district court as to that in this case?

MR. ROGOW: That it did not adversely affect the market. It did not supplant the original Orbison-Dees song. It did not impair its market. The Sixth Circuit, Justice O'Connor, basically recognized that there were no facts in this case adduced by Acuff-Rose to show that its market for the original song had been materially impaired.

QUESTION: Shouldn't the market be defined more broadly to include all the possible adaptations that the copyright owner might want to make or to license? I mean, there could be, you know, rock adaptations of waltzes and so on.

MR. ROGOW: Justice Souter, I don't have any difficulty with a broad definition of the market. What's lacking in this case is any proof that any market for the Orbison-Dees song was harmed.

If the defendant raises the affirmative defense of fair use parody, then the first thing the defendant must show is that it is a parody, and then the four factors are certainly relevant: [the purpose and character of the use; the nature of the copyrighted work; the portion of the work used; and "the effect of the use on the potential market for or value of the copyrighted work."]

This is a parody. The purpose is parody. Parody is important. Parody is a creative force. That's the purpose.

The [character] of the work is commercial, so that would enter into the equation, but it should not be a presumption that completely eviscerates the rest of the factors. And the Sixth Circuit said in the last line of its opinion: "Because this was blatantly commercial, it cannot claim fair use." That simply goes too far.

It will be recalled that the lyrics and the music were substantially altered, though the nub of the song and lyrics—that which is necessary to make the connection in the audience's mind to the original—was used. But two separate issues shouldn't be confused here. Using parts of the song as referents and the amount used in light of the new work's purpose seem to go directly to the definitional/constitutional question of genre, or parody. But the commercial use of the parody and its effect on the market for the original song don't seem to pertain to the parody question but rather the distinct and separate question of harm to the original authors or, in this case, the current copyright holder, Acuff-Rose. And under the copyright law, the author is entitled to protect use of the work in other markets—say in the rap market. This is what a derivative use of a copyrighted work is . . . say, an essay enlarged and republished as a book.

The main point in the oral-argument exchange, though, is that a parody that is disruptive of a market is no less a parody than one that isn't. Not all parodies are protected against liability for infringement. Indeed, the fair use statute doesn't use the word *parody*.

QUESTION: Mr. Rogow, does commercial use have any independent significance for you, or does it really weigh in evaluating the effect of the use on the potential market for the copyrighted work?

MR. ROGOW: Justice Ginsburg, it—it has both. It's—obviously, the courts have had difficulty with [this]. But commercial use is independently something to look at: Is this a commercial use, as opposed to a nonprofit use, an educational use? So it would be something to look at, but it's not decisive.

But the [separate question of harm to the copyright holder's market], which this Court has said is the single most important factor, that's the key, I think, Mr. Chief Justice, to protecting the copyright holder's interest. Has he or she been harmed? Has their market been harmed or supplanted?

QUESTION: And what was your evidence with respect to the derivative market, to rap works? Suppose there would be another rap version of this composition. Would that be a fair use?

MR. ROGOW: Not if it was not a parody. I mean the threshold is, is this a parody. Just simply a rap version of "Oh, Pretty Woman" would not qualify under the fair use doctrine. That would be mere copying for a commercial use, and no—

QUESTION: Different lyrics, some variation in the musical presentation—would that infringe anyone's copyright at this stage, suppose there were another version?

MR. ROGOW: It would make out a prima facie case for the plaintiff of copyright infringement. The defendant would then have the burden of—

QUESTION: Which plaintiff? Suppose we have a rap version now that has different lyrics than the 2 Live Crew, slightly different presentation of the music, and the claim is made this is a parody of the parody?

MR. ROGOW: Of the parody? That would be entitled to a fair use claim. There's nothing the matter with making fun of the people making fun of the original. In fact, that is, if we believe in—in creativity, if we believe in some humor—

QUESTION: Does Campbell have a copyright in the parody?

MR. ROGOW: He has a copyright on the album, which would include, presumably, the parody.

QUESTION: Is the underlying theory of your case that if there is a market to be exploited, in this case 280,000 copies, and it can be exploited best through a parody, that it is essentially fair that the person who creates the parody receives 100 percent of the profit?

MR. ROGOW: No. The thrust of my case, Justice Kennedy, is that if a parody is a creative, true parodic work, then it is entitled to be called a fair use unless there is evidence that it has materially impaired or supplanted the market for the original.

The original does not hold the absolute right to preclude any other use of that original work. And the fact that 280,000 or 2,000 records were sold is not the decisive fact here.

CHIEF JUSTICE REHNQUIST: Thank you, Mr. Rogow.

The questions at the heart of the case—what is the expressive value of parody and in light of its value what does parody mean, what protection it should receive, and how does the relatively technical element of genre help decide such cases—were elusive, hardly explored in any depth in the argument. Perhaps this was because the Court saw the case as one involving only the meaning of a law of Congress, not the larger questions of freedom of expression under the First Amendment. But that simply won't work in the long run, for the Constitution controls acts of Congress, and if they are inconsistent with one another, the Constitution prevails.

In thinking about another genre—Karen Finley's performance art or expressionist painting—there is not the luxury of making assumptions about genre or perceptions of audiences. The question to ask in the 2 *Live Crew* case is whether the adaptation of the original song was cognitively or emotionally transforming, resulting in a new meaning lodged not in the intention of Roy Orbison and William Dees but in the sensory perceptions of a listener. Is the kind of transformation assumed in parody on par with that produced by art or aesthetic expression?

The Court will continue to struggle with these questions in the second half of the oral argument, when the lawyer for the copyright holder, Acuff-Rose, presents his case.

MR. ROSDEITCHER: Mr. Chief Justice, and may it please the Court: This Court has stated unequivocally that every commercial use of copyrighted material is presumptively unfair. Now, there's been no discussion of that here, and in fact it's overlooked. In the petitioner's view, once it's a parody you look to the impairment of the market. And I'm going to come to impairment of the market, because there's substantial evidence of impairment of the derivative market, including the market for rap versions.

But I'd like to talk about the significance of that commercial presumption. My view of the presumption is a little subtler than I think petitioners give us credit for, or even give the Sixth Circuit credit for. I believe that the commercial use presumption means something like this. You have to look at the commerciality to see what purpose the so-called parodist or news reporter or critic or commentator is [seeking to achieve].

There's a wonderful article by Judge [Pierre] Leval [a widely respected federal judge in New York] in which he modestly reassesses his own opinion on the Salinger letters case, and he acknowledges he made an error. [The case involved the use of a few selected letters by J. D. Salinger in a biography.] Judge Leval originally concluded that the use was transformative—from personal correspondence by a famous writer to biography—and thus was a fair use of the letters. But upon further reflection he saw something else in reviewing the record, and that was that the letters were also being used to dazzle, to have a good read, not just for the purpose of biography, but to sell the work for the expressive value of the underlying copyrighted material.

That's what happened in *Harper & Row*. The *Nation* was engaged in news reporting, but the court said that the *Nation* went further and was exploiting the 300 words taken verbatim from President Ford's book for their expressive value so that people would know it's Ford speaking.

Now, that's what happened here. They took my client's music, partly for parody, let's assume that. But they took the music not just for parody. After all, they were selling a rap album. There's no suggestion anywhere in this record that they were selling a parody record. They were selling a rap album to an audience—what they described as an audience of urban black youth or disaffected black urban youth. Not that it was directed to a parody audience but directed to a wide audience for rap music.

Rap music is danceable music. Rap music needs music. And they took our music.

Mr. Rosdeitcher's theory is plain enough, though a little elaboration might help here. He claims that 2 Live Crew took the song mostly to sell it into the rap market. The parody, if any, was incidental to the rap music market purpose. Converting a rock song into a rap version is to change it, but it is not a fair use because the rap version of "Oh, Pretty Woman" would be a derivative use, and the right to sell (or not) a derivative use is the copyright holder's alone. A painter may permit a run of prints, a derivate use of the art reflected in the original painting; he or she can also prohibit it, and that's the end of the matter.

What if someone did a print run of a copyrighted painting (say, for fun, the *Mona Lisa*), but then added a moustache on the print drawn from the original *Mona Lisa* for humorous effect: would that be a parody and therefore "fair use"? When the right to control derivative works overlaps with a fair use, which prevails? The answer might depend on whether parody (a genre of criticism under fair use, according to the Court) is important to the aims of copyright or free speech or whether it is more important than the author's right to license prints or rap versions in a derivative market so that others can have access to the image. It might concern whether criticism is the same as transformation in meaning, giving something new rather than criticizing something old. Is parody (perhaps an elliptical form of criticism) a "genre" distinct from rock music or ballad ("Oh, Pretty Woman") in the same way that a rap version would be a distinct genre from a rock version? Arguably a rap version would be a new and transcending kind of sensual and aesthetic experience. A parody whose value is criticism would be largely cognitive in its goals, thus not sensually new, except to the extent that 2 Live Crew unnecessarily employed rap to "dazzle" its cognitive point (and make more money in a new market) with sensual meaning too, a tactic that should be entitled to no extra credit beyond the criticism expressed. If this is so, then the new genre of rap should outweigh the new genre of parody because it yields wholly new sensual meaning that cannot be achieved without the original music. At least with art and aesthetic expression, it can be argued that the substantively transforming and sensually transcending new meaning counts most.

QUESTION: Well, now, just let's stop a moment and inquire. Suppose you had somebody who simply writes critical commentary—very straightforward, not a parody—about somebody else's work, and he wants to sell his critical piece. Can it be a fair use?

MR. ROSDEITCHER: Yes.

QUESTION: It's perfectly commercial.

MR. ROSDEITCHER: Yes, it can be a fair use. Let me go back to Judge Leval's example, and then we use our example. The author was using the Salinger letters for a biography, but as [Judge Leval] pointed out, they went further, they took too much. They did more than just take enough to serve the interests of biography. They were anxious to sell the beauty and dazzling quality of the letter.

And what I'm saying in this case is it's not just that they profited from the parody. They profited here, in addition, because they needed music, and they needed dazzling, good music, and they took one of the great rock and roll classics—

"Dazzle" is not transformation for purposes of the fair use provisions of the copyright act and arguably not for the First Amendment either, says Mr. Rosdeitcher. At least with respect to parody as criticism, this proposition has great force: the volume is turned up, but nothing new is said. How about with art? What if someone takes Karen Finley's performance and gives it greater pizzazz—more lights, more lewdness and nudity, music—and then calls it parody because it makes Finley's skilled and more tempered act look ridiculous. How much should this count as criticism? Is this really what transformation—here, to criticism—should mean (as opposed to wholly new perception or meaning)?

QUESTION: I thought we had accepted the fact that this was a parody.

MR. ROSDEITCHER: Your Honor, you can have a parody that takes too much. I think that is the great danger. One can write parodic lyrics and take all the music or most of the music and sell and sell and profit by and exploit and take advantage of the music [in the rap market]. And if it's fair use, they get the profit, they get a copyright [for the rap version] on their recording. They presumably will claim a copyright on the derivative work that we can't, because it's allegedly fair use and fair game, so that anybody, any other rap artist—

QUESTION: Why isn't a parody of the whole thing more persuasive than just a few phrases? I mean, if you're going to have parody as a fair use at all, it seems to me you might be much more effective using the whole thing than just a phrase.

MR. ROSDEITCHER: What's going on in this case is not about parody. I'll accept there's a parody there. This case is about selling rap music by—in the words of one of the scholars that we refer to, Professor Light—fusing a street message with pop music.

And he gives a wonderful example of how this whole phenomenon started, and it throws light on what's happened here. There was a very famous hard rock song called *Walk This Way* by Aerosmith. Another group, another rap group, Run DMC, decided that they would change that into a rap song. They actually hired the guitarist from the Aerosmith group to do it, and they did it. They made a rap song with hard rock music, and they sold it—it was the greatest rap hit, at that time, ever. And I'd like to read you what Mr. Light concludes from this and how he describes what happened thereafter in rap. "Rap was established as a viable pop form, at least as long as its connections to the traditional rock and roll spirit were made explicit."

Now, that's what happened here. They took our music in order to have a free ride on our good music and make a profit from our good music. The record shows that they already had released two albums, and that they were now going to release their third. The two other albums were very successful commercially, both of them had gone gold, one of them was close to platinum, they were high up on the rap charts—not on the parody charts, on the rap music charts.

And they told us if you give us a license, we will sell this to hundreds of thousands of new homes. Now, they did have a track record. They had a track record of selling lots and lots of records. My client decided that it did not think this was a good way to exploit this market and exercised their right as copyright owners to say no, a right which is absolutely essential if they are to have a marketable copyright.

I take that history, and I add to [it] the fact that they then took our song. Now, the amount of song has been underplayed by petitioners, it's been underplayed by the district court. When you listen to these two tapes, the first thing you hear when you hear the Orbison and Dees record is a wonderful, powerful, dynamic, jolting guitar riff that is so famous and begins that work. That guitar riff then is played throughout the Orbison and Dees work, and then you hear the "Pretty Woman" melody, which is very familiar.

They took the guitar riff. Now, in the Orbison and Dees work they play it ten times. They played it sixteen times. At one point they play it eight times. They played it because it's one of the most wonderful, danceable, dynamic musical works of rock and roll—this record of Orbison and Dees was one of the all-time hits—and they played it over and over again to dazzle, to have a good hear, to have a good dance. And then they say we can now profit and free ride on the genius of Roy Orbison and Bill Dees. That's what they were about.

When they sold the record, they didn't [label it] parody, they didn't give it another name. They called it "Pretty Woman," they dropped the word "Oh." If you look at their letter, they think the name of our song is "Pretty Woman." They asked us for a license on "Pretty Woman," written by Roy Orbison and Bill Dees. It's published by my client. In terms of market, they were [just] trying to exploit "Pretty Woman" by Roy Orbison and Bill Dees.

This is a good and interesting argument. The point really is that 2 Live Crew is using "parody" as a label, but it's not parody. It is instead taking part of the song "Oh, Pretty Woman" as a means of improving their own rap song and their album. How do we know whether there is truth in this assertion (other than that it makes a certain amount of sense on the face of it)? We don't even know for sure what the Court and the lawyers think the meaning of parody is. Is it just making fun; or is it making fun plus another larger point; or is it criticism, which might mean something more cognitive and analytical whether conveyed metaphorically or literally? Is putting a mustache on the *Mona Lisa* really enough?

QUESTION: Mr. Rosdeitcher, I presume there were reviews in various periodicals of the rap version? I'd be curious to know whether it was recognized in those reviews as a parody or just another rap or music.

MR. ROSDEITCHER: There is nothing in the record. But, Your Honor, if I can go off the record, I originally bought this record when I was in the running for coming onto this case. I went into Sam Goody, and I went to the rap section, and I pulled this off the shelf next to 2 Live Crew's other rap songs. That's where it's viewed. That's where it's sold. So there's no question that there's a rap market and that they exploited it and that that injures us. That injures a potential market that we have. The standard—

QUESTION: Well, counsel, do we look to the market for the original work and whether that's supplanted?

It should be recalled that copyright protects the author's right to control publication of the original work—say, a book—as well as publication of "derivative works," which the copyright law defines as a work "based upon one or more preexisting works, such as a translation, musical arrangement, dramatization, . . . or any other form in which a work may be recast, transformed, or adapted." Under this definition, Mr. Rosdeitcher argues that a rap version of "Oh, Pretty Woman" would be a derivative work controlled by the holder of the copyright on the original work, in this case Acuff-Rose. Luther Campbell, copyright owner for the 2 Live Crew rendition of "Pretty Woman" in rap, claims that using part of the derivative right controlled by Acuff-Rose (transformation to rap) and adding in parody or *implied* criticism of the original work makes 2 Live Crew's version a fair use "for purpose of criticism." Why should fair use override an author's derivative use rights? And just how much criticism is needed, and how explicit must the criticism be to overbalance the derivative right, is something that is greatly concerning the Court.

In the end, the Court will say that "2 Live Crew's song reasonably could be perceived as commenting on the original or criticizing, to some degree." "Could be perceived" and "to some degree" represent a pretty slim reed on which to rest Campbell's claim.

The Court keeps probing, looking for an answer.

MR. ROSDEITCHER: You look at the market. In this case you look at the market for rap. And I'm prepared to look at that market for rap because they, themselves, have made the case that there is a rap market for a rap version of our rock and roll classic. We have in the record evidence of the interest of a rap group called the Brothers Make 3 in making a rap version of our song and fusing our music. This is a classic way in which rap music is given a mainstream appeal. So there is a rap market.

And then—then you have to ask yourself what's the evidence of any potential injury? Now, they had the burden of proof here. They did not carry the burden of proof.

Let me come back to this commercial use now. First of all, I think there is a situation where commercial use may actually sweep the boards on all of the factors. In this case, we showed not just that they made a profit from the parody, but that when you take the amount they used of it, the way they displayed it, how they played this music not just a background to the singing of the lyrics but in wonderful virtuosity and displays and dazzling displays in the middle and at the end, [the conclusion is] that they were selling *this* music. It reflected also in how they marketed it.

Now, in that circumstance, I believe that that it is not a fair use.

It is notable that the word *parody* is not used in the copyright statute. The claim instead is that parody is a genre of speech that at least for purposes of the 2 *Live Crew* case is focused on criticism of the original work. So parody is not technically dispositive of fair use. And the small amount of parody, the implication rather than express statement of criticism, and the fact that the criticism took the form of making fun of the original, rather than defending and explaining faults in the original work, all combine in Mr. Rosdeitcher's argument to downplay the importance and substance of the criticism and leave bare the dominant fact of transformation of the original into a rap version, which is Acuff-Rose's right, not Campbell's.

A theme underlying the arguments but not explicitly pursued is transformation. One might argue, as Mr. Rogow did, that 2 Live Crew's version transformed the meaning and sensory perception of the original "Oh, Pretty Woman." It created new ideas and new speech, indeed new sensory meaning and aesthetic perception, and thus should be protected against a derivative copyright claim by Acuff-Rose. The current story pursues this later, but the argument from a purely free speech perspective is very strong, for the new version is new speech that old speech should not be able to snuff out with the assistance of the law—depending, of course, on how and whether, in fact, it gave rise to new aesthetic and artistic meaning.

But it is less clear that the argument works under the copyright law. That law describes derivative versions of the original as "transformative." It does not use that term for fair use, which seems to focus more descriptively on certain forms of publication—education, news, criticism—that serve public interests but generally do not extinguish the value of the original work or its derivatives. It is the Supreme Court, not the statute, that has introduced the term *transformation* into fair use, thus effectively broadening the scope of fair use. But that is hardly dispositive of Acuff-Rose's claim, for if the derivate use being protected by the original copyright holder is transformative and if the fair use (parody with but a light connection to what is ordinarily meant by criticism of art) is likewise transformative, the choice between competing transformations can hardly be said automatically to favor the infringer over the copyright holder.

All of this is simply to say that the questions in the case are very confusing, very complex, and exceedingly important for both copyright policy and the First Amendment.

QUESTION: May I ask you one question there about the similarity of the two works and so forth? Do you think their version changed the basic melody or fundamental character of the work, within the meaning of the statute?

MR. ROSDEITCHER: Yes.

QUESTION: But it didn't entirely supplant it.

MR. ROSDEITCHER: It changed it but it created a record which would compete with any rap version we would create. It could be parody. But, you know, rap has many messages. Rap has humor. It has acerbic criticism of society. According to the record, 2 Live Crew has a message.

They've exploited our work for a profit, they're free riding on our music, and in addition, they have impaired a market which we are entitled to exploit. This is music. Music's lifeblood is adaptability. What makes a song in the 1960s a great song may not make it a great song in the 1970s, and as the record shows, we then had the song done in the hard rock style, from the soft rock to the hard rock. And now we're in the eighties and nineties, and they've shown that you can now take a rock song and, as many rap artists have done, convert it to a rap song.

QUESTION: May I ask one last question? At the outset of your argument you acknowledge that you would agree this was a parody. How do you define parody when you make that concession?

MR. ROSDEITCHER: I would limit it to parody that is critical of the underlying work, because I think that's a sensible limitation.

QUESTION: In your example, I think it was Aerosmith's [music that] progressed or regressed to rap.

MR. ROSDEITCHER: Yes.

(Laughter.)

QUESTION: Under the definition of parody that's been submitted to us, would you not expect that it could be argued that [the rap version of Aerosmith's song] was a parody?

MR. ROSDEITCHER: It could be. In fact, any change in the lyrics that's funny seems to me to be a parody. It makes ridiculous the original situation. It could be read back to criticize the original because if it's funny, it's mocking it, poking fun at it, and therefore it would be a parody, and it would be fair use, and they could profit by it.

Thank you, Your Honors.

CHIEF JUSTICE REHNQUIST: Thank you, Mr. Rosdeitcher.

As Mr. Rosdeitcher returns to his seat, it can be with satisfaction that he has made a clear and very effective argument, and it has ended on a high note, implicitly at least. He is asked whether the conversion of Aerosmith's record to rap, without more, might qualify as parody and thus criticism. He agrees, because it could be understood as funny or mocking the original. If this is so, the whole case falls apart analytically. If it might be understood that publication of an original in a different form, that different form itself might qualify as a form of criticism for purposes of fair use—even though mocking criticism only, like the mustache on the *Mona Lisa*—then fair use will have swallowed up all of the author's right to control derivative uses, and indeed it will have come close to digesting much of copyright itself. Campbell wouldn't be in court; and he wouldn't have to argue that parody and criticism were his aim in adapting the lyrics. He could just do a rap version without even having to ask Acuff-Rose because converting a song into rap from another genre such as rock (or country or classical) could reasonably be perceived to be mocking or funny and thus "criticism" "to some degree." This, Mr. Rosdeitcher might well believe, is enough of a warning to force the Court to pull back and rethink the parody issue from the beginning.

But in this, Mr. Rosdeitcher will be both surprised and disappointed.

CHIEF JUSTICE REHNQUIST: Mr. Rogow, you have four minutes remaining.

MR. ROGOW: This Court's opinions say there must be some meaningful likelihood of future harm to the copyright holder, and *Harper & Row* gives life to that formulation. In *Harper & Row*, the market was supplanted. *Time* magazine decided not to pay $12,500 to Harper & Row because the *Nation* had taken President Ford's words and published them, copied them without permission.

That gives, I think, the framework for deciding this case. Meaningful likelihood of harm, there is none here. I hear this talk about how they might want to do a rap version at some point. There's nothing to keep them from licensing a rap version. But this is a parody—

There is nothing new here, and that's often a good reason to waive rebuttal, for if you've said it before and repeat it again, nothing but trouble can come of it. And trouble is what Mr. Rogow gets, at the hands of Justice Scalia, who swoops in hard.

QUESTION: No, but Mr. Rosdeitcher is right that the reason people bought this record and the reason the record was sold to them was largely for the music and not for the subtle parody. [Under that view] they have suffered a loss. That money should have been their money rather than your money. You're making money from their music, if he's right about that premise.

MR. ROGOW: And there's no reason to think that he is right.

This is one cut out of ten cuts on the record. The 2 Live Crew album was not named Pretty Woman, it was named *As Clean as They Wanna Be*. So this kind of argumentation about what might be, what might have occurred, why they sold it, how they sold it, is completely belied by any facts in this record.

QUESTION: You mean it would be a different case if they had packaged this as a separate tape with only the "Oh, Pretty Woman" on it?

MR. ROGOW: Not necessarily. We would still have fair use, and we would still argue fair use. But it would look much different in terms of how fair was it, if they were trying to confuse people. This is a record that's out there. One cut uses "Oh, Pretty Woman" and makes fun of it. Was that fair? We submit it is fair unless they can show that their market was materially impaired, supplanted.

And how could they do [that]? They could do it by showing that they had someone to whom they were going to license this. But the truth is they don't want to license this as a parody. And one can understand that. Most authors don't want to give a license to someone to make fun of their work—

QUESTION: Don't they simply have to show that there was someone to whom they *could* license it?

MR. ROGOW: They do need to show, as in *Harper & Row*, that there is some meaningful likelihood that there is someone to whom they would [or could?] license this. And that is completely—

QUESTION: Or *you* needed to [make the contrary showing]. I thought you conceded last time around that this is *your* burden. You have to show that there is no market that they could exploit that you have made an inroad on by virtue of this recording.

MR. ROGOW: No, Justice Ginsburg. Our burden is to make some showing that this would not impair their market. The ultimate burden is upon them to show they were injured by the loss of a market, just as *Harper & Row* showed they were injured by the publication in the *Nation*.

CHIEF JUSTICE REHNQUIST: Thank you, Mr. Rogow. The case is submitted.

Oops. Saying nothing would have been very wise. Mr. Rogow really got slaughtered—actually, he slaughtered himself. First, another group had asked Acuff-Rose about doing a rap version of "Oh, Pretty Woman," as the oral argument itself revealed. That's ample proof that they could have sold that derivative form, coupled with the claim that Campbell's unauthorized recording has supplanted the rap market now. Second, in response to Justice Ginsburg's statement that Campbell in any event had the burden of proof, Mr. Rogow could say nothing, other than to dissemble a bit.

Fortunately for Mr. Rogow, cases are not won or lost on debating points, and slip ups are not decisive. The Court is informed by the lawyers' briefs and, particularly in this case, perhaps, by the oral arguments in which a justice's concerns and uncertainties can be aired and probed with the lawyers. But in the end the justices make their own decisions independent of what the lawyers say.

And so the Court did. On March 7, 1994, four months after oral argument but well before the end of the Term, the Court issued its opinion. The decision was unanimous—a startling fact to many people. There was but one separate opinion, a full concurrence by Justice Kennedy, who agreed with all of the others but observed, too, that the implied criticism that may have existed "to some degree" was a pretty thin reed upon which to rest the decision in the case and too thin to extrapolate much from it in future cases.

> Justice Souter delivered the opinion of the Court.
>
> It is uncontested here that 2 Live Crew's song would be an infringement of Acuff-Rose's rights in "Oh, Pretty Woman," under the Copyright Act of 1976 but for a finding of fair use through parody. [A]s Justice Story explained, "In truth, in literature, in science and in art, there are, and can be, few, if any, things, which in an abstract sense, are strictly new and original throughout." Every book in literature, science, and art borrows, and must necessarily borrow, and use much which was well known and used before. The central purpose of this investigation is to see, in Justice Story's words, whether the new work merely "supercede[s] the objects" of the original creation, or instead adds something new, with a further purpose or different character, altering the first with new expression, meaning, or message; it asks, in other words, whether and to what extent the new work is "transformative."
>
> Suffice it to say now that parody has an obvious claim to transformative value, as Acuff-Rose itself does not deny. Like less ostensibly humorous

forms of criticism, it can provide social benefit, by shedding light on an earlier work, and, in the process, creating a new one.

The germ of parody lies in the definition of the Greek *parodied*, quoted in Judge Nelson's Court of Appeals dissent, as "a song sung alongside another." Modern dictionaries accordingly describe a parody as a "literary or artistic work that imitates the characteristic style of an author or a work for comic effect or ridicule," or as a "composition in prose or verse in which the characteristic turns of thought and phrase in an author or class of authors are imitated in such a way as to make them appear ridiculous." For the purposes of copyright law, the nub of the definitions, and the heart of any parodist's claim to quote from existing material, is the use of some elements of a prior author's composition to create a new one that, at least in part, comments on that author's works. If, on the contrary, the commentary has no critical bearing on the substance or style of the original composition, which the alleged infringer merely uses to get attention or to avoid the drudgery in working up something fresh, the claim to fairness in borrowing from another's work diminishes accordingly (if it does not vanish). . . .

The fact that parody can claim legitimacy for some appropriation does not, of course, tell either parodist or judge much about where to draw the line. The threshold question when fair use is raised in defense of parody is whether a paretic character may reasonably be perceived. Whether, going beyond that, parody is in good taste or bad does not and should not matter to fair use.

While we might not assign a high rank to the paretic element here, we think it fair to say that 2 Live Crew's song reasonably *could be perceived as commenting on the original or criticizing it, to some degree.* [Emphasis added.] 2 Live Crew juxtaposes the romantic musings of a man whose fantasy comes true, with degrading taunts, a bawdy demand for sex, and a sigh of relief from paternal responsibility. The later words can be taken as a comment on the naiveté of the original of an earlier day, as a rejection of its sentiment that ignores the ugliness of street life and the debasement that it signifies. It is this joinder of reference and ridicule that marks off the author's choice of parody from the other types of comment and criticism that traditionally have had a claim to fair use protection as transformative works.

Parody presents a difficult case. Parody's humor, or in any event its comment, necessarily springs from recognizable allusion to its object through distorted imitation. Its art lies in the tension between a known original and its paretic twin. When parody takes aim at a particular original work, the parody must be able to "conjure up" at least enough of that original to make the object of its critical wit recognizable. What makes for this recognition is quotation of the original's most distinctive or memorable features, which the parodist can be sure the audience will know. Once enough has been taken to assure identification, how much more is reasonable will depend, say, on the extent to which the song's overriding purpose and character is to parody the original or, in contrast, the likelihood that the parody may serve as a market substitute for the original.

It is true, of course, that 2 Live Crew copied the characteristic opening bass riff [or musical phrase] of the original, and true that the words of the first line copy the Orbison lyrics. But if quotation of the opening riff and the first line may be said to go to the "heart" of the original, the heart is also what most readily conjures up the song for parody, and it is the heart at which parody takes aim.

This is not, of course, to say that anyone who calls himself a parodist can skim the cream and get away scot free. In parody, as in news reporting, context is everything, and the question of fairness asks what else the parodist did besides go to the heart of the original. It is significant that 2 Live Crew not only copied the first line of the original but thereafter departed markedly from the Orbison lyrics for its own ends. 2 Live Crew not only copied the bass riff and repeated it but also produced otherwise distinctive sounds, interposing "scraper" noise, overlaying the music with solos in different keys, and altering the drum beat.

When the second use is transformative, market substitution is at least less certain, and market harm may not be so readily inferred. Indeed, as to parody pure and simple, it is more likely that the new work will not affect the market for the original by acting as a substitute for it ("superced[ing] [its] objects").

We do not, of course, suggest that a parody may not harm the market at all, but when a lethal parody, like a scathing theater review, kills demand for the original, it does not produce a harm cognizable under the Copyright Act. Because "parody may quite legitimately aim at garroting the original, destroying it commercially as well as artistically," the role of the courts is to distinguish between "[b]iting criticism [that merely] suppresses demand [and] copyright infringement [that] usurps it."

But the later work may have a more complex character, with effects not only in the arena of criticism but also in protectable markets for derivative works, too. In that sort of case, the law looks beyond the criticism to the other elements of the work, as it does here. 2 Live Crew's song comprises not only parody but also rap music, and the derivative market for rap music is a proper focus of enquiry. Evidence of substantial harm to it would weigh against a finding of fair use, because the licensing of derivatives is an important economic incentive to the creation of originals.

It was error for the Court of Appeals to conclude that the commercial nature of 2 Live Crew's parody of "Oh, Pretty Woman" rendered it presumptively unfair. No such evidentiary presumption is available to address either the first factor, the character and purpose of the use, or the fourth, market harm, in determining whether a transformative use, such as parody, is a fair one. The court also erred in holding that 2 Live Crew had necessarily copied excessively from the Orbison original, considering the paretic purpose of the use. We therefore reverse the judgment of the Court of Appeals and remand the case for further proceedings consistent with this opinion.
It is so ordered.

Well! After the thorough, even laborious discussion of fair use and parody and transformation and after extended analysis of the issues raised by the facts of the *2 Live Crew* case, the Court declines to decide whether 2 Live Crew's use of "Oh, Pretty Woman" infringed Acuff-Rose's copyright or not. Instead it left that decision to the court of appeals, which is instructed to reconsider the case and decide it in a manner consistent with the rules set out in the Supreme Court's opinion. As it turned out, the court of appeals passed the hot potato to the district court.[10] The Supreme Court thus made the bullet but ordered the lower court to bite it. One can't help but be a little—even a lot—sympathetic with the district-court judge, who must now make some sense of the "little of this, little of that" new rules.

Justice Kennedy, concurring.
Under the Court's opinion, parody may qualify as fair use only if it draws upon the original composition to make humorous or ironic commentary about that same composition. It is not enough that the parody use the original in a humorous fashion, however creative that humor may be. The parody must target the original, and not just its general style, the genre of art to which it belongs, or society as a whole (although if it targets the original, it may target those features as well). This prerequisite confines fair use protection to works whose very subject is the original composition and so necessitates some borrowing from it.
It will be difficult, of course, for courts to determine whether harm to the market results from a parody's critical or substitutive effects. But again, if we keep the definition of parody within appropriate bounds, this inquiry may be of little significance. If a work targets another for humorous or ironic effect, it is by definition a new creative work. Creative works can compete with other creative works for the same market, even if their appeal is overlapping. [This] underscores the importance of ensuring that the parody is in fact an independent creative work, which is why the parody

must "make some critical comment or statement about the original work which reflects the original perspective of the parodist—thereby giving the parody social value beyond its entertainment function."

The Court decides it is "fair to say that 2 Live Crew's song reasonably could be perceived as commenting on the original or criticizing it, to some degree." While I am not so assured that 2 Live Crew's song is a legitimate parody, the Court's treatment of the remaining factors leaves room for the District Court to determine on remand that the song is not a fair use. As future courts apply our fair use analysis, they must take care to ensure that not just any commercial takeoff is rationalized *post hoc* as a parody.

With these observations, I join the opinion of the Court.

Upon reading the Court's opinion, one might well conclude that it is questionable copyright law but possibly good First Amendment law—or that by importing transformation so heavily into fair use, the Court imported the First Amendment into copyright law. With art and aesthetic speech, the First Amendment concerns seem to turn on ideas of transformation and new meaning drawn from what otherwise would be a mere representation . . . beautiful, perhaps, but without additional significance or meaning. From this perspective, one can say that the Court's job in the 2 *Live Crew* case was to find new meaning, transformation beyond the original, representation to something else in the minds or senses of the audience, and to do so with thoroughness, sensitivity, and particularity and, yet, to stop short of the boundary between judicial competence and Holmes's forbidden field of judicial incompetence to judge the quality of art and the beautiful (or ugly). Justice Souter's opinion suggests in this respect that courts can identify art but not judge it.

From a First Amendment perspective, a number of questions need to be asked. First, what exactly is the transformation in 2 Live Crew's "Pretty Woman"? Second, is the transformation to be judged by what a reasonable person "could perceive," by the audience's actual interpretation, or by 2 Live Crew's intent in making the rap song? Finally, why is parody needed at all if transformation is accomplished?

Justice Souter is clear on the transformation that "could be perceived . . . to some extent." The new meanings, for him, were (1) the naivete of the "original of an earlier day" or (2) the original's ignorance of "the ugliness of street life and the debasement that it signifies." Maybe so. But the Court provides little assurance to the skeptic. Such an intellectual interpretation may be the one that occurs to a Supreme Court justice, highly educated and existing in an elite vacuum, but what of those of us who regularly listen to rap, take its lyrics as they are given, and enjoy the beat? The naivete of the original "Oh, Pretty Woman" or the song's failure to embody the ugliness of street life and sexual debasement seem at least a few steps removed from what will likely be heard on 2 Live Crew's song, which is a comment on ugliness and debasement in itself—maybe even a repulsive reaction that reflects the sweet love that also exists (and thus interprets the song as a parody on rap, not vice versa).

Or maybe the new meaning is just the juxtaposition of one sentiment (sweet love) with the vulgarity of rap. Is this enough? Or is this what, by common practice and definition, much rap music does because of the inherent message of rap itself, unassisted by parody? If, for the Court, parody directed to the original song is essential, yet juxtaposition is part of what rap is, then all rap versions of nonrap music are paretic (under a very broad definition) and transformational. This is a conclusion that is hard to square with the fair use statute but that may be in harmony with the First Amendment.

How does one go about determining meaning—in this case the meaning(s) of a rap song for purposes of transformation analysis? One can start by saying that the meaning must consist of more than the text; if it doesn't, there is no transformation—or re-representation. So one must look beyond text. The Court says that one must look to what a "reasonable" person would or could perceive the meaning to be. The problems with this formulation are many, but two stick out. First, a "reasonable" person exists largely in the mind of the Court, in this case Justice Souter. He is surely reasonable, but he is not ordinary or average, and he is likely not a member of the group of persons who listen regularly to rap music. How is he, then, to reach out and capture a full picture of a reasonable person and then apply that person's understanding to 2 Live Crew's "Pretty Woman"?

One might instead look beyond text to context: to whom, when, and how the music is played, and why it is appreciated by those who buy it or come to hear it. This is an apt description of an approach that asks what the audience actually understands the song to mean and therefore whether there actually was transformation and of what kind. Such an undertaking is far from impossible in the judicial setting, but it requires the right decision makers and, more important, it requires actual evidence instead of imagination. The best justification for the Supreme Court's "community standards" approach to a jury's judgment of obscenity is precisely to determine what a community (here of rap fans) would conclude as to meaning *in fact*. There was nothing of this sort in the Court's opinion in the 2 *Live Crew* case, and no instruction that the district court to which the case was returned should undertake such an inquiry.

Finally, in seeking meaning one might look to the author's intent—in this case Luther Campbell's explanation of what he intended his use of the original song to say to listeners. Of course, there are real difficulties here, for the author's intent may be shaped by what later happens after the record is released, it might be calibrated to the law, and its potential unreliability as a guide likely requires some other evidence to test veracity. More basically, however, the author's intent is an unreliable guide to what the listeners actually hear, and what they actually perceive is the ultimate question to be answered. Campbell might intend rap parody. A listener might hear rap soul. Indeed, five different listeners might hear five different things.

If transformation is the necessary question, however, the endless potential for idiosyncratic meanings in an audience must somehow be domesticated into one or a few most common ones. Can that be done? Not easily, as this discussion suggests. Parody, whatever its specific meaning, is even too evanescent to rely upon in the 2 *Live Crew* case. But rap, as opposed to rock, isn't. These genres are sufficiently universal in perception and difference to say with certainty, that whatever specific transformative meaning a listener gives the particular lyrics or beat, for example, rap and rock are different and different in ways going to mode and mood as well as strict form.

So the last question is, why does the case have to hinge on parody? In truth, it doesn't. Even the fair use statue doesn't use the term. For First Amendment purposes, moreover, the transformativity question isn't constrained by such limitations as comment or academic history and the like. Transformation in a sensual or aesthetic sense will do, at least for art like "Oh, Pretty Woman," and rap from rock certainly involves re-representation of the original.

This seems true whatever the meaning or message is.

Would such an approach destroy copyright? I think not. And it would certainly go a long way to vindicating the First Amendment.

DANGEROUS ART

Virginia v. Black

538 U.S. 343 (2003)

AT THE OUTER EDGE of the free speech universe is an area populated by the most lawless and dangerous speech. It is an area that includes incitement to terrorism or revolution, Holocaust denial, racism, and other forbidden domains of contemporary expression. In the political arena, it includes speech that goes beyond advocacy of violence and disruption to direct incitement to violence against law, institutions of government, abortion providers, and the like. It includes also cartoons of Mohammad and representations of bestiality, subordination, obscenity, and defamation.

In the art world, it includes all of these same forbidden domains, many of which fall under the term *blasphemy*, speech dangerous not to person or property but to the security of belief and identity and spirit. The *Oxford English Dictionary* defines *blasphemy* as "profane speaking of God or sacred things; impious irreverence . . . against anything held 'sacred.'"[1] One might also think of blasphemy as a threat to or intimidation of fundamental beliefs.

In this distant First Amendment zone, the United States Supreme Court has crafted an outpost of freedom, believing that if the boundaries of such speech are not carefully and protectively established, the very foundation of free speech can crumble. The boundary was firmly set in 1969 in a case involving a Ku Klux Klan leader standing hooded before a burning cross and fellow Klan members threatening future "revengence" against "niggers and jews." The Court declared the speech protected by the First Amendment, stating that the freedom of speech does not "permit [government] to forbid or proscribe advocacy of the use of force or of law violation except where such advocacy is directed to inciting or producing imminent lawless action and is likely to incite or produce such action." With the requirements of direct advocacy, specific intent, action, and imminence of illegal action, the Court erected a high wall protecting freedom of speech even in the distant zone.

Speech threatening belief is always fair game under the First Amendment; only if speech directly produces imminent lawless acts may it be prohibited. This is the famous "clear and present danger test."

Thirty-four years later, however, in another Ku Klux Klan case—this one involving the visually powerful aesthetic force of a burning cross in public view, the Court appeared to step back, encouraged to do so by a fundamental belief—in this case, racial equality—and the power of speech to threaten that belief and to intimidate those who hold it. The Klan speech was not heard, nor was action imminent. Instead, the speech consisted of an image—the burning cross—and the revulsion, insecurity, and fear felt by those who witnessed it. The case was an example of the power and danger of some ideas, and the Court's felt need to protect against such expression, notwithstanding the First Amendment.

Our attention in this story—really a set of stories—will be directed to dangerous and intimidating speech, speech, as I described it above, that produces a "threat to or intimidation of fundamental beliefs." Threat and intimidation may take on various shades of meanings, but the underlying ideas are stable. Beliefs, however, even fundamental ones, change. Many believe that a basic function of art is to threaten and intimidate, to shake and upset fundamental beliefs, and to do so through the powerful aesthetic medium of the image and the transformative and re-representational potential of art.

Andres Serrano did more than shock and cause revulsion by his picture *Piss Christ*. He threatened core beliefs. He intimidated those whose identity rested on them. He undermined basic assumptions of the social order. Is his image different than the burning cross? Is it less threatening? Is religious conviction different than ideological conviction?

Alison Young describes the aesthetic and emotional response to *Piss Christ*:

> The picture on the gallery wall does not literally touch the spectator; however, the visceral response to artworks such as *Piss Christ* . . . can be interpreted as the shudder arising from an image which transcends the cushioning effect of the fact of representation and threatens metaphorically to touch the spectator. . . .
>
> This is the dynamic of "aesthetic vertigo." Rather than provoking a simple "disgusted" response, artworks such as . . . *Piss Christ* . . . make the spectator dizzy, teetering on the verge of a representational abyss . . . The desire to judge these artworks not only as disgusting but also as indecent, or obscene or blasphemous, is a desire for the reinstatement of the law (of

2. *Piss Christ*, by Andres Serrano. ©A. Serrano. Courtesy of the artist and the Paula Cooper Gallery, New York.

community, of religion, of representation) and a continued segregation of images into the sanctioned and the unwarranted.[2]

Our journey stretches over a long period of time. It will introduce different beliefs and different social orders. We begin with the burning cross, an image whose power genuinely partakes of art and aesthetics—aesthetics of the ugly as well as the beautiful. We will then examine the medium of film and its dangerous power. Following that we will turn the clock much further back to Edouard Manet's *Olympia* and even further back to Boccaccio's *Decameron*. Powerful and dangerous "texts" all.

• • •

We begin with a burning cross and a Ku Klux Klan gathering in Virginia. The focus will be on the burning cross, not the Klan gathering, for what is at issue is the image of the cross, visible from 300–350 yards away on a rural state highway, a silent but powerful message to the few passersby who noticed it, including the sheriff, who proceeded to arrest the Klan leader on the spot. He was arrested for displaying a burning cross in public view with intent to intimidate, a felony in Virginia.

3. Ku Klux Klan rally.

Ordinarily a burning cross is not thought of as art. But it partakes of central features of art: It is an aesthetic and skillful image for communicative purposes. It evokes sensual and emotional responses, and its messages are surely transformative or re-representational of the plain fact of a cross on fire. It is a very powerful, shocking, and dangerous image, not unlike, in many ways, the image of Christ on a cross in urine. If the latter is art, must the burning cross be, too?

Virginia Postrel has written wisely and usefully on the subject of aesthetics (not necessarily art).

> Aesthetics is the way we communicate through the senses. It is the art of creating reactions without words, through the look and feel of people, places, and things. Hence, aesthetics differs from entertainment that requires cognitive engagement with narrative, word play, or complex, intellectual allusion.
>
> Aesthetics shows rather than tells, delights rather than instructs. The effects are immediate, perceptual, and emotional. They are not cognitive, although we may analyze them after the fact. As a midcentury industrial designer said of his field, aesthetics is "fundamentally the art of using line, form, tone, color, and texture to arouse an emotional reaction in the beholder."
>
> Whatever information aesthetics conveys is prearticulate—the connotation of the color and shapes of letters, not the meanings of the words they form. Aesthetics conjures meaning in a subliminal, associational way, as our direct sensory experience reminds us of something that is absent, a memory or an idea. Those associations may be universal, the way Disney's big-eyed animals play on the innate human attraction to babies. Or they may change from person to person, place to place, moment to moment.
>
> Although we often equate aesthetics with beauty, that definition is too limited. Depending on what reaction the creator wants, effective presentation may be strikingly ugly, disturbing, even horrifying.
>
> Because aesthetics operates at a prerational level, it can be disquieting. We have a love-hate relationship with the whole idea. As consumers, we enjoy sensory appeals but fear manipulation. As producers, we'd rather not work so hard to keep up with the aesthetic competition. As heirs to Plato and the Puritans, we suspect sensory impressions as deceptive, inherently false. Aesthetics is "the power of provocative surfaces," says a critic. It "speaks to the eye's mind, overshadowing matters of quality or substance."
>
> But the eye's mind is identifying something genuinely valuable. Aesthetic pleasure itself has quality and substance. The look and feel of things tap deep human instincts. We are, as Brown says, "visual, tactile creatures." We enjoy

enhancing our sensory surroundings. That enjoyment is real. The trick is to appreciate aesthetic pleasure without confusing it with other values.[3]

Our inquiry here is not whether a burning cross is art but rather whether, art or not, images and representations can be too powerful to countenance in the law, notwithstanding the First Amendment. And it is on this question that the Supreme Court's decision in the burning-cross case, *Black v. Virginia*, is mightily, and perhaps disturbingly, instructive.

• • •

The Supreme Court heard oral argument in the burning-cross case on December 11, 2002. The Court was then, as it had been for many years, deeply divided. William H. Rehnquist was the Chief Justice. He was accompanied on the conservative side of the Court by Justices Antonin Scalia and Clarence Thomas. In the center of the Court were Justice Sandra Day O'Connor, who would author the opinion, and Justice Anthony M. Kennedy. On the more liberal side were Justices John Paul Stevens, Ruth Bader Ginsburg, Stephen Breyer, and David H. Souter. But the conventional liberal/conservative characterizations would not hold up in the end (as is often the case).

The lawyers arguing in support of the Virginia law banning intimidating cross burning were William Hurd, the State Solicitor for Virginia, and Michael Dreeben, Deputy Solicitor General of the United States. For the arrested Klan leader, Barry Elton Black, the case was argued by Rodney Smolla, a widely respected First Amendment scholar and then-dean of the University of Richmond Law School.

The Chief Justice was not able to attend the argument, so it was conducted by Justice Stevens, the next most senior Justice. Justice Stevens called Mr. Hurd to present his argument first.

MR. HURD: Justice Stevens, and may it please the Court: Our Virginia cross-burning statute protects a very important freedom, freedom from fear, and it does so without compromising freedom of speech. Our statute does not ban all cross burning, only cross burning used to threaten bodily harm. And our statute does not play favorites. It bans cross burning as a tool of intimidation by anyone, against anyone, and for any reason. Surely, for all the reasons why we can ban threats of bodily harm, one hundred times over we can ban this exceedingly virulent weapon of fear.

QUESTION: In this case, what evidence, other than the burning itself, was there to show intimidation?

MR. HURD: Klan leader Barry Black heard that—he's from Pennsylvania—and he heard that down in Carroll County, blacks and whites were holding hands on the sidewalk. And so he came down, and the Klan had this event. They chose a spot near an open stretch of highway where they erected a thirty-foot cross. And they burned it at night with a loudspeaker and talk about taking a .30/.30 and randomly shooting blacks.

QUESTION: Now, was that—did that intimidate everyone who drove by in their passenger vehicle or—let's put it this way—racial minorities who drove by in their passenger vehicle? All of those were intimidated?

MR. HURD: Whether or not there was actual intimidation of minorities who drove by was not clearly established by the record. There was evidence in the record that a black family did drive by, pause, saw it, and took off at a higher than normal rate of speed.

QUESTION: Yes, but surely they were in no fear of immediate violence, and our—our Brandenburg line of cases says there must be an element of immediacy before you can punish speech by reason of its content.

MR. HURD: Well, we believe, Your Honor, that if you read into the threat jurisprudence an immediacy element, then . . . you would constitutionalize threats when someone said, "I'm going to kill you, but it won't be for a little while." Surely that can't be the case. A threat, say, against the President would be constitutional so long as the time when the threat was going to be delivered was delayed.

QUESTION: Well, that may be a different . . . so in your view if a burning cross is just put on a hill outside of the city, everybody in the city can be deemed intimidated?

There are a number of questions swirling around here . . . and breeding some confusion. The first is the word *intimidate*, defined as "to render timid, inspire with fear; to overawe, cow." *Intimidation*, in turn, is "the action of intimidating or making afraid; the fact or condition of being intimidated; now, *esp.* the use of threats or violence to force to or restrain from some action, or to interfere with the free exercise of political or social rights."[4] The terms are decidedly ambiguous, ranging from being rendered afraid, timid, or cowed to fearing for one's safety. The second confusion involves intent. Under the law, the cross burner must intend to intimidate. Must the intent concern a known person or victim, or a general group of people, or simply a known likelihood that someone might be intimidated? And, finally, there is actual intimidation—say, fear of racially based violence. Must actual intimidation occur in order for the burning cross to be extinguished and those burning it to be jailed? Or is intent alone enough? If there is actual intimidation, need intent still be proved?

In fact, none of these questions can be answered from the cross-burning statute or, for that matter, from the Supreme Court's treatment of it in the case. The burning cross in the case was 300–350 yards back from the road; relatively few cars drove by on the out-of-the-way rural highway; one black family did drive by, slowed to see the cross, and sped back up right away. There was no evidence of actual intimidation if, as the Court often seems to assume, intimidation means directly threatening use of force against a person. There was no discussion of how intent to intimidate should be proved, except that it couldn't be proved simply by the defendant burning a cross. There was no talk by the Court of requiring imminence of harm to one or more persons.

All in all, the facts and issues were pretty loosey-goosey, yet they would be good enough, the Court said, to justify jailing the cross burner and censoring his speech/image. The image was simply too powerful for the Court to protect its use. How about Jesus in urine? Or Mohammed in urine?

MR. HURD: Your Honor, the burning cross carries not merely a message of intimidation but a threat of bodily harm soon to arrive.

QUESTION: Why doesn't Virginia just have a statute making it a crime to threaten bodily harm that's soon to arrive, burning cross or not?

MR. HURD: We could have such a statute, Your Honor, but the availability of other options does not mean the option we have chosen is unconstitutional.

The question is a fair one, and the answer isn't entirely pretty. If the law were a general law prohibiting criminal threats—say threats of bodily harm to another—it could be applied to a case of cross burning but only upon a showing that a threat to an *identifiable and known person's life or safety* was specifically intended by the burner at the time of the burning, and that the intended *threat caused harm to the person in fact*. Neither of these things were proven in the *Black* case, and neither were required by the Virginia cross-burning law. The fact is that the Virginia law could catch virtually all cross burning and thus was much more attractive to those who wanted the image of the burning cross banned.

QUESTION: Well, just to make it clear, anytime in Virginia a burning cross is put near a highway, that is an—a criminal offense.

MR. HURD: Your Honor, it is a criminal offense to burn a cross with intent to intimidate [in] a public place. A *public place* is defined in our statute—actually on a jury instruction—as being [in] public view [whether on private property or not].

QUESTION: And *intimidate* means to cause fear of violence at some unspecified time in the future to some unspecified people.

MR. HURD: To instill fear of—of bodily harm. The specificity of the people is not hard to figure out. It's whoever burns the cross is the one who is delivering the threat, Justice Kennedy.

Justice Kennedy is homing in on the uncertain scope of the law—the fact that the intent need not be specific to a person or group, that the harm of intimidation need not occur immediately (if ever), and that intimidation covers a lot of potential ground. Is the law really about the cross-burner's act or about the burning cross's message however disseminated?

QUESTION: Supposing he burned a circle, he could not be convicted on the same evidence?

MR. HURD: He could not. A burning circle, unlike a burning cross, carries no particular message.

QUESTION: May I ask you about a case of immediate concern? You have said that the burning cross is a symbol like no other. And so this is a self-contained category. What about other things that are associated with the Klan? For example, the white robes and the mask? Are they also symbols that the State can ban, or is there something about the burning cross that makes it unique?

MR. HURD: Justice Ginsburg, there are several things about the burning cross that make it unique. First, it is the symbol that the Klan has used to threaten bodily harm. The connection, if you will, in our history is between the burning cross and ensuing violence, not so much between people wearing white sheets and ensuing violence.

It may not be quite that clear. There are plenty of images associated with violence over the course of history. How about the cross and the Inquisition? The swastika?

MR. HURD: In terms of delivering symbols and delivering threats, a burning cross really is unique. It says, we're close at hand. We don't just talk. We act. And it deliberately invokes the precedent of eighty-seven years of cross burning as a tool of intimidation.

Burn anything else. Burn the flag. Burn a sheet. The message is opposition to the thing that the symbol unburned represents. Burning a cross is not opposition to Christianity. The message is a threat of bodily harm, and it is unique. And it's not simply a message of bigotry. It's a message that. . . bodily harm is coming. That is the primary message—

QUESTION: It sounds to me like you're defending the statute on the ground that the message that this particular act conveys is particularly obnoxious.

MR. HURD: Obnoxious? Justice Stevens, we have a lot of obnoxious speech, and it's all perfectly fine. This is not obnoxious speech. This is a threat of bodily harm. Justice Souter made the point [that] the Government may punish certain types of expressive conduct even though that conduct is associated with a particular point of view. Those who burn draft cards typically oppose the draft. Those who engage in sidewalk counseling typically oppose abortion. But we can impose restrictions on those activities. Similarly, we can ban cross burning as a tool of intimidation even though many people who practice cross burning may also carry with that cross burning some message of bigotry. But the primary message—the fundamental message is a threat of bodily harm.

And this is not something that we just made up. Cross-burning has that message because for decades the Klan wanted it to have that message because they wanted that tool of intimidation. And so it rings a little hollow when the Klan comes to court and complains that our law treats that message—treats that burning cross as having exactly the message that they for decades have wanted it to have.

And so, we do believe that our statute is—is quite constitutional. They may have a political rally with a burning cross, but what they cannot do is use a Klan ceremony as a way to smuggle through real threats of bodily harm with a specific intent to intimidate.

JUSTICE STEVENS: Thank you, Mr. Hurd.

One can burn a cross at a political rally, and it's protected speech, but at a Klan meeting, it isn't? Why is a Klan group standing around a burning cross 300–350 yards back from a county road, too far away to be heard, more intimidating than seeing a political rally using the burning cross, up close? The distinction doesn't make a lot of sense: Is intimidation more likely at one place than another? Is the intent likely different? The First Amendment demands more than Mr. Hurd has given if the government is prohibiting an image or a message and jailing the messengers.

Without saying so in the argument, the Court seemed inclined to treat the burning cross as an image with a message and, thus, speech; the problem was that the burning cross had too dangerous and hateful a message, and for that reason it should not receive the protection of the First Amendment.

It appears that the last bastion of free speech protection in the lawless outer zone, the clear and present danger test, is neither so clear nor so present in the modern Supreme Court. It will be up to Mr. Dreeben, representing the United States, to make sense out of this apparent confusion.

JUSTICE STEVENS: Mr. Dreeben.

MR. DREEBEN: Thank you, Justice Stevens, and may it please the Court: Virginia has singled out cross burning with the intent to intimidate because it is a particularly threatening form of such conduct. History has revealed that cross burning has been used as a tool to intimidate and put people in fear of bodily violence in a way that no other symbol has been used.

QUESTION: Is it a defense under the statute for someone to prove that they didn't intend to threaten anyone but just purely to express a viewpoint?

MR. DREEBEN: The statute does not reach cross burning when it is done solely for the point of expressing a particular view. But a cross-burning statute like this functions on the theory that a signal to violence or a warning that violence will come is not protected within the First Amendment. It is a prohibited form of conduct, and when done as here by an act of putting a flaming cross in a place with the intent to actually put somebody in fear of bodily harm, it's not a form of protected conduct that directly implicates the First Amendment.

This exchange goes to the very heart of the matter, whether the object of legal concern is a burning cross or a shocking, disquieting aesthetic image—even a work of art. The justices understand the issue: Must the expression produce illegal acts of violence by known persons as a direct and imminent consequence of the display of the cross, or is it enough that the image is intended to produce fear in someone with respect to violent acts that might occur at an indefinite time—and indeed might be caused by some other intervening agent? To put it another way, is the State's purpose in enacting the law to prevent illegal acts of violence, or is it to prevent an image that may produce fear in the mind of some viewers, even though violent acts are very unlikely to occur as a result? Mr. Dreeben says that it is the latter—fear instilled by the cross coupled with intent that fear be produced—which is likely no more than proven foreknowledge that it *may* occur.

The exchanges that follow probe the distinction. Justice Scalia has started things off. During the exchanges, a number of things should be kept in mind, for they are discussed later. First, are images particularly powerful because of their frequent appeal to the "immediate, perceptual, and emotional," not the cognitive or reasoned, as Postrel says? Are images "prerational [and often] disquieting"? Second, where does meaning come from—especially the meaning of an image? Does intent of the author have any place in ascertaining meaning? Third, should harm be based on belief-mediated responses that take the form of disquiet or fear, no matter how undifferentiated or unlikely its actual fruition? Might the answer be different if the mediated belief is based on a history of experience with lynching, killing, assault, as opposed, say, to a history of Holocaust or slaughter in the Crusades?

QUESTION: Is it unlawful in Virginia to put somebody in fear of bodily harm in some other fashion, not to burn a cross, but to say I'm going to lynch you? Is that unlawful in Virginia?

MR. DREEBEN: Justice Scalia, my understanding of Virginia law is that it has a written-threats statute which would cover any threat of any kind in writing, but it does not have a general intimidation or threat statute that would reach other means of oral expression.

QUESTION: It's sort of peculiar, isn't it?

MR. DREEBEN: Well, what Virginia has done is take something which has historically been used as a particularly dangerous means of intimidation because it has so often been followed up by actual violence and establish a prohibition that is limited to that. Rather than sweeping in other classes of speech that may raise questions when you come close to the line of whether it is or isn't intimidating and therefore might chill free expression, Virginia has chosen to focus on what conduct occurred within its borders that caused particular harms.

QUESTION: Is there an immediacy component to that as there is with assaults?

MR. DREEBEN: No, there is not, Justice Kennedy, and it's crucial to underscore why that is. The harms that can be brought about by threat statutes are not only putting somebody in fear of bodily harm and thereby disrupting their movements but providing a signal that the violence may actually occur. It may not occur tomorrow, the next day, or next week, but it's like a sword of Damocles hanging over the person who has been threatened. And in that sense it creates a pervasive fear that can be ongoing for a considerable amount of time.

QUESTION: This statute was passed in what year?

MR. DREEBEN: 1952 originally.

QUESTION: Now, it's my understanding that we had almost one hundred years of lynching and activity in the South by the Knights of Camellia and the Ku Klux Klan, and this was a reign of terror, and the cross was a symbol of that reign of terror. Isn't that *significantly greater than intimidation or a threat?*

MR. DREEBEN: Well, I think they're coextensive, Justice Thomas, because it is—

QUESTION: Well, my fear is, Mr. Dreeben, that you're actually understating the symbolism of and the effect of the cross, the burning cross. I indicated, I think, in the Ohio case that the cross was not a religious symbol and that it was intended to have a virulent effect. And I think that what you're attempting to do is to fit this into our jurisprudence rather than stating more clearly what the cross was intended to accomplish and, indeed, that it is unlike any symbol in our society.

MR. DREEBEN: Well, I don't mean to understate it, and I entirely agree with Your Honor's description of how the cross has been used as an instrument of intimidation against minorities in this country. That has justified fourteen states in treating it as a distinctive—

QUESTION: Well, it's actually more than minorities. There's certain groups. And I—I just—my fear is that—there was no other purpose to the cross. There was no communication of a particular message. It was intended to cause fear and to terrorize a population.

MR. DREEBEN: It absolutely was and for that reason can be legitimately proscribed without fear that the focusing on a burning of a cross with the intent to intimidate would chill protected expression. In the Virginia statute the focus is not on any particular message. It is on the effect of intimidation, and the intent to create a climate of fear and, as Justice Thomas has said, a climate of terror.

QUESTION: So your argument would be the same even if we assumed that the capacity of the cross to convey this message was limited to certain groups, blacks, Catholics, or whatnot.

MR. DREEBEN: I would, Justice Souter . . .

QUESTION: But it seems to me from this argument, if the message is as powerful as Justice Thomas suggests it is—and I'm sure he's right about that— why is it necessary to go beyond the message itself? Why wouldn't it still be proscribable even if the person burning it didn't realize all of this history, just did it innocently, but it nevertheless had that effect? Why do you need the intent? If the message is as powerful as we're assuming as it is, why isn't that a sufficient basis for just banning it?

MR. DREEBEN: It might well be, Justice Stevens, but I think that a law that is more tailored, as this one is, and reaches those acts of cross burning where it is the very intent of the actor to put a person or group of people in fear of bodily harm makes it quite clear that the statute aims at the proscribable feature of that conduct and not at the protected feature, namely race-based hatred.

JUSTICE STEVENS: Thank you, Mr. Dreeben.

Well! Some of the justices seem to be falling all over each other to sympathize with Justice Thomas's strong feelings about the burning cross, even to the point at which they ask whether the State couldn't just ban burning a cross, period. Justices Stevens and Souter seem enthusiastic about a flat ban at any time, any place, by anyone. And they are the liberals on the Court. But their view is the logical one if, as many seem to believe, the problem is the power of the image itself—what it says and does apart from any human agency. But can the forbidden image be limited only to the burning cross?

Mr. Dreeben offers a tepid agreement but nevertheless tries to stay on narrower and safer ground of intent to intimidate, distinguishing it from "protected . . . race-based hatred." One might wonder, though, whether the fear of harm from the cross can be so easily separated from expression of race-based hatred.

We now turn to Dean Smolla who, judging by the argument so far, clearly has a lot of convincing to do—and indeed a lot of teaching of the justices about their prior principles of free speech.

JUSTICE STEVENS: Mr. Smolla, we'll hear from you.

MR. SMOLLA: Justice Stevens, and may it please the Court: At the heart of our argument is that when the State targets a particular symbol or a particular symbolic ritual, it engages in content and viewpoint discrimination of the type forbidden by the First Amendment.

QUESTION: What about the symbol of brandishing an automatic weapon in somebody's face?

MR. SMOLLA: Justice Scalia, there is a fundamental First Amendment difference between brandishing a cross and brandishing a gun. The physical properties of the gun as a weapon add potency to the threat, and so if the State makes a threat committed with a firearm an especially heinous type of threat, it is acting within the confines of what is permissible. But the properties of the cross are not physical properties, and the burning elements of a burning cross are not what communicate the threat.

QUESTION: How does your argument account for that fact that the cross has acquired a potency which I would suppose is at least as equal to that of the gun?

MR. SMOLLA: Justice Souter, I think that our argument is that in fact it works the reverse way, that what the cross and the burning cross have acquired as a kind of secondary meaning, somewhat akin to the way that trademarks acquire secondary meaning in intellectual property law, are a multiplicity of messages. Undoubtedly a burning cross identified as the trademark of the Ku Klux Klan carries horrible connotations of terrorism of the kind—

QUESTION: But it—it carries something else, doesn't it? It's not merely a trademark that has acquired a meaning. Isn't it also a kind of Pavlovian signal so that when that signal is given, the natural human response is not recognition of a message, but fear?

MR. SMOLLA: No, Your Honor. Respectfully I think that that overstates what is being communicated. Any symbol in its pristine state that has gathered reverence in our society—the American flag, the Star of David, the cross, the symbols of government—is a powerful, emotional symbol in its revered state.

QUESTION: But they don't make—they don't make you scared for your own safety. And if you start with the proposition that the State can, in fact, prevent threats that scare people reasonably—for their own safety, this is in a separate category from simply a symbol that has acquired a potent meaning.

MR. SMOLLA: Your Honor, the word *scared* is important in answering your question because it's what we mean by being scared, or what we mean by being intimidated. If I see a burning cross, my stomach may churn. I may feel a sense of loathing, disgust, a vague sense of being intimidated. . . . But that's not fear of bodily harm.

QUESTION: How about a cross on your lawn? If you were a black man at night, I dare say that you'd rather see a man with a rifle than see a burning cross on your front lawn.

MR. SMOLLA: Your Honor, I concede that. However, as powerful as that point is—and I accept the history that Justice Thomas has recounted, and that the United States recounts in its brief—as powerful as all of those points are, there's not a single interest that society seeks to [achieve] in protecting that victim that cannot be vindicated as well, with no fall-off at all, by content-neutral alternatives, not merely general run-of-the-mill threat laws, or incitement laws, or intimidation laws which may have an antiseptic and sterile quality about them.

It may be recalled that a fundamental principle of free speech is that when government seeks to prevent an evil (here, fear for safety), government should seek to do so by regulating conduct first, and only if the evil is great and cannot be substantially prevented by conduct regulation should the government even think about regulating speech to prevent the harm. And even then the First Amendment prohibits the regulation of speech in virtually all cases.

This principle may partly result from a conviction that "mere" speech is harmless, though that is hardly true in all instances. It may also result from a belief that other speech can counter hateful and frightening ideas better than the hand of the criminal law. Finally, it may result from a recognition that virtually all speech is ambiguous: It conveys many different messages to various viewers or audiences, and thus it is hard to ascribe direct and clear causation to a word or symbol's relationship with an act. This is the ground on which Dean Smolla must make his stand, and he does so very, very well.

QUESTION: But why isn't this just a regulation of a particularly virulent form of intimidation? And why can't the State regulate such things?

MR. SMOLLA: Your Honor, it is not a particularly virulent form of intimidation.

QUESTION: Well, it is for the very reasons we've explored this morning. What if I think it is? Why can't the State regulate it?

MR. SMOLLA: Because, Justice O'Connor, it is also an especially virulent form of expression on ideas relating to race, religion, politics—

QUESTION: Yes, but what was made a crime was the burning it with a particular motivation, wasn't it? It wasn't the mere act.

MR. SMOLLA: And at the core of our argument, Justice Scalia, is the claim that the First Amendment prohibition of viewpoint discrimination [or censorship] encompasses not only [use of words to state a view], but also the singling out of a symbol because symbols acquire meaning in precisely the same way that words acquire meaning.

QUESTION: And so the question before us is whether burning a cross is such a terrorizing symbol in American culture that . . . it's okay to proscribe it.

MR. SMOLLA: That is a fair characterization of the question. And there is no getting around the fact that the harm the government seeks to prevent here indubitably flows only from the formation of this symbol.

QUESTION: So I would think then that if the test suggests that you cannot have a statute which says you cannot use the words, "I'll kill you," with an intent to kill somebody or threaten him, then there's something wrong with the test, not that there's something wrong with the statute.

MR. SMOLLA: Your Honor, take the words, "if you do that again, I swear I'll kill you." Those words in a given context might be breakfast banter, might be a joke. It might be something a teacher says to a student, or might be a true objective threat. And a core element of this Court's commitment to freedom of speech has been to separate abstract advocacy from palpable harm.

QUESTION: Well, I guess . . . you have a very interesting point. And as I've been thinking about it, it seems to me that a difficulty, a possible difficulty, with it is that the First Amendment doesn't protect words. It protects use of words for certain purposes. And it doesn't protect, for example, a symbol. It protects a thing that counts as a symbol when used for symbolic purposes.

MR. SMOLLA: That's correct.

QUESTION: So just as it doesn't protect the words, "I will kill you" but protects them when used in a play but not when used as a threat, so it doesn't protect the burning of the cross when used as a threat and not as a symbol. And now we have a statute that says you can use it as a symbol, but you can't use it as a threat. And therefore, the First Amendment doesn't apply. Now, if that's the right analysis, then what's your response?

MR. SMOLLA: Your Honor, that—everything you said up until the very end we would accept.

I have a—I have a hunch I have to at least say that much.

(Laughter)

Justice Breyer, it comes to this, that you cannot make the judgment that this law in its actual impact only penalizes those acts of cross burning that result in threat. It certainly chills a wide range of expression, as it did in this case, that cannot plausibly be understood as a threat of bodily harm in any realistic sense. Every time the Ku Klux Klan conducts one of its rallies, at the height of its rally, it burns a large cross, and it plays a hymn such as the "Old Rugged Cross," or "Onward Christian Soldiers" or "Amazing Grace," and this is a ritual that it engages in. Now, it is inconceivable—there is absolutely nothing in this record that says that every time the Klan does that, that is, in fact, a true threat.

QUESTION: No, it isn't, so long as the Klan doesn't do it in sight of a public highway or on somebody else's property, there's not a chance that this statute would apply to them.

MR. SMOLLA: Your Honor, but all the statute requires is that it be visible to others. And, of course, the First Amendment value here in our view is that speech, particularly disturbing and offensive speech that runs contrary to our mainstream values, is ineffective unless it is put out to the world where others can see it. As Justice Brandeis said [many years ago,] you don't make the world safer by driving the speech of hate groups such as the Ku Klux Klan underground. The burning cross, whether it's the nineteenth-century burning cross before the Klan began or today, introduces a symbol—first of all, just a cross before we get to the burning part, a symbol that you must concede is one of the most powerful religious symbols in human history. It is the symbol of Christianity, the symbol of the crucifixion of Christ. When the cross is burned, in much the same way as when the flag is burned, undoubtedly the burner is playing on that underlying positive repository of meaning to make the intense negative point, often a point that strikes as horrible and as evil and disgusting, but that's what the person is trying to do.

QUESTION: Mr. Smolla, there's a huge difference between a flag and a burning cross. The flag is a symbol of our government, and one of the things about free speech is we can criticize the President, the Supreme Court, anybody, and feel totally free about doing that. But the cross is not attacking the government. It's attacking people, threatening their lives and limbs. And so I think you have to separate the symbol that is the burning cross from other symbols that are critical of government, but that aren't a threat to personal safety.

MR. SMOLLA: Justice Ginsburg, I only partially accept that dichotomy. In fact, when the Klan engages in cross burning, it [conveys] a mélange of messages. Yes, to some degree, it is a horizontal message of hate speech, the Klan members attacking Jews and Catholics and African Americans and all of the various people that have been the point of its hatred over the years. But it has also engaged in dissent and in a political message. If you remember in *Brandenburg* [the prior cross-burning case involving the KKK], the Klan speaker, Brandenburg, said, "if the Congress doesn't change things, some revenges will have to be taken." In this case, President [Bill] Clinton was talked about by the Klan members. Hillary Clinton was talked about by the Klan members. Racial preferences and the idea that they're using taxes to support minority groups. There is a jumble of political anger, of—

QUESTION: It's your argument, I take it, that if you actually have a statute that criminalizes the use of particular words or the burning of a symbol, even if you qualify that by saying it's criminal to use them for certain purposes, you've monopolized those words because people who are using them from different purposes will be afraid to use them.

MR. SMOLLA: And not merely monopolize, Justice Breyer, but chilled the use of that combination of words or chilled the use of that symbol—

QUESTION: Yes. All right. I see your point.

JUSTICE STEVENS: Thank you, Mr. Smolla. The case is submitted.

Smolla acquitted himself well—brilliantly, even. The burning cross is an image—here 300–350 yards from a rural road not heavily traveled—and an image either contains or is used to send a message—to speak, in short. But few, if any, messages have only one message, and the burning cross is not an exception to this rule. To ban the image, therefore, is to ban all possible messages, good, bad, or in the middle; it is, therefore, to deprive a message of force or full meaning. Images shock. Speech shocks. That is one of the reasons we have a First Amendment.

Art, a form of aesthetic image, shocks, disorients, re-represents, evokes prerational emotion and feeling. It works just like the burning cross, which is a powerful aesthetic image, even if it is not art.

Even if an image has but one coherent meaning, would we be justified in prohibiting it because of viewers' (some viewers but not all) reaction—a feeling of isolation, uncertainty, fear of what is coming? Is it with feelings and beliefs that we must concern ourselves, protecting us from certain feelings with the assistance of state and censor?

On the other hand, there are certain cultural and deep personal truths—Justice Oliver Wendell Holmes Jr., the skeptic, called them his "can't helps"—truths like equality and the value of life. Such truths may be deemed foundational and, thus, unreproachable lest the very order of society be fatally undermined. Do we really lose all that much by preserving these truths through prohibiting certain ideas, like the message of the burning cross? Can't there be an exception to the general rule for just a few of the worst and most harmful ideas and images that convey them with the brutal force of emotion? Only a few. Like lynching, arson, and hanging on the tree outside the Black family's house? Who could blame the Supreme Court for agreeing to that?

• • •

The Supreme Court issued its decision on April 7, 2003. The decision was a jigsaw puzzle of opinions, none of which received five votes. But a common denominator was found in the basic conclusion and reasoning voiced by Justice O'Connor, who authored the opinion for the Court: Burning a cross in public view with intent to intimidate can be prohibited. The more interesting implications, however, lie in the details.

> Justice O'Connor announced the judgment of the Court and delivered the opinion of the Court with respect to parts I, II, and III, and an opinion with respect to parts IV and V, in which the Chief Justice, Justice Stevens, and Justice Breyer join.

> To this day, regardless of whether the message is a political one or whether the message is also meant to intimidate, the burning of a cross is a "symbol of hate." And while cross burning sometimes carries no intimidating message, at other times the intimidating message is the *only* message conveyed. . . . In sum, while a burning cross does not inevitably convey a message of intimidation, often the cross burner intends that the recipients of the message fear for their lives. And when a cross burning is used to intimidate, few if any messages are more powerful.

> "True threats" encompass those statements where the speaker means to communicate a serious expression of an intent to commit an act of unlawful violence to a particular individual or group of individuals. The speaker need not actually intend to carry out the threat. Rather, a prohibition on true threats "protect[s] individuals from the fear of violence" and "from the disruption that fear engenders," in addition to protecting people "from the possibility that the threatened violence will occur."

> Intimidation in the constitutionally proscribable sense of the word is a type of true threat, where a speaker directs a threat to a person or group of persons with the intent of placing the victim in fear of bodily harm or death. Respondents do not contest that some cross burnings fit within this meaning of intimidating speech and rightly so. The history of cross burning in this country shows that cross burning is often intimidating, intended to create a pervasive fear in victims that they are a target of violence.

> It does not matter whether an individual burns a cross with intent to intimidate because of the victim's race, gender, or religion or because of the victim's "political affiliation, union membership, or homosexuality." A ban on cross burning carried out with the intent to intimidate is proscribable under the First Amendment.

4. *Nazi Drawing #17*, by Mauricio Lasansky, courtesy of Lasansky Studio, Iowa City, Iowa.

5. *Nazi Drawing #29*, by Mauricio Lasansky, courtesy of Lasansky Studio, Iowa City, Iowa.

The key to Justice O'Connor's opinion is this language: "The speaker need not actually intend to carry out the threat. Rather, a prohibition on true threats 'protect[s] individuals from the fear of violence' and 'from the disruption that fear engenders,' in addition to protecting people 'from the possibility that the threatened violence will occur.'" The cross burner—or the artist, for that matter—need only be aware of the likelihood of intimidation and intend it in that sense. He or she need not intend to carry out any act of harm or violence nor know anything more than that a group exists some members of which will be intimidated. This is a "true threat," to use the Court's First Amendment terminology, only in the sense that, for someone at some time, the sense of threat will be real.

In the political realm, one must wonder whether Holocaust denial would qualify as a true threat. In the artistic realm, the possibilities are equally broad: a photo or painting of a lynching, Mauricio Lasansky's Nazi drawings, damnation of a religion or central belief. That these examples cannot be dismissed as qualifying as true threats speaks volumes.

> Justice Souter, with whom Justice Kennedy and Justice Ginsburg join, concurring in the judgment in part and dissenting in part.
>
> It is difficult to conceive of an intimidation case that could be easier to prove than one with cross burning, assuming any circumstances suggesting intimidation are present. The provision, apparently so unnecessary to legitimate prosecution of intimidation, is therefore quite enough to raise the question whether Virginia's content-based statute seeks more than mere protection against a virulent form of intimidation. It . . . bars any conclusion "that there is no realistic [or little realistic] possibility that official suppression of ideas is afoot," [thus, the law] can only survive if narrowly tailored to serve a compelling state interest, a stringent test the statute cannot pass; a content-neutral statute banning intimidation [rather than a particular form of intimidating speech] would achieve the same object without singling out particular content.

The issue raised in the opinions of Justices Stevens and Souter is whether a law that singles out intimidation by cross burning from the much-wider categories of intimidation—for example, intimidation based on gender or religion—is invalid because it selects one kind of intimidation or one point of view from all others. Justice Stevens concludes that picking out just one "particularly virulent" form of intimidation and prohibiting it is fine. Justice Souter disagrees. The result of their disagreement, however, is not that intimidating cross burning is constitutionally protected but rather that it should be prohibited as part of a larger set of intimidating images or messages. This is small solace.

Justice Thomas, dissenting.

In every culture, certain things acquire meaning well beyond what outsiders can comprehend. That goes for both the sacred, see *Texas v. Johnson*,[5] describing the unique position of the American flag in our Nation's two hundred years of history, and the profane. I believe that cross burning is the paradigmatic example of the latter.

Although I agree with the majority's conclusion that it is constitutionally permissible to "ban ... cross burning carried out with the intent to intimidate," I believe that the majority errs in imputing an expressive component to the activity in question. In my view, whatever expressive value cross burning has, the legislature simply wrote it out by banning only intimidating conduct undertaken by a particular means. A conclusion that the statute prohibiting cross burning with intent to intimidate sweeps beyond a prohibition on certain conduct into the zone of expression overlooks not only the words of the statute but also reality.

This statute prohibits only conduct, not expression. And, just as one cannot burn down someone's house to make a political point and then seek refuge in the First Amendment, those who hate cannot terrorize and intimidate to make their point. In light of my conclusion that the statute here addresses only conduct, there is no need to analyze it under any of our First Amendment tests.

Justice Thomas's opinion is notable for two reasons. First, he classifies cross burning—and indeed all other forms of intentional intimidation by expressive conduct—as conduct, not speech. As such, the First Amendment does not apply to a law prohibiting such acts. The expressive part of the conduct—a burning cross or presumably a painting or an act like Karen Finley's, has no speech component at all. And government's power to regulate such acts is broad and need not meet any special kind of constitutional scrutiny. Such acts can be regulated just like, for instance, spitting on the sidewalk to emphasize a point.

His second conclusion is not inconsistent with Justice O'Connor's opinion for the Court, but it is more explicit. *Intimidation* is a legal term that includes the sacred and the profane—cross burning that instills fear as well as flag burning that defaces the sacred, thus instilling another kind of hate and revulsion and, indeed, also fear. Would a photograph of Christ on the Cross in urine qualify? With the proper intent to defame and threaten religious conviction, it would seem so.

6. *Piss Christ*, by Andres Serrano. ©A. Serrano. Courtesy of the artist and the Paula Cooper Gallery, New York.

The Court has previously decided that flag burning as a means of expression is protected by the First Amendment, but that decision does not preclude the possibility, indeed the likelihood, that other forms of threatening through defamation of the sacred could be prohibited—perhaps defaming the sacred belief in equality or the sacred practices of religion.

• • •

The current story has focused on the cross-burning case because the central question in the case involves the power of image as expression. To put the point a bit differently, the case involves the power of aesthetic expression, expression that communicates at a sensual, non- or pre-rational level, appealing to emotion and noncognitive understanding or interpretation. The burning cross certainly qualifies under this description. Much, if not most, art does as well.

Many elements contribute to the power of the aesthetic in expression, whether the expression takes the form of a painting, a photograph, a play, a poem, music, or even a book, which is also capable (though, as Marshall McLuhan explains, less often) of sweeping the reader to an aesthetic sense transcending the cooler medium of cognition. In the *Virginia v. Black* case, history, and specifically the historically grounded cultural meaning attached to the burning cross, played a large role, especially for those who by virtue of race had deeply internalized the brutal connotations. This suggests, too, that the construction of meaning resided not in the image, or even very much in the "author's" intent, but in those persons who witnessed the burning cross in public view. Intention had little if anything to do with the image and resulting fear that arose in the viewer; instead intention has mostly to do with the law's ascription of guilt and the possibility (a bare one at best) that the public cross burning was inadvertent or that the burner was truly, although almost impossibly, unaware of the image's power and meaning.

The meaning—lynching, burning, violent racism—lay not in the image itself when viewed as a bare text. It instead arose from it in a transformative act of mental recall and construction or belief mediation. It arose, as with the St. Patrick's Day Parade, out of thin air, variously constructed in malignant or benign form by the various persons who viewed it. Of those harmed by the image, some were repulsed, some called up hate, and perhaps some—only "some," an unknowable number to the cross burner—were frozen in fear for themselves, their families, their way of life, their friends, their nation. Of this latter group, nothing specific can be said about their particular and unique individual perception. But for the Court, *likelihood* was enough. This, of course, is the difficulty presented by such terms as intimidation, blasphemy, indecency, and obscenity, to name but some.

The artist claims, with justification, that art is powerful in its evocation and impact. As an expert practitioner of the aesthetic and re-representational, the artist can claim that image and imagination are the means of aesthetic transformation—the necessary means, in fact. The forms of artistic power— the works of art—are not all malignant. But many are, and the line between the benign and malignant is a shadowy and, more important, changing one. By this, I mean that malignancy in art, if I may use the term as shorthand, is object, time, place, history, and culture bound. After all, *The Adventures of Tom Sawyer* looks a good deal different to our sense of the forbidden today than it did one hundred years ago, or even twenty-five years ago.

This discussion of the image of the burning cross presents two fundamental questions. If, in the context presented in the *Black* case, the burning cross was not art, its image was necessarily emotionally powerful, perceptually re-representational, and sensually evocative. How can we describe the difference between the burning cross and art? How can we explain a distinction between the burning cross and Serrano's *Piss Christ?* Certainly not in terms of power or emotion or sensual force or re-representation. Yet, if we are to privilege powerful art but not the burning cross, a line between them will have to be drawn, at least in the law.

A related question is why the freedom of speech should protect either example. As we already know, art itself fits uncomfortably within the history and purposes of the First Amendment. It needn't have any coherent message; indeed, in a sense it shouldn't have such a message, as meaning lies in the mind of the beholder. In its aesthetic evocation, art is difficult to distinguish from a beautiful sunset or an ugly thunderstorm—except that its creation—advertent or not—is a product of man's imagination. The purely aesthetic, however, has been given a place under the First Amendment: "Fuck the Draft" on a jacket is protected speech, including (even especially because of) the word *fuck*, which, according to the Court, adds force and emotion to the underlying message of disdain for the draft. The aesthetic, in other words, is connected to the cognitive—the message—and alters its force, though not its meaning.

Can it be that the aesthetic, when attached as a word equivalent, a force, or feeling, to a written message is protected as free speech . . . and for all of the cognitive self-governing justifications underlying the First Amendment? But the aesthetic, when unconnected with a coherent message communicated by a speaker or creator, is not protected? Is aesthetic use of words or messages protected but art not protected, at least unless it has a generally understood cognitive meaning? If art consists of meaning in the mind and imagination of the viewer or listener or reader only—a fine piece of music, a painting evoking feelings of hate or blasphemy or contemplation of the beautiful or sublime—must it lie outside the protection of the First Amendment? Or must it at least justify its place under that guarantee in very different terms calling upon very different purposes? Might it have to draw, for example, on an analogy between art and religious belief and feeling rather than free speech? Perhaps so.

In the following pages we will ply these waters with an emphasis on the culture- and history-bound quality of the forbidden image and its transcendent power as speech under the First Amendment. This inquiry begins with Giovanni Boccaccio and *The Decameron*, moves on to Edouard Manet and *Olympia*, and then turns to more recent times with film censorship and the film *The Miracle*, directed by Italian neorealist film director Roberto Rossellini.

THE DECAMERON

Giovanni Boccaccio was born in 1313, the illegitimate son of a Florentine banker in a small town of Certaldo, located southwest of Florence. Growing up in a prosperous household, Boccaccio benefited from a good education that continued when, in his teens, he moved with his father to the southern Italian city of Naples.[6] The French potentate Robert of Anjou ruled Naples during that time and transformed the city into a cultural hub where Italian, French, and eastern cultures mixed.[7] The Angevins built fortresses, opened universities, stimulated trade, and generally spurred art and culture in southern Italy.[8] Boccaccio's awakening as a writer may be traced to these years in Naples.

While in Naples, Boccaccio assisted his father in the banking trade. Unwilling to pursue that vocation, Boccaccio also began the study of canon law. That career did not take, either, and he eventually turned to writing. Boccaccio's return to Florence in the early 1340s marks the beginning of his serious literary output. A defining moment in the history of that illustrious city occurred shortly thereafter when, in 1348, the plague struck Florence, as well as the rest of Italy and Europe. The city lost over a third of its population and was ravaged socially and economically. Twenty-five million died across Europe, while Boccaccio himself lost his father and stepmother to the plague, as well as many of his friends.[9]

In the 1350s, Boccaccio found employment as a Florentine diplomat. He visited other Italian city-states and crossed the Alps to represent Florence before Popes Innocent VI and Urban V in Avignon, the southern French city that was the seat of the papacy from 1309 to 1377. In 1361, he was unable to gain any further diplomatic appointments and thereafter retired to his town of birth, where he retreated into solitude. With his reputation as "the father of Italian prose" solidified, he returned home to concentrate on living a simple life of meditation and prayer.[10] During these years, he continued to write and to maintain his friendship with Petrarch, the Italian scholar and "father of humanism," whom he had met years earlier. Boccaccio died in 1375 in Certaldo.

Of the various phases of Boccaccio's prolific life, it was the period between 1349 and 1351 that is perhaps the most significant from a literary perspective. Boccaccio composed *The Decameron* during this time, his most famous and most important work. Recognized—along with the writings of Dante and Machiavelli—as a crowning achievement of Italian literature, *The Decameron* is an early example of "modern" literature before the flowering of the Italian renaissance.

Set against the backdrop of the plague, *The Decameron* tells the fictional story of seven young women and three young men who flee plague-infested Florence for the countryside, where they pass the time by telling stories—ten stories told on each of ten days, one hundred stories in all. Each character is king or queen of the group for the day, which comes with the privilege of choosing the topic of the storytelling for the day. Over the course of the ten days, the group tells love stories that end tragically, love stories that end happily, or on the seventh day, for example, stories about wives playing tricks on their husbands. The result is a book of fables, fanciful tales that explore the range of human emotions—wit and ingenuity, love and lust, passion and hatred—that portray Italian merchant life and the nobility and peasant classes, and frequently mock the clergy.[11]

During Boccaccio's time, *The Decameron* was popular among the middle classes. It was generally ignored by the upper classes and in serious literary circles.[12] Such ambivalence reflected the source and inspiration for Boccaccio's stories. The author looked to the medieval period, rather than the classical world, for his source material.[13] He drew his stories from medieval texts and those peasant fables "beloved by the populace."[14] In contrast to Dante's *Divine Comedy*, whose exploration of the afterlife is inherently otherworldly, Boccaccio's tales are distinctly human, exploring the foibles and follies of everyday life in often exaggerated and comic fashion. Despite—or perhaps because of—their ribald qualities, Boccaccio's stories endured the test of time, as later writers and dramatists such as Chaucer, Shakespeare, and Keats borrowed from Boccaccio for their own works.[15]

For a fourteenth-century literary classic, one of the unique—or notorious—aspects of the book is its treatment of love and sex. The Decameron's novellas are filled with stories of irrepressible youthful love, but also of carnality and lust. Breaking with Italian literary tradition, Boccaccio features these themes openly in several of his stories, portraying them as natural and universal impulses that self-imposed asceticism is powerless to suppress.[16] Boccaccio's portrayal of sexuality in The Decameron is particularly poignant in light of the prevailing approaches to the subject in fourteenth-century Europe, which saw sex as more of a problem than anything else.[17] Premarital fornication was, of course, forbidden during this period. However, one Italian city went so far as to prohibit men from admiring women in church, while a statute from another town attempted to forbid men from approaching women on the streets.[18] These laws reflected the medieval-Christian ideal of the subordination of the sexual to the spiritual.

By contrast, the actualization of irresistible carnal desire is brought to the fore in several of the stories in The Decameron. Love is intimately associated with sex, not divorced from it. The tales of sexual licentiousness also coincide in some cases with a portrayal of the religious establishment as a depraved bunch. Although officially required to remain celibate, few clerics honored that commitment during this period.[19] Boccaccio's tales perhaps reflected the reality of the situation but took things to an exaggerated level to great comic effect. Boccaccio features clerical depravity in one tale (the first story of the third day) in which an enterprising young man feigns to be dumb in order to secure a position as a gardener in a convent where the nuns use him to satisfy their sexual needs. In one of The Decameron's most notorious tales (the tenth story of the third day)—which was edited or removed in some later editions—a devout hermit named Rustico tricks an unknowing young woman into believing that coitus represents an act of Christian piety.[20] The hermit is eventually undone, as the story goes, because his stamina is no match for her zest for religious devotion. Boccaccio employs religious imagery in this story and in others for similarly perverse ends, while he elsewhere parodies saints, sainthood, and the power of relics and impugns dogma, effectively "reversing Christian teaching about sex."[21]

Despite its reputation as the "first modern work of pornography," *The Decameron* did not immediately elicit the ire of the papacy.[22] Girolamo Savonarola, an Italian religious reformer, burned *The Decameron* in Florence in 1497 as part of his general purge of immoral writings, paintings, and other art associated with the renaissance in Italy.[23] Such fanaticism was atypical for the age, however.[24]

The papacy's first serious attempt to ban the work arose as part of the Church's reaction to the Reformation, when, in 1559, it was placed on the list of banned books—the *Index Liborum Prohibitum*.[25] Although the list was primarily concerned with heretical writers, *The Decameron*, it seems, was banned not primarily for its obscene content but rather for its depiction of the sexual depravity of nuns, bishops, and monks.[26] Given that Martin Luther's challenge to Catholicism was motivated in part by the perceived corruption of the papacy, the Church found Boccaccio's portrayal of the clergy to be particularly subversive.[27] For example, the Council of Trent—the Catholic theological council that met several times in the mid-sixteenth century to respond to the Protestant challenge—disapproved only of portions of the text.[28] As to editions in which the clerics where changed to laypersons, the book was not subject to ban.[29]

By the nineteenth and twentieth centuries, the Church had loosened its grip somewhat on public morality. But legislatures filled the gap, passing measures banning *The Decameron* by means of anti-obscenity statutes. *The Decameron* was proscribed at times in Great Britain, where destruction of the book was attempted as late as the 1950s.[30] In the United States, the text fell under state and federal obscenity law. The Federal Anti-Obscenity Act of 1873 was commonly known as the Comstock Law for Anthony Comstock, the postbellum anti-obscenity crusader who pushed the legislation through Congress and won appointment as a special postal inspector to enforce the law.[31] The statute prohibited the mailing of "[e]very obscene, lewd, lascivious, or filthy book, pamphlet, picture, paper, letter, writing, print, or other publication of an indecent character."[32] Comstock targeted *The Decameron* in particular, claiming that its novellas, the "lascivious products of ancient writers," set "our youth wild with passion."[33] These prohibitions were enforced on a variety of occasions at the turn of the twentieth century.[34] It was the subject of litigation in Massachusetts during this time and also in New York, where the work was declared not obscene.[35]

MANET'S *OLYMPIA*

When the French painter Edouard Manet presented his *Olympia* to the Paris Salon in 1865, he was unprepared for the negative reception the now-famous painting would receive. In a story that is now famous in the history of art, critics excoriated *Olympia*, a modern painting that, ironically, intended to invoke the memory of a revered Renaissance classic—Titian's *Venus of Urbino*.

Manet is widely regarded as having helped push art into modernity, his life a dividing line between the traditional and the modern.[36] *Olympia* represents a "founding moment" in this transition.[37] Born the son of a judge but a lackluster student, Manet scorned his father's profession. After a short flirtation with joining the French navy, he began his pursuit of a life in painting. Throughout his career, Manet maintained his "high bourgeois" roots, never adopting the bohemian lifestyle of some of his contemporaries.[38] Manet hungered for official approval and considered admission to the Salon to be the mark of an

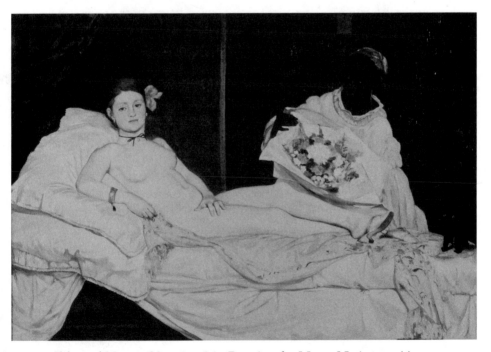

7. Eduoard Manet, *Olympia,* 1863. Reunion des Musee Nationaux / Art Resource, New York.

accomplished artist.[39] The Salon was France's official exhibition of art, held annually in Paris. Created by Louis XIV in 1663, the Salon was the focal point of the art world in the mid-nineteenth century and drew submissions from around the world.[40] Because the French state retained controlled over which pieces to admit to the exhibition, the Salon's tastes favored the conventional.

The Salon refused Manet's first attempt to submit *Olympia*. Manet then paired the painting with a religion-themed piece entitled *Christe insulté par les soldats* (Christ Mocked by the Soldiers).[41] This time he was successful. *Olympia* was accepted for display in the Salon in 1865, and it caused a great uproar.[42] The painting was instantly lambasted by its critics. The response among the viewing public was similarly virulent. At the time, Manet complained to his friend and renowned poet Charles Baudelaire, "[A]buses rain upon me like hail.... I have never before been in such a fix.... [A]ll this outcry is disturbing and clearly somebody is wrong."[43]

Why such a reaction, particularly for a now-revered painting that currently hangs in the halls of the Musée d'Orsay? *Olympia*, after all, is a nude— and there is no more ubiquitous subject in painting than the nude female form.[44] Moreover, the painting deliberately attempts to evoke Manet's celebrated Renaissance artistic antecedents, a connection that Manet assumed the sophisticated Parisian audience would make.[45] Although generally missed by his contemporaries, the link with the famous Venetian master Titian is unmistakable. Shortly after the Salon closed, one commentator, for example, labeled the painting "Venus with the Cat."[46]

"Venus," of course, refers to Titian's famous painting *Venus of Urbino*, housed in the Galleria degli Uffizi in Florence. Venetian art was popular in France during the nineteenth century, and the *Venus of Urbino* was known and widely reproduced during the period.[47] Manet himself had traveled to Florence and had made copies of Titian's painting, as well as other masterworks. Manet's imitative intentions are suggested by the fact that he unveiled *Olympia* along with *Christe insulté par les soldats*. Titian had apparently simultaneously presented two similarly themed works to Emperor Charles V in 1547, in which he intended to evoke the duality of the sacred and the profane.[48]

Titian's painting—titled after the Roman goddess of love—depicts a woman reclining on bed, surrounded by the accouterments of the Renaissance-era palace. The nude gazes invitingly at the viewer. Her pose appears less divine than erotically pliant. Her skin is milky white, and she is characteristically full bodied. The nude delicately guards her femininity with an adroitly placed hand while a small, apparently sleeping dog rests beside her.

Inside the grand room, a woman and girl are peering into a large *cassone*, a richly gilded or painted chest given to a wealthy bride on her wedding.

Olympia's compositional structure resembles the *Venus of Urbino* in many respects. But *Olympia* is not the idealized subject Titian created. The woman in *Olympia* is a courtesan—a prostitute for the Parisian upper classes. The name *Olympe*—the French version of the Italianized *Olympia*—was a frequent alias for prostitutes and courtesans in Paris at the time.[49]

Olympia is pictured in a position of repose not dissimilar to *Venus*. But in contrast to Titian's stylized canvas, the aesthetic sensibilities of Manet's piece are wholly different. They challenge the viewer, reversing traditional expectations about the portrayal of female nudity on canvas.

Olympia, like Titian's *Venus*, looks out at the viewer. In contrast to the *Venus's* seductive, erotic gaze, *Olympia's* does not seem to be an inviting or submissive one. She appears distinctly self-possessed, almost defiant. With one hand, she guards her sex but does so firmly, without the casualness Titian portrays in his work. One of her slippers has already fallen off—or been removed—perhaps suggesting to a viewer that she is already preparing for a male visitor. She is joined by a black maid-servant, bringing her a prominent bouquet of flowers. This bouquet, some viewers in 1976 suggested, has just arrived from one of her recent male visitors.[50] She sports an exotic flower in her ear, perhaps an orchid—a touch that critics have speculated conveys a sense of exoticism or is a subtle injection of the phallic into the painting.

Whereas a sleeping dog kept the Venus company in Titian's painting, a black cat at the foot of the chaise stares at the viewer. Where a dog represented stylized marital fidelity in Titian's work, it might be thought that the black cat suggests promiscuity in Manet's case[51]—the association of the feline with female sexuality. The nude's skin bears a yellowish tint, perhaps suggesting that she suffered from syphilis, which causes such discoloration, an affliction that was common in Paris at the time and that prostitutes were blamed for spreading. One contemporary described her body as having "the livid tint of a cadaver displayed in the morgue."[52] The shape of her body is unmistakably realistic. A short woman, her legs and body are slender. This suggests that her diet does not permit her to attain the healthy body to which the European viewer would have been accustomed—at least, in nude representations of persons from the upper classes. One author has termed her "emaciated."[53]

Manet had taken an icon and transformed it. In selecting Titian's work as a subject, Manet intermingled "contradictory ideas: classical and modern, mythic and actual, genre and portrait, precision and fluidity."[54] Where Titian depicted sensual romanticism, Manet depicted sex—an image of a prostitute following a visit by a patron. *Olympia* presented Paris with an image of a naked prostitute rather than the idealized nude.

Manet's break with his audience's aesthetic expectations was not lost on his contemporary critics. Viewing a model "stripped" of her "feminine qualities," the audience found the painting so bizarre and ridiculous so as to evoke laughter.[55] One viewer apparently found himself unable to describe the painting: "I can say nothing about her in truth, and do not know if the dictionary of French aesthetics contains expressions to characterize her."[56] Though most missed the connection to Titian, contemporary audiences sensed enough from the painting to know they generally didn't like it. Critics labeled her a "sort of female gorilla" or as lacking human form.[57] Titian's *Venus* clearly evokes none of these reactions—that painting is otherworldly.

But precisely what was it about the realism that audiences confronted in *Olympia* that elicited such scorn? Art critics and historians propose a variety of explanations, each of them rooted in the thesis that Manet's painting roiled its viewers' expectations—social, artistic, and gender. What "eluded their frame of reference"[58] was perhaps that Manet had inserted an apparently lower-class prostitute into the role of the idealized nude, disturbing nineteenth-century class associations.[59]

Alternatively, *Olympia*'s relationship with the viewer—her apparent lack of submission to the male eye—is one of disconcerting rejection of the onlooker. As one art historian has proposed, while Titian's *Venus* is "voluptuously available," *Olympia* seems to be fully in control of her body, free to accept or reject the favors of her suitors.[60] Another observer agrees that Manet presents a subject whose "blatant readiness to be consumed as an erotic commodity" is perhaps subordinate to her "taut, self-assured, commanding pose" that "appears to defy appropriation."[61] *Olympia* challenges the viewer by her refusal to be the object of gawking or fetishism.[62]

Olympia challenged and threatened to undermine deep-seated social and cultural expectations about sexuality and class, at least among the intelligentsia. It revealed their falsity. The price Manet paid for doing so was great controversy and ultimately the inability to sell *Olympia* during his lifetime.

After Manet's death, it was acquired by the French government, which owns it to this day. It is now widely considered Manet's finest work.

THE MIRACLE

In the seminal case of *Joseph Burstyn Inc. v. Wilson*,[63] the United States Supreme Court addressed whether and how the First Amendment to the Constitution protects filmmakers and their art. The Court's subject was a movie by the famous Italian director Roberto Rossellini entitled *Il miracolo* (The Miracle).

Rossellini, born in Rome in 1906, is widely regarded as one of Italy's greatest directors and a founder of the Italian neorealist style of filmmaking. Neorealist cinema emerged following World War II, and its films typically depict the struggles of lower-class life. Rossellini's 1945 *Roma, cittá aperta* (Rome, Open City), one of his most critically acclaimed works that portrays the everyday challenges of residents of Rome living under German occupation, exemplifies this style. Rossellini's involvement in the cinema began in the 1930s in fascist Italy, during which time he made six films, only one of which survives.[64] Rossellini filmed documentaries, including one on the rise of Louis XIV for French television and another in 1957 on modern India. But Rossellini was also well known for his well-publicized love affairs, including one affair with Ingrid Bergman, which later led to marriage.

The object of the dispute in *Burstyn*, Rossellini's *Miracle*, is only forty minutes long. A short picture and the second of two episodes of the two-part film *L'Amore, The Miracle* stars Anna Magnani in the role of a "demented goat herder."[65] The plotline in *The Miracle* explicitly melds the sacred and the sexual.[66] The film finds the protagonist tending to her herd of goats when she encounters a bearded stranger. Delusional, she believes the stranger to be Saint Joseph, there to take her to heaven. He serves her wine, and at the height of her delusions, the vagrant ravishes her. This carnal encounter is for her an episode of religious ecstasy.[67] Uncertain whether the experience was a dream or reality, she descends from the hilltop and into town. The village women later discover that she is with child, a pregnancy she believes to be a divine gift. She thereafter suffers abuse from the townspeople for her belief and flees town to live in a cave. When her delivery is imminent, she wanders through the village but—like Christ's ascent to Calvary—turns toward a church on a high hill to deliver, lumbering toward it and crying out for God.[68] She finds a side entrance to the church and enters. In the dramatic culmination of the film, she gives birth to a son whom she believes to be a saint.[69]

Italians greeted the film with ambivalence upon its release in 1948. *The Miracle* was not popular at the Italian box office, nor did it attract significant negative attention from Italian authorities.[70] The Vatican's censorship agency, the Catholic Cinematographic Centre, did, however, describe the film as "an abominable profanation from religious and moral view-points."[71] But the Vatican, which under the Italian Constitution had the power to have the State suppress films, cleared the movie for showing, as did the Italian government.[72]

The Miracle met a different reception in the United States. Although the film won awards in Europe and in the United States and enjoyed positive reviews in the New York Times and from various academic commentators, other segments of society denounced it. The motion-picture division of the New York State Education Department first licensed the movie without subtitles in March 1949. However, paired with two other short films in a trilogy entitled The Ways of Love, The Miracle was first shown on November 12, 1950, at the Paris Theatre on Fifty-eighth Street in New York City upon its second licensing.[73] Shortly after its showing, it came under attack from the Catholic archdiocese of New York, which excoriated The Miracle as "an open insult to the faith of millions of people in this city and hundreds of millions throughout the world," and from the National Legion of Decency, a Catholic organization advocating film censorship.[74] Cardinal Spellman, archbishop of New York, added that "the perpetrators of The Miracle unjustly cast their blasphemous darts of ridicule at Christian faith and at Italian womanhood, thereby dividing Religion against Religion and race against race."[75] Critics did not stop with mere verbal denunciations. The Catholic War Veterans, the Holy Name Society, and others picketed the Paris Theatre, which also received a number of bomb threats and had its phone line cut.[76]

The first attempt to suppress the film proved ineffective. New York City's commissioner of licenses threatened to suspend the Paris Theatre's license and ordered the film withdrawn.[77] The New York Supreme Court ruled shortly thereafter that the commissioner of licenses lacked the power to censor movies.[78] The uproar over the film caused the New York State Board of Regents, which had supervisory authority over the New York State Education Department, to review the film. The chancellor of the board requested that three of its members analyze the film and report on whether there existed grounds for finding the film "sacrilegious."[79] The three-member committee concluded that The Miracle was indeed sacrilegious.[80] The Regents then ordered that the theater show cause why its license should not be suspended.[81] The Regents formally rescinded the Paris Theatre's license to exhibit The Miracle on February 16, 1951, finding that "the mockery or profaning of . . . beliefs that are sacred to any portion of our citizenship is abhorrent to the laws of this great State."[82]

Joseph Burstyn Inc., which owned the exclusive rights to distribute *The Miracle* in the United States, challenged the board's actions. The New York courts upheld the Board of Regents' determination on the grounds that the film was sacrilegious.[83] The stage was set for a challenge in the United States Supreme Court.

The Supreme Court disposed of the case promptly and with apparent ease, declaring the decision of the Board of Regents unconstitutional. The Court's opinion was brief and, frankly, narrow. The action of the board denying the license constituted, the Court said, a prior restraint of speech—an act in the form of censorship that is rarely countenanced by the First Amendment. The film was protected under the First Amendment "as an organ of public opinion" whose protection is "not lessened by the fact that [films] are designed to entertain as well as to inform."[84] The board's standard of "sacrilegious" was too vague and potentially open-ended to serve as the basis for government prior restraint of speech, the Court said, adding "It is not the business of government in our nation to suppress real or imagined attacks upon a particular religious doctrine, whether they appear in publications, speeches, or motion pictures."[85]

The opinion was far from a ringing endorsement of the proposition that art is protected speech, as opposed to its informative dimension, and hardly a recognition that the aesthetic is as valuable as the cognitive. The board's misguided attempt to protect the integrity of a religious doctrine (divine conception) in the name of sacrilege is hardly the same as a claim of intimidation and fear stemming from blasphemy. The Court's opinion left room for prohibiting the latter.

DANGEROUS ART

Art can be dangerous—as much, if not more so, than less emotional and visual forms of speech. The dangers—intimidation, fear, revulsion, spurred violence, moral decay—are real. They are, to be sure, highly circumstantial and deeply cultural in identity and incidence, but it will simply not do to elide the danger problem by disputing the fact of danger or claiming that art, as opposed to other forms of expression, never produces harm.

Each generation, of course, has its own dangers. The fear and uncertainty instilled by undermining social norms in *Olympia* or blasphemy in *The Decameron* or sacrilege in *The Miracle* are different only in time and culture and belief from that instilled in the mind of a black person by the burning cross. The denial of one's personhood and individuality by racist or sexist or homophobic speech effects an exclusion from society and an impediment to work, learning, and freedom just as condemnable today as the earlier examples were in their time.

It is tempting to prevent such harm by prohibiting its agent, whether speech or art. To this end, the European Union recently announced a decision that will make punishable in each member state the following intentional conduct:

> (a) publicly inciting to violence or hatred directed against a group of persons or a member of such a group defined by reference to race, colour, religion, descent or national or ethnic origin;
> (b) the commission of an act referred to in point (a) by public dissemination or distribution of tracts, pictures or other material;
> (c) publicly condoning, denying or grossly trivialising crimes of genocide, crimes against humanity and war crimes ... directed against a group of persons or a member of such a group defined by reference to race, colour, religion, descent or national or ethnic origin when the conduct is carried out in a manner likely to incite to violence or hatred against such a group or a member of such a group.[86]

The EU law would prohibit Serrano's *Piss Christ* and paintings or cartoons of Mohammad or Salmon Rushdie's *Satanic Verses* or *The Decameron* or *The Miracle*. Like some university speech codes in the United States, the law represents today's version of blasphemy, which is simply a definition of those ideas that a culture deems unspeakable and those values it deems unchallengeable at any point in time.

If anything, the sensory and emotional and often visual or re-representational nature of art makes it more powerful and less susceptible to the cooling impact of cognitive expression and reason. It is an entirely different experience to read about a burning cross than to witness it firsthand or to see its image on film or canvas. *Olympia* challenges and undermines social conventions more efficiently and effectively than any essay or book on the subject could have done. The visual and fictive force of the novel or short story—genres spawned by *The Decameron*—threatened Catholicism more effectively than a series of essays about the sexual hypocrisy of monks and priests.

Thus, a set of choices is left that everyone would prefer not to face. Either artistic expression is treated just like any other form of speech and subject it to restrictions, broad or narrow, that are visited generally on speech (like decency, intimidation) or art is exempt from restrictions that are based on dangers it produces because art is, well, art, even though it is every bit as likely, if not more so, to produce harm than nonartistic expression.

The first alternative would allow avoidance, at least for these purposes, of the definitional question of what is art or even good art. Art is simply a form of free speech indistinguishable from all others. But the price to be paid would be high if, as may well be the case, art is peculiarly likely to challenge conventions and enter forbidden aesthetic domains that, for speech, can be regulated.

The latter view—affording distinct and often special protection from restriction to artistic expression—is more palatable for those who value art above much else. But it requires that there be judicially manageable criteria by which artistic and aesthetic expression can be identified and the importance of which can be judged. And this requires, finally, that we squarely confront the surprisingly difficult questions of the purposes served by art and their relation to the purposes served by the First Amendment guarantee of freedom of speech.

ART AND ITS VALUE

Art is viewed by many scholars and philosophers as a genre of expression that relies in the first instance on emotion or sensuality (appeal to the senses as distinguished from cognition), that its message lies in the mind of the audience, and specifically that it appeals to imagination, re-representation, or new or altered perception or understanding. Art in this view is transformative in a special way. Perhaps the most articulate proponent of this view is John Dewey, the foremost pragmatic philosopher of the twentieth century and author of the famous book *Art as Experience*.

> Art is the living and concrete proof that man is capable of restoring consciously, and thus on the plane of meaning the union of sense, need, impulse and action characteristic of the live creature. The intervention of consciousness adds regulation, power of selection, and redisposition. Thus it varies the arts in ways without end. But its intervention also leads in time to the idea of art as a conscious idea—the greatest intellectual achievement in the history of humanity.[87]

Man lives in a world of surmise, of mystery, of uncertainties. "Reasoning" must fail man—this of course is a doctrine long taught by those who have held to the necessity of a divine revelation. Keats did not accept this supplement and substitute for reason. The insight of imagination must suffice. "This is all ye know on earth and all ye need to know." The critical words are "on earth"—that is amid a scheme in which "irritable reaching after fact and reason" confuses and distorts instead of bringing us to the light. It was in moments of most intense esthetic perception that Keats found his utmost solace and his deepest convictions. This is the fact recorded at the close of his Ode. Ultimately there are but two philosophies. One of them accepts life and experience in all its uncertainty, mystery, doubt, and half-knowledge and turns that experience upon itself to deepen and intensify its own qualities—to imagination and art. This is the philosophy of Shakespeare and Keats.[88]

Art is a quality of doing and of what is done. Only outwardly, then, can it be designated by a noun substantive. . . . The *product* of art—temple, painting, statue, poem—is not the *work* of art. The work takes place when a human being cooperates with the product so that the outcome is an experience that is enjoyed because of its liberating and ordered properties. Esthetically at least:

> [W]e receive but what we give,
> And in our life alone does nature live
> Ours is her wedding garment; ours her shroud.[89]

Art is a mode of prediction not found in charts and statistics, and it insinuates possibilities of human relations not to be found in rule and precept, admonition and administration.

> But art, wherein man speaks in no wise to man,
> Only to mankind—art may tell a truth
> Obliquely, do the deed shall breed the thought.[90]

Plato, Immanuel Kant, and others took a similar view, though their emphasis was on the sensuous and perceptual hallmarks of art and less on the transformative or re-representational character of its effect on the audience. For them, art was the object (painting, poem) and its sensual evocation. It lay only partly in the interpretation or construction of an audience that gives it new emotional meaning and power. Yet, for Plato, it was the latter qualities that made art dangerous.

Yet another view of art rests its existence, fundamentally, in the artist's or creator's intention. This is not a view that anything intended as art is, therefore, art. Such a view would be hopelessly overbroad and, at the same time, underinclusive. But the intention view does have a well-grounded pedigree in First Amendment theory: speech, including art as a form of speech, is an individual act of liberty and free will that should be protected, at least, in the service of creative liberty—a liberty possessed not by the interpreter but by the speaker, the artist. This concept is both acknowledged and critiqued by Ronald Dworkin, perhaps the most famous philosopher of our day, in his famous work *Law's Empire*.

> [T]he author's-intention method of artistic interpretation is disputed even in its most plausible form. Many critics argue that literary interpretation should be sensitive to aspects of literature—the emotional effects it has on readers or the way its language escapes any reduction to one particular set of meanings—whether or not these are part of its author's intention even in the complex sense. . . . And even those who still insist that the artist's intention must be decisive of what the "real" work is like disagree about how that intention should be reconstructed.
>
> Here is one answer to that question. Works of art present themselves to us as having, or at least as claiming, value of the particular kind we call aesthetic: that mode of presentation is part of the very idea of an artistic tradition. But it is always a somewhat open question, particularly in the general critical tradition we call "modernist," where that value lies and how far it has been realized. . . . Some critics . . . [reject] values of tradition and continuity in which an author's place shifts as tradition builds, and argue for a retrospective interpretation that makes the best reading of [a] work depend on what was [seen] a century later. Still more radical challenges, which insist on the relevance of the social and political consequences of art or of structuralist or deconstructionist semantics . . . , seem to reject the enterprise of interpretation altogether. . . .
>
> I mean only to suggest how the argument over intention in interpretation, located within the larger social practice of contesting the mode of art's value, itself assumes the more abstract goal of constructive interpretation, aiming to make the best of what is interpreted.[91]

Intention can't govern the question of art or its meaning. Intention is rarely ascertainable or reliable, and over time, it may be irrelevant. More basically, it misfits the very nature and value of art, which goes not to the liberty of the artist but to the liberty of the audience engaged in its own, often idiosyncratic and time- and culture-bound ascription of meaning. Intention may well be an important element of that exercise of meaning-giving, but it may not. And intention can take on too many meanings itself to play more than a supportive role. In this sense, the Supreme Court's decision in the *Hurley* case was surely correct: that the meaning of the St. Patrick's Day Parade rested with those who viewed it, each bringing their experience, culture, values, and emotions to the undertaking. Meaning thus does not come "out of thin air," as the Court's opinion might imply, but it is just as surely not a product of the intentions of the parade organizer.

THE CONSTITUTIONAL VALUE OF ART

We have alluded many times before to the uncomfortable relationship between art and free speech. The difficulty is a product of the historical record, in which free speech was seen as an important instrument of democratic self-governance and a means by which, in the competition of ideas, political (and economic and social) views could be shaped and tested in the reasoned and essentially cognitive process of public and private discourse. Faith, it is said, is the predominant business of the religion guarantees. To qualify for protection (or full protection) under the free speech guarantee, therefore, art must serve the masters of truth, of individual freedom, of political self-realization, and of the process of self-governance. The cognitive and reasoned prerequisite for protected speech has allowed scholars and courts alike, including the Supreme Court, to exclude obscenity and much indecent speech from the First Amendment, as well as speech that is of such power—perhaps aesthetic power—that it directly produces illegal conduct or defined harm, such as intimidation.

Art is not, by any fair standard, purely cognitive, and, indeed, it would exclude much art to require that it be shown to have some predictable or intended cognitive message or effect. Art's appeal to the senses makes it inherently dangerous because powerful and unpredictable. And artistic expression may but need not concern issues of self-governance and political democracy.

Yet, the intuitively grim conclusion that art is not a form of free speech has led the Supreme Court and thus many scholars to assert, with a large degree of analytical foot-stomping, that art is protected by the First Amendment. Exactly why this is so and what forms and types of art are protected remains largely a constitutional mystery.

At this juncture, two alternative views present themselves. The first is that art is, qualitatively, distinct from speech. It is not the handmaiden of self-government or reasoned liberty. It exists instead on a different plane from democratic theory, the makings of which are imagination and mystery and the purely sensory—the ineffable, perhaps.

Yet, this highly abstracted conception of art seems somehow incomplete. It lacks Dewey's pragmatic insistence that art must ultimately connect to the world in which we live, though in special ways. For Dewey, the connection between art and individual self-government may not be as difficult as it might first appear. Free speech, after all, rests on the assumption of individual free will and liberty of belief. It rests on the capacity for free political and economic and social and personal and religious beliefs, which, then, serve the self-governing objectives of representative democracy.

Free will is not a function only of cognition and reasoned views. It is a function, too—and perhaps even more so—of individual identity grounded in perception, imagination, and creativity. Without these qualities, an individual's free beliefs consist of little more than the more factually correct or logically reasoned choice, a relatively mechanical conception of freedom. Imagination, creativity, and a capacity to perceive the world and what it contains in a personal and unique way give articulable and defensible—that is, cognitive and reasoned—conclusions for both life and individuality. Genius is said by some to be the capacity to see the world differently, a bit off-center, connected in unappreciated ways. The account, perhaps fable, of Isaac Newton seeing an apple fall but perceiving and then understanding it differently in terms of gravity illustrates the point. Albert Einstein's perception of the relativity of speed and time and mass originated in a re-representational perception of common events.

The point is not that art must serve such ultimately scientific or cognitive ends to qualify for protection or that the apple was art to Newton. It is instead that imagination is foundational to self-identity—who we are and why, even—and to knowledge and intelligence and insight and creativity. These things are not separate from the capacity to think and conclude, but, as Anthony Damasio and others have observed, they are inextricable parts of our mental processes.[92] Art produces re-representation; it fosters interaction between the sense and the sensible, faith and reason, sensuousness and cognition. Art produces truth, in the sense that it produces new ways of seeing and believing and feeling. It is as essential to the quest for truth, political or otherwise, as is reason and discourse, as Dewey lays out in several places throughout his book *Art as Experience:*

> There is no art without the composure that corresponds to design and composition in the object. But there is also none without resistance, tension, and excitement; otherwise the calm induced is not one of fulfillment. In conception, things are distinguished that in perception and emotion belong together. The distinctions, which become antitheses in philosophic reflection, of sensuous and ideal, surface and content or meaning, of excite-

ment and calm, do not exist in works of art; and they are not there merely because conceptual oppositions have been overcome but because the work of art exists at a level of experience in which these distinctions of reflective thought have not arisen.[93]

[T]he art characteristic of a civilization is the means for entering sympathetically into the deepest elements in the experience of remote and foreign civilizations. By this fact is explained also the human import of their arts for ourselves. They effect a broadening and deepening of our own experience, rendering it less local and provincial as far as we grasp, by their means, the attitudes basic in other forms of experience.[94]

Every well-constructed object and machine has form, but there is esthetic form only when the object having this external form fits into a larger experience.[95]

Shelley said, "The imagination is the great instrument of moral good, and poetry administers to the effect by acting upon the causes." Hence it is, he goes on to say, "a poet would do ill to embody his own conceptions of right and wrong . . . in his poetical creations. . . . By the assumption of this inferior office . . . he would resign participation in the cause"—the imagination. It is the lesser poets who "have frequently affected a moral aim. . . ."[96]

Art is a mode of prediction not found in charts and statistics, and it insinuates possibilities of human relations not to be found in rule and precept, admonition and administration.

> But art, wherein man speaks in no wise to man,
> Only to mankind—art may tell a truth
> Obliquely, do the deed shall breed the thought.[97]

In a way, perhaps, art can be squared—indeed *must* be squared—with the purposes of the First Amendment. But what makes this conclusion possible is a view of art that is distinct and separate from free speech as it has been conventionally defined. And it is that irony that has been the nub of the constitutional problem of art and free speech.

Can we protect art as free speech and at the same time argue that art is special speech? Can we argue that art's constitutional protection must be differently understood and perhaps effectively greater than many other forms of protected speech? It is this question that is the subject of the next story.

This last chapter will come full circle, returning to the various meanings of art and understandings of aesthetic expression. In the process we will ask whether it is possible to define art and to define it independently of judging its quality—its goodness or badness. Can art be distinguished from craft, skill from aesthetic re-representation? And the last chapter turns also to the important practical question that has been explored in so many ways in these pages: Should art qualify as speech under the First Amendment? Judged by what standard? And with what degree of protection or privilege from the hands of the law?

All of this and a bit more is considered in the context of J. S. G. Boggs, a currency artist extraordinaire. Are Boggs's "bills" art or craft only? How do they differ from Andy Warhol's painting of Campbell's soup cans? Or an ad for smoking, like the Marlboro Man? Can their quality as art be distinguished from, say, their quality as skill? In 1946, the art critic Clement Greenberg said about artist Edward Hopper, "Hopper simply happens to be a bad painter. But if he were a better painter, he would, most likely, not be so superior an artist."[1]

ART AND CRAFT

J. S. G. Boggs v. Bowron

J

S. G. BOGGS is a currency artist. Currency art, a subspecies of *tromp l'oeil*—a fancy French expression meaning "fool the eye"—has a relatively long tradition in America and elsewhere, particularly Europe. It is said to have fully blossomed in America with the populist resistance to paper money following the Civil War, a cause made memorable with William Jennings Bryan's "Cross of Gold" speech. J. S. G. Boggs is perhaps its finest, and surely its most famous, practitioner.[1]

Boggs's currency art is often vivid, obvious, funny, satirical. It is remarkably detailed in its rendition of currency design, accomplished by hand on various paper stocks. Much of it is quite subtle in its differences from real currency—differences in coloring or shading, signature, or motto. Many of the American Boggs Bills, as they are often called, could easily escape notice as artistic rendition rather than the real item. Deception, or fooling the eye, could thus be alleged—even counterfeiting—except for two very important things. First, the bills are only one-sided. Second, Boggs never tries to "spend" the bills. Instead he openly and only after engaging a person—perhaps a waiter or merchant—in a discussion of the bills, "sells" them in exchange for goods or services. The merchant or "buyer" can hold the bill as art or sell it for a considerable sum two or three days later when contacted by an earnest collector to whom Boggs has sold the receipt, change from the transaction, and the identity of the buyer (for a significant sum as well).

James Stephen George Boggs was born Steve Litzner in 1955 in New Jersey. He lived with his mother and stepfather, moving from place to place and finally ending up in Florida, where his stepfather was a citrus grower and later an investor. James never graduated from high school; he had been kicked out of eleventh grade, "accused of starting a riot in the auditorium." He worked at a printing company, wrote a play, managed a rock group, entered a

8. Boggs Bills. Courtesy of J. S. G. Boggs and the Sherry Frumkin Gallery, Santa Monica, California.

management-training program with Holiday Inn, and studied accounting at Miami University in Oxford, Ohio. But business just didn't work for him, so he returned home to study art at a community college. Thereafter, he spent time in the art culture of London. In 1979, he was admitted (on special terms given his lack of a high-school degree) to Columbia University's art program. He "received a degree" at Columbia, to which he adds, "I mean I have a piece of paper—a blank one. They gave it to me a year later on condition I'd leave. I kept signing up for classes for which I didn't have prerequisites—studio art, economics, Russian—and they said ' . . . you have to take these other required courses, too. Take it or leave it.' So I left it." His friend in the admissions office told him, "'You're right, There's nothing more we can offer you, you don't need it, you're already a master.' He laughed, opened his drawer, and handed me a blank diploma. I was on the next flight back to London."[2]

Back in London, he did odd jobs and after a few years started painting full-time—portraits, objects, even some abstract paintings. He did not begin creating currency art until a few years later, in 1984.

> [H]is inspiration came on a visit to Chicago's Art Expo, as he waited for the bill in a coffee shop, idly doodling a copy of a one-dollar bill on his table napkin. "Wow, that's great," said his waitress—a muse in uniform—as she presented him with a 90¢-bill for his cup of coffee. "Can I buy it?" "It's not for sale," snapped Boggs—then, softening at her disappointment, he agreed she could have the drawing of the dollar in payment for his coffee. As he was leaving, she called out, "Wait, you're forgetting your change" and handed him a ten-cent piece. This dime he kept, under glass, much as billionaires frame the first dollar they ever earned.[3]

Boggs had performed his first act of currency performance art, a form of "art" that was to make him widely known around the world, including especially widely known to the police on three continents. His "art" consisted, as the *New Yorker* put it, of three questions: "What is art? What is money? What is the one worth and what the other?"

Brendan Bernhard of the *LA Weekly* describes a typical Boggs transaction:

> I'd met Boggs for the first time earlier in the day over lunch with [Lawrence] Weschler at a Caribbean restaurant called Bamboo—a lunch Boggs had paid for with a one-sided, patently fake, orange $50 bill. Not that doing so was easy. First of all, he'd had to explain to our waiter, Hugo, that his name was Boggs, that he was an artist who drew pictures of money, and that, with Hugo's permission, he would like to pay for our meal with this

particular artwork, which, taken at its face value, would not only pay for the meal but also net Boggs some $15 in real change. Hugo seemed tickled by this idea, mainly because he had no intention of going along with it. "It's pretty nice," he told Boggs, smiling as he examined the blank side of the $50 note, "but it's not real. It's just a piece of paper."

At which point Boggs had pulled out a regular dollar bill, placed it on the table, and pointed out that it, too, was just a piece of paper.

"Yeah, but it's green," Hugo said sensibly. Then he suggested that "In Fun We Trust," the motto emblazoned on another bill Boggs showed him, might read better as "In Fuck We Trust." At this, Weschler threw up his hands, shot me a look that said, *You see what incredible things people come up with when you go to lunch with Boggs?* and slid back in his chair to laugh a delighted, burbling laugh.

Eventually, when a kind of friendly stalemate had been reached, Hugo went to talk to the manager. The manager looked at the bill, considered the situation for a moment, shrugged, and said, "Sure, why not?"

Boggs had just paid for lunch.[4]

And without their knowing it, the manager or Hugo or both of them would have the chance to reap substantial profit when contacted, a few days later, by a Boggs collector and offered $500.00 or more for the bill. When combined with the receipt and change from the Boggs Bill sold to the collector by Boggs and then framed, the resulting "art" could be worth as much as, indeed more than, $10,000.

Part of Boggs's wide reputation comes not from his currency art and transactions but from his criminal prosecutions for counterfeiting. Boggs was tried on the equivalent of counterfeiting charges in England and Australia, where he was acquitted after trial, and he has been the subject of protracted investigations by the Secret Service, the Treasury Department, and the Justice Department in the United States.

In England, Boggs began drawing likenesses of British pound notes and using them for exchange. He was told of the requirement that permission be granted before facsimiles of the notes could be drawn and published, so while he didn't like it, he sought the Bank of England's permission, which was promptly, and unceremoniously, denied. Undeterred, Boggs continued drawing the notes (one-sided, always with variations from the real) and was, predictably it seems, arrested and charged with using a likeness of Bank of England notes without authorization.

Following his arrest, Boggs was questioned by a chief inspector of New Scotland Yard:[5]

CHIEF INSPECTOR: This afternoon from the Young Unknown's gallery, I took possession of a number of drawn items which resembled Bank of England currency. Did you paint or draw these items?

BOGGS: The works of art are original works from my own hand and are not reproductions, nor are they currency.

CHIEF INSPECTOR: But you agree that some of the items contain many if not all of the detail of Bank of England currencies?

BOGGS: A painting of a horse may contain depictions of details created by God, yet you would not place a saddle on that painting.

CHIEF INSPECTOR: This appears to me to be a painting of a [pound] note. It appears to my mind to be an attempt to reproduce an item similar to genuine British currency. Did you draw or paint that article?

BOGGS: It is my job to allow my thoughts and feelings to be expressed and communicated through the visual work of my hands. For art to be true and just and honest, I must allow my inner self out.

CHIEF INSPECTOR: Did you draw or paint it?

BOGGS: Inspector, I truly don't mean to be difficult. The work originates in a hidden and subconscious part of my being. I've gone into my mind to the place where art originates, and it is a very expansive place: I am only just beginning to explore it.

CHIEF INSPECTOR: Did you, with your hand, with a pen, pencil, or paintbrush, irrespective of the reasons, paint, draw, or colour this item?

BOGGS: If you are asleep and you have a dream, are you then responsible for the creation of that dream? I have bled onto this piece of work.

CHIEF INSPECTOR: It appears to me that certain criminal offences have been committed, in particular, producing reproductions of Bank of England notes, without authority. I must again caution you that *you* are not obliged to say anything but what you do say will be taken down in writing and given in evidence.

BOGGS: I am an artist, not a criminal. If I have committed an offence, it is the crime of being born which was not my choice.

The chief inspector and the Bank of England were apparently unimpressed. Formal charges were filed and the matter was set for trial.

In the criminal jury trial, one of Boggs's experts "made the helpful distinc-

tion between 'reproduction' (mechanical and exact copying, to produce a facsimile of the original) and 'representation' (making a picture of a subject)":

> If I sit down with my watercolours and draw a tree, I am representing
> it. Nobody is expected to compare my drawing with a real tree, although,
> if I am lucky, there may be people who admire the fidelity and truth with
> which I have represented the tree—the way its branches go, the colour
> of the leaves, and so forth. This simple distinction will, I hope, clarify the
> nature of what Boggs has been doing in these works. The Bank of England
> is putting itself in the position of the silly bird which, in Pliny's story, flew
> down and pecked at a bunch of grapes painted by Zeuxis, believing them
> to be the real thing.[6]

And another testified that Boggs's work reflected both *tromp-l'oeil* and performance art: "Boggs's work belongs to the tradition which raises the question
of the relationship of the picture to the thing represented. The meaning, as
with all true works of art, must be supplied by the viewer, but they inescap-
ably raise questions of the relation of art to money and money to power. The
banknote is intended to exude anonymity and authority. Boggs's drawings
instantly and overwhelmingly exude individuality."[7]

In his closing argument, Boggs's lawyer eloquently drove the point home
to the jury.

> When Andy Warhol depicts tins of Campbell's soup, more precisely than
> Boggs depicts banknotes, he does not "reproduce" the label on Campbell's
> soup. He is presenting an image which makes people think about mass-
> production and common experiences and advertising messages, about be-
> ing left on the shelf in a supermarket society; in short, about their life,
> rather than about the nutritional ingredients of Campbell's soup. When
> Van Gogh, that anguished and tormented artist, painted a picture of irises,
> he could have had no idea that in 1987 his picture would be sold for £25
> million to Alan Bond. A life-size photograph, a true "reproduction," can
> be bought for a few pounds. So can real irises. For £25 million you could
> have thousands of real irises delivered every day for the rest of your life.
> The Bank of England would say, "Oh, that Van Gogh original is a repro-
> duction of the irises growing in a field in the South of France in the spring
> of 1876." The art critic might say the picture is not about irises at all, it's
> about human anguish, about rage against the squalor and shortness of our
> life compared with the eternal beauty and refulgence of nature. We don't
> know what Mr. Bond thinks. It may be no more than a good investment, or
> a reminder that he has more money than other people. And money brings

us back to Boggs. What is he saying, when he talks like Van Gogh of "bleeding into his pictures"?[8]

At the close of the trial, the firm and unyielding judge all but ordered the jury to convict Boggs, who had, it must be said, distributed a facsimile of the British currency in the face of the express refusal of the Bank of England to authorize such acts, which is almost exactly what the criminal law said. Yet, after no more than ten minutes of deliberation, the jury returned to the courtroom and acquitted Boggs of all charges.

Could it be that art is safer in the hands of a jury—at least a common-sense British jury—than in the hands of limited government or independent judges?

More evidence of that may be provided by Boggs's experiences with the United States government, which has been at once less brutal, yet much more devious and, thus, destructive. The U.S. government—Treasury Department, Justice Department, Secret Service—has lodged no criminal charges, made no arrests, held no trials. But the Secret Service has seized a great many of Boggs's pictures and refuses to return them on grounds that they are contraband. The government follows Boggs's actions, even showings of his work, seizing further works, blocking showings, and threatening further legal action. This is all a bit like taking one's property or liberty for commission of a crime but never getting around to filing a criminal charge or holding a trial.

Boggs has tried unsuccessfully on a number of occasions to force the government to return his art or enjoin it from prosecuting him, but to no avail. Federal courts have consistently held that his United States currency art fits within the broad and technical language of the counterfeiting laws, and therefore, the judges claim, they are in no position to question the seizures of his art in the absence of an adjudication of a particular work or a particular transaction in a criminal trial, which the government won't pursue.[9] Most likely, the government is perfectly satisfied by the *in terrorem* (fear-inducing) results of its current actions and sees no need (and great risk, considering the results in England and Australia) to take any further steps. Checkmate is the word that comes to mind.

• • •

Is Boggs's work art? If so, are the drawn bills art, or does the "art" instead consist of the bills *accompanied by* a proposed transaction in which the value of Boggs's bill compared to a real bill is discussed and, ultimately, judged by the merchant? In other words, does the art lie in the performance, not the thing itself—a skillfully crafted, clever item? Finally, in answering these questions, is it possible to avoid making a judgment about the *quality* of Boggs's art?

Are Boggs's bills art? There is little room for doubt that Boggs is a master at his craft. His craft is drawing astoundingly detailed copies of currency and altering them in very subtle or very obvious ways: a JSG Boggs signature instead of the Secretary of the Treasury, a different perspective on a famous government building pictured on the back of many bills, a different interpretation of a face or a motto, a different color, a different size, or any of many other variations. Boggs clearly is, in the common usage of the phrase, an artist. But are his bills art, or are they instead skilled craft?

The argument that the bills are craft, just like a very fine cabinet or a perfect print, rests on the premise that the bills themselves do not carry an artistically transformative meaning, a sensual response that leads to deeper or different meaning on an aesthetic or cognitive level. Boggs's bills evoke surprise and even awe at the skill they reflect but, in common perception, at least, nothing more. They are, to be sure, inherently re-representational but, in a limited way, as a painting of a beautiful landscape may represent only the actual scene, evoking feelings only of familiarity, beauty, peace, or fear.

The argument that art consists of more than skill and beauty but also requires sensual response evoking imagination and re-representation rests on a simple but contestable premise. It is that much in the world reflects high skill and beauty or remarkableness, reflecting the expanding limits of human capacity: an evocative advertisement, a skilled painting of a barn, a computer game, a fine piece of furniture, an iPod, a strikingly beautiful automobile, a lawyer's brief, a complex commercial transaction, even, not to mention beauty in nature, like the intricate and always unique fern or a sunset. But at base these are all ordinarily representations of reality or reflect the use of complexity, beauty, or other emotions to describe the reality, like a car, and induce feeling and desire and want, not imaginative transformation.

It will be obvious to any reader that this argument and the distinctions on which it rests are slippery, at best. Is a lawyer's brief different from poetry or literature simply because it has a different form or a specific purpose or utilitarian character? Might it not become poetry or literature to another audience at a different time and place? And fine furniture can clearly be considered art. Is a car's design and attractiveness easily distinguishable from original architecture in its beauty or appeal to the senses, even its "imaginativity"? In such difficult cases, the argument might go, one could appeal to the purpose served by the thing or the purpose of its creator or the aims of its audience. Such subordinate criteria are certainly possible and, indeed, are common fodder in constitutional law and free speech theory. But they are not terribly accurate substitutes for the essential inquiry into the types of emotion and imagination and re-representation that claims to be art. And it is, after all, not so much the artist's intention (it is always to create art, even in an advertisement) but the audience's reaction and perception that counts.

But art, in the view of aesthetes and philosophers, does exist in a realm beyond skill and representation. As John Dewey put it:

> The existence of art is concrete proof ... that man uses the materials and energies of nature with intent to expand his own life, and that he does so in accord with the structure of his organism—brain, sense-organs, and muscular system. Art is the living and concrete proof that man is capable of restoring consciously, and thus on the plane of meaning, the union of sense, need, impulse and action characteristic of live creatures.[10]

> Whatever conditions are such as to prevent the act of production from being an experience in which the whole creature is alive and in which he possesses his living through enjoyment, the product will lack something of being aesthetic. Now matter how useful it is for special and limited ends, it will not be useful in the ultimate degree—that of contributing directly and liberally to an expanding and enriched life.[11]

The principal counterargument to this highly conceptual and idealized conception of art is, in the main, the denial of art itself. Art, the argument goes, is simply a reflection of human skill seen through the prism of culture and politics. Art is a social and cultural construct, a reflection of valued skills and aesthetic experiences given special stature through the norms and characteristics of a specific culture—a reflection of relationships of primary values and power and social organization. The quite beautiful and original bird feeders I recently purchased are not seen in our culture as art but instead as aesthetically pleasing alone. But in a culture of birdwatchers, or even birds, they may be positively mind-altering. Art, then, might be described as akin to religion: a thing resting on belief and faith socially or environmentally constructed—an ephemeral and false prophet, perhaps.

This argument and others of its kind should not be lightly dismissed. The gods one believes in are, many would say, social constructions. One need not look too deeply in the various faiths of human history to see truth in the observation. Only if history is seen as progress can one entertain the conceit that his or her God today is the final truth and ultimate incarnation of religious belief and values. The aesthetic and beautiful were different for the Greeks than for African tribes or Native Americans and so on.

But the cultural and political view of art—that art is but an icon of a class structure or economic and social order—need not be seen as negating the idea of art, even Dewey's ideal of art. The question "What is art?" is, surely, a culturally grounded one, and the answer, too, is often culture and time specific. That fact, however, is not inconsistent with the possibility that there exists a form of communication that transcends skill and evokes deep aesthetic reaction and re-representational meaning—re-representational of the known reality, values, circumstances, and organization of a specific culture. The mysteries of the cosmos were different for the Greeks than for us today: the Earth actually revolves around the sun; the cosmos is dynamic. The ineffable has changed and taken on new meanings. So also with what is commonly described as high art or fine art. Art, like religion, is that which lies beyond current boundaries of knowledge (themselves social and cultural facts).

Now return to Boggs's bills and the second line of inquiry. If the bills do not, themselves, reflect more than high skill, it remains to be asked whether, in combination with the Boggs transactions, the bills are transformed into art. The very point of the transactions, indeed, is to alter and elevate the significance of the bills—are they just pretty paper and remarkably skilled images, like real currency, or do they have value, like currency, but *different* value? And what is the source of their value (Boggs Bills and currency alike)? Is the source of value a falsehood or a cultural construct or a transactional device, for example? Can't this be said about both Boggs Bills and currency? Is the source of value an act of faith? Or are Boggs Bills simply a skilled copy of currency, valuable only by government decree? Which is more lasting? What, in the end, is the nature of "value"? These are surely re-representational and transformative meanings. But do they stem from the bills or from the intellectual and political discourse accompanying them? Are the bills the repository of the mystery of value or simply rhetorical devices, much like the images in an effective advertisement or the display of a burning cross? Must art transform without outside assistance?

If the combination of the skillful bills and the discourse about value can be seen as an instance or object of art, it would perhaps be best described as performance art. This, it will be recalled, was Karen Finley's claim, which the Supreme Court implicitly accepted: her acting and nudity or humor and words, combined into a performance, were art. Boggs's art, too, is often described as performative. Can the combination of skill in presentation and political expression, neither of which, alone, may constitute art as Dewey and others describe it, become something new that is sensually evocative and re-representational? Surely so.

But what if the transformational meaning of the art is the message of the explicit political speech itself and thus would be perceived, though perhaps with different force, without the skilled presentation? There is danger lurking in blithely counting this as art. Is a political demonstration or Boston's St. Patrick's Day Parade art because the demonstration or parade differently or more dramatically communicates express political messages? In the famous case of *Cohen v. California*,[12] involving a young man wearing a jacket with "Fuck the Draft" imprinted on the back, Supreme Court Justice Harlan said that "much linguistic expression serves a dual communicative function: it conveys not only ideas capable of relatively precise, detached explication, but otherwise inexpressible emotions as well. If fact, words are often chosen as much for their emotive as their cognitive force." Harlan was speaking of speech, not art.

Perhaps the difficulty of drawing lines in the performative setting is a danger that must be accepted and controlled in other ways, lest musicals or opera be dethroned. Even Shakespeare. Much art is, after all, performative in that it involves multiple senses and complex combinations of stimuli: opera, theater, music, dance, sculpture, to give but a few examples. Or perhaps, in our culture and society, such emotionally transformative performative acts, if skillfully done, are art because, and so long as, we so deem it. If art is, to at least some degree, a *cultural* artifact, reflecting standards of taste, values, and limits of knowledge, and if art relies upon the emotional and transformative interpretation of the audience, it would not be unjustified to rest its definition partly on social and cultural habits and preferences. The drawing of such lines was left, in the *Finley* case, to the art panels of the National Endowment for the Arts, thus reflecting the importance of the panel members' knowledge of artistic practices in the culture and the public attitudes that reflect their acceptance *as art*. In Boggs's case, that question was effectively given to the juries in England and Australia. In the United States, at a threshold level at least, Boggs's artistic fate was left to judges "versed only in the law," as Supreme Court Justice Oliver Wendell Holmes said. Whether the question would be given to a jury at a later stage of a prosecution in the United States, then, is a matter of considerable importance. It is also a matter of considerable doubt, art being, arguably, a question of constitutional definition, not strictly of fact, and thus for judges ultimately to decide.

What is at stake in all of this is whether there exists a category of expression that can be identified as art, as distinguished from ordinary speech or visual, electronic, aural, or other forms of expression. Only if art can be set apart can the Constitution be read as affording it a distinct form of privilege from legal prohibition or regulation. If it cannot, art will be subject to the ordinary protective rules of the First Amendment, but those rules, as illustrated by the *Finley* case, the *Jenkins* case, the *2 Live Crew* case, and the burning-cross case, fall short of the mark many would set for artistic expression. This question is next for discussion in the Boggs case and requires thought about two fundamentally important questions. First, if art can be set apart from the ordinary rules of free speech protection and afforded greater, perhaps absolute, privilege under the First Amendment, how could such a rule be justified? The second question, perhaps contingent on the answer to the first question, is whether the greater freedom afforded art would have to rest on the quality of the art, not just on its status as art.

Art can, the argument goes, be set out as a special category of expression. It rests not on cognition but on emotion and sensory perception. It is aesthetic in its character and impact on the audience. And out of the aesthetic quality of art come the evocation of imagination and re-representation or transformation of meaning from the image or sound or words themselves to a distinct *perception* resting on both imagination and understanding "quicken[ed] ... to an indefinite, and yet ... harmonious activity." This result is as much culturally determined as it is intrinsic and thus relies in the end on the perception and reaction of the audience, which itself exists in a specific culture.

This definition of art is offered not as true, perfect, or proven but as a generally tenable premise—not the only one and certainly not incontrovertible by those who would deny art a special place—upon which the question of legal protection or privilege necessarily depends. If art is not distinct from all other speech, the only thing that can be done is fall back on the general free speech rules, imperfect as they may be, or even deny purely sensory expression with no cognitive meaning any status under the First Amendment.

Assuming that the premise (that art can be set apart from other speech) is generally sound, the next question is how an absolute or higher legal privilege for it can be explained. The essence of the explanation begins with the premise of free speech law: Speech is expression that has an identifiable speaker who intends to communicate a specific message to an audience that reasonably understands *that message*. From this premise, legal judgments of the cognitive meaning and value of an instance of speech, and its resulting consequences, can be judged, and responsibility can be fairly assigned to the speaker. If I cry "Fire!" in a crowded theater, the audience's understanding is pretty unambiguous, the message of the speaker is clear, and the harmful consequences can fairly be assigned by the law to the speaker, who can be punished and whose speech can be prohibited. From this analytical premise, virtually all free speech doctrine flows, the only remaining questions being the value of the speech, the causal relationship between the speech and harm, the magnitude of harm, and the purpose of the government in regulating it.

Art need not—indeed *can* not—reflect any of the speaker-message-audience premises of classic speech law. As seen in *Dale*, the Boy Scouts' case, messages can be constructed by other means than the speaker's intent. And as seen in *Hurley*, the St. Patrick's Day Parade case, a nominal speaker may not even intend to speak or have any message at all in mind. Instead, the audience is in control of meaning. By the terms of the definition of art used here, it is clear that art need not have an origin in an intentional artistic expression by an artist, it need not have, and perhaps ordinarily does not have, a coherent cognitive message, and its meaning and consequences are lodged firmly in the minds of the audience—those who witness a work of art and experience its emotional and transformative power in ways unique to each individual interpreter. The Campbell's soup can was not art until Andy Warhol laid his hands and creativity on it. The same is true for the toilet bowl, the Marlboro Man, or ancient depictions carved on stone walls. Who is the artist, the creative agent, for a genre of architecture only now considered important?

What is "the message" of the Campbell's soup can? Andy Warhol may have something coherent and cognitive in mind (though perhaps not), but is its quality as art dependent on the "reasonable" viewer understanding that particular message, grasping Warhol's particular meaning? And what is, after all, the meaning of the Campbell's soup can in today's culture and in the perception of today's viewers? Is it likely that there is one common understanding? Are answers to these questions any clearer with Manet's *Olympia*, scorned as blasphemous and socially disruptive when it was first revealed, but now occupying pride of place as a masterpiece in the French museum? Or *The Miracle?* Or *The Decameron*, deemed by many to be the origin of the fictional short story and novel forms?

All of these questions can also be asked of Boggs's work. He would say—indeed, he has said—that his bills themselves send a message about currency and its value and about the very nature of value. At the risk of the message being a bit too subtle or confused with a suspected con, perhaps, Boggs accompanies his bills with a dialogue designed to spur re-representation and imagination by his audience. But control remains firmly in the hands of the audience—indeed, nine out of ten people want nothing to do with the bills. If Warhol placed a plaque beside one of the Campbell soup paintings, explaining the general cultural and social meanings he had in mind, would the painting be any less art? And are Boggs's messages of value and culture and social habit—evocative as they are—any different than Andy Warhol's?

If the premises of free speech doctrine—a speaker, a message, understood by an audience—do not apply, then an opening is left to craft a different set of constitutional rules for art instead of the current speech-centered ones. The argument might look something like this: With art, it is often, perhaps even usually, impossible (indeed fruitless) to identify the "speaker." An artist may, in fact, be the creative agent, but his or her creativity has unleashed not *a* meaning but instead an *instrument* through which a new order of perception and meaning can be found. Can the artist be held responsible for that which he or she knowingly can't control or even anticipate? Manet's confusion at the response to *Olympia* was caused by those critics and viewers who saw the painting as strictly representative of reality. The reaction was, one might say, short term and wrong-headed, but was it Manet's fault? Did it deprive Manet's work of the status of art? Hardly. Boccaccio's *Decameron* was censored as blasphemy for many, many years (though it was widely read from the very beginning—just not by judges, it seems). To think of it today as blasphemous or even as sexually scandalous would be ridiculous. Instead, it would more clearly evoke the imagination and wider perception of institutions and social hypocrisy by virtue of its aesthetic beauty and force. Is *The Miracle* no more than a denial of virgin birth?

The point is that with art as we have conceived it, there is no one to blame, no single message to judge, no probable consequence or harm to measure. There is instead an agent who unleashes an aesthetic, interpretive *process* that yields no single, no lasting, and certainly no universal meaning. There is an object—poem, painting, photograph—that has fostered a *process* of creative interpretation by individual members of an audience. How can the law assign meaning and responsibility in such circumstances? It can only, I think, look to the individual viewer and hold that person responsible for his or her acts that were occasioned by the art, but not because the art caused those acts or even the person's perceptions, but because the meaning given by that person was his or her meaning, the consequences of which he or she, and no one else, should account for. If a man rapes a woman after a Karen Finley performance, is his ignorance her fault?

To these qualities of art should be added the argument, made numerous times already, that in fostering imagination, re-representation, and new meaning or significance, aesthetic rather than purely cognitive expression, art serves the purposes of the First Amendment. It fosters creativity, imagination, and new ways of seeing and thinking. It is a fundamental instance of individuality and free will and the capacity to perceive and to change perception. Without these qualities, freedom and self-government would be tragic failures.

The argument that art is distinct in these fundamental ways from speech leads to a striking conclusion. It is that art itself, and artists as agents of artistic perception, should be absolutely privileged under the First Amendment, absolutely free from legal sanction for their work. This is not because they earn or deserve absolute privilege or even because what they do expressively is more important than political speech or something else. It is instead because absolute privilege is the logically necessary consequence of the qualities that make art distinct from other expression.

This conclusion does not mean, of course, that *claimed* art can never be regulated or prosecuted. Art and the perceptual process it occasions are culturally situated as well, perhaps, as intrinsic. Therefore, it can be argued that the culture must be free, within strict limits, to place limits on it. To use an example from our discussion of obscenity, it should be possible (as the Supreme Court says it is) to argue that *Sex Kittens* is not protected as art, because it evokes nothing more than it represents—only lust—but *Carnal Knowledge* is art because it evokes more new meaning and differently. This is not an easy task, but it is one that simply must be undertaken if true art is to receive the higher protection it deserves.

As for J. S. G. Boggs, one might say that grounds exist for viewing his bills and even his performances as craft, not art. But that conclusion is far from obvious. His performances do, after all, have the qualities of transformation built on the aesthetic response to the bills he offers, accompanied by the dialogue. And two lay juries in Western countries and cultures have deemed with stunning speed and assuredness his work to be art—and have judged the interests and motives of the governments to be petty at best. Can it be that the result could be any different in the United States? And should government's escape from this ultimate judgment by too-clever lawyering—seizing but not prosecuting—be permitted?

J. S. G. Boggs would say no. Most other people, I think, would agree.

JUDGING ART AND
ITS QUALITY
REFLECTIONS ON ART
AND FREE SPEECH

T SHOULD COME AS no surprise to the readers of this book that most of the legal questions about art arise in the two contexts of sex and cultural offense (cultural blasphemy may be a better descriptor). What should be made of this? And can a better understanding of it help in thinking about art and free speech? Are the categories of sex and cultural offense exceptions to a general rule of protection for art? Are they categories not worthy of special legal concern? Or are they instances of the failure of art itself?

In the main, the state's impulse to censor and regulate art has been inspired by sexual representations, some explicit and others implied but powerful: Karen Finley, the nude dancer, *The Decameron, Olympia*, and others. One can look at these special instances in two related ways. First, sexual art (in its time and place) may deeply offend social mores and threaten social arrangements: the class structure of France, the Catholic Church, the family, sexual limits, even political power. The offending art strikes at those values and settled arrangements, instilling fear and undermining the felt security of the governing order. Why does this happen, and how is it to be dealt with?

With obscenity, the United States Supreme Court has agonized its way through this problem, though not in so many words, and has settled upon a rule, or test, that on reflection may hold something of an answer. Obscenity, the Court says, is that which appeals to the prurient interest in sex, offends community values, and does not represent serious artistic expression. As legal tools, these criteria are often too loose and complex and perhaps even internally inconsistent. But as a general matter they may be sound.

The problem with much—though certainly not all—sexual art is that the sexuality may get in the way of the sensual re-representation that must occur in art. The nude dancer may be aesthetically pleasing, and her dance may be highly skilled, but in its barroom context, can one say that it represents for those viewing it in context anything more than a visceral impulse centered on the thing itself—on the nudity and prurient suggestiveness? It is not a *form* of expression that encourages the audience to enter a quite different domain of re-representation. One might say that the barroom audience's imagination is focused like a laser beam on copulation. In *Carnal Knowledge*, however, this imaginative domain was claimed (rightly, I think) to be the emptiness of sex as a mere object or experience pursued by two friends whose life seemed to revolve around it.

Most obscenity, as opposed to sexual artistic representation, appeals to the prurient interests—that is, that which the object or the performance itself represents—with such directness and force that it usually negates the claim of aesthetic, sensual, and re-representative imagination or insight. This is the conclusion offered, at least, by a number of serious and widely respected First Amendment scholars. I don't think it mere happenstance that their view corresponds with the distinction explored here between aesthetic art that spurs imagination and re-representation and art that does no more than describe that which it represents—art that, at best, can be described as cognitive speech (subject to ordinary speech restrictions). Obscenity is an inquiry conducted in legal proceedings by a jury and in a community— ignorant people, as the lawyer in the *Carnal Knowledge* case unfortunately described jurors. But one must wonder how an art critic, if asked, would try to explain the underlying difference between Finley's act and the nude dancer's act in a bar. The two explanations—the Court's and the critic's—would likely have much in common once the linguistic differences were stripped away.

A similar approach might be applied to the other and more culturally fluid forms of blasphemy, whether directed at religion or at class or, today, at the forbidden territory of racism and sexism and homophobia. Are Robert Mapplethorpe's homoerotic works blasphemy—culturally dangerous in their message—or are they art? What about the picture (an actual picture) of Mohammed on a cross in urine? Can they be evaluated in the same way as obscenity and sex? Is the offensiveness expressly depicted so dominant that it negates the very possibility of artistic transformation, in intent or in effect? Or is the audience's emotive—even violent—reaction simply evidence of aesthetic ignorance? Those who see only the object itself, not its transformative significance, should not be able to arm themselves with the iron fist of the law. And who is to decide where the line between ignorance and bigotry lies? A jury? Art panels? Critics? Judges "trained only in the law"?

ART AND THE CONSTITUTION

Is there a way to dig beneath the surface and see the obscenity and blasphemy questions more clearly as they arise in the setting of art? Perhaps so. One way would be to separate art that fits the *speech* paradigm from art that doesn't fit it and then to focus more clearly on the First Amendment value that should be attached to the *nonconforming* art under a different paradigm. Such a separating out of art might be accomplished, at least in a rough-hewn way, by identifying two distinct types of art.

The first type I call propositional art. This is art that itself simply makes a cognitive statement or argument by the artist to an audience. Such art may be only representational of an object, or it may serve as an emotive augmentation of a proposition, like "Fuck the Draft" rather than "I Detest the Draft." Whatever form it takes, such art operates in a linear fashion: It contains *a* coherent message intended by the artist and understood by the audience. For example, a cartoon of Mohammed wearing a bomb for a hat contains a clear proposition: Islam is violent. Another example is a Thomas Nast cartoon.

9. Thomas Nast, "Compromise with the South," *Harper's Weekly,* September 3, 1864, 572. Wood engraving.

Although many such skillful and creative representations are often thought of as art, they present little difficulty under the First Amendment. They are clearly "speech" in the sense that they communicate an intended message or meaning to an audience and should, thus, be protected as free speech.

The second type of art—with which this book has been mostly concerned—is what might (for a lack of a better term) be called nonpropositional art. It conveys no single representation or message, and those viewing the art will not usually understand it as doing so (and shouldn't understand it as doing so). Nonpropositional art functions at the sensual and not just cognitive level, spurring imagination and re-representation of the presented object (or musical score or dance, and the like) and yielding a message or meaning that is the creation not of the artist's propositional intention but the viewer's independent construction. Mauricio Lasansky's *Nazi Drawing #17* fits in this category. Meaning arises for the viewer from the aesthetic or emotional qualities of the work, which evokes imagination and re-representation. It is this nonpropositional form of art that faces the most difficult and important challenges in finding protection under the speech guarantee of the First Amendment, for it does not fit the propositional model that characterizes *speech* as the Supreme Court has used the term.

Indeed, it is nonpropositional art that most accounts for the Supreme Court's reluctance to bring art into the First Amendment. But if nonpropositional art—which I henceforth call art or aesthetic art—is viewed in isolation, a number of arguments about its constitutional value can be made. The first is that art should be protected by the First Amendment because of its link to individual imagination and creativity. Second, art should be protected by the First Amendment *as art*, not speech—that is, if and when it can be practically identified in law, its protection should be based on distinct constitutional premises and should take distinct form. The third argument is that the Supreme Court can interpret the free speech guarantee to protect art. If one accepts these arguments or premises, then only one major question remains, and it is perhaps the most difficult and important question that constitutional protection for art, as art, requires to be answered: How can art be defined and distinguished from the forms of "art" that already are protected because they fit the free speech paradigm? These arguments, or questions, are discussed in order.

Art spurs imagination and re-representation of the objective; it is, perhaps, intrinsic to creativity. Art is incapable of domestication. Only destruction will do. It rests on emotion and the senses. Art is a representation perceived not mainly through cognitive faculties but instead through the senses

10. *Nazi Drawing #17*, by Mauricio Lasansky, courtesy of Lasansky Studio, Iowa City, Iowa.

unconstrained by reason. An object or performance that can be called art is an instrument through which the presented object is assimilated through the senses and becomes re-represented as something distinct, a perception or understanding grounded in an act of imagination. Like Yo-Yo Ma playing Bach in the woods. Like Jan Vermeer's *Girl with a Pearl Earring*. John Dewey comments, "The *product* of art—temple, painting, statue, poem"—to which one might add music, theater, opera, literature, dance, and more—"is not the *work* of art. The work takes place when a human being cooperates with the product so that the outcome is an experience that is enjoyed because of its liberating and ordered properties."[1]

Art is more than skill; indeed it is different altogether from skill. It was said of Edward Hopper, and specifically of his painting *Nighthawks* (1942), that "Hopper simply happens to be a bad painter. But if he were a better painter, he would, most likely, not be so superior an artist."[2] *Nighthawks* is art because of its evocation of feeling and understanding and imagination—about the place, the people, the world in which they exist. A better painting would have disturbed the evocativeness of the scene. Hopper's skill was in presenting an object as an instrument of sensual understanding and imagination.

Was Andy Warhol's art the perfection with which he painted the Campbell's soup can? He loved Campbell's soup; he ate it for lunch nearly every day; everyone ate Campbell's soup, from the president to Liz Taylor to the bum; the soup is the same for all of them. He also said, "Making money is art, and working is art and good business is the best art." He loved Los Angeles and Hollywood: "Everything's plastic. I love plastic. I want to be plastic."[3]

Art, Dewey thought, is experience at its highest level. Art is imagination let loose. This is the work of the aesthetic in art, the purely sensual. And this is why art is valuable and dangerous.

So we come to the core of the problem of art and free speech. Art is in its very nature an instrument of sensual representation loosed as an engine of imagination—whether on matters of pure aesthetics or beauty or peace or economics or politics or meaning. If this is so, then art's place in the First Amendment is doubtful, and the reasons it is doubtful stem, as Plato said, from the emotive and unpredictable consequences art spawns in the individual viewer. First Amendment speech has always been a realm of reason. Alexander Meiklejohn, one of the greatest free speech theoreticians of the twentieth century, said that free speech is not a guarantee that everyone can say what they want but rather that everything *worth* saying be said. Unregulated talkativeness, even emotiveness, is not free speech. Notably, Meiklejohn

11. Jan Vermeer, *Girl with a Pearl Earring* (1665).
Royal Picture Gallery Mauritshuis, The Hague.

12. Edward Hopper, American, 1882–1967, *Nighthawks*, 1942, Oil on Canvas,
84.1 x 152.4 cm, Friends of American Art Collection, 1942.51. Photograph by
Robert Hashimoto. Reproduction. The Art Institute of Chicago.

13. Andy Warhol, "100 Campbell Soup Cans," 1962.

concluded that art was not speech protected by the First Amendment (though he later recanted).[4]

If speech is reasoned, and art is not; if speech can be analytically broken down into a speaker, *a* message, and a *comprehending* audience, and art cannot because it lacks a speaker, a message, a single, reasoned, comprehending audience; if meaning follows emotion with art, while emotion follows meaning with speech—if the meaning of art rests with an unknowable and transient audience—then how can art be protected by the speech guarantee of the First Amendment?

This question becomes all the more difficult when one sees that the kind of protection that befits art is significant immunity from the law. By this, I mean immunity of the art and the artist for those harms that may flow from art: violence, blasphemy, racial hatred and intimidation, political or cultural revolution.

Why so? Because of the nature of art itself. Art can emerge from an object never intended as art. Say, the Marlboro Man, which has become an artistic icon—evocative, like Manet's *Olympia*, perhaps, of a time and culture. Or the urinal, that most pragmatic and functional of devices, which in the hands of Marcel Duchamp makes a point, some say, about the ontological structure of sculpture. By conferring the status of "art" on a urinal, Duchamp transformed it as sculpture yet simultaneously undermined conventions of meaning and aesthetics. Much like Warhol's Campbell's soup can. Their "message" is their value as an instrument that unleashes the viewer's own, perhaps idiosyncratic, leap of imagination and perception. (In the case of the urinal, we can at least hope so.)

With speech, the law can assign fault and cause, and it can thus get its hands on regulating it by regulating the messenger and the message. Indecency— dirty words and images—may be the cause of dirty thoughts and moral decay, the Supreme Court says.

This is so, the Court also says, with Karen Finley's performance "art," which includes posing nude but covered with chocolate (at least for those who do not see the chocolate as a metaphor for feces, Tawana Brawley, and so forth) and then with tinsel because women must always be dressed for dinner. The impact of indecent *speech* on the audience, the Court assumes, can be identified and judged as a causal consequence of the speech and, thus, the speaker's act of communicating it. This is also so, it is said with greater justification than with Finley, with much hard-core pornography, in which

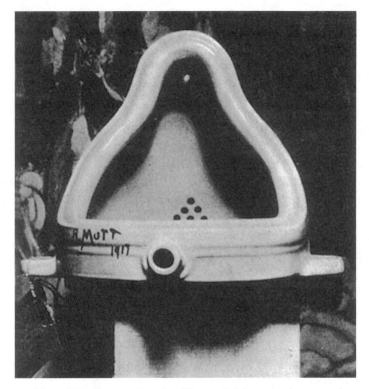

14. Marcel Duchamp, *Fontaine* (Fountain) (1917), photograph by Alfred Stieglitz.

lust is the message, and the admittedly emotional response of lust is the consequence. Dirty pictures, dirty deeds.

The political revolutionary inciting a crowd to violence is engaging in a speech act the cause and consequences of which can be judged in terms of the words used; the legal responsibility can be placed on the speaker, the inciter, like the Ku Klux Klan burning a cross in public, or the utterer of racist speech. Here emotion—aesthetics—follows and indeed serves the message.

None of this is possible with art. Art must be free just as an act of imagination must be free—inherently so. And it *should* be free because it is an act of imagination and creativity in which the agent of the message and its consequences is the individual viewer, not the artist. Dewey calls the "*idea* of art as a conscious idea the greatest intellectual achievement in the history of humanity."[5]

15. Karen Finley, photograph by Timothy Greenfield-Sanders.

Despite the individual and cultural role and value of art as a form of expression, its constitutional home, if there be one, must lie in the First Amendment's guarantee of freedom of speech. And "speech" in its paradigmatic constitutional form has presented the problem for art. To solve that problem, the constitutional meaning of "speech" must be read more

16. Ku Klux Klan rally.

broadly, both linguistically and, as important, distinctly from the cognitively grounded self-governing roots of the speech guarantee. Can the Supreme Court create an interpretation of the First Amendment to protect art *precisely because* it is an unleashed exercise of emotion and re-representation and imagination in the mind of the audience—a form of expression deserving its own, quite different standard of protection?

On this question, on the Supreme Court's power to interpret the First Amendment to include artistic expression, one comes face-to-face with Justice Antonin Scalia and *his* Constitution, a Constitution of strict construction and tight obedience to the text. Justice Scalia is the father of the form of strict constructionism that has come to be known as "textualism."

To understand the problem presented by textualist modes of constitutional interpretation, we must begin with an account of constitutional interpretation by the Supreme Court and the boundaries that should be placed on it. The account reflects the last twenty-five or so years of Supreme Court nomination fights, culminating, perhaps, with John Roberts's memorable metaphor of the umpire. "Judges," he said, "are like umpires. Umpires don't make the rules; they apply them. The role of an umpire and a judge is critical. They make sure everybody plays by the rules. But it is a limited role. Nobody ever went to a ball game to see the umpire."

Textualism's now-ascendant view of judicial power strictly confines the Supreme Court's duty when interpreting the Constitution. The Court must look to the words used and their meaning and follow them soldier-like regardless of the consequences. The First Amendment states, "Congress shall make no law . . . abridging the freedom of speech, or of the press." The text uses the phrase *freedom of speech*. *Speech* is the operative term, and for those wedded to the text only, speech means speech, not art. If it were not so, the argument goes, the Supreme Court would have the power creatively to reword the Constitution to fit its idea of the good. The Court, it is said, is the *least democratic* branch, and therefore it must also be the *least dangerous* branch.

As with the various schools of religious interpretation, textualism is not a monolith. There are many variations, some of which warrant mention, as they are important to understanding the problem the Supreme Court faces when attempting to include art within the word *speech*.

First, there is textualism meant literally. Just the words. Speech is speech, not art. But words are notoriously ambiguous, as is language itself. And words are nothing, really, without context. For Justice Clarence Thomas, the strictest of strict constructionists on the Court, the fact that most language is ambiguous is not a problem. For him, the presence of ambiguity simply means that the courts should back off and leave the interpretation, if any, to the elected branches.

A second variation of textualism looks to the Constitution's words understood in the context of the author's—the framers'—intent. Did the framers intend art when they wrote speech? Probably not. Did they mean the word *equality* to include race, gender, sexual orientation, or even the vote? Although this second variation—called intentionalism—was for many years the prevailing view, it ultimately proved to be a largely futile exercise. Records of Constitutional Convention are imperfect; most of the framers didn't speak to all the major issues, they just voted; and, anyway, the mind of man is ultimately ineffable. The mind of woman, too.

To shore things up in a more objective way, the next variant of textualism became the meaning of the words *to the framers*—those who authored the words and voted on them. When the framers used the term *equality*, or the term *speech*, what was the general meaning of the term at the time? But here the problems are legion, not the least of which are the regional variations in linguistic usage among the framers. Did *equality* mean *nondiscrimination* based on race or, instead, "separate but equal"? Did *speech* mean *art* or *obscenity* or *falsehoods*? More embarrassingly for the Court, the Constitution's meaning may turn on the choice of dictionary of the period upon which one should rely. Believe it or not, there are some Supreme Court decisions that rest on dueling dictionaries (never the *OED*, of course!). It's hard to image the Constitution coming to this.

The unseemliness of this pursuit of dictionary-determined textual meaning led finally to today's dominant view of textualism, which is dubbed *public meaning*. Public-meaning textualism, as it is called, is Justice Scalia's brainchild. The public meaning of the text relies on the common objective understanding of the words used in the populace—in the culture of the time when the words were written.

In the American frontier culture of the late 1700s, art wasn't thought of very much at all, much less was it thought of as speech. But there are even bigger problems with *public meaning*. Which public does the Supreme Court choose? Men only? Property owners, who were the voters? Educated men, of whom there were few? Literate men, of whom there were more but still a distinct minority? Illiterate men as well? How about women? Slaves? So much for objectivity, much less representativeness of the polity that is governed by the Constitution and its amendments.

Finally, there is one other school, still primarily focused on the text but willing to look beneath and beyond the words to divine the original underlying *purposes* of words. This might be dubbed *original purpose textualism*.

Purpose-based textualism asks why freedom of speech was included. Or the phrase *equal protection of the law*. What purposes did the words embody? Once the purposes are divined, extrapolation to new meanings can be undertaken. Under this view, the Supreme Court has considerable creative power when interpreting the text of the Constitution. Indeed, it likely has too much creative power, for purpose-based interpretation knows no limits. What is the purpose of the equality guarantee ... better yet, what are all of the possible purposes? Separate but equal? Equal opportunity? Protection of minorities? And so forth. If one picks a purpose, there will often be a vast range of possible meanings to be built upon it.

How about free speech? The text of the First Amendment says speech—not art. The historical and cultural meaning at the time of the Bill of Rights almost certainly excluded art, thus in all likelihood foreclosing any purpose that would fairly extend the guarantee to art *as art* and not ordinary speech. At the time, the speech guarantee was seen as an essential means for the dissemination of information and opinion upon which voters could be educated and cast their ballots. Reasoned discourse. Maybe speech means, in its purpose, talk only about politics. If so, art is likely out.

But maybe the purpose of free speech is to guarantee individual free will and liberty. If so, art might well find a place. But, as Judge Robert Bork well put it, why doesn't speech-as-liberty encompass *all* conduct, at least conduct that reflects free choice and doesn't harm others? There is really no good answer to that question. Free choice, then, might include art in the speech guarantee or the liberty guarantee, but the costs of such an expansive protection for virtually all forms of conduct would likely preclude the very idea itself.

In the alternative, maybe the purpose of free speech was to foster an educated public and thus educated public decisions, political or not. This view of free speech (proposed by some scholars and justices) might include art. But it would also enable, indeed compel, government to *regulate* expression in the name of truth, fairness, balance, value, and the like. Even decency. Art doesn't fit these ideas well at all.

That's textualism in a nutshell. It wasn't a prevailing—or even very respectable—theory forty years ago, at the end of the Warren Court. But, today, textualism seems to have swept the boards: Even the most liberal constitutional scholars genuflect to it. Ours is now a world of strict, intentionalized, definitionalized, culturalized, and purposivized (!) textualism. Only lawyers and philosophers could create such a constitutional world— perhaps not even philosophers!

But textualism is not the only theory of constitutional interpretation. Indeed, in the mind of many scholars, it is not needed or even desirable as a limitation on judicial power. The principal alternative to textualism, and notably the methodology employed by the Supreme Court over more than two hundred years of constitutional interpretation, entertains new meanings *of the text* that are grounded in broad historical patterns of social and cultural change and that are broadly accepted *today* as reflecting values upon which the founding principles of our democracy rest. Equality *today*, for example, means nondiscrimination based on race as well as affirmative action. It does not include separate but equal (Jim Crow), even if it did at one time.

This historically and culturally grounded approach contains objective constraints on the creativity of the Supreme Court. It ties to the text but not a text consisting only of ossified rules writ by the dead hand of the past. The Constitution instead is seen as a covenant with the *future*. And the Court's interpretive power is at its strongest with those open-textured and thematic terms in the Constitution, such as equality, speech, religious freedom, due process, liberty, and war.

But even if the Supreme Court's discretion is bounded under this approach, the textualists say the problem is that it is the *judicial* branch that is doing the interpreting. Their central argument is that judicial power must, in a democracy, be limited because judicial power is undemocratic. The judiciary occupies a realm beyond politics: the neutral umpire, whom no one comes to see. The Supreme Court does not fit the ideas of representative democracy, where the polity is given responsibility for governing and making the fundamental choices about the social and political order in which we live.

This is a powerful and in many respects sound argument. Judicial power, especially the power to interpret—that is, alter—the Constitution, *is* decidedly nondemocratic, decidedly nonmajoritarian. But if the argument is strong and sound, is it *that* strong and sound? Does limited judicial power foreclose *any* creativity? Does it prohibit a court's power to interpret the word *speech* to mean, also, *art*, and to protect art differently than speech? I think not.

The American Constitution is in fact neither democratic—nor even representative—and it certainly is not majoritarian. What we think of as American democracy is no more and no less than the assemblage of constitutional provisions that assign and limit power in the Constitution. Americans elect presidents by the decidedly undemocratic electoral college— wisely, I think, but that's another matter. Americans elect representatives in the legislative branch by elections that under no circumstances could be characterized as democratic, given voter turnout, voting disqualifications, and the failure of the Constitution to bind those elected to the will of the majority (to the extent it is voiced meaningfully). The Senate is quite intentionally nonrepresentative of popular will. Congress is governed by minority interests: supermajority cloture requirements in the Senate; powers of committees and party leaders; vetoes by the president; delegated lawmaking power to unrepresentative administrative agencies, where most law is made today.

And how does the Constitution allocate power? It does so *inefficiently*—and often to the branch least able to execute it boldly. The power to *make* war—to *fight* it—is given to the president, but the Congress has the power to regulate the military forces. The power to *declare* war is given to Congress, that ungainly babble of varying interests and talents. No lean, mean fighting machine here. The president is given the power to veto the democratic choices of the legislative branch. The courts are given the power to enforce the Constitution and laws, even in the face of legislative or executive insistence to the contrary. But courts have no power broadly to enforce their will against the other branches. The fact is that the Constitution is, in fact, a messy and theoretically ugly business. There are no perfectly crafted and executed theories there. None were intended. And the United States is better off for it.

And what about the nature of judicial power? It is clear in the Constitution itself that the Supreme Court has the power to interpret the Constitution even in the face of executive and legislative and popular resistance. This doesn't mean that the Court can do whatever it wants with the Constitution, but it is an important starting point. The power of interpretation, no matter its breadth, is the power of creativity in making law.

How creative? Strict constructionists, tied to the literal text, say, "Not very." The words or intentions or understandings at the time of the Constitution must control as a means of restraining the power of the appointed and independent courts. But there are two things that must be said about this view of judicial power.

First, textualism sees the Constitution as a pact with the past. But that is not the only or even the best way to see it. It is instead a covenant with the future, wrought by those who were savvy and wise enough to know that the future would present new problems of governance and who were idealistic enough to believe that the Constitution might last for hundreds of years. For them, hundreds of years would reach backwards to the time of Henry VIII and even further to the time of feudalism. Can a frozen text ever adapt to such change, at least without large doses of flexibility?

Second, if the Constitution is to be adaptable, where should the power of adaptation be lodged? Constitutional amendment is provided for in the Constitution, but it is a purposefully onerous and dangerous business, requiring large public demands for change and agreement by a supermajority (three-fourths) only rarely seen in the Constitution's history.

So there must be room for intermediate and gradual change over time. Such a power, even if narrow, is dangerous. Yet, there are indisputably thematic parts of the Constitution that imply, even require, adaptation: the guarantee of equality, of due process, of liberty, of separation of church and state and its frequent competitor, religious freedom. Freedom of speech, too—perhaps even especially. These are the parts of the Constitution that represent *an idea's* covenant with the future. They contain ideas or themes that, by any fair measure, will *have to* evolve, will have to change in a way that defies adaptation through the ungainly and dangerous process of constitutional amendment.

Indeed, many of these ideas are distinctly countermajoritarian. Like free speech. Or worse yet, free art!

So where to lodge the power of adaptation and interpretation? The place it has been lodged from the very beginning of the nation is in the least dangerous branch, the judicial branch. The Supreme Court is highly educated, principled in the way it functions, bound by its own prior decisions, committed to reasoned explanation of its interpretations, independent of the prevailing political winds of the day, bound to a text that is often open textured but still constraining, but a branch of government that is, nevertheless, part of the larger tides of social and political change over time.

More important, however, are other, more practical—even messier— reasons. The Supreme Court has no power of the purse. Its budget, even its ability to function, depends on Congress (a fact demonstrated on more than one occasion in history when Congress simply cancelled the Court's Term). The Court has no army, it has no legislative power—indeed its public support consists only of what respect it *earns* by its work. The Court's enforcement power consists, figuratively, of an octogenarian United States marshal with canes.

The judicial branch, in short, is the least *dangerous* branch. It is both wise and weak, creative but truly constrained. For the Supreme Court to overstep its power would be to court disaster for the Court itself. Where better to lodge the momentous power to adapt the Constitution to the tides of historical and cultural change?

The expansion of speech to include art reflects the evolved and evolving habits and attitudes of the society at large over a period of more than two hundred years. Art is, today, a major source of expression and ideas. It is a central feature of the creativity that American culture so prizes. From a time when there was no broad private market in art—only patrons—we have evolved to a time when the private market in art is pervasive. Public and private museums have blossomed, making art accessible to everyone. Doing art, owning art, viewing art, and arguing about art are all part of the American national discourse, cultural identities, collective acts of imagination. The very *idea* of art, Dewey says, is foundational in American culture. In such an environment, it would be foolish, and foolishly narrow minded, to deny art its place in the Constitution—or to deny the Supreme Court the power—indeed the duty—to say so.

JUDGING ART

We began our inquiry with the question: What is art? We have spent a great deal of time trying to understand it and describe it and to distinguish art in its sensual and aesthetic form from its more common form of pure representation or aesthetic embellishment of a cognitive proposition. If, for present purposes, one accepts the basic concept underlying the propositional/nonpropositional distinction, the question remains whether that distinction can be captured and administered as a matter of constitutional law and by whom. This is Justice Oliver Wendell Holmes Jr.'s question: Can judges "trained only in the law" play a role in defining, judging, and protecting art as free speech under the First Amendment? Holmes was deeply skeptical. But he may not have been aware of what is at stake if today's cognitive paradigm of speech is the only source of protection for art under the First Amendment.

Holmes's statement was, characteristically, captivatingly put. The same can be said more recently for Justice Scalia's statement: "For the law courts to decide 'What is Beauty' is a novelty even by today's standards." But just because two brilliant and linguistically captivating justices said so doesn't make them right. Whether one agrees with them depends, among other things, on the nature of the protection the First Amendment might afford and the soundness and manageability of the criteria by which art might be identified.

It is a fair reading of Holmes and Scalia to say that it was to the question of judging aesthetic and artistic *quality* that their remarks were directed. A distinct question is whether the *boundaries* of art can be legally defined in acceptable and accurate terms and whether its protection can be assured without requiring judges or juries to judge the relative *quality* of a given work of art.

Perhaps so. If art is seen as more than a skillful and even beautiful depiction of an object but instead as an instrument that effectively and aesthetically lures the audience to engage in an act of new imagination, to cull up new meaning, art can be seen as a process engaged by an object or performance and thus more than the object itself. Edward Hopper's visual aesthetic in *Nighthawks* draws us into imaginings about the couple in the diner and the lone man.

Leonardo da Vinci's *Mona Lisa* captivates with the unfathomable and alluring smile. It is not the object but where it takes us. In this sense art, at its highest levels, at least, may be universal, as Immanuel Kant thought. But whether at high or low levels, art partakes of the same character as an instrument of aesthetic appeal and imagination, even if its power to do so is more transient.

17. Edward Hopper, American, 1882–1967, *Nighthawks*, 1942, Oil on Canvas, 84.1 x 152.4 cm, Friends of American Art Collection, 1942.51. Photograph by Robert Hashimoto. Reproduction. The Art Institute of Chicago.

If the essential nature of art can so be captured and then protected by a wise and forgiving set of legal rules, then Holmes and Scalia will have been partly, at least, wrong. The legal "fact" of art, not its specific quality, will be enough to know in the law. It is, in short, the fact of artistic interpretation, not its result, that matters. And for that question, it may be preferable to have judges "trained only in the law" than to have judges trained in the arts. Perhaps juries, too. Aware of their limitations of knowledge, judges and juries may just be more prudent in their own judgments and aware that the interpretive agent of art is the audience, the culture, and the assemblage of often idiosyncratic meanings assigned by individual imagination.

This seems to have been the result in J. S. G. Boggs's prosecutions in England and Australia. One shouldn't, of course, overgeneralize. But it might also be noted that in the United States, with perhaps the strongest history of speech protection in the world, Boggs's claim of art is not even tested, much less vindicated, because the political branches are doing everything possible to avoid defending their actions before judges or juries.

Crafting a standard, process, and evidentiary system by which art might seek protection *as art* may well be possible. Even desirable. We must at least hope so. For in a highly legalized and communication-based culture, there is no way that art will be able to escape the grip of law.

NOTES

INTRODUCTION

1. *Bleistein v. Donaldson Lithographing Co.*, 188 U.S. 239, 251 (1903).
2. *Pope v. Illinois*, 481 U.S. 497, 505 (1987) (Scalia, J., concurring).

STORY 1. PERFORMANCE ART

1. Beth Potier, "Karen Finley Provokes, Reveals in Lecture," *Harvard University Gazette*, February 14, 2002.
2. Ibid.
3. Ibid.
4. Ibid.
5. "The World According to Karen Finley," *Nation*, April 7, 2006.
6. C. Carr, "The Karen Finley Makeover," *Village Voice*, November 8–14, 2000.
7. Potier, "Karen Finley Provokes."
8. Ibid.
9. Ibid.
10. *Oxford English Dictionary*, Oxford University Press, 2008, http://www.oed.com/ (accessed November 1, 2008), s.v. "Art."
11. Nick Zangwill, "Aesthetic Judgment," *Stanford Encyclopedia of Philosophy*, Stanford University, October 22, 2007, http://plato.stanford.edu/entries/aestheticjudgment (accessed November 1, 2008).
12. Ibid.
13. The oral arguments in this case and the cases that follow are taken from the official transcripts maintained by the Supreme Court. The author has selectively edited the transcripts for purposes of this book and has also made detailed changes in the text for purposes of grammar, syntax, and clarity only. Where the changes are of possible use to the reader, appropriate editing marks have been included.
14. *Rosenberger v. University of Virginia*, 515 U.S. 819 (1995). The Supreme Court chose to treat the University of Virginia case as a free speech case rather than a free exercise of religion or an establishment clause case. This was a debatable choice, but in the current volume, we will accept it. I have written on the

case and the speech-versus-religion problem elsewhere in *How Free Can Religion Be?* (Urbana: University of Illinois Press, 2006).

15. This paragraph was a footnote that the author inserted into the text for purposes of clarification.

16. For a thorough discussion of this point, see story 7, "Dangerous Art," infra.

17. Alison Young, *Judging the Image* (New York: Routledge, 2005), 42, 44.

18. *Bleistein v. Donaldson Lithographing Co.*, 188 U.S. 239, 251 (1903).

19. *Pope v. Illinois*, 481 U.S. 497, 505 (1987) (Scalia, J., concurring).

STORY 2. THE ARTISTIC TURN?

1. Religious speech is included within these broad categories of "political" speech, but direct religious speech like proselytizing and ceremonial expression are often separately (or additionally) considered under the establishment and free exercise of religion clauses of the First Amendment.

2. *Abrams v. United States*, 250 U.S. 616, 630 (1919) (Holmes, J., dissenting).

3. Alexander Meiklejohn, *Free Speech and Its Relation to Self-Government* (New York: Harper and Bros., 1948; Clark, N.J.: Lawbook Exchange, 2001), 24–27, 39.

4. David Richards, "Free Speech and Obscenity Law: Toward a Moral Theory of the First Amendment," 123 U. Pa. L. Rev. 445, 62 (1974).

5. Thomas Emerson, *The System of Freedom of Expression* (New York: Random, 1970), 7.

PART 2. "WHAT MATTER WHO'S SPEAKING?"

1. Samuel Beckett, *Texts for Nothing* (New York: Grove, 1967), 81, 85.

STORY 3. SOURCES OF EXPRESSION

1. Benoit Lewis-Denizet and Erik Meers, "The Model Boy Scout," *Advocate*, 757, April 14, 1998, 46–51.

2. Ibid.

3. "*Boy Scouts of America v. Dale, James*, 06/28/2000" *On the Docket*, U.S. Supreme Court News, Medill School of Journalism, Northwestern University, http://otd.oyes.org/cases/1999/boy-scouts-america-v-dale-james-06282000 (accessed December 5, 2008).

4. Lewis-Denizet and Meers, "Model Boy Scout."

5. The Supreme Court's answer in the license-plate case, *Wooley v. Maynard*, 430 U.S. 705 (1977), was that the pacifist was protected against liability for covering the motto on his license plate.

6. The status or existence of the "message" itself is, in fact, an open question that should have been dealt with more thoroughly by the Court. Dale did not speak, nor did he intend to speak; the same goes for the Boy Scouts. The case seems to involve a totally fabricated message—indeed, the Court is really talking about stigma. And the problem with stigma is that it's the effect of broader social structures. Neither the Boy Scouts nor Dale, as individuals, can will it into existence as some finite message intended to be expressed.

7. Karol Berger, *A Theory of Art* (Chicago: University of Chicago Press, 2000), 236.

8. Alexander Meiklejohn, *Political Freedom* (New York: Harper, 1960); Owen Fiss, "Why the State?" 100 Harv. L. Rev. 781 (1987); Cass R. Sunstein, *Democracy and the Problem of Free Speech* (New York: Free Press, 1993); Daniel A. Farber, "Free Speech without Romance: Public Choice and the First Amendment," 105 Harv. L. Rev. 554 (1990); *Red Lion Broadcasting Co. v. FCC*, 395 U.S. 367 (1969); *Virginia State Board of Pharmacy v. Virginia Citizens Consumer Council*, 425 U.S. 748 (1976); *Miller v. California*, 413 U.S. 15 (1973).

9. C. Edwin Baker, *Human Freedom and Liberty of Speech* (New York: Oxford University Press, 1989); Martin Redish, "The Value of Free Speech," 130 U. Pa. L. Rev. 591 (1982); Steven H. Shiffrin, *The First Amendment, Democracy, and Romance* (Cambridge, Mass.: Harvard University Press, 1990); *Abrams v. United States*, 250 U.S.616 (1919) (Holmes, J., dissenting).

10. The classic formulation of this approach is found in the definition of obscenity, which excludes from the constitutional definition of speech material that "lacks serious literary, artistic, political or scientific value." *Miller v. California*, 413 U.S. 15, 24 (1973). Commercial speech, in contrast, is given some constitutional stature under the First Amendment but only because of its instrumental informational value and thus not if it misleads or is false. *Virginia State Board of Pharmacy v. Virginia Citizens Consumer Council*, 425 U.S. 748 (1976).

11. Robert C. Post, "Meiklejohn's Mistake: Individual Autonomy and the Reform of Public Discourse," 64 U. Colo. L. Rev. 1109 (1993); Robert C. Post, "Managing Deliberation: The Quandary of Democratic Dialogue," 103 Ethics 654 (1993).

12. Anthony Damasio, *Descartes' Error: Emotion, Reason and the Human Brain* (New York: Putman, 1995); Anthony Damasio, *The Feeling of What Happens: Body and Emotion in the Making of Consciousness* (New York: Harcourt, 1999).

STORY 4. SPEAKING OUT OF THIN AIR

1. The following discussion of *Hurley* is drawn in part from R. Bezanson and M. Choe, "Speaking Out of Thin Air: A Comment on *Hurley v. Irish-American Gay, Lesbian and Bisexual Group of Boston*," 25 COMM/ENT 149 (2002).

2. Charles Simic, "Making It New," *New York Review of Books*, August 10, 2006, 10.

3. The council itself applies for and receives a permit from the city every year to organize and conduct the parade. Through 1992, however, the city allowed the council to use the city's official seal and directly funded the parade. 515 U.S. 560–61.

4. Kevin Dwyer, "'Do Your Job': A Talk with Wacko Hurley," *South Boston Online*, http://www.southbostononline.com (accessed July 29, 2006).

5. *Hurley v. Irish-American Gay, Lesbian and Bisexual Group of Boston*, 515 U.S. 561.

6. J. L. Austin, *How to Do Things with Words*, 2nd ed., ed. J. O. Urmson and Marina Sbisà (Cambridge, Mass.: Harvard University Press, 1975), 6.

7. Austin refers to verifiable statements of fact—statements that do nothing in themselves or that have no necessary force—as "constative" statements. Ibid., 1–3.

8. When Austin began the Harvard lecture series documented in the book *How to Do Things with Words*, he crafted a dichotomy between a performative and constative statement, suggesting that no overlap existed between the two senses of speech. See ibid., 1–11. By the end of the lecture series, Austin rejects this dichotomy in favor of a more generalized speech-act theory that tracks the various degrees of illocutionary force effected by various statements:

> We said long ago that we needed a list of "explicit performative verbs"; but in the light of the more general theory we now see that what we need is a list of illocutionary forces of an utterance. The old distinction, however, between primary and explicit will survive the sea-change from the performative/constative distinction to the theory of speech-acts quite successfully. For we have since seen reason to suppose that . . . [we can sort] out those verbs which make explicit . . . the illocutionary force of an utterance. . . . What will not survive the transition . . . is the notion of the purity of performatives: this was essentially based upon a belief in the dichotomy of performatives and constatives, which we see has to be abandoned in favour of more general families of related and overlapping speech acts.

Ibid., 149–50. For additional discussion of Austin's speech-act theory and a critique of the constative/performative dichotomy, see Stanley Fish, *Doing What Comes Naturally: Change, Rhetoric, and the Practice of Theory in Literary and Legal Studies* (Durham, N.C.: Duke University Press, 1989), 37–67.

9. *Hurley v. Irish-American Gay, Lesbian and Bisexual Group of Boston*, 515 U.S. 568 (emphasis supplied).

10. Ibid. (emphasis supplied).

11. Eric Donald Hirsch Jr., *Validity in Interpretation* (New Haven, Conn.: Yale University Press, 1967), 5–6.

12. *Hurley v. Irish-American Gay, Lesbian and Bisexual Group of Boston*, 515 U.S. 557, 570–71 (1995).

13. Ibid., 575.

14. Ibid., 574.

15. John Durham Peters, *Speaking into the Air: A History of the Idea of Communication* (Chicago: University of Chicago Press, 1999), 61. Peters says, "The Christian doctrine of communication is a doctrine of broadcasting, of single turns, expended without the expectation that one good turn deserves another."

16. James W. Carey, *Communication as Culture* (New York: Routledge, 1992), 15.

17. Ibid., 9.

18. Ibid., 23.

19. Ibid., 25.

20. Ibid., 34.

21. Carey explains, "A ritual view conceives communication as a process through which a shared culture is created, modified, and transformed. The archetypal case of communication is ritual and mythology . . . art and literature. . . . A ritual view of communication is directed not toward the extension of messages in space but the maintenance of society in time . . . ; not the act of imparting information or influence but the creation, representation, and celebration of shared even if illusory beliefs." Ibid.

22. Ibid., 28.

23. Ibid., 33.

24. Ibid., 44. Lee Bollinger, *The Tolerant Society: Freedom of Speech and Extremist Speech in America* (New York: Oxford University Press, 1986), 67–71.

> The Supreme Court understands the premise that communicative practices are central to the existence of a democratic polity, in part because linguistic connectivity is a basic element of the tissue of civility and a precursor to democratic enfranchisement. Precisely because of this realization, the Court in *NAACP v. Button*, 371 U.S. 415 (1963), held that membership in the NAACP (plus its affiliates and staff) constituted a "mode[] of expression and association" protected by the First Amendment. Ibid., 428–29. Justice Harlan dissented, arguing that the activities of the NAACP are more akin to conduct than speech and should not be protected. Ibid., 453–55. Participation in the organization articulated an effective political statement (especially given the historical context of 1963) and constituted a legitimate form of political expression.
>
> Awareness of linkages between communicative practices and democratic culture may also lend credence to the notion of "low value" speech articulated most recently by Justice Stevens. *R.A.V. v. City of St. Paul*, 505 U.S. 377, 416 et seq. (1992) (Stevens, J., concurring in the judgment). In *Young v. American Mini Theatres*, 427 U.S. 50 (1976), and *Renton v. Playtime Theatres*, 475 U.S. 41 (1986), sexually explicit, nonobscene speech was thought to have less social

value than political speech because sexually explicit nonobscene speech failed to occupy a "core" position in relationship to democracy. Cases from *Valentine v. Chrestensen*, 316 U.S. 52 (1942) to *Central Hudson Gas v. Public Service Commission*, 447 U.S. 557 (1980) also demonstrate a belief, at least by a majority of the Court, that commercial speech is less valuable to a democratic ideal than, for example, traditionally conceived political speech.

25. Carey, *Communication as Culture*, 17.

26. *Hurley v. Irish-American Gay, Lesbian and Bisexual Group of Boston*, 515 U.S. 573.

STORY 5. POLITICS AND COMMUNITY

1. This chapter is an adaptation of "The Artist," a chapter in the author's book *Speech Stories: How Free Can Speech Be?* (New York: New York University Press, 1998), 115–49.

2. Ulric Neisser, "The Process of Vision," *Scientific American* 3 (September 1968): 204, 214.

3. Christian Metz, "Aural Objects," *Yale French Studies* 60 (1980): 24, 32.

STORY 6. GENRE: RAP AND ROCK

1. "Nasty as He Wants to Be, No More," *Orange County (California) Register*, January 9, 2000.

2. "Luther Campbell," *Contemporary Musicians*, ed. Julia M. Rubiner, eNotes .com, 2006, http://www.arts.enotes.com/contemporary-musicians/campbell -luther-biography (accessed November 1, 2008).

3. Alan Light, ed., *The Vibe History of Hip Hop* (New York: Three Rivers, 1999), 268–70.

4. Ibid.

5. "Luther Campbell."

6. Ibid.

7. The following lyrics came from appendix B to the Supreme Court's opinion 510 U.S. 569, 594–96 (1994).

8. For an excellent general discussion of the changes in copyright and their implications for increased First Amendment scrutiny of the copyright law, see Raymon Shih Ray Ku, "F(r)ee Expression? Reconciling Copyright and the First Amendment," Case Western Reserve L. Rev., forthcoming, Case Legal Studies Research Paper, no. 06-25, December 19, 2006, rev. December 3, 2007, http:// ssrn.com/abstract=952374 (accessed November 1, 2008).

9. Section 106 of the Copyright Act provides in part:

Subject to sections 107 through 120, the owner of copyright under this title has the exclusive rights to do and to authorize any of the following:

(1) to reproduce the copyrighted work in copies or phonorecords;

(2) to prepare derivative works based upon the copyrighted work;

(3) to distribute copies or phonorecords of the copyrighted work to the public by sale or other transfer of ownership, or by rental, lease, or lending.

A derivative work is defined as one "based upon one or more preexisting works, such as a translation, musical arrangement, dramatization, fictionalization, motion picture version, sound recording, art reproduction, abridgment, condensation, or any other form in which a work may be recast, transformed, or adapted. A work consisting of editorial revisions, annotations, elaborations, or other modifications which, as a whole, represent an original work of authorship, is a 'derivative work.'" 17 U.S.C. § 101.

Section 107 of the Copyright Act describes limitations on exclusive rights relative to fair use.

Notwithstanding the provisions of sections 106 and 106A, the fair use of a copyrighted work, including such use by reproduction in copies or phonorecords or by any other means specified by that section, for purposes such as criticism, comment, news reporting, teaching (including multiple copies for classroom use), scholarship, or research, is not an infringement of copyright. In determining whether the use made of a work in any particular case is a fair use the factors to be considered shall include—

(1) the purpose and character of the use, including whether such use is of a commercial nature or is for nonprofit educational purposes;

(2) the nature of the copyrighted work;

(3) the amount and substantiality of the portion used in relation to the copyrighted work as a whole; and

(4) the effect of the use upon the potential market for or value of the copyrighted work.

The fact that a work is unpublished shall not itself bar a finding of fair use if such finding is made upon consideration of all the above factors. 17 U.S.C. § 107 (1988 ed. and Supp. IV).

10. The Supreme Court sent the case back to the circuit court, which, in turn, sent it back to the district court after determining that further district-court proceedings would be necessary. 237 F. 3d 297 (1994). No further proceedings appear to have taken place, and it is likely that the dispute was settled.

STORY 7. DANGEROUS ART

1. *OED*, s.v. "Blasphemy."

2. Young, *Judging the Image*, 42 (see story 1, n. 17).

3. Virginia Postrel, *The Substance of Style: How the Rise of Aesthetic Value Is Remaking Commerce, Culture, and Consciousness* (New York: HarperCollins, 2003), 6.

4. *OED*, s.v. "Intimidation."

5. *Texas v. Johnson*, 491 U.S. 397, 422–29 (1989) (Rehnquist, C. J., dissenting).

6. Vittore Branca, *Boccaccio: The Man and His Works*, trans. Richard Monges (New York: New York University Press, 1976), 9.

7. Ibid., 57.

8. Francis Macmanus, *Boccaccio* (New York: Sheed & Ward, 1947), 34–35.

9. Thomas Caldecot Chubb, *The Life of Giovanni Boccaccio* (New York: Boni, 1930), 160.

10. Ibid., 128.

11. Branca, *Boccaccio*, 202.

12. Ibid., 200.

13. Ibid., 203.

14. Ibid., 202.

15. Macmanus, *Boccaccio*, 199.

16. John Charles Nelson, "Love and Sex in the *Decameron*," in *Philosophy and Humanism*, ed. E. P. Mahoney (New York: Columbia University Press, 1977), 340, 344.

17. James A. Brundage, *Law, Sex, and Christian Society in Medieval Europe* (Chicago: University of Chicago Press, 1997), 490.

18. Ibid., 491–92, 517. Brundage adds that these laws reflected "the belief that women possess unquenchable sexual appetites, that they were more likely to seek illicit sexual satisfaction, and that they were more often than not the root and source of marriage problems and sexual immorality." Ibid., 548.

19. Ibid., 536.

20. Nelson, "Love and Sex," 343.

21. Ibid., 344.

22. H. Montgomery Hyde, *A History of Pornography* (New York: Farrar, Straus, and Giroux, 1964), 65, quoted in Kevin W. Saunders, "The United States and Canadian Responses to the Feminist Attack on Pornography: A Perspective from the History of Obscenity," 9 Ind. Int'l & Comp. L. Rev. 1, 20 (1998).

23. Norman St. John-Stevas, *Obscenity and the Law* (London: Secker and Warburg, 1956), 5.

24. Ibid.

25. Maurice Amen, "Church Legislation on Obscenity," 10 Cath. L. Rev. 109, 117 (1964).

26. Saunders, "United States and Canadian Responses," 20.

27. Macmanus, *Boccaccio*, 196.

28. Amen, "Church Legislation on Obscenity," 119.

29. Saunders, "United States and Canadian Responses," 27.

30. St. John-Stevas, *Obscenity and the Law*, 112, 129.

31. Margaret A. Blanchard and John E. Semonche, "Anthony Comstock and his Adversaries: The Mixed Legacy of This Battle for Free Speech," 11 Comm. L. & Pol'y 317, 327 (2006).

32. Ibid.

33. Ibid., 341 (citing Anthony Comstock, *Traps for the Young*, ed. Robert Bremner (Cambridge, Mass.: Belknap Press of Harvard University Press, 1967), 171.)

34. "Notes," 70 Alb. L. J. 225, 229 (1908–9); "Decameron," HalfPrice Books, Records, Magazines, 2006, http://deletecensorship.org/decameron.html (accessed November 1, 2008).

35. *Commonwealth v. McCance*, 41 N.E. 133 (Mass. 1895); *In re Worthington Co.*, 62 N.Y. St. Rep. 115 (N.Y. 1894).

36. Beth Archer Brombert, *Edouard Manet: Rebel in a Frock Coat* (Boston: Little, Brown, 1996), xiii.

37. T. J. Clark, "Olympia's Choice," in *Titian's "Venus of Urbino,"* ed. Rona Goffen (New York: Cambridge University Press, 1997). Another author remarks, "The painting instantiates aesthetic strategies that have in subsequent works come to mark modernism's departure from Renaissance perpetual-realism." Robert W. Witkin, "Constructing a Sociology for an Icon of Aesthetic Modernity: Olympia Revisited," *Sociological Theory* 15, no. 2 (July 1997): 108.

38. Michael Fried, *Manet's Modernism* (Chicago: University of Chicago Press, 1996), 1.

39. Otto Friedrich, *Olympia: Paris in the Age of Manet* (New York: Harper Collins, 1992).

40. Ibid., 14.

41. Ibid., 169.

42. Brombert notes, "The storm of abuse unleashed by Le Déjeuner [sur la herbe] pales in comparison with Manet's submissions to the Salon of 1865." *Edouard Manet*, 168.

43. Phylis A. Floyd, "The Puzzle of Olympia," *Nineteenth-century Art Worldwide*, 2004–5, http://www.19thc-artworldwide.org/spring_04/articles/floy.shtml (accessed November 1, 2008), 1.

44. Theodore Reff, *Manet: Olympia* (New York: Viking, 1976), 50.

45. Ibid., 48.

46. Anne Coffin Hanson, *Manet and the Modern Tradition* (New Haven, Conn.: Yale University Press, 1977), 98.

47. Reff, *Manet*, 50. Reff indicates that Venetian art was more popular than other schools. He describes the *Venus of Urbino*: "For the nineteenth century this painting was the nude." Ibid., 94.

48. Theodore Reff, "Meaning of Manet's Olympia," *Gazette Des Beaux-Arts* 63 (February 1964): 116.

49. Sharon Flescher, "More on a Name: Manet's 'Olympia' and the Defiant Heroine in Mid-Nineteenth Century France," *Art Journal* (Spring 1985): 27.

50. Reff, *Manet*, 101.

51. Alan Krell, "The Fantasy of Olympia," *Connoisseur*, 195, Aug. 1977, 300 (discussing the significance of the black cat at Victorine Meurent's bedside). Hanson comments, "The cat, on the other hand, hissing to alarm the approaching visitor, is a recognized symbol of irresponsible love." *Manet*, 98.

52. T.J. Clark, *The Painting of Modern Life: Paris in the Art of Manet and His Followers* (Princeton, N.J.: Princeton University Press, 1989), 96 (quoting from the contemporary publication *Le Monde Illustré*).

53. Reff, *Manet*, 57.

54. Brombert, *Edouard Manet*, 120.

55. Reff, *Manet*, 15 (citing a contemporary account of viewers' reactions to the painting); Clark, *Painting of Modern Life*, 95 (describing Manet's removal of Meurent feminine qualities and noting that one critic suggested that "never has anything so ... strange been hung on the walls of an art exhibition").

56. Clark, "Olympia's Choice," 136.

57. Clark, *Painting of Modern Life*, 92, 94.

58. Clark, "Olympia's Choice," 136.

59. This appears to be T. J. Clark's thesis: "I shall end the chapter by arguing that class was the essence of Olympia's modernity and lay behind the great scandal she provoked." *Painting of Modern Life*, 88, 100.

60. Brombert, *Edouard Manet*, 145.

61. Charles Bernheimer, "Manet's Olympia: The Figuration of Scandal," *Poetics Today* 10, no. 2 (Summer, 1989), 255–77.

62. Ibid., 274.

63. *Joseph Burstyn Inc. v. Wilson*, 343 U.S. 495 (1952).

64. Peter Bondanella, *The Films of Roberto Rossellini* (New York: Cambridge University Press, 1993), 2.

65. *Burstyn v. Wilson*, 343 U.S. 509.

66. Ibid.

67. Tag Gallagher, *The Adventures of Roberto Rossellini* (New York: Da Capo, 1998), 253.

68. *Burstyn v. Wilson*, 343 U.S. 509; Gallagher, *Adventures*, 253.

69. Gallagher, *Adventures*, 253.

70. Ibid.

71. *Burstyn v. Wilson*, 343 U.S. 509.

72. Gallagher, *Adventures*, 368.

73. *Burstyn v. Wilson*, 343 U.S. 511; Edward de Grazia and Roger K. Newman, *Banned Films: Movies, Censors and the First Amendment* (New York: Bowker, 1982), 231.

74. Gallagher, *Adventures*, 367.

75. Ibid., 368.

76. *Burstyn v. Wilson*, 343 U.S. 513; Gallagher, *Adventures*, 368.

77. de Grazia and Newman, *Banned Films*, 232.

78. *Joseph Burstyn Inc. v. McCaffrey*, 101 N.Y.S. 2d 892 (N.Y. 1951).

79. De Grazia and Newman, *Banned Films*, 232; Ira H. Carmen, *Movies, Censorship, and the Law* (Ann Arbor: University of Michigan Press, 1966), 48.

80. *Burstyn v. Wilson*, 343 U.S. 499.

81. Ibid., 516.

82. Ibid.

83. *Burston v. Wilson*, 104 N.Y.S. 2d 740, 746–47 (N.Y. 1951).

84. *Burston v. Wilson*, 343 U.S. 495, 502 (1952).

85. Ibid., 505.

86. Council of the European Union, *Council Framework Decision 2008/ . . . /JHA on Combating Certain Forms and Expressions of Racism and Xenophobia by Means of Criminal Law*, 16771/07, *Droipen* 127, February 26, 2008, 6, available at www .eclan.eu/Utils/ViewFile.aspx?MediaID=43E&FD=4E (accessed December 1, 2008).

87. John Dewey, *Art as Experience* (New York: Perigee, 1934), 26.

88. John Keats, "Ethereal Things," quoted in Dewey, *Art as Experience*, 34–35.

89. Samuel Taylor Coleridge, "Dejection: An Ode," April 14, 1802, quoted in Dewey, *Art as Experience*, 222–23.

90. Robert Browning, "The Ring and the Book," quoted in Dewey, *Art as Experience*, 363.

91. Ronald Dworkin, *Law's Empire* (Cambridge, Mass.: Belknap Press of Harvard University Press, 1986), 59–61.

92. Damasio, *Feeling of What Happens*.

93. Dewey, *Art as Experience*, 166–67.

94. Ibid., 346.

95. Ibid., 355.

96. Ibid., 361.

97. Browning, quoted in ibid., 363.

PART 4. GOOD ART

1. Clement Greenberg, quoted in Avis Berman, "Hopper," *Smithsonian*, July 2007, 58.

STORY 8. ART AND CRAFT

1. Some information on *J. S. G. Boggs v. Bowron* is from an unpublished opinion, D.C. Circuit, (October 12, 1995).

2. Quotations from Lawrence Weschler, *Boggs: A Comedy of Values* (Chicago: University of Chicago Press, 1999), 15–16.

3. Geoffrey Robertson, *The Justice Game* (London: Chatto and Windus, 1999), 265.

4. Brendan Bernard, "Making Money: The Conceptual Art of J. S. G. Boggs," *LA Weekly*, August 6–12, 1999. Lawrence Weschler is the author of *Boggs: A Comedy of Values*, the wonderful book about Boggs.

5. Robertson, *Justice Game*, 269–70.

6. Ibid.

7. Ibid.

8. Ibid.

9. For example, *Boggs v. Rubin*, no. 97–5313 (D.C. Circuit 1998); *Boggs v. Bowron* (unpub. dec., D.C. Circuit, October 2, 1995); *Boggs v. Bowron*, 842 F. Supp. 542 (D.C. 1993).

10. Dewey, *Art as Experience*, 26.

11. Ibid., 27.

12. *Cohen v. California*, 403 U.S. 15 (1971).

JUDGING ART AND ITS QUALITY: REFLECTIONS ON ART AND FREE SPEECH

1. Dewey, *Art as Experience*, 222.

2. Clement Greenberg, quoted in Berman, "Hopper," 58.

3. Andy Warhol, quoted at http://thinkexist.com (accessed November 1, 2008).

4. Meiklejohn, *Free Speech*, 15–16, 24–27, 39.

5. Dewey, *Art as Experience*, 26.

INDEX

RANDALL P. BEZANSON is the David H. Vernon Distinguished Professor of Law at the University of Iowa. His books include *How Free Can the Press Be?*; *How Free Can Religion Be?*; *Speech Stories: How Free Can Speech Be?*; *Taxes on Knowledge in America: Exactions on the Press from Colonial Times to the Present*; and *Taking Stock: Journalism and the Publicly Traded Newspaper Company.*

The University of Illinois Press
is a founding member of the
Association of American University Presses.

Composed in 10/13.5 Janson Text
with Meta display
at the University of Illinois Press
by Jim Proefrock
Designed by Dennis Roberts
Manufactured by Thomson-Shore, Inc.

University of Illinois Press
1325 South Oak Street
Champaign, IL 61820-6903
www.press.uillinois.edu